SOUTHWEST ARKANSAS
3 8430 00
M000017451
HEMPSTEAD COUNTY LIBRARY
HOPE, ARKANSAS

PETITIONS FOR LAND FROM THE SOUTH CAROLINA COUNCIL JOURNALS

VOLUME I:1734/5-1748

97:1257

BY

BRENT H. HOLCOMB

SCMAR
COLUMBIA, SOUTH CAROLINA
1996

Copyright 1996 Brent H. Holcomb

SCMAR
Columbia, South Carolina

ISBN 0-913363-25-1
Library of Congress Catalog Card Number: 96-69860

Copies may be ordered from
Brent H. Holcomb
Box 21766
Columbia, SC 29221.

INTRODUCTION

Ever since the first time I used a Council Journal in 1971 to find the petition of my own immigrant ancestor of 1752, I have seen the need for abstracts of these petitions to aid genealogical and historical researchers. Since no ships passenger lists survive, the Council Journals are the best source for finding information on the arrival of immigrant ancestors. Additionally, all of the petitions for land are important. Some indicate migration to South Carolina from other provinces; some indicate slave holdings of low-country planters; still others give information on persons who died before their land titles could be perfected and the heirs are named. In the council journals there are many Indian matters, matters to do with treason, the Spanish problem, persons at the fort, expenses, etc., but this volume contains abstracts or transcriptions only of petitions concerning land. The exceptions are some petitions which would be of interest such as that of Jeremiah Theus who petitioned for compensation for his translating the petitions of German speaking applicants.

Prior to the year 1755, land was granted to persons coming into the province of South Carolina on a "headright" of 50 acres per person, whether they were male, female, free or slave, white, or black. From the British Public Records Office (BPRO) film, Volume 24, page 314, we have instructions to Governor James Glen in March 1750/1 "His Majesty's Governours by these Instructions are direct to proportion all the Grants according to the number of Persons White or Black that each Grantee has in his family, and to allow fifty acres for each person...."

Readers need to be aware that the Gregorian calendar was not adopted by England and the British colonies until the year 1752. Prior to 1752, the year began on March 25. From January 1 through March 25 of each year, a dual indication was used, such as 25 January 1747/48. The latter year corresponds to current usage.

Where the original volumes are paginated, page numbers are indicated. Where pagination is lacking, the petitions must be located by the date of the meeting of the council alone.

The writer graciously acknowledges that the British copies of the Council Journals are Crown copyright and the information from those volumes is used with the permission of the Controller of Her Majesty's Stationery Office, the document references being CO 5/437, 5/438, 5/440, 5/441, 5/442, 5/444, 5/451 and 5/455.

Brent H. Holcomb
July 8, 1996

PETITIONS FOR LAND FROM THE SOUTH CAROLINA COUNCIL JOURNALS

Meeting of 25 January 1734/5

Read the Petition of Brice McCleland and 8 other Persons desirous to Settle in the Township of Williamsburgh. Ordered that Col'o Parris do furnish the Pet'rs with such Provisions &c as are allowed to other settlers in the Townships upon producing to him the attorney Generals Certificates how much Land they have sworn themselves Qualifyed for.

Meeting of 5th February 1734/5

Read the Petition of James McCance praying such allowance &C as is given to other persons who are to Settle at Williamsburgh. Ordered That Col'o Parris the Publick Treasurer do furnish the said Pet'r with such Provisions &C as are allowed to other Settlers in the New Townships and the said Ordered sent attested by the Clerk of this Board for the Treasurer.

Meeting of 7th February 1734/5

Read the Petition of Wm. Chambers, Hugh Graham, and James Garmony, praying an Allowance of Provisions in the same Proportion as is allowed to other Settlers at Williamsburgh where they are going to settle. Resolved that the above Pet'r being within the number of those persons represented to this Board by a message of yesterday from the Commons House that colo Parris do send an order to James McCance and other lately gone to Williamsburgh to supply the said Pet'r with a proportionable part of the Provisions, Tools &C out of that delivered them lately on their going to settle in the said Township.

Resolved that no New Comers, which are Intitled to His Majestys Bounty shall receive any part thereof for the future except Immediately on their arrival they apply for the same and settle in such Township as they shall be ordered by his Ex'cy and the Council and that they do give in their names and the number of Persons in their respective familys on Oath to the Publick Treasurer and Shall deliver an attested copy thereof to this Board and that the List so returned by the Treasurer be entered in this Council Book.

Meeting of 12th Feb'ry 1734/5

Read the Petition of David Johnson in behalf of himself and the rest of the Poor Protestants lately Settled in the Township of Williamsburgh and also the Petition of William James, David Henderson, and Rob't Irwin Inhabitants in the said Township both setting forth, that sev'l People had setled Cow Pens and kept large stocks of Cattle in the said Township which consume the herbage of the Township and was a great oppresion on the Inhabitants thereof praying relief...

Meeting of 27th Feb'ry 1734/5

Read The Petition of Eliz'a Ward Widdow in behalf of her son John Ward, son and Heir of Jonathan Ward Planter deceased, praying that a Grant be passed in the name of the said John Ward for 488 acres of Land in Craven County admeasured and laid out by warrant to her late Husband. Ordered that the hon'ble Mr. Secretary Hammerton do prepare a Grant pursuant to the Prayer of the said Petition and the Platt thereunto annexed.

Capt. John Garnet having applied to this Board and represented that he had a Warrant by Virtue of His Family Right for 500 acres in one of the Townships and that he had bought a Warrant of 1000 acres from Mess'rs William and George Saxby which he desired might be joynd in a new warrant with the other 500 acres in one of y'e Townships. Resolved That the same cannot be Granted, being contrary to His Majestys Instructions relating to the Settling the Townships.

Meeting of 7th March 1734/5. P. M.

Read The Petition of James Gordon setting forth that Several Protestants are lately arrived from Philadelphia in order to settle at the New Township of Queensborough and praying they may have the same allowance of Provisions &C as other settlers have. Read also the said James Gordons Memorial of what things are wanted for the better Regulation of the said Township and Resolved that a Proclamation do Issue to forbid any persons setting without warrant and to authorize all Magistrates to remove them. Resolved that all persons applying for warants for Land in any of the Townships shall bring a certificate from some Magistrate in or near the said Townships of their Qualification to which they shall also make oath before a warrant be granted.

Meeting of 20th March 1734/5

Read The Petition of John Stubbs praying for 100 acres of Land in the Township of Williamsburgh where he is settled and Ordered that the attorney General do sign a Fiat for 50 acres of Land in the place where the Petitioner is setled, he having no Family right for any more.

Read the Petition of Peter Faure praying for a warrant of survey for Lands in Edisto Township in virtue of His Family right being six persons and Ordered that the attorney General do Issue a Fiat in the usual manner pursuant to the Prayer of the said Petition.

Meeting of 21st March 1734/5

His Maj'st Hon'ble Council taking into Consideration the Complaint of Susanna Gregory widdow of the late Theophilus Gregory Esq'r Master in Chancery representing that One Deane a Deputy Surveyor had run out some

Land for her late Husband some months before His death which happened about nine months ago yet he has not returned the Platt of the Land so run out into the Surveyor Generals Office. Ordered that the Clerk of this Board do write to the said Dean to make a return of the s'd Platt forthwith.

Meeting of 21st March 1734/5 P. M.

Read The Petition of Benj'a Savage and Thos Lamboll Esq'r in behalf of Anne James and Sarah Smith Infants praying a Warrant to the Surveyor Genl to lay out to them 31 foot in Breadth of the Platt or water Lott lying Eastward of the Bay of Charles Town and fronting the Pet'rs part of the Two Lotts No. 1 & 2 in order to have a Grant for the same. Ordered the Prayer of the Petition be Granted on the usual Conditions and that the attorney Gen'l do prepare the proper Fiat for the same.

Read the Petition of James Fisher praying Lands in the Township of Williamsburgh for 23 persons in Family and he renouncing all the benefit to New Comers. Ordered that the prayer of the said Petition be Granted and that the Attorney Gen'l do Issue a Fiat for y'e same.

Meeting of 26th March 1735

Read the Petition of Cap't Skrine praying 800 acres of Land being His Family right in the Township of Queensborough. Ordered that a warrant issue pursuant to the Prayer of said Petition.

Read the Petition of Alex'r Goodbee for Lands in Waccamaw Township and refferd the same to the Attorney Gen'l.

Meeting of 29th March 1735

Read the Petition of Tho's Wright praying a Warrant for a Low water Lott and ordered the same.

Upon reading the Memorial of James Gordon and the List of persons that came over with him. Orderd That the Commissary do Supply 21 poor Protestants arrived from Pensilvania and settled at Queensborogh with 8 Bushels of Corn and 1 Peck of Salt P Head as also the same Quantity of Corn and Salt to 27 Poor Protestants imported last year by the said Gordon and now by him made free, agreeable to a List delivered by him to this Board. And a Copy of this order was delivered to the said Mr. Gordon.

Meeting of 26th April 1735

Upon reading the Petition of Thos Hall, Richard Hall and John Basnet Setting forth that they have run out Several Tracts of Land in the Township of Williamsburgh, pursuant to warrants granted them for that purpose and praying Directions to the Surveyor General to cause one of his Deputys to Survey and return Platts of the Town Lotts and other Lands in s'd Township mentioned in the said Warrants. Ordered that the Surveyor General do Direct the Deputys by him appointed for each Township to make a return of the full quantity of Land layd out for each Family in One Platt with a Certificate of the same, including also the number of the Town Lott on the same Platt and return the same in the said Surveyor Generals office pursuant to the Governors warrant for that purpose.

Read the Petition of William Donning, Winifred Anderson, George Donning and Benjamin Donning praying that the warrant give out by his Ex'cy the Governor for 6050 acres dated the 27th Feb'ry 1733 to Thos Donning Esq'r Since Deceased may be Cancelld and a New Warrant for 5750 acres may be Directed to the Surveyor General to admeasure to them the said Quantity of 5750. Which is Granted proving their Family Right.

Meeting of 9th May 1735

Read The Memorial of Captain George Anson, Attorney to John Roberts, Esqr, assignee to the Rt. Honble John Lord Carteret. Took the sane into Consideration and Resolved that whereas the two Baronys mentioned in the said memorial have some time since been run out by Virtue of his Late Ex'cys Warrant De Bene Esse and Platts thereof returned into the Surveyor Gen'ls Office and no reason appearing to this Board why the Surveyor General should not certifye the same or that the said Plats so Certifyed can give any Now or Additional force to the Grants from the late Lords Proprietors to the R't Hon'ble The Lord Carteret for the same. Orderd that the surveyor General do certify the said Platts provided they are surveyd and returned agreeable to His Majestys Instructions relating to Lands.

Mr. Robert Finley applyed to this Board and produced a warrant Signd by His Last Ex'cy for 2000 acres of Land praying he may have a fresh warrant to run out the said two Thousand acres in the Township of Williamsburgh being a New Comer. It was Orderd that the Hon'ble Mr. Secretary Hammerton do prepare a warrant for so much land in the said Township as the Mr. Finley shall prove himself Entitled to by His Family Right and that he likewise have a warrant for the overplus of the said 2000 acres in the said Township on proviso that he do qualify himself for the same and on Condition he shall pay the Kings Quit Rents and enters into Bond as usual, the former warrant being cancelld.

Meeting of 13th May 1735

Read the Petition of Othniel Beale in behalf of himself and Col'o George Lucas and Refferd the Consideration thereof until there is a fuller Council, so far as relates to Mr. Beale and as to Col'o Lucas, It was Ordered that a

Grant pass to him for y'e 1150 acres prayed for on Wacamaw Neck, which has been run out for him, the Platt of which was produced in Council.

Meeting of 29th May 1735

His Maj'tys Hon'ble Council taking into Consideration the Petition of Mary Smith widow and relict of Rich'd Smith late of Craven County deceased, wherein among other things she prays a Grant may pass to her for a Tract of One thousand four hundred and fifty acres of Land in Craven County admeasured to her late Husband by virtue of His Late Excellencys Warrant, and the Surveyor Gen'ls Precept, a platt of which now remains in the said Surveyor Gen'ls Office. Orderd that a warrant do Issue to the Surveyor Gen'l to resurvey and admeasure unto the said Mary Smith the above mentioned 1450 acres and that the Platt returned in the Surveyor Gen'ls Office for Richard Smith with the Warrant for the same be cancelld.

Read the Petition of Tho's Farrington praying he may have a Warrant for Surveying 550 acres of Land in the Township of Williamsburgh, in lieu of a warrant granted him in the month of Nov'r 1733 for the like quantity of acres. Orderd. That a Warrant do Issue pursuant to the Prayer of s'd Petition in proportion to his Family right.

Meeting of 30th May 1735

Upon a Hearing between Silas Wells and James Thompson about a disputed tract of Land of 400 acres in Colleton County and the partys haveing agreed between them to appoint each of them a Surveyor to resurvey the said tract. It was Ordered That the Grant signed for the said Silas Wells for the said Tract of land but stoped in the Secretarys Office the said Thompson having Enterd a Caveat against the said Wells having the same, be delivered by the Secretary or his Deputy to the said Wells.

Meeting of Tuesday the 3d of June 1735

Read The Petition of the Hon'ble James Kinloch Esq'r praying a Short Day may be appointed for a hearing on a Caveat entered by the Petitioner against D'r Daniel Gibsons having a Grant for 670 acres in Craven County. Ordered That the same be heard on Thursday morning next.

Meeting of Thursday the 5th of June 1735

Read The Petition of Elias Foissin and William Swinton Esq'r relating to some Lands Caveated by the Hon'ble Mr. Chief Justice Wright in Craven County and praying the said Caveat may be overruled for the reasons mentioned in the said Petition and that regular Grants may pass to the Pet'rs for those lands. Orderd. That Tuesday the 24th inst. be appointed peremtorily for the Hearing the said Petition and in the mean time that Mr. Chief Justice be served with a copy of the said Petition and that unless just cause be then shewn by the said Chief Justice against the said Petitioners having their Grants, that the s'd Grants do pass to the Pet'rs as prayed for.

Meeting of Friday the 6th of June 1735

Read the Petition of Nicholas Haynes praying a Grant may pass to him for 300 acres of Land in Craven County for him surveyd before the Townships were layd out on Santee River, but now taken in in one of them.

Read also the Petition of Captain Othniel Beale praying a Grant for two Tracts containing 1000 acres run out by him on his Family Right on Pedee River, both which were referrd to the Attorney Gen'l that he may make out a Special Fiat with the Quit Rents pa'ble from the date of the Grant, the said 1000 acres having been run out before the Township was marked on Pedee River.

Read the Petition of Col'o Purry, John Francis Chifelle, Isaac Bonial, Lewis Grineke and John Rodolph Purry, praying they may have Warrants for Lots in the Town of Purisburgh, and the Land they are Intitled to in that Township by their Family Rights and referd to the Attorney Gen'l to Examine & Granted allow'g serv'ts to be part of y'e Family.

Read the Petition of Andrew Rutledge Esq'r praying a warr't for 3350 acres of Land in the Township of Williamsburgh and a Town Lott by Virtue of His Family Right and refferd the same to the Attorney Gen'l that he may make out a Special Fiat with the Quit Rent made payable from the date of the Grant for 1000 acres in Williamsburgh, 1000 acres in any other Township, and that he have a Warrant for the remaining Quantity he prays for for any vacant land.

Meeting of 26th June 1735

Read the Petition of Benj'a Carter, Robert Whitford, John Shell, Thos Weekley, Ezechiel Cox, Jos'h Lyons, James Tellier, and Jos'h Robertson. And on considering the matters therein containd, they representing they had run out Lands by virtue of his late Excy's warrants, which they had occupied for some years before the Township on Santee River was markt out, when their said Lands were taken in within the Limits of the said Township. His Hon'r and His Maj'tys Hon'ble Council were of opinion that Special Grants do pass for each of the Pet'rs as by them prayed for.

Orderd That Wm James Le Bas has a Special Grant pass to him for 200 acres of Land at a place commonly calld Bell Broughton with the Limits of the Township on Santee River in consideration that he has had a settlement there for many years past, and that he has such a considerable stock of Cattle &C on the spot as will enable him fully to supply the new Inhabitants settled and which shall hence forward settle in the said Township upon paying His Majestys usual Quit Rents.

The Hon'ble Joseph Wragg Esq'r having applyed to this Board and represented that Paul Jenys Esq'r and himself were administrators to the estate of Noah Hurt Blenco and praying a Grant may pass to the said Jos'h Wragg and Paul Jenys Esq'r for 500 acres of Land on Chehaw River. Ordered that the Hon'ble Secretary Mr. Hammerton do forthwith prepare a Grant accordingly n order it may be signd in Council.

Read the Petition of Thos Ellery setting forth that he is Intitled to 500 acres of Land by purchase from His father in Law Mr. John Moore, situate at English Santee and that the Front of His the said Pet'rs Land has been run in the name of the Heirs of David Peyre, which he apprehends is void, and prays that he may have a special war't for running out his Front Land, to the end a Grant may be made to him (after due notice given to the Heirs of David Peyre) that he may be heard on the first day Publick notice is given, that the Council will sit and her Caveats. Ordered that Mr. Sec'ry Hammerton do forthwith prepare a special warrant accordingly.

Read the Petition of Rich'd Alleyn, Gen't, praying a warrant for 2000 acres of Land in Santee Swamp lying uncultivated. Resolved That the consideration of the same be putt off till the afternoon.

Meeting of Friday 27th June 1735

Read the Petition of Hannah Lawrence widow of James Lawrence of this Province deceasd, praying she may have a Direction to the Attorney Gen'l to prepare and make out Special fiat that the Pet'r may have a Grant for 500 acres of Land which by a warrant from his late Ex'cy and the Surveyor Gen'ls precept on the same was run out for her late Husband but he dying before a Grant could pass for the said number of 500 acres to him the said James, that she may by virtue of the said Fiat be Entitled to that Land. Resolved. That it is the opinion of this Board that the Pet'rs request is reasonable and ought to be Grant. Orderd. That the Attorney Gen'l do make out a Special Fiat pursuant to the Prayer of the Petition.

The Hearing on a disputed Low water lott between Mr. Lamboll and Col'l Brewton, Mr. Lamboll in behalf of same infants to whom he was Guardian, being taken in to consideration and Council being heard on both sides. The Partys were acquainted by His Majestys Hon'ble Council that it was their opinion, as it was likely a matter of that nature would not again appear before them, that it would be the best way for the contending partys to compromise the Dispute between them in an amicable manner before the next meeting of the Council, on failure of which the Council would then proceed to pass their Judgement on the merit of the said Cause. To which the Partys agreed.

The mem'l of Sebastian Zouberbuhler of the Canton of Appenzel in Switzerland sheweth That your memorialist being Imployd by many of the Protestant Inhabitants of the Canton of Appenzel in Switzerland to come to this Province in order to find our a proper place for a considerable number of them to come and settle on, makes the following proposals

1st That one of the Townships on Santee River be set apart for such as shall come from the said Canton of Appenzel to settle and that they be admitted to have Lands therein agreeable to his Majestys Instructions.

2d That the first hundred familys that come in this Province from the said Canton shall be provided with Provisions Cattle and Tools in the same manner as the Inhabitants of Purisburgh have had, and y't that said Hundred familys shall be in this Province by December 1736.

3d That the Town Lotts and other Lands to which the said first hundred will be entitled by layd out to them clear of all Charges and that the Titles to the said Lands be made at the Expence of this Province.

4th That two hundred Familys more shall come and settle in the Township where the other hundred Familys settled with all convenient speed, who will I believe be followed by many more.

5th That a proper person be appointed by your Hon'rs and at the Publick Charge to show your Memorialist the Townships on Santee and Wateree Rivers and that he may have leave to choose the Townships he thinks most proper for the use of the People he designs to bring in.

Resolved upon reading the above memorial that provision by made for the first hundred Familys to be provided for according to the desire of the memorialist and that a Resolution of this Board be prepared under the seal of this Province and delivered unto the said Memorialist but that the Township where those people settle is to be Edisto or Santee Township which of the two the Memorialist shall think proper.

Meeting of Thursday the 17th July 1735

Read The Petition of Thomas Lambol Esq'r praying for Land in one of the Townships in proportion to his Family Right, consisting of Eight persons. And reffered the same to the Attorney Genl.

Read The Petition of McElveny[?] praying a Town Lott and 400 acres of Land in the Township of Williamsburgh by virtue of His Family Right consisting of 8 persons. And reffered the same to the Attorney Genl.

Meeting of Friday the 18th July 1735

Read the Petition of Phillip Peyre in behalf of Judith Peyre praying a warrant for 600 acres of Land in this Province and refferd the same to the attorney genl.

Read The Petition of David Henderson and James Armstrong praying a Special warrant for 50 acres of Land they are Intitled to bey a Family right as is further expressed in the said Petition. Ordered that the Attorney Genl do make out a fiat forthwith pursuant to the prayer of the said Petition.

P. M. Read the Petition of James Robert and John Dubose representing that Noah Serre has run his line thro' the Petrs Lands &c.

Meeting of Saturday the 19th July 1735

His Maj'tys Council having sent for the Chief of the Switzers lately arrived in Cap't Piercy in order to settle in one of the new Townships the Commissary was also sent for, and they all attending, the Township of Edisto was proposed to them as the most proper and convenient place for them to settle in, but the said Swiss desiring they might have leave to view both that and the Township marked out on Santee River and might be permitted to chuse which of y'e two they should like best, they were permitted so to do.

And the Commissary had Directions to Provide the said Swiss with Provisions according to the Regulation made for that purpose, and to take care that proper Carriadges be forthwith got to carry the said Provisions and also the baggage of the said Swiss to the Township they shall settle on.

His Hon'r the Lieutenant Governor being inform'd that several of the Swiss dyed of the small pox and there was a Child on shore who was then full of it, which Child dyed of the same in the afternoon, and that sev'l of the Swiss were gone into the place where the Child lay. His Hon'r directed some of the Justices of the Peace and Constables immediately to go towards the said place and keeping at a moderate distance from the same, hinder the people within the house where the Child lay from coming out, and any person without, from going in. And a lone inhabited House about three miles from Charles Town was Immediately put in order to receive the persons who were in the infected House, or such who might be taken with the small pox to which place they were conducted this day and a watch se over the House, to prevent any Communication with the same.

Meeting of Wednesday the 6th Aug't 1735

Read The Petition of William Brockington in behalf of Sarah Johnson his Granddaughter praying a Grant may pass in her name in lieu of one Signed for Joseph Johnson for 500 acres in Craven County thro' mistake the 13th of May last, altho' he dyed the latter end of March preceding, which makes the said Grant void in Law. Orderd That the Hon'ble Mr. Secretary Hammerton do upon Surrender of the above Grant in the name of Jos'h Johnson prepare a Grant for the said Land in the name of William Brockington in trust for Sarah Johnson daughter of the said Joseph Johnson.

Meeting of Thursday the 7th Aug't 1735

Read. The Petition of Henry Wood and orderd That a Special Warrant be granted according to His Qualification in Waccamaw Township upon his Surrender of a Warrant formerly granted him for 400 acres.

Read the Petition of James Linus praying that a warrant he has for 550 acres may be changed into a Township warrant, which was orderd.

Read the Petition of James Reynolds praying he may be allowed to run out by virtue of His Family Right 140 acres overplus Land in a Platt returnd for his Father, to which his Father is consenting. Which was Granted.

Read a Paper signd by Benj'a Whitaker Esq'r called Reasons offered in behalf of Sarah Johnson Daughter and Heir at Law of Joseph Johnson deceasd against William Brockingtons obtaining a Grant for a Tract of Land in the Parish of Prince Frederick in Craven County and praying a Grant may pass to the said Brockington in trust for the said Sarah Johnson. Ordered. That a Grant do pass for the same in the name of Sarah Johnson.

Meeting of Friday the 8th Aug't 1735

The Hon'ble Joseph Wragg Esq'r producing to this Board a Platt of 6000 acres of Land in Berkley County surveyd by order of the said Wragg on a Warrant from the late Lords Proprietors and Certifyed the 18th day of Feb'ry 1723 by Col. John Herbert late Deputy Surveyor, which 6000 acres is bounding to the southward on Lands of Alex'r Skene and Francis Yonge Esq'r to the westward on William Stead to the northward on Mr. Willoughby Gibbes and to the Eastward on lands not then layd out. It being the opinion of this Board not to pass any Grant for the said six thousand acres of land on the Proprietors Rents, and that the said Wragg being desirous to take up and cultivate the said Lands on his Majestys Quit Rents. It is therefore ordered that a special warrant for the said Six thousand acres of Land in Berkley County be Issued to the said Wragg to resurvey the said Land, that a Grant may pass to him for the same.

Meeting of Wednesday the 3'd Sep'r 1735

Upon a hearing between Thomas Lambol Esq'r in behalf of the Children of ____ Smith deceasd against Col. Brewton about a Low water Lott before the Bay of Charles Town, claimd by both partys, Mr. Whitaker and Mr. Greeme for the said Smiths Children and Mr. Pinckney, Mr. Allen, and Mr. Rutledge in behalf of Col. Brewton, and having heard council on both sides It was the

Opinion of His Maj'stys Council do not think proper to pass a grant to either, but leave them to support their Title at Law as they shall think proper.

Upon a hearing between the Heirs of the late John Lloyd Esq'r and Capt. Dry about a Tract of Land disputed between them, The Council was of opinion that a Grant do pass for Capt. Dry.

Mr. Whitaker applyed on behalf of Peter Johnson praying the Grant may pass for 750 acres in Craven County Which was agreed to and orderd accordingly.

Orderd Likewise that Mr. Thos Butlers Grant for 566 acres in Granville County do pass, the Caveat being withdrawn.

And Also the Grant for Jane Monger for 500 acres in Colleton County.

And also the Grant for 653 acres to James Ferguson the Caveat against him being withdrawn.

Mr. Greeme moved this Board in the behalf of Isabella Lea (now Finch) about a Caveat entered by Mr. Brian against her having a Tract of Land of 300 acres in Granville County and the said Brian being present, and acknowledging that he had no exception against her having a Grant for the same. Orderd That she have a Warrant for resurveying the said Tract in Order a Grant may pass for the same.

Meeting of Thursday the 4'th Sep'r 1735

On hearing a Caveat enterd by Mr. Whitaker in behalf of Sarah Johnson against Brockington Council being heard on both sides

Orderd That a Special Grant be prepared for 520 acres of Land in Craven County for Sara Johnson widdow of Joseph Johnson during her natural Life and the Reversion of the same to Sara Johnson daughter of the said Joseph and Sarah Johnson her Heirs and assigns for ever.

Mr. Graham moved That the Caveat Enterd by Thomas Jones against James Fergusons having a Grant for 200 acres of Land in Colleton County may be dismissed in case the said Jones doth not appear to support it.

Read the Petition of Paul Bruneau praying a Special Grant for 900 acres of Land in Craven County run out by David Peyre His Father in Law, which Peyre dyed before a Grant could pass to him and which land for valuable considerations the Heirs of y'e said Peyre have Enterd into Bonds to make a good Title in behalf of y'e Pet'r. Orderd that a Special Grant do pass to the said Paul Bruneau, pursuant to the Prayer of His Petition.

Meeting of Friday the 5'th Sep'r 1735

The matter in dispute between the Hon'ble Col. Fenwicke and Anthony Mathews Jun'r and Jonathan Brian in relation to Lands on Pocotaligo Neck was heard and the argument of Council on both sides. After a full hearing The question was put Whether the Order of Council of the 6th Sep'r 1733 on the said disputed Land shall stand or whether there shall be a rehearing. Resolved and ordered that the Order of Council of the 6th Sep'r 1733 shall stand and that Grants do pass to Anthony Mathews Jun'r and Jonathan Brian accordingly.

Whereas the Hon'ble Arthur Middleton Esq'r did on this day make application to this Board that his Majestys Grant might pass to him the said Arthur Middleton for certain overplus Lands containd within the Bounds of a Certain Lott in Charles Town heretofore granted by the late Lords Proprietors of this Province unto Jonathan Amory Gent: the Fee simple whereof by divers mesne conveyances is now vested in the said Arthur Middleton and is distinctly known in the model of the said Coven by the No. 199 and is butting and bounding to the eastward on a lott formerly belonging to the aforesaid Jonathan Amory now in the possession of __________, to the Westward on a lot heretofore belonging to Jonathan Pendarvis, now in the possession of Ann Allein and the Heirs of Tweedie Somerville, to the northward on a Lot formerly of Capt. Edee now in the possession of Mr. Joseph Wragg and to the southward on a street that leadeth from Cooper to Ashley River now called Queen Street... Charles Pinckney Esq'r in behalf of himself and all and singular the res of the inhabitants of Charles Town did enter a caveat against any Grant being passed to the said Arthur Middleton or any other person for any vacant or unoccupied lands on the north side of Queen Street lately called Dock Street in Charles Town between the Lands of the said Arthur Middleton and Joseph Wragg Esq'rs and for reason for Entring the said Caveat did sujest and set forth that the said Lands of the said Arthur Middleton bounding to the southward on Dock Street aforesaid contained as mentioned in his grant only half an acre English measure and that between the said half acre of land and the land of Joseph Wragg Esqr bound to the north on a marsh on Cooper River was more than one acre of land vacant and unoccupied to which land it was humbly presumed the Inhabitants of Charles Town in General ought to be preferd to a Grant prefferable to any single or private person... It is the Opinion of this Board that the aforesaid Arthur Middleton by virtue of the original grant to the aforesaid Jonathan Amory and the sev'rl mesne conveyances under which he claims is well entitled to all the lands which are contained within the said circumjacent Boundarys... that his Majestys Grant do forthwith pass for the overplus Land to the said Arthur Middleton, and that the aforesaid Caveat be dismissed.

Upon consideration of the Petition of Mr. Rich'd Allein setting forth that the was a considerable quantity of Low Lands lying waste and uncultivated fronting sev'l parts of upland belonging to the said Richard Allein on Santee and which has layd waste and uncultivated during all the time of the late Lords Proprietors and ever since, His Maj'tys purchasd of the soils of this Province being of little use or benefit but to the owners of the uplands in regard to the frequent Inundations and over flowings of Santee River which happen twice a year and sometimes oftener, and y't he was willing to become his Maj'ts Tenant for the same and praying a Grant for the said Lands. it is therefore orderd that a Special warrant do Issue to His Majestys Surveyor Genl for laying out unto the said Richard Allein all the swamp or low land fronting a part of 1200 acres of Land and 500 acres of Land belonging tot he said Richard Allein in the Parish of St. James down Santee River in order that a Grant be passed to the said Richard Allein for the same at the usual Rents.

Meeting of Friday the 5'th Sep'r 1735 P. M.

Upon application made to this Board by William Brockington praying that he may have a warrant for 500 acres of Land n lieu of the 520 disputed between him and Sarah the widdow of Joseph Johnson which said 520 acres was adjuged by this Board to the said widdow and in reversion to her daughter Sarah granddaughter of y'e said Brockington. Ordered that a Warrant do Issue to the said Brockington for 500 acres prayed for.

Read the Petition of George Logan Esq'r against Mary Smith widdow of Richard Smith Esq'r relating to a grant of 1450 acres issued to her, which land the said Logan lays Claim to by virtue of the will of the said Richard Smith. Heard the Council in behalf of the said Logan, and also on behalf of the said Widdow Smith and after several arguments. The Council for Mary Smith proposed to deliver up their Clients Grant for the said Land to this board, reserving to themselves the Rights of Applying De Novo in her behalf. Which being agreed to by both partys the Cause was dismissd.

Read the Petition of John and Thomas Conn praying Grants for the overplus land containd in their respective Platts which Overplus Land has been run out for Dr. Martin. And Orderd that Grants do Issue to the Pet'rs and that Dr. Martins Grant be suppressed.

The Members of His Majestys Hon'ble Council representing to His Hon'r the Lieut. Governor that they attended on all occasions for the service of His Majesty and the urgent affairs relating to this Province and in the mean time their own private affairs were neglected and sufferd, without having an allowance of any kind for such their attendance therefore thought they were justly intitled and deserved some part of His Majestys Lands in such manner as they are Granted to other His Majestys Officers. For the Hon'ble Arthur Middleton, William Bull, Alex'a Skene, James Kinloch, Robert Wright, Jno Fenwicke, Joseph Wragg, Thomas Waring and John Hammerton Esqr, for admeasuring to each of them 6000 acres of Land.

Meeting of Saturday the 6'th Sep'r 1735

On a Hearing on a Caveat Enterd by John Givens against Dan'l McGregorys having a Grant of 700 acres of Land in Craven County situate on Washee Neck. Orderd That the said Caveat be allowed, and that the said Lands be resurveyd to the said Givens or His Assigns in order for a Grant passing for the same.

Mr. Ellery moved in behalf of Danl Cartwright against Mr. St. Johns having a Grant for Land run out for him at the Head of Pocotaligo River. It was ordered that there be a resurvey of the said Lands within twenty days.

Mr. Pinckney moved again the Cause of Logan Heir to Richard Smith Esq'r against Mary Smith widow of the sd Smith on a further Information and upon a Caveat enterd by the attorney for the widdow Smith against recording y'e Grant for Richard Smith. The further hearing thereof be put off till the next meeting of the Council.

Read the Petition of Susanna Gregory widdow of the late Theophilus Gregory Esq'r praying that a Grant may pass in her name for 1000 acres of Land run out to her late Husband. Which was orderd accordingly.

Meeting of Tuesday the 2'd Oct'r 1735

The Hon'ble John Fenwicke Esqr one of His Maj'ts Council representing to this Board that he had had a platt of 1500 acres of Land in the Surveyor Genls office for about two years, the lying there so long being occasiond by a Claim Mr. Thomas Elliot made before this Board to part of the said Land, but the said Fenwicke agreeing to let said Elliot have 50 acres of that Land, they have amicable made up the matter and their differences. That there are parts of two tracts of Old Granted Land which of late appears to be within the Lines of the said 1500 acres which ought to be set off the same before the new platt pass the said office. That he is desirous to divide the remainder of the new land into two platts vizt 500 acres thereof to Mr. Edward North or any family warrant where the said Fenwicke shall direct and the rest on his own warrant which can be of no disadvantage or lessening to the Kings Rents.

That he has layd these sev'l matters before James St. John Esq'r Surveyor Genl and desired him to Issue his Precept to one of his Deputys to resurvey the said Land agreeable to the above articles but the said Surveyor Genl has refused absolutely to do the same without an order of Council. Orderd that the Surveyor Genl do cause the said platt of 1500 ares to be resurveyd in the manner proposed by the said Col. Fenwicke.

Jesse Badenhop, Clerk of His Maj'ts Hon'ble Council applyed to his Hon'r and Council representing that as Chief Officer of this Board, he with great submission believed himself deserving of His Majestys Bounty of Land as has been granted to other officers. Orderd that two warrants do Issue of the said Badenhop, the one for 100 acres and a Town Lot at Williamsburgh, and that other for 100 acres in the Township of Waccamaw together with a Town Lott therein.

Meeting of Friday the 17'th October 1735

Read the Petition of Richard Hall praying a Warrant for 1000 acres of Land in Consideration of the Hazards, Labor, Expence and Loss of time in coming from, returning to ,and coming back from Great Britain &C with Hemp and Flax seed, with a full design to propogate the Grown thereof in this Province. It being the opinion of His Majestys Council that the Pet'rs allegations were trued, and that he was a very industrious and useful subject. Orderd. that Mr. Sec'ry Hammerton do Issue a warrant unto the said Mr. Hall for one Thousand acres in any Township excepting the Township of Orangeburgh, Savanna Township and y'e Townships on the So side of Santee River.

Resolved That None of the Inhabitants of this Province shall have any Lands in the Townships on the So Side of Santee or the Township of Orangeburgh and Savanna Town the said Townships being reserved Intirely for New Comers.

Read the Petition of John Ballentine and also the Petition of John Reynolds Both setting forth that they have no Lands in this Province either in their own right or otherwise and praying they may be permitted to run their Family Right in some of the New Townships. It was orderd that the Prayer of the Petition be granted and that the Land they are qualified for by their Family Right be run in any Township, excepting those of Orangeburgh, Savanna Town, or the Townships on the So Side of Santee River.

Application being made to this Hon'ble Board by Antonio Albergotty, praying he may be allowed one Years Provisions Extra as a settler at Purisburgh for self and Family. Orderd That the Commissary Genl do Compute what the amount of the said allowance is, and pay it in money to the said Albergotty, for which the said Commissary shall have an order on the Publick Treasurer. Saturday the 18'th Oct'r 1735.

Read the Petition of Abraham Crouch wherein he Complains that having run a Tract of 500 acres of Land Hugh Butler Esq'r run out all the Swamp fronting the said 500 acres upland, by which the Pet'r is put in great difficultys. Orderd that y'e said Pet'n be sent to the Attorney Gen in Order a Fiat be drawn for the special warrant as prayed for.

Thursday the 27'th Nov'r 1735

Read the Petition of Magdelene LeNud praying a Grant may pass to her eldest son Albert LeNud for 400 acres of Land on Cedar Creek run out by her late Husband by virtue of a warrant for which no Grant did pass he dying soon after running out the same. Orderd The same be Granted and that the Surveyor Gen'l do Certifie the Platt in the manner prayed for.

Read the Petition of Jacob Moon praying a Warrant for 400 acres and a Town Lott in some of the Townships pursuant to his Family Right. Which was Granted excepting the Township set a part by Resolution of Council.

Read the Petition of Richard Draycott and Edward Carpenter praying a Warrant for 100 acres of Land to be admeasured to them Jointly. Which was Granted.

Read the Petition of Joseph Moody praying a Town Lott and 550 acres in one of the Townships. Granted excepting the Townships set a part by Order of Council.

Read the Petition of Will: Porter praying a Warrant of Survey for Lands in one of the Townships he having 13 persons in Family.. Granted excepting the Township set a part.

Read the Petition of Charles Starnes praying a Warrant for 500 acres of Land and a Town Lott in one of the Townships by virtue of His Family Right. Orderd excepting the Township set a part.

Read the Petition of Elias Horry Sen'r and referrd the Consideration thereof till to morrow.

Friday the 28'th Nov'r 1735 P. M.

Upon a full hearing of the disputed Land between the Hon'ble Mr. Chief Justice and Messrs Foissin and Swinton in Craven County. Orderd that the said Foissin have a Grant for His 700 acres and it appearing to this Board that the Chief Justice regularly applied to the said Swinton to Survey for him the Land Swinton now claims, who refused to do it, upon which the said Chief Justice Enter his Caveat prior to the said Swinton's Survey and the Surveyor Generals Certificate, which was obtained without notice given thereof to Mr. Chief Justice. Orderd That a Warrant Issue to the Surveyor Genl to admeasure the 350 acres Claim by Mr. Swinton in Craven County butting and bounding to the northwest on John Greens Land, to the No East on William Swintons Land, to the So East on Pedee River and to the So West on Black River unto Mr. Chief Justice.

The hearing between the Hon'ble Mr. Kinloch and the Heirs of Danl Gibson deceasd relating to a Tract of Land disputed by the said Heirs as mentioned in the Minutes of this Board of the 5th Sep'r last came on and council being heard on both sides, Orderd That Grants do pass to the Hon'ble Mr. Kinloch for the said Lands.

Upon reading the Petition of Will: Brockington relating to Lands he has been seized of in Craven County praying a Grant may pass to him for the same. It was Orderd that the Lands prayed for be resurveyd that a Special War't do Issue to the Surveyor Genl for that purpose.

Read the Petition of Eliz'a Hammerton widdow of the late Wm Hammerton, Naval Officer, of the Part of Charles Town representing the Low Circumstances she and her son were left in, Her Late Husband good behaviour in his office, and humbly praying for 500 acres of Land and a Town Lott in any of the Townships in trust for her son. And His Maj'tys Council being of opinion that her request is very reasonable and her Case very Compassionate. It was orderd That the Prayer of the said Petition be granted to the said Mr. Hammerton in trust for her son and that a Warrant do pass for the same in any Township excepting those set apart.

Read the Petition of Nath'l Johnson Esq'r, Publick Register of the Province, praying he may be Indulged in the same manner as other officers are by a warrant for such a quantity of his Maj'tys Lands as this Hon'ble Board shall think proper. Orderd that a warrant do Issue to the said Mr. Johnson for 2000 acres of Land in order a Grant may pass to him for y'e same.

Read the Petition of Francis Goddard praying a Warrant of Survey for a Town Lott and 1700 acres in any of the Townships being Entitled to that quantity by his Family Right. Orderd that a Warrant Issue accordingly excepting the Townships by an order of Council.

Meeting of Saturday the 29'th Nov'r 1735

Read the Petition of Charles Lowndes Esq'r setting forth that he has 10 persons in Family for which he has hitherto had no Land and praying a Warrant of Survey for 500 acres of Land. And the said Petition was Rejected.

Read the Petition of Phillip Peyre setting forth that Hugh Butler has by a survey Endeavoured to take away all the Front of 500 acres of Land possessed by his Mother and praying a Special warrant of survey for the same that a Grant may pass for it. Which was Granted and orderd accordingly.

Read the Petition of Joseph Barry gentleman praying a Town Lott and 250 acres of Land in the Township of Williamsburgh in virtue of His Family right and so much more as this Board shall judge proper in consideration of his having been very Industrious in Educating and teaching a great many of the youth of this Province. Ordered That 500 acres of Land in the said Township be granted to y'e said Mr. Barry together with a Town Lott in the same.

Meeting of Saturday the 29'th Nov'r 1735 P. M.

Read the Petition of Elias Horry Sen'r praying new Grants for Several Tracts of Land he has been seized of and had Grants for from the late Lords Proprietors which were burnt when his House was burnt down.

Meeting of Monday the 1'st Dec'r 1735

Read the Petition of Martha and Will Ramsey son of the said Martha setting forth they had obtaind a warrant for 400 acres of Land in this Province and that they were desirous of surrendering the same, praying that in lieu thereof they may have a warrant for y'e same number of acres to them joyntly in any of the Townships together with two Town Lotts. Granted for any of the Townships excepting such are set apart.

Read the Petition of Edw'd Shrewsbury praying a warrant for 650 acres of Land in any of the Townships, he being Intitled to that quantity by his Family Right. Granted excepting the Townships set a part.

Wednesday the 3'd Dec'r 1735

Upon motion made to this Board by Tho's Ellery of Council for Dan'l Cartwright, representing that on the 6th of Sep'r last It was orderd in Council y't the 1500 acres of Land layd out to Dan'l Cartwright y'e 26th Feb: 1734 should be resurveyd which was accordingly done by John Andrews one of the Deputys to James St. John Esq'r Surveyor Genl on the 17th day of Sep'r last. It appearing to this Board by the return of such survey that about 200 acres of the said 1500 acres is already Granted to John Tripp & that 345 acres more part thereof is since the said Cartwrights survey layd out to the said James St. John Esq'r. Orderd. That the said James St. John do Immediately Issue his precept that the said 1500 acres of Land be resurveyd and a return thereof made to the Board sometime in January next and that such survey do distinguish what part of the said Land is layd out to any & what person since Cartwright's original survey, to the end a Grant may pass to him of such much thereof as is not already Granted and Enterd of Record in the Secretarys office and y't whatever Quantity may be wanting to make up Cartwrights original 1500 acres be layd out to him out of any vacant Land Lying contiguous to or adjoyning his old Platt.

Read the Pet'n of John Maylor praying 200 acres of Land in one of the Townships by virtue of His Family right. Which was Granted excepting the Townships set a part.

Meeting of Thursday the 4'th Dec'r 1735

Read the Petition of Thomas Stone praying 650 acres of land may be Granted him, being His family Right. Granted proving his Family Right to that Quantity.

Meeting of Saturday y'e 6'th Dec'r 1735

Read the Petition of Ann King widdow of Cap't John King, praying she may have a Warr't in her name for 650 acres of Land, in lieu of a warrant Issue to her late Husband as His Family right, which she is willing to Surrender. Which was Granted and Orderd accordingly.

Meeting of Thursday the 11'th Dec'r 1735 P. M.

Read the Petition of George Nicolas praying that as he had a Warant for 2500 acres of land which he has since been informed belongs to the Heirs of Mr. French therefore he is willing to Surrender the said Warrant and prays he may have a warrant for the same number of acres in one of the Townships. And the Prayer of the said Petition was Granted excepting the Townships already excepted.

Read the Petition of Sabina Rowse praying 350 acres of Land and a Town Lott in any of His Majestys Townships. Granted excepting as usual, she proving her Family Right.

Meeting of Friday the 12'th Dec'r 1735

Read the Petition of Col'o Sam'l Prioleau setting forth that he had a Grant for 3250 acres of Land in Granville County which now appears to be within the Parish Line of Purisburgh, for which reason he is willing to surrender the said Grant and in lieu thereof to have a Warrant issue to him for the like number of acres of Vacant Land in any part of this Province.

Meeting of Monday the 15'th Dec'r 1735

Read the Petition of Robert Hall Esq'r Provost Marshall, praying so much Land in One of the Townships as to the Council shall seem meet, together with a Town Lott, He being one of His Majestys Officers. Orderd that he have a warrant for 1600 acres of Land and a Town Lott in any of the Townships to the No'ward of Santee River vizt. 1000 acres as one of His Maj'tys Officers and 600 acres which he is Intitled to by His Family Right.

Meeting of Thursday 15th of Jan'ry 1735/6

His Maj'tys Hon'ble Council taking into their consideration the Pet'n of Elias Horry Sen'r read in Council the 29th of Nov'r last. Orderd That the Pet'r do

Support what he prays for in his Petition by the Rent Roll Law and by Examining the Records in the Secretarys Office, when his Maj'tys Council will give their Opinion thereon.

P. M.

Read the Petition of James St. John Esq're Signed by himself as Deputy Auditor praying a Warrant for so much of His Maj'tys Lands as to this Board shall seem meet, the same favour having been granted to other His Majestys Officers. Orderd That the said James St. John have a warrant Issue to him for 1000 acres on Vacant Land as Deputy Auditor to his Maj'tys in this Province.

Read the Petition of Anthony Hugget praying a Warrant for Land as has been Granted to other Officers he being Marshall of His Majestys Court of Vice Admiralty. Orderd That a Warrant do Issue to the said Anthony Hugget for 500 acres of Land and a Town Lott in the Township of Williamsburgh.

Meeting of Friday the 16th of Jan'ry 1735/6

Elias Horry Esq'r attended this Board in order to Support the Merits of His Petition as mentioned in the Minutes of Yesterday, which he the said Horry having done to the satisfaction of this Board, by producing Copys of the Grants for the Lands mentiond in his said Petition from the Secretary and Registers Office of this Province. It is therefore orderd That a Special Warrant do Issue in the name of the said Elias horry for the quantity of Land he prays for in his Petition in order the same be resurveyed, and that upon the return of a Platt duely Certified a Grant be signd for the same.

Heard a Caveat Enterd by the Hon'ble Arthur Middleton Esq'r against Col'o Blake and others mentioned in the said Caveat their having a Grant for 6000 acres on the neck of Colafina Creek or thereabouts & his Maj'ts Council heaving heard arguments on both sides. Resolved That the said 6000 acres of Land be allowed and Granted to Colonel Black and others with him Joynd.

His Hon'r the Lieuten't Gov'r at the humble request of the Heirs of Will: Yorke deceased produced a Platt for 300 Acres of Land in Berkley County run out in the Life time of the said Will: Yorke, who dyed before a Grant could pass to him for the same.

Orderd That the Surveyor General do Certifie the said Plat in the name of Will'm Yorkes widdow, and the eldest son of William Yorke Deceased, in order a Grant do pass in their names for the said Land.

Meeting of Saturday the 17th of January 1735/6

A Grant for 650 acres of Land for Jonathan Bettison being produced to this Board, and His Maj'tys Council being of Opinion that the said Tract of Land ought to be resurveyed, in Order to be satisfied whether the said Land is bounded as mentioned in the Surveyor Generals Certificate annext to the said Grant. Orderd That the Surveyor Gen'l do direct one of His Deputys to resurvey the s'd Tract of Land accordingly, and that the said Surveyor Gen'l be Served with a copy of this minute.

Read The Petition of Henry Chifelle Minister of Purisburgh praying he may have the same favour shewn him as other ministers in this Province, in having a warrant for 1000 Acres of Vacant Land granted him. Orderd. That a Warrant do Issue to the said Chifelle for 1000 Acres of Vacant Land in this Province, provided he conforms with the Liturgy of the Church of England.

Meeting of Wednesday the 28'th of January 1735/6 P. M.

Read the Petition of George Andrews praying a Town Lott and 300 acres of Land in any one of the Townships his family right sworn to. And refferd the same to the Attorney General.

Read The Petition of Benj'a Jones praying his Family right consisting of Eleven persons in one of the Townships. And refferd the same to the Attorney General.

Read The Petition of Ann Blakeway praying her family Right consisting of her self and nine Slaves in one of the new Townships. Granted the Swearing to her Family Right in any of the Townships, excepting Orangeburg hand Savanna Town, and the Townships on the South side of Santee River.

His Maj'tys Council taking into Consideration the Pet'n of Sev'l Switzers and others who came to Purisburgh in order to settle there, in the month of Oct'r 1734 praying a further allowance of Provisions, having been unable to raise any for want of their Lotts being run out. Orderd. That the Commis: do provide the Pet'rs with half a years Provision more.

Meeting of Thursday the 29th of January 1735/6

On a Motion made by Mr. Greeme in behalf of Mr. Bugnion minister of Santee, praying his Grant may be signd for some Lands he has run which are supposed to be in or near the Township or Orangeburgh, which the Swiss are now Settling. Orderd that nothing shall be done in that affair, till Mr. Haig the Deputy Surveyor do appear at this Board and satisfy the Council whether the said Bugnions Land is within the s'd Township.

A Motion was made for hearing the following Caveats Vizt.
The Caveat Keating against Deane
The Caveat Keating against Singleton.

By consent of Council on both sides. Orderd That the said two Caveats be heard Peremptorily on Wednesday next and that all partys concernd do attend accordingly without further notice.

On the Hearing of a Caveat relating to Lands in Craven County in Dispute between Capt. Anthony White and Will: Screven, bounding on one side on John Greens Land. Resolved that if Mr. Lane the Deputy Surveyor declares on oath that he run & markd the three Lines mentiond so to be run in Whites Platt before Robertson began his Survey for Scriven, then the said White to have a Grant for the same, otherwise he is to withdraw his Pretentions.

Orderd That a Warrant Issue for admeasuring to Benj'a Whitaker Esq're 200 acres of Land as Judge of the Vice Admiralty.

Meeting of Friday the 30'th of January 1735/6

Read the Petition of Dan'l McGregor, praying a Grant for 500 acres of Land on Santee River now possessed by Sam'l Ash. Orderd. That the said Sam'l Ash have notice to attend this Board some day next week.

Read The Petition of Col'o Prioleau praying Grants may pass to him for three Lotts in Beaufort Town No. 304, 305, and 312. Which was granted he proving the allegation of His Petition and no other person claiming the said Lotts.

Read the Petition of Joseph Lowell praying for 350 acres of Land and one Town Lott in the Township of Waccamaw he having Seven persons in Family Sworn to which was granted he proving His Family right on oath before His Majestys Attorney General. The said Lowell accordingly produced the Attorney Generals Certificate.

Read also the Petition of Greenwood Mallory praying for 400 acres of Land and a Lott in the Township of Waccamaw, he having Eight persons in his family sworn to. Ordered That a Warrant do Issue to the Pet'r according to the Prayer of his Petition.

The Revd. Mr. Bugnion having Surrendred to this board a warrant he had obtained for 750 acres of Land and one Town Lott in the Township of Orangeburgh. Orderd That in lieu thereof a Warrant do Issue to the said Bugnion for 100 acres and a Town Lott in the Township of Williamsburgh.

Meeting of Tuesday the 3'd of February 1735/6

Read the Certificates of Col'o Purry and Mr. Abercromby Certifying that Jacob Bouet [Bonet?] was Intitled to 50 acres and One Lott and that ____ Madeleine was also Intitled to 250 acres both in Purisburgh. Orderd That Mr. Secretary do prepare Warrants for the above named persons.

Meeting of Wednesday the 4'th of February 1735/6

Read the Petition of Mary Shillitor widdow praying a Grant for 300 acres of Land in or without any of the Townships to the Northward of Santee River. Orderd that the same be Granted and that Mr. Secretary Hammerton do prepare a Warrant accordingly.

Read the Petition of Jane Eldridge praying 600 acres of Land in any of His Majestys Townships, she having a Family Right for that number. Resolved. That the Prayer of the Petition be granted in any of the Townships not excepted. Orderd That a warrant do Issue accordingly.

Read the Petition of Childermas Croft praying a warrant for 600 acres of Land in any of the new Townships, he having a Family Right for that number of cares. Orderd. That a warrant do Issue to the Pet'r he swearing to His Family Right before the Attorney Gen'l in any Township except Orangeburg, Savanna or the Townships on the South Side of Santee River.

Read the Petition of Joseph Crell praying 350 acres of Land in one of the New Townships being his Family Right sworn to by him before the Attorney Gen'l. Orderd That a warrant of Survey do Issue to the Pet'r for the same.

Read The Petition of Thos Howard praying for 450 acres of Land and a Town Lott in Pedee Township he having Sworn to his Family Right for that number of acres before John Wallis Esq'r one of His Maj'tys Justices of the Peace. Orderd That the Prayer of the Petition be Granted and that a warrant do Issue to the Pet'r accordingly.

Meeting of Thursday the 5'th of February 1735/6 P. M.

His Maj'tys Council taking into Consideration the disputed Land between Edw'd Keating & Richard Singleton and having heard Council on both sides. And it appearing to this Board upon Oath that Rich'd Singleton had been in possession of the Land in dispute for Eleven years and had purchased the Right to the said Land from ____ Allen, who was posses'd of the same Sev'l years. Orderd. That a Grant do pass to the said Rich'd Singleton for the said Land.

A Caveat was heard Edw'd Keating against Dan'l Dean about a disputed Tract of Land and having heard Council on both sides. Orderd. That the further Consideration thereof be putt off till tomorrow morning.

Meeting of Friday the 6'th of February 1735/6

The Cause moved yesterday by Charles Pinckney Esq'r Council for Capt't Gordon against the Hon'ble Mr. Hammerton, Benj'a Whitaker Esq'r, and

Joseph Hurst, was again argued this day by Council on both sides. Resolved. That the further hearing of that Cause be put off to next Thursday sev'night.

The Caveat heard last night, Keating against Dean was taken into Consideration and put of till y's afternoon, then to be further considered.

P. M.

Thomas Jenkins having been Sworn to His Family Right before William Drake Esq'r and praying he may have a warrant for 300 acres of Land in the Township of Kingston on Waccamaw River pursuant to his said Right. Orderd. That a warrant Issue to the said Thomas Jenkins accordingly.

Nicholas Franks having Sworn to His Family Right before the attorney General and produced to this Board the said Attorneys Certificate for 500 acres of Land and praying the said number of acres may be allotted him in one of the New Townships, he never having had any Land bay virtue of his said Family Right. Orderd. That a warrant Issue to the said Franks for 500 acres of Land in any of the Townships excepting the Townships or Orangeburgh and Savannah (calld New Windsor) and the Townships to the southward of Santee River.

Upon hearing the Humble Petition of Sam'l Commander, Joseph Commander, John Commander, Elisha Scriven and Hannah his wife, this day preferrd to the Hon'ble the Lieuten't Governor in Council for the reasons therein mentioned. It was Orderd that a Special Warrant do Issue under the Hand and Seal of the Hon'ble the Lieutenant Governor directed to the Surveyor Gen'l of His Majestys Lands authorizing and requiring him to lay out and admeasure unto Joseph Commander three sev'l Plantations or Tract of Land each containing 500 acres that is to say one Plantation or Tract of Land containing five hundred acres situate in Craven county on the north side of Black River butting and bounding as by a Platt thereof Certified by Francis Yonge Esq'r late Surveyor General to the late Lords Proprietors of the 24th day of Oct'r 1717 appears. And also one other Plantation or Tract of Land containing 500 acres situate in Craven County aforesaid on the north side of Black River butting and bounding south upon the said River, East upon the Land now or late of Francis Goddard, north on the Land late of Sam'l Commander deceased, west on the Land now or late of John Russ, as by a Platt thereof Certified by the aforesaid Francis yonge Esq'r on the aforesaid 24th day of October 1717 also appears. And also one other Plantation or Tract of Land containing 500 acres situate in craven county aforesaid on the north side of Black River being an Inland Plantation butting and bounding as appears by a Platt thereof also certified by the aforesaid Francis Yonge on the aforesaid 24 day of October 1717. And also to lay out and admeasure unto John Commander one other Plantation or Tract of Land containing 500 acres situate in Craven county aforesaid on the North side of Black River, butting and bounding South upon the said River, east upon Lands now or late of

Landgrave Smiths, north upon the Lands late of the said Sam. Commander deceased commonly called the Deep Gully and also to lay out unto Elisha Scriven and Hannah his wife one other plantation or tract of Land containing 500 acres situate in Craven County aforesaid on the north side of Black River, being an Inland Plantation butting and bounding southwardly on Lands now or late of William Brockington, Easterward on Lands now or late of joseph Singleterry, and on all other sides not heretofore laid out, as by a Platt thereof also Certified by the aforesaid Francis Yonge on the said 24th day of October 1717 appears. all which said Lands were lately in the possession and occupation of Saml Commander deceased. And it is further orderd that when the Lands aforesaid shall be admeasure and layd out, His Majestys said Surveyor Gen do return Platts thereof duely Certified to His Majestys Lieuten't Governor in Council to the End that Grants may pass for the same according to the Prayer of the aforesaid Petition if no cause shall be then shewn to the Contrary. And it is further Orderd, That the Clerk of this Board do Issue Publick Notice, that if any person or persons whatsoever, has any Rights, Title, Interest, Property Claim, or demand whatsoever of in, or to the aforesaid lands, or any ____ that they Enter their Claim in the Secretarys Office on or before the 3d Wednesday in March next ensuing, and that such notice be affixed at the Door of the Church of the Parish of Prince George Wyneau for 3 Sundays successively and that return thereof be made upon Oath to this Board.

Mr. Whitaker moved in the behalf of John Musgrove, praying Grants may be sign'ed to him for the Land he is Intitled to, disputed by George Logan. Orderd that Grants be signed in the name of John Musgrove and that they be recorded in the Secretarys Office, but not delivrd or Copys thereof grant to him, until the Right is decided at Common Law.

His Majestys Council took into Consideration the cause of Edw'd Keating against Dan'l Dean argued this morning. It was Resolved and Orderd That a Grant do pass to Dan'l Dean for the s'd Land.

Meeting of Saturday the 7'th of Feb'ry 1735/6

Read the Petition of Phillip Massey setting forth that he has a family of Ten persons five White and five Negros and is desirous to Cultivate and Settle a Town Lott and 500 acres of Land in any of the New Townships to the northward of Santee River & prays a war't for the same. Orderd. That the Prayer of the said Petition be Granted, the Petitioner making oath before the attorney General that his Family Right Intitles him to that Quantity of Acres.

Meeting of Tuesday the 10'th of Feb'ry 1735/6

Read The Petition of John Elliot, Bricklayer, praying a warrant for 300 acres of Land to which he is Intitled by His Family Right of Six persons in any of the Townships or any other part of this Province. Orderd. That a Warrant of

Survey do Issue to the Pet'r for 300 acres of Land in any of the New Townships excepting Orangeburgh and New Windsor and the Townships to the Southward of Santee River.

Meeting of Wednesday the 11'th of Feb'ry 1735/6

Read a Certificate Signd and Sworn to before James LeBas Esq'r by Rob't Gosling, setting forth that he was a New comer and desiring fifty Acres of Land in Amelia Township and a Town Lott. Orderd. That a warrant of Survey do Issue to the Pet'r as prayd for.

P. M.

Read the Petition of John Cahusac praying His Family Right consisting of Six persons in one of the New townships or on vacant land in this Province, he having no Land therein. Orderd. That a Warrant of Survey do issue to the Pet'r for 300 acres in any of the New Townships except Orangeburgh, New Windsor and the Townships to the Southward of Santee River or on vacant Land at his option.

Read the Petition of John Virtue, Gunsmith, praying his Family right consisting of three persons (he never having had any Land in this Province) in one of the Townships or on vacant Land. Orderd That a warrant do Issue to the Pet'r for 150 acres of Land in any Township or on vacant Land at his option excepting the Township of Orangeburgh and New Windsor & the Townships to the Southward of Santee River.

Meeting of Thursday the 12'th of Feb'ry 1735/6

Read the Petition of Tho's Dale Esq'r praying for a warrant of Survey for such quantity of Land in some of the Townships as his Hon'r the Lieutenant Governor and His Majesty's Hon'ble Council shall think fit, he being one of the Assistant Judges. Orderd. That a Warrant do Issue to him for 600 acres and a Town Lott, in virtue of His Family Right in any of the New Townships except Orangeburgh & New Windsor and that Townships to the southward of Santee River.

Meeting of Friday the 13'th of Feb'ry 1735/6

Upon read the Petition of Landgrave Edmond Bellinger praying that Grants may be passed to him for sev'l tracts surveyd in the year 1728 & 1729 under his Patent. Orderd. That the said Bellinger do lay before this Board Platts of the sev'l Tracts of Lands surveyd under His Patent as mentioned in his said Petition for their Consideration.

Upon hearing a Caveat Enterd by Ed'wd North against Mr. Stobo's having a Grant for 1800 acres of Land situate on the Head of Ashepoo River in the

Great Swamp. Orderd. That the said Mr. Stobo have a grant for the said 1800 acres of Land.

P. M.

Read the Petition of John Dart, merchant, praying he may have liberty to surrender a Warrant he is possessed of for 500 acres of Land in this Province obtaind from his late Exc'y as his family right and in lieu thereof have a warr't for 1000 acres of land in one of His Majesty's New Townships, his Family being Increased. Orderd That the Prayer of the Petition be granted and that a warrant of survey do issue to the Pet'r on his proving his Family Right and that he has no Lands in this Province & in any Township except those of Orangeburg, New Windsor and those to the Southward of Santee River.

Read the Petition of Edward Thomas praying he may have a warrant for 500 acres of Land for his Family Right in one of his Majestys Townships he designing to cultivate the same. Orderd. That he proving his Family Right a Warrant of Survey do Issue to the Pet'r for 500 acres of Land for his Family Right on vacant Land out of the Townships he being already possessed of Lands in the Province.

Read the Petition of Thomas Cordes praying 1800 acres of Land in any Township not excepted being his Additional Family Right. Orderd. That he proving his additional Family Right, a warrant do issue to him for 1800 acres on vacant Lands out of the Townships he being already possessed of Lands in this Province.

Read the Petition of John Croft praying a Grant for some Land in one of the Townships in Consideration of his having served His Majesty and this Province in Sev'l stations and been very Serviceable to the Publick in Interpreting between the Spaniards from the Spanish Colonys and this Province on affairs relating to the same. The Board being sensible his allegations were true It was Orderd That a warrant Issue to the said John Croft for 500 acres of Land in any of the Townships, excepting Orangeburgh, New Windsor, and the Townships to the Southward of Santee River.

Meeting of Saturday the 14'th of Feb'ry 1735/6

Mr. John Dart having surrendered up his warrant for 500 acres of Land and at the same time produced a Certificate signd by James Wedderburgh Esq'r in the absence of Mr. Attorney General for his Family Right. Orderd That a Warrant of Survey do Issue to the said John Dart as directed in the minutes of yesterday.

P. M.

Read the Petition of Mrs. Hargrave praying a warrant for 500 acres part of a warrant for 100 acres Granted to her late Husband in the year 1732. Orderd That Mr. Sec'ry Hammerton do prepare a Warrant for the aid 500 acres being the remaining part of the warrant for 1000 acres aforementioned, with a Lot in the Township of Williamsburgh.

Meeting of Monday the 16'th of Feb'ry 1735/6

Emanuel Smith applied to this Board and Represented that he had a Grant for 550 acres of Land in Colleton County signd by his Late Ex'cy Gov'r Johnson y'e 23'd day of May 1734 but upon a Survey of the said 500 acres it appeared that great part thereof had been before run out for other persons therefore prays that he may on his surrendring the said Grant have a Warrant for Surveying so much of the said Tract as shall appear to be vacant and also a warrant for surveying on any vacant land so much as shall make up the quantity of 550 acres. Orderd. That the Pet'r do return a Resurvey of so much land as is vacant for which a Grant shall pass to him on his surrendring the Grant he has already for 500 acres and that he have a Warrant to take up as much Land elsewhere as falls short of the said 550 acres.

Read the Petition of Purchas Hendrick widdow setting forth that one James Berry has obtaind Letters of Administration to her late Husbands estate without her knowledge and praying the said Letters of Administration may be revoked and new Letters of granted to her. Orderd. That the Pet'r and the said Berry attend the Governor in Council on the 26th inst.

Read the Petition of Cath: Rennie widdow setting forth that her late Husband had a warrant for his late Ex'cy Gov'r Johnson for surveying of a Lot and 500 ares of Land in the Township of Williamsburgh but that before a Grant could pass to him for y'e same her said Husband dyed and praying a warr't may pass in her name for the s'd quantity of 500 acres and a Town Lott in the said Township. Orderd. That a warrant do pass in the Pet'rs name as prayed for, she delivering up the former warant passed to her late Husband.

P. M.

The Hon'ble Joseph Warr Esq'r produced to this Board the Two foll'g instruments praying at the same time a warrant or Warrants should Issue to him for the number of acres in the s'd Instruments mentioned which being read It was Orderd That a warrant do Issue to the Surveyor Gen'l to admeasure to the said Joseph Wragg Esq'r the quantity of 12,000 acres of land as mentioned in the said Instruments....

Instrument dated 26 Nov'r 1722 to give to "our Secretary Richard Shelton" a Barony or 12,000 acres for 21 years service.

Meeting of Wednesday the 25'th of Feb'ry 1735/6

Read the Petition of John Wilson setting forth that after the Indian war on the Encouragement given by an Act of Assembly for encouraging persons to come over and settle here, he accordingly came into this Province and had a warrant granted him for 300 acres of Land, which was run out for him but could not obtain a Grant for the same, the Land Office being shut up and therefore praying a warrant may Issue to him for 300 acres and his Family Right in the Township of Williamsburgh. Orderd that a Special Warrant do Issue to the Pet'r for 500 acres of Land in the Township of Williamsburgh in consideration of the allegations in his Petition including in the said 500 acres his family Right.

P. M.

Read the Petition of Thomas Upham seting forth that he being possessed of Purchases Receipts and Platts of Survey of Two Tracts of Land under the Late Lords Proprietors viz't One of 300 acres in Granville County and another of 300 acres in the said County both butting and Bounding as Expressed in the warrants signd by Thos Yonge, Esqr., then Surveyor General and praying a Special warrant for a resurvey of the s'd Lands in order he may obtain a Grant for the same, under and Lyable to His Maj'ts Quit Rents. Orderd. That the attorney Genl do draw out a Special Warrant pursuant to the Prayer of the Pet'r for resurveying the said Tracts of Land in order Grants may pass to him for the same.

Nathaniel Johnson Esqr having obtaind a Warrant for 2000 acres of vacant land Signd the 29'th Nov'r last, and praying he may on the Surrender of the said Warrant obtain one for the same number of Acres in the name of John and Edmond Atkin. Ordered that a Warrant for 2000 acres of vacant Land and not under Patent do Issue to the said John and Edmond Atkin on Surrendring the aforesaid warrant.

Mr. Rutledge moved in the behalf of Col. Thomas Lynch praying the said Lynch may have Grants annexed to six Plats of 500 acres each in Craven County which he purchased from the Late Lords Proprietors in the year 1717 and were accordingly surveyd to him as appears by a Certificate of Francis Yonge Esquire then Surveyor Genl dated the 19th of August 1718 and which the said Linch has settled long since, and payd Taxes and Quit Rents for the same.

Read the Petition of Rebecca Yonge, praying 300 acres of Vacant Land in this Province being thereto Intitled by Her Family Right Sworn to. Orderd. That a warrant do Issue to the Pet'r for 300 acres of Land as prayd for she Proving her Right before the Attorney General.

Meeting of Thursday the 26'th of Feb'ry 1735/6

His Maj'tys Hon'ble Council taking into Consideration the motion made yesterday by Mr. Rutledge in behalf of Colo. Thomas Lynch and he the said Lynch having proved upon oath to the satisfaction of this Board agreeable to the Quit rent Law (which provides that persons in his case shall produce Purchase Receipts for the Purchas money of the Land so by them claimd, and make oath before the Governor for the time being, that Land was Surveyd and ascertaind to him, them, or His or their Heirs &C and that no other Land whatsoever is held by him or any other person whatsoever by virtue of the said Warrant or purchase Receipts, and that he or they have constantly payd the usual Taxes for the same) that the sev'l Platts and other Instruments by him produced Intitled him to the Quantity of acres by him claimd viz't 3000 acres. IT was Orderd. That a Form of a Grant be drawn by the Attorney Gen'l in order a Grant or Grants may pass to the said Colo. Lynch for the number of Acres above mentiond.

Meeting of Friday the 27'th of Feb'ry 1735/6

Read the Petition of John Arthur setting forth that he has a family now in this Province consisting of Ten persons for which hitherto he has had no Land, and praying a warr't of Survey for 500 acres of Land in some of His Maj'tys New Townships and the Pet'r producing the Attorney Generals Certificate that he had sworn to His Family Right for that number of acres. Orderd That a warrant of Survey do Issue to the Pet'r for 500 acres of Land in any of the New Townships, excepting Orangeburgh, New Windsor, and the Townships on the So side of Santee River.

Read the Petition of Joshua Joully setting forth that he has now Eight persons in Family for which he has hitherto had no Land, and praying a warrant for 400 acres of Land in some of His Maj'tys Townships, and the Petitioner having Sworn to his Family Right before the Attorney Genl. Orderd That a warrant of Survey do Issue to the Pet'r for 400 acres of Land in any Township, excepting Orangeburgh and the Townships on the South side of Santee River.

Read the Petition of Hercules Coyle shewing that he has two purchase Receipts for 100 acres of Land in the Lords Proprietors time, and praying he may have a Grant for 100 acres of Land, he being willing to pay the same Quit Rent as was payd in the Lords Proprietors time. Orderd. That the said Coyles Petition be Grant, he complying with the Directions of the Quit Rent Law.

Read the Petition of John Baxter setting forth that he has lived two years in this Province, and being willing to promote the Settlement of the same with Industrious Protestants, prays he may have a warrant for 1500 acres of Land in any of the Townships he being ready to be bound in any penalty their Hon'rs shall think fit, to bring over in the Space of one year 30 persons to settle the said Number of Acres. Orderd. That the Prayer of the Petition be Granted on his entring into Bond to Import the said number of Persons, agreable to the Kings Instructions, and to settle agreeable thereto Death and other unforeseen accidents excepted.

Read the Petition of Dan'l Butler, Messenger of this Board, praying that in Consideration of his having been sev'l years Messenger of this Board and served in that Station faithfully to the best of his Power, he may be Indulged with such a Quantity of Land in one of the New Townships as their Hon'rs shall Judge proper, together with a Town Lott. Orderd. That a warrant do Issue to the said Dan'l butler for 300 acres of Land and a Town Lott in any of the Townships except Orangeburgh and the Townships on the So. Side of Santee River, or on vacant Land at his Option.

Read the Petition of Mary Gledow praying a warrant for her Family Right consisting of herself and one Servant in the Township of Williamsburg together with a Town Lott. Orderd. That a warrant do Issue to the said Mary Gledow for One hundred Acres of Land and a Town Lott in the Townships of Williamsburgh as prayd for in her Petition.

Read the Petition of Christian Gatlieb Priber setting forth that he has a Family of Six persons in this Province and also a wife, four children and one servant in Saxony, and praying he may have a Warrant of Survey for his whole Family right viz't that in this Province, and also that in Saxony aforementioned, in the Township of Amelia. Orderd. that the Pet'r have a Warrant Issue to him for his Family Right now in this Province, including also his Family in Saxony, he entring into Bond that the Family he has in Saxony Shall come over into this Province, and settle within two years and that his goods shall be sent to the said Township without any Charge to him.

Read The Petition of Several of the Inhabitants of Williamsburgh setting forth that by an Instruction to them given, they run out 400 acres for a Town and Common and run their Tracts of Land bounding on the said 400 acres where they settled, and they being Informd. there was an order for enlarging the said Common which would take away their Houses, and the Lands they have Cleard & prayd a Stop may be put to y'e Same.

His Majestys Council taking the same into Consideration, and being Satisfied that the Pet'rs would be great Sufferers in any Alteration was made int he laying out of that Town, and also that the Resolve of Council of the 19th August last relating to the fixing of Townships was made after they were settled. Orderd. that upon these Considerations the Said Town remain as it was first layd out that none of the Setlers Lands may be Encroached upon.

Read the Petition of Elinor Mortimer setting forth that she has Eighteen persons in family, all in her own absolutely right for which she has not ever had any Land in this Province, and therefore prays a warrant may issue to her

HEMPSTEAD COUNTY LIBRARY
HOPE, ARKANSAS

for 900 acres of Land in the Township of Kingston, and the Pet'r having produced the Attorney Gen'ls Certificate, proving on oath her said Right. Ordered. that a Warrant do issue to the Pet'r for 900 acres of Land in the Township of Kingston as prayed for.

Meeting of Wednesday the 3'd of March 1735/6

Read the Petition of James Hartley, setting forth that he has Seventeen persons in Family as appears by the Attorney Genl's Certificate for which having no Land, he prays he may have a Warrant Issue to him for 850 acres of Land in the Township of Queensborough. Orderd. that a Warrant do Issue to the Pet'r for 850 acres of Land in the Township of Queensborough, pursuant to the Prayer of the Petition.

Read the Petition of James McCance, setting forth that he has been in this Province since Sep'r 1732, that he is now Settled in Williamsburgh, and has six persons in family for which he has not run out any Land, and praying a Warrant for 300 acres of Land and a Town Lott in the said Township of Williamsburgh. Orderd. That a Warrant do Issue to the Pet'r for 300 acres of Land and a Town Lott in the Township of Williamsburgh, pursuant to the Prayer of his Petition.

Rad the Petition of John Jamesson praying a Warrant for 1000 acres in any Township he designing to bring over twenty Protestant subjects to settle the same, and being willing to Enter into Bond in such Penalty as shall be thought proper to perform the same in the Space of One year, and praying likewise that his Account for runing Lands for the Poor Settlers of Williamsburgh may be taken into Consideration and orderd. to be payd. Resolve that that part of the said Jemmessons Petition relating to the Land he prays for on his entring into Bond be rejected. Resolved That the said Jemmessons accounts do lye upon the Table in order to be Audited.

Read the Petition of Richard Purcel praying 300 acres of Land pursuant to the Act of Assembly passd Immediately after the Indian War for encouraging people coming into this Province to settle, and also his Family Right consisting of nine persons in the Township of Williamsburgh. orderd. That a Warrant of Survey do Issue to the Pet'r for 450 acres of Land and a Town Lott being his Family Right, sworn to before His Majestys Attorney Gen'l in the Township of Williamsburgh, but that his Prayer for the 300 acres on the Encouragement of the Act, be Rejected.

Read the Petition of William Ferguson praying a Warrant of Survey for 400 acres of Land and a Town Lot by virtue of His Family Right, in the Township of Williamsburgh he having Sworn to his said Right before his Majestys Attorney Genl as appeard by the Certificate and the Pet'r having no Lands in this Province. Orderd. That a Warrant do Issue to the Pet'r for 500 acres and A town Lott in the Township of Williamsburgh.

Meeting of Thursday the 4'th of March 1735/6

Read the Petition of Benj'a Carter praying a Warrant of Survey for 100 acres of Land in Amelia Township in Berkley County. Orderd. That a warrant of Survey do Issue to the Pet'r accordingly.

Read The Petition of Ezechiel Cox praying a warrant of Survey for 100 acres of Land in Amelia Township for his Family Right. Orderd. That a warrant of Survey do Issue to the Pet'r pursuant to the Prayer of His Petition.

Read The Petition of William Tilly praying a warr't of Survey for 200 acres of Land in Amelia Township for his Family Right. Orderd. That a warrant of Survey do Issue to the Pet'r in Amelia Towns'p.

Meeting of Wednesday the 17'th of March 1735/6

Read the Petition of George Tabart praying that as he has obtained his Hon'rs arrant for 250 acres of Land and a Town Lott in Purisburgh having 5 persons in Family he may receive for himself and his said Family the Benefit of His Maj'tys Bounty of Provisions and Tools to Enable them to settle and Cultivate the said Lott and Lands. Orderd. that the Prayer of the said Petition be Granted.

Read the Petition of Isaac Amyand praying such part of His Majestys Lands as to this Hon'ble Board shall seem meet in one of the New Townships, he being one of His Majestys Officers. Ordered. that a Warrant do Issue to the Pet'r for 1000 acres in any Township not excepted.

Read the Petition of Stephen Proctor praying a warrant for 800 acres of Land and a Town Lott in Waccamaw Township in lieu of the same quantity of acres run out by virtue of His Family Right in Granville County which happen'd to be within the Limitts of Purisburgh Township, and for that reason could not obtain a Grant for the same. Orderd that the Prayer of the Petition be Granted upon the Pet'rs Surrendring the former Warrant.

Read the Petition of James Wedderburn praying a warrant for 1000 acres of Land in any of the Northern Townships, he being one of His Majestys Officers as Clerk of the Crown, Pleas &Ca. Orderd That a Warrant do Issue to the Pet'r accordingly for 1000 acres of Land.

Read the Petition of Thomas Maddock praying his Family Right consisting of Eight persons (which right he had swore to before his Maj'tys Attorney Gen'l) in any of His Majestys Township.l Orderd. That a Warrant do Issue to the Pet'r for 400 acres of Land in any Township Excepting Orangeburgh, and the Townships to the Southward of Santee River.

Meeting of Thursday the 18'th of March 1735/6

Read the Petition of Thomas Lowndes gen't setting forth that by Mesne Conveyances from Thomas Rutherford, he has a Right to 12,000 acres of Land in this Province, which right was proved in Council, Her Majesty the Queen present, a copy of the Order of Council being annexed to the Petition, and praying a warrant of Survey for the same. Orderd. That Mr. Secretary do prepare a warrant of Survey for 12,000 acres of land in the same of the said Thomas Lowndes, directed to His Majestys Surveyor Gen'l to answer the purport of the said Order of Council. the Pet'r by himself or his Attorney, producing to this Board the original Order of Council mentioned in his Petition.

P. M.

On reading the Petition of William Weekley setting forth that upon employing a Lawful surveyor to run the Land left to him by his Father, which Land was Granted by the late Lords Proprietors near twenty years since, and likewise setting forth that one Thomas Bollen stopped the Chain and threatened to Trouble the Surveyor if he proceeded further on the said survey. It was Resolved and Orderd That the Pet'r is at Liberty if he thinks fit to Employ a Surveyor to resurvey the said Tract of Land and that in case the Pet'r in pursuance of this order and Resolution meets with any Loss, hindrance or Molestation, that he be at Liberty to Right himself at Common Law.

Meeting of Friday the 19'th of March 1735/6

Read the Petition of Captain Thomas Henning setting forth that he has a Family of Twenty Two persons for which he has had not Land in this Province and being determind to settle in the same with his said Family, he humbly apprehends himself Intitled to the benefit designd by his Majesty to those who come into this Province to settle the Townships And praying that a warr't of survey do pass to him for Eleven hundred acres and a Town Lott in any of his Majestys New townships not excepted by Resolution of Council. Orderd. That a Warrant do Issue to the said Cap'n Henning for 1100 acres of Land and a Town Lott in any of the New Townships excepting Orangeburgh and the Townships to the Southward of Santee River, the Pet'r qualifying himself before his Majestys attorney General for that number of acres, and surrendring his former warrant of 1100 acres on vacant lands.

Meeting of Wednesday the 24'th of March 1735/6

Upon a Motion made by Benj'a Whitaker, Esq'r for grants to pass to Jos. Commander for 548, and 446 acres to John Commander for 439 acres and to Elisha Scriven for 423 acres, all which Lands were resurveyd, pursuant to an Order of this Board to the Several persons aforesaid, It was Orderd that

Grants do pass accordingly to the persons aforementioned for the number of Acres as above.

Robert Hume Esq'r Attorney for Thomas Lowndes Gent: having produced to this Board the Original Order of Council dated at Kensington the 9'th of July 1735 pursuant to an order of this Board of the 18th Inst. which said Original Order of Council was Compared with a Copy of the same annext to the said Lowndes's Petition, and allowed to be an Exact and true copy of the Original Order of council aforesaid. Orderd. That the Secretary of this Province do forthwith Comply with the Order of council of the 18'th of March inst.

Meeting of Thursday the 25'th of March 1736

His Majestys Hon'ble Council taking into Consideration the Petition of Isaiah Overy a person Intitled to run out 200 acres of Land in the Township of purisburgh, complaining the one Staples a Deputy Surveyor for the said Township, instead of Shewing him to run out the said Land within the Limits of the said Township Directed him to run out the said 200 Acres on Land which now proves to be without the said Township which after being performed by one Ross another Deputy Surveyor the Pet'r carried his Family and settled upon the same and now Prays to have a Grant for the said 200 acres, but as this Board is not satisfied whether the said Land may not have been Granted already to some other person Orderd that the Prayer of the Petition be granted so far, that the Pet'r is allowed to remain in quiet Possession of the said Land until it appears that it has been Granted heretofore to some other Person.

Meeting of Thursday the 26'th of March 1735/6

Read the Memorial of the Hon'ble Joseph Wragg Esq're setting forth that the memorialist by virtue of a Grant from the Late Lords Proprietors to John Danson Esqr of two Baronys containing each 12,000 acres of Land English measure, lying and being on the Lands commonly known and distinguished by the name of Yamasee Lands, on the Conditions as in the said Grant is fully Expressed and that he by virtue of the said Grant did cause two Baronys of 12,000 acres each to be surveyd and laid out on the said Yamassee Lands fronting Port Royal River as appears by Platts thereof Layd before this Board Certified by John Frip, a Deputy Surveyor, the 20th of May 1730, and the memorialist Setting forth, likewise that he has great reason to believe Sev'l Encroachments have been made on the said Baronys, and praying a warrant of Resurvey to His Majestys Surveyor General to resurvey and new mark the Lines, which he conceives will prevent the like Inconvenience for the future. Orderd. That a Special Warrant do Issue to His Maj'tys Surveyor Gen'l to Resurvey or Cause to be resurveyd and new markt the Lines of the said Baronys as prayed for and mentiond in the Memorial and that Platts of the said Resurvey be forthwith returnd to this Board.

William Greenland representing to this Board by Thomas Ferguson, a Deputy Surveyor, that the said Surveyor that the said Surveyor had made a mistake in a Platt of 373 acres of Land Certified by the Surveyor y'e 27th Day of January 1732 of about 60 acres short of the quantity, and in order to clear up the same the said Ferguson layd before this Board a just & regular Platt of the said 373 acres as it ought first to have been. It is therefore Orderd that the said Just and regular Platt be carried to y'e Surveyor General and that he the s'd Surveyor Gen'l do Certifie the same under the date the first Platt was Certified, he Cancelling the said first Platt, and that at the request of the said Greenland the Secretary is also Orderd to take off the Seal from the Grant affixed to the first mentiond Platt in order that the regular Platt aforesaid may be affixed to the said Grant, and layd before This Board to be returnd to the said Greenland.

P. M.

His Majesty's Hon'ble Council took into Consideration the Hearing of the Caveat enterd by the Hon'ble Mr. Kinloch against Atkins and others, having Grants for Lands by him the said Kinloch Surveyd and run out by virtue of a Warrant for 9150 acres. Orderd. that Mr. Kinloch have 3249 acres of Land being the quantity remaining in his warrant for 9150 acres and that a Grant or Grants do pass to him for the same.

Heard a Cross Caveat between Mr. Whitaker and Cap't James Gordon. And the Partys agreeing among themselves, no further notice was taken of the same by the Board.

A Caveat entered by Ca't Gordon against Jos'h Hurst for 1050 acres of Land in Craven County butting and bounding on the South on Peter smiths land and on the East on Will Whitesides North Easterly on Edw'd Bullard Land was taken into Consideration. And on Heading the Partys on the above Caveat and it appearing that 1000 acres of the said 1050 acres was surveyd in the said Hurst's name by the Deputy Surveyor without any Lawfull Authority from the said Hurst and it also appear to this Board that the said 1050 acres of Land was duely surveyd to the said James Gordon. It is therefore Orderd that the Certificate of James St. John Esq'r surveyor Gen'l annexed to the Platt of the said James Gordon dated the 7th day of April 1734 be withdrawn and that the said Surveyor Gen'l do make a Common General Certificate to the said James Gordon of the said Platt of 1050 acres of Land in order that a Grant do pass to the said James Gordon for the same.

Heard a Caveat Enterd by Catherine Lenee against Dan'l Crawford, and hearing Council on both sides. It was Orderd That a Grant do pass to the said Crawford for the Land in dispute as mentiond in the said Caveat.

Upon reading the Petition of James Abercromby Esq'r praying a Special Warrant for 500 acres of Land in the Township of Queensborough, Surveyd for one Solomon Hughs, for that the said Solomon Hughs was accused of feloniously taking and Carying away two Negro men Belonging to William Heatly of Craven County, Cooper, and that the said Hughs had never applied for a rant for said Land, but was fled out of the Province to escape the Punishment due for so great a Crime.

It appearing to this Board that the said William Heatly was the person Injurd, and a great Sufferer by the said Hughs, and a motion being made by the Hon'ble Mr. Wragg, a member of this Board and a Creditor of the said Heatly, that a Special Warrant may Issue to the said Heatly for the said 500 acres of Land, Surveyd for the said Hughs, as some recompences for the Damage done him.

Orderd that a Special Warrant do pass to Will: Heatley for 500 acres of Land Surveyd to Solomon Hughs in the Township of Queenborough in order that a Grant do pass to him for the same.

Meeting of Saturday the 27'th of March 1735/6

Mess's Greeme and Whitaker moved that the Sev'l Caveats enterd by Will: Bellinger against Col'o Joseph Blake, James Kerr, Walter Izard Esq'r Sen'r and Walter Izard Esq'r Jun'r might be heard and determind. And the said hearing came on, and Council being heard on all sides. It was Ordered that grants do pass to Col'o Blake and Mr. Kerr, and that there be a Resurvey of the Lands formerly Survd. for the s'd Izards Sen'r and Jun'r it being apprehended the former Survey Includes some Lands granted to Mr. Hasel.

Read the Petition of Robert Cole praying a Grant for the Lands therein mentiond. Orderd. That the said cole do attend this board with his purchase receipt and other papers relating to the said Lands in order to be considerd by this Board.

Read the Petition of David Mongin praying an allowance of Provisions for himself and Family on his removing into the Township of Purisburgh. Orderd that Provisions be allowed to all the white persons in the Petitioners Family on his settling them in the said Township.

Meeting of Thursday the 8'th of April 1736

Read the Petition of John Brookes and Thomas Binder praying they may have Warr'ts the former for 150 acres and a Lott in Pedee Township and the latter for 50 acres and a Lott in the s'd Township.

Read the Petition of Allen Wells Signd by His Attorney Nath: Wickham Esq'r praying a Warrant for 1200 acres of Land in one of the Townships. Ordered. that the said Petition do lie upon the Table, till the said Wells appears at this Board and satisfies his Majestys Council that his Allegations are True.

Meeting of Friday the 9'th of April 1736

Read the Petition of Charles Hart Esq'r praying he may have a Warrant for 500 acres of Land granted him by Governor Craven and also his Family Right amounting to 400 acres more. Ordered that a Warrant of Survey do Issue to the said Charles hart for 1000 acres on Vacant Lands.

Col'o Stevens attorney to Col'o Sam'l Horsey appeared at this Board and produced an order of Council dated at Kensington the 9'th day of July 1735 on a Report from the Right honb'e the Lords of the Commee of Council on Plantation affairs which is as followeth...

By order of council of the 3d April 1734 referring to this Comm'e a Report made by the Lords Commm'rs for Trade and Plantations upon the Petition of Col'o Sam'l Horsey, the Lords of the Com'ee this day took the same into their Consideration and do find that the said Petition set forth that on the 26th day of Dec'r 1726 the Lords Proprietors of Carolina signed a warrant to make him a Landgrave and to Grant him four Baronys of 48,000 acres of Land but that the Pet'r being then concernd in Solliciting a Surrender of the Province of So Carolina to his Majesty from the late Lords Proprietors, he did not attempt to take up the said Lands at that Junction, being desirous to avoid every thing which might give any Obstruction to the proposed surrender, chusing rather to depend on His Majestys Goodness for the perfecting his Grant, when his Majesty should be in full Possession of the Province wherefore the Pet'r most humbly prayd His Majesty in regard to his good Services in Solliciting and perfecting the said Surrender, and the great Trouble and expence he has been at upon that account for which he has never received any Consideration, that his Majesty would be Graciously pleasd to Direct that a Grant might be made to him of the Lands Comprized in the above mentioned warrant of the Late Lords Proprietors, in such manner as his Majesty in his Great Wisdom should think fit, that he might be enabled to pursue his Intention of making a Settlement in the said Province... Her Majesty this Day took the said Report into Consideration and was pleasd with the Advice of His Maj'tys Privy Council to approve thereof and to order as it is hereby orderd That the Governor or Commander in Chief of His Majestys Province of So Carolina for the time being do Cause a Grant to be made to the Pet'r His Heirs and Assigns of 48,000 acres of Land in that Province, upon the Sev'l Conditions proposed by the said Report. Ja: Vernon.

Meeting of Saturday the 10'th of April 1736

Evan Hopkins took his Oath before the Council that he had four persons in his Family viz't himself, his wife and two Children for which he never as yet had any Land. Orderd That a Warrant do Issue to the said Evan Hopkins for 200 acres of Land and a Town Lott in the Township of Williamsburgh.

Meeting of Wednesday the 14'th of April 1736

Read the Petition of Phillip Delegall of the Independ't Company at Beaufort praying a Lott in Beaufort Town. Orderd that the Prayer of the Petition be Granted, and that he have a vacant Lott in that Town.

Meeting of Friday the 16'th of April 1736

Mr. Baxter moved this board that the 1500 acres for which he had an order of Council in any of the Townships be layd out in three different Tracts of 500 acres each in any of the Townships on Pedee and Black River. Orderd that the said Baxters request be Granted.

On a Motion made by Richard Allein in behalf of Henry Peroneau and James Osmond surviving Executors and Devisees of Arthur Hall Esq'r deceased against Joseph Seabrook praying that the two Caveats or Claims exhibited by the above mentioned Claimants against the said Defendent Seabrook may be heard. Ordered that the same be heard at this board on the 6th of May next.

Meeting of Saturday the 8'th of May 1736

Read the Petition of John Fairchild praying that in Consideration of a Tract of 49 acres layd out to his late Father but not Granted, he dying soon after the s'd Tract was layd out he the Pet'r may have a Special Warrant to resurvey the same in Order to obtain a Grant for it. Ordered that the Petition be Granted and that a Special Warrant do issue to the Pet'r accordingly.

Read The Petition of Peter Hume praying a Warrant may Issue to him for 950 acres and a Town Lott in the Township of Williamsburgh he having nineteen persons in Family for which he has never had any Lands, which family Right he proved before Mr. Secretary Hammerton. Orderd that the Prayer of the Petition be Granted and that a Warrant do issue to the Pet'r for nine hundred and fifty acres and a Town Lott in the Township of Williamsburgh as prayed for.

Read the Petition of Joseph Crell praying 150 acres of Land in the Township of Fredericksburgh, having Sworn to His Family Right of 3 persons. Ordered that a warrant do issue to the Petitioner accordingly.

Read the Petition of John Lining praying a warrant for 1200 acres and a Town Lott in any of the New Townships in lieu of a warrant for survey granted him for 1150 acres of Land, he having purchased One negro since. Orderd that the Prayer of the Petition be Granted and that a Warrant do Issue to the Petitioner in any Township except Orangeburgh and the Townships on the south side of Santee River, the Pet'r proving His family Right on Oath before the Attorney Gen'l and Surrendring at this Board the first Warrant.

Read the Petition of Allen Wells praying 700 acres of Land in any of the Northern Townships he having Swore to his Family Right before the Attorney General. Orderd That the Prayer of the Petition be Granted and that the Warrant be for 1200 acres of Land and a Lott in any of the Townships north of Santee River he having produced a purchas Receipt for 500 acres for which he made Oath he never yet has had any Land.

Read the Petition of Alex'r and Isaac Chauvin praying that Special Grants may pass to them for one Tract of Land of 150 acres for another Tract of Land containing 150 acres for another Tract of Land containing 150 acres on Black River and for another Tract of Land containing 350 ares in St. James's Parish Santee, all which Tracts were admeasured to their late Father, who dyed before he could obtain Grants for the same and who by his last will and Testament devised all his Lands to the Pet'rs. Orderd that the Prayer of the Petition be granted and that Special Grants do pass accordingly.

Read the Petition of Thomas Wally, Herman Kolb and Tilman Kolb, praying a Warrant for 50 acres of Land each may pass to them in the Township of Queensborough. Orderd That Warrants do pass to the Pet'rs accordingly.

Read the Petition of Ruth Glasbrooke praying a Grant may pass to her for the use of her three Children of 418 acres of Land laid out to her late Husband, who dyed before a Grant could pass to him for the same. Orderd That a Grant be prepared in the name of the said Ruth Glasbrooke in trust for the 3 Children of Martin Glasbrooke.

Read the Petition of Thomas Taylor praying one Thousand acres in the Township of Williamsburgh Township, he having swore to His Family Right before the Attorney General.Ordered That a Warrant of Survey do Issue to the Pet'r as prayd for.

Read the Petition of William Row praying 300 acres of Land in the Township of Kingston, he having Sworn to his Family Right before the Attorney Gen'l.

Read the Petition of Thomas Charnock setting forth that by virtue of Two Warrants y'e One for 500 acres the other for 450, he had caused to be admeasured to him the said Tracts, and had Improved them &ca. and praying a Grant may pass to him for the Same. Orderd That the Petition do Lye upon the Table until it is known if the Land be within the Township of Queensborough.

Read the Petition of Mary Carmichael widdow of John Carmichael deceased, praying a New Warrant in her name for 850 acres of Land in Lieu of one for the like Quantity, granted to her late Husband for His Family Right, no part of which was Executed in his Life time. Orderd that the Prayer of the Petition be Granted, and that a Warrant do Issue in the Petitioners name accordingly, upon her surrendring the former warrant.

Read the Petition of Stephen Bedon setting forth that he has a Warrant for His Family Right of 1100 acres of Land, but having made no use of the said Warrant and having no Land in this Province, prays he may have a New Warrant to run the said 1100 acres of Land in some of the New Townships to the northward of Santee River. Orderd that the Prayer of the Petition be Granted, on his Surrendring his former warrant.

Read the Petition of Stephen Andrews praying 350 acres of Land in any of the Townships to the northward of Santee River, being his Family Right swore to before the Attorney Gen'l. Orderd that a Warrant do Issue to the said Stephen Andrews pursuant to the Pray'r of His Petition.

Read the Petition of Jeremiah Coutinno, praying a warrant may Issue to him for 300 acres of Land His Family Right consisting of six persons swore to before Peter Paget, Esqr. Orderd that a Warrant do Issue to the Pet'r accordingly.

Meeting of Wednesday the 12'th of May 1736

Read the Petition of William Tunker praying a Warrant for 300 acres of Land in any of the Northern Townships he having swore to His Family Right before the Attorney General. Orderd That a Warrant Issue to the Pet'r accordingly.

Meeting of Friday the 14'th of May 1736

The Hon'ble Mr. Skene having Surrendred to this Board two Platts of one Thousand acres each in Berkley County the greatest part of the said Land having been Granted to other persons and praying he may have two Warrants Issue to him for one thousand acres of Land in lieu thereof, in one of the Townships or Elsewhere. Orderd that Warrants do Issue to the said Mr. Skene accordingly.

His Majestys Council taking into Consideration a Grant signd for James St. John Esq'r for 345 acres of Land in Colleton County the 29th of Nov'r 1735 which was stoped it being apprehended the said 345 acres were run on Lands belonging to Dan'l Cartwright, and it having since appeard to this Board that the s'd 345 acres were actually part of the Lands belonging to the said Cartwright and Mr. St. John Aquieseing therein, the said Grant was this day Cancelld in Council.

Meeting of Saturday the 15'th of May 1736

Application being made to this Board by Capt. John Croft praying that his Warrant for 500 acres of Land in any of the Townships not excepted may be Changed for a warrant for 1000 acres in any of the Townships not excepted as aforresaid. Orderd That a warrant do Issue to the said Croft for 1000 acres and a Town Lott in any of the Townships not excepted upon his Surrendring his former warrant for 500 acres as aforementioned, this Board being of Opinion that said Croft is deserving of that Indulgence for the many Services he has done to the Publick, without having received any fee or reward for the same.

Read the Petition of John Williams, praying a warrant for 100 acres of Land in Amelia Township he having two persons in Family, as appears by his Oath before Thomas Ferguson, Esqr. Ordered That a warrant do Issue to the said John Williams for 100 acres in Amelia Township as prayd for.

Meeting of Tuesday y'e 18'th of May 1736

Read The Petition of Richard Ash and Will: Levingston Esq'rs Executors of the last will and Testament of Sam'l Ash late of Charles Town deceased setting forth that John Givens was Several Years possessed of a Tract of Land containing by Estimation 700 acres more or less in Craven County and payd Tax for the same That the said John Givens Impowered his son in Law Thomas Bennet to sell and dispose of all his Lands and Tenements in this Province who continued in Possession of the said Land and payd Tax for the same till on a Valuable Consideration to him payd by the said Sam'l Ash he made over his right to the said Ash of the said Tract. That Dan'l McGregory run out that said Land upon which a Caveat was Enterd in the name of Thomas Bennet against any Grant being passed to the said McGregory for the said Land, which Caveat was argued before his Maj'stys Hon'ble Council the 6th of Sep'r last, and it was decreed that the said Tract of Land should be granted to the said John Givens or His Assigns, and that the said Saml Ash died considerably indebted to Sev'l persons far beyond what his personal Estate will amount to. Therefore praying a Special Warrant may Issue tot he Pet'r to run out the said Tract of Land in order it may be Granted them to sell and dispose of for the use of the said Ash's Creditors. Orderd That a Special Warrant do Issue pursuant of the Prayer of the said Petition.

Read the Petition of Laurence Royal praying a warrant of Survey for 200 acres of Land in Amelia Township having proved his Family right before the Attorney Gen'l. Orderd That a warrant issue to the said Royal as prayd for.

Read the Petition of John Chevillette praying a warrant of Survey for 450 acres of Land in Purisburgh Township, being his Family Right Sworn to before the attorney Gen'l. Orderd That a warrant of Survey do issue to the said Chevillette pursuant to the Pray'r of his Petition.

Read the Petition of Jacob Woolford setting forth that John Browne deceased had in his Life time 1500 acres of Land layd out to him by virtue of a Warrant from his Late Ex'cy Robert Johnson Esq'r as appears by a Platt thereof now in the Surveyor Gen'ls Office. That the said John Browne dyed before a Grant could pass to him for the same and by his last Will and Testament nominated the Pet'r Sole Executor and Residuary Legatee of all his real and Personal Estate, after paying his Debts, That the said Browne dyed much Indebted to Sev'l persons. Therefore, the Pet'r prays in order he may be Enabled to fulfill the True Intent of the said will by disposing of the said Land for Payment of the said Brownes Debts he may obtain a Special Grant of the Land so Surveyd to the said Browne. Orderd. That a Special Grant do pass to the Pet'r as prayd for.

Meeting of Thursday the 20'th of May 1736

His Maj'tys Hon'ble Council took into Consideration the Pet'n of the Rev'd Mr. Thomas Morret praying a warrant for 1000 acres of Land, the same number of Acres having been allowed to other the ministers of the Church of England. Orderd That a warrant Issue to the said Thomas Morret accordingly.

Read the Petition of the s'd Thomas Morret clerk praying a warrant for 250 acres on his family right proved before the Attorney Gen'l and further praying he may have leave to Surrender his Platt for 700 acres heretofore run out on Mr. Dansons Barony, and have a warrant to run out the said number of acres elsewhere. Ordered that the Pet'r on surrendring his Platt of 700 acres mentioned to be run on Mr. Dandsons Barony, a warrant do Issue for laying out to him 700 acres of Land on any Vacant Land, and that a warrant do also Issue to him for 250 acres on vacant land also being his family right.

Meeting of Friday the 21'st of May 1736

Orderd That the Hearing on the disputed land between William Elliott Jun'r and Will: Dry come on at 9 o Clock tomorrow morning, of not other business Interfere.

Orderd. That the Attorney Gen'l do make out a Special Fait in the name of Eliz'a Jennys late Eliz'a Raven for 1000 acres of Land in Craven County in lieu of that for the same number of acres in the said County made out and Issued to the s'd Eliz'a Raven now Jennys in order a Grant do pass to her for the same.

Read the Petition of Charles Purry praying a Warrant for 50 acres of Land and a Town Lott being his family Right, proved before Peter Lafitte Esq'r Justice of the Peace at Purisburg. Orderd That a Warrant do Issue to the Pt'r pursuant to the Prayer of his Petition.

Read the Petition of John Chilcot and also the Petition of Dominick Murphy praying each of them have a Town Lott in Beaufort. Orderd That the merits of the said Petition be taken into Consideration with the rest of the Claims for Lotts in the said Town.

Meeting of Monday the 24'th of May 1736

Read the Petition of David Browne praying 200 acres of Land and a Town Lott in one of the Western Townships. Orderd That a Warrant do Issue to the Pet'r for 200 acres of Land and a Town Lott in any of the Townships excepting Orangeburgh and the Townships to the Southward of Santee River.

Read the Pet'n of Anth: Stark praying an additional quantity of Fifty acres of Land in the Congree Township as an additional family right for a Child born to him. Orderd That a warrant do Issue to the Pet'r pursuant to the Prayer of y'e Petition.

Meeting of Wednesday the 26'th of May 1736

Mr. Whitaker in behalf of Mr. Dry against Mr. Elliot, appeard at this Board, touching the Vacant land in dispute between them and having heard Council on both sides and His Maj'tys Council being of Opinion that Mr. Dray and John Cockfield had an Equal Right to the Vacant land, which lies between the Lands of s'd Dry and cockfield to the westward of the said Drys Land. Ordered that the said Land be resurveyd and equally divided between the said Dry and Cockfield and Plats thereof returnd, that Grants may Issue to each of them.

Meeting of the 27'th of May 1736

Mr. Allein moved that the Caveat enterd by Henry Peroneau and James Osmond surviving Executors and Devisees of Arthur Hall Esq'r deceased against Joseph Seabrooke may now be heard. Orderd. That the same be heard tomorrow morning.

Read The Petition of Mr. Stephen Bull, praying that he may surrender a Grant for 700 acres of Land, which is found by Mr. Bryans late survey to be within the 6 miles of the Townships of Purisburgh, and that he may obtain a warrant to lay out a like Quantity of Land in other part of the Province. Orderd That a Warr't do Issue pursuant to the Prayer of the Pet'n on his delivering up the said Grant, and that the Secretary do Indorse this Order on the back of the Record of the said Grant in his office.

Meeting of Saturday the 29'th of May 1736

Mr. Whitaker moved that the Caveat Enterd by Cooper against Wigfall might be withdrawn and that a Grant do pass to the said Wigfall. Orderd that a

Grant do pass to the said Wigfall for the Land Caveated, if the person Caveating do not shew reasons to the Contrary with the Space of one Month from this day.

On reading the Petition of Mr. Will: Elliot, Mr. Pinckney moved that the Order of Council of the 26th Instant relating to the vacant Land in dispute between him and Mr. Dry may be set aside and reheard. Orderd That the said Order of the 26th Inst. be set aside and that the Lands in dispute be resurveyed within two months from this Day and that all partys concernd have notice thereof to attend the Survey.

Orderd That a Warrant do Issue to Paul Jenys Esqr, Speaker of the Commons House, for 200 acres of Land on any vacant Land in this Province, and that Mr. Secretary do prepare the same.

Meeting of Wednesday the 16'th of June 1736

Read the Petition of Sarah Woodward, widdow, Isaac Chardon and Mary his wife, shewing that Richard Woodward at his Death was seized of two Tracts of Land the one containing 382 Acres of Land in Colleton County and the other containing 500 acres in the said County, and praying a warrant of resurvey of the said two Tracts, and that the Pet'rs may obtain a Grant for as much Land as shall appear to be containd within the Boundarys of said Platts, at such Quit Rents as are reservd on the said Original Grants. Orderd that a Warrant of Resurvey do Issue accordingly, in order that a Grant may pass as prayd for, on such Quit Rents as shall be concluded on by this Board.

Read the Petition of James Delas, Agent for Mr. Danl Vernezobre, praying a warrant for 2000 acres of Land in Purisburgh he having qualified for that Quantity as sworn by the said Delass, before the Attorney Genl. Orderd That a warrant do Issue accordingly to the Petr in the name of Daniel Vernezobre.

Read the Petition of Duncan McQueen praying 600 acres of Land in this Province he having 12 persons in his Family Sworn to. Orderd That a Warrant do Issue to the Pet'r accordingly.

Orderd That for the Future all petitions to the Governor and council for Land shall after Qualification sworn to before the Attorney Gen'l or in his absence before any other Magistrate be sent by the said Attorney Genl together with the Fees due thereon to the Clerk and Messenger of the Council to the said Clerk of the council, in order the same may be layd before this Board for their Direction thereon.

Upon reading the Petition of Sev'l of the Inhabitants of Williamsburgh, setting forth y't they expect many of their Relations and friends from Ireland to settle in that Township and praying no warrants may issue for that Township till their arrival. Orderd. That no warrants do Issue for the s'd Township of Williamsburg before the 1st of Oct'r next.

Meeting of Tuesday the 22'd of June 1736

Read the Petition of John Rivers praying 300 acres of Land, being Intitled to that Number by His Family right Sworn to. Orderd That a Warrant do Issue to the Pet'r for 300 acres of Land as prayed for.

Read the Petition of Joseph Jolley praying 600 acres of Land in one of the Townships being his family right Sworn to. Orderd That a Warrant do Issue to the Pet'r for 600 acres of Land in any of the Townships excepting Orangeburgh, Williamsburgh or the Township on the South side of Santee River.

Read the Petition of Thomas Gallway praying a Town Lott and 250 acres of Land in any Township to the norward of Santee River. Orderd. That a Warrant of Survey do Issue pursuant to the Prayer of the Petitioner excepting the Townships excepted.

Read the Petition of Robert Thorpe Esq're praying two Town Lotts in Beaufort in Granville County. Orderd. That the said Petition do lye upon the Table till the matter relating to the Lotts in Beaufort is taken into Consideration.

Meeting of Wednesday the 23'd of June 1736

Read the Petition of Will: McMullin praying a warrant for 200 acres of Land his Family right sworn to. Orderd That a Warrant do Issue to the Pet'r pur't to the Prayer of the Petition.

Read the Petition of Abraham Michau praying a warrant for 400 acres of Land his Family right sworn to. Orderd That a Warrant do Issue to the Pet'r pursuant to the Prayer of the Petition.

Read the Petition of John Fitch praying a warrant for 300 acres of Land his Family right sworn to. Orderd That a Warrant do Issue to the Petitioner pursuant to the Prayer of the Petition.

Read the Petition of Anne Ursel Keller and Frederick Preacher praying 100 acres of Land being their Family right sworn to. Orderd That a Warrant do Issue to the Pet'r pursuant to the Prayer of His Petition.

Read the Petition of Tho's Lake praying a warrant for 1550 acres of Land his Family right sworn to, in one of the Townships. Orderd That The same do lie upon the Table untill the Pet'rs attorney do prove the number of Persons the Pet'r has in family in this Province.

Meeting of Thursday the 24'th of June 1736

Read the Petition of Joseph Blake, Esq'r, praying that in Consideration of His readiness to submit to His Majestys pleasure in Surrendring His Proprietorship in this Province, he may have a warrant Issue to him for such a quantity of Land and on such Terms and Conditions as this Board shall think fit. Orderd That a warrant do Issue to the said joseph Blake Esq'r for 6000 acres of vacant land Subject to His Maj'tys Quit Rents as usual.

Meeting of Thursday the 1'st of July 1736

Read the Petition of Andrew McCleland praying his Family right consisting of 15 persons Swore to in one of the Townships pursuant to his Majestys Royal instructions. Orderd That a warrant do Issue to the Pet'r for 750 acres of Land in any of the New Townships, excepting Orangeburgh and the Townships on the South side of Santee River.

Meeting of Friday the 2'd of July 1736

Read The Petition of Saml Commander, John Commander, Burtonhead Boutwell & Eliz'a his wife, and the Prayer of Their Petition appearing to His Majty's Hon'ble Council Just and reasonable It was Orderd That Grants do pass as prayd for by the Pet'rs.

Read the Petition of Giles Holliday praying such a Quantity of Acres of his Majestys Land as their Hon'rs shall Judge proper, he being one of His Majestys Officers, as Register of the Court of Vice admiralty. Orderd That a Warrant do Issue to the Pet'r for 500 acres of Land in any Township excepting Orangeburgh or the Townships on the South side of Santee River.

Read the Petition of William James, praying that the Lands formerly run out to one Archibald Hamilton deceased may be run and Granted to him in Trust for the use and benefit of a dissenting minister during the time he officiates in the Township of Williamsburgh. Orderd That the attorney General do prepare a Special Fiat in order that a Grant do pass in the name of the said William James, Capt. Thomas Hall and John Witherspoon in trust for the dissenting Minister aforesaid.

Read the Petition of John Salter setting forth that he has no Land in this Province neither in His own right or his Familys and therefore prays a warrant of Survey for 500 acres of Land in one of His Majestys Townships. Orderd That the Prayer of the Petition be Granted and that a warrant do Issue to the Pet'r for the Survey of 500 acres of Land in any of His Majestys Townships except Orangeburgh and the Townships on the South side of Santee River.

Meeting of Saturday the 3'd of July 1736

Read the Petition of Margaret Postel widdow praying a Warrant of Survey for 1450 acres of Land in virtue of her Family right sworn to by John Garnier in behalf of the said Margaret. Orderd That the prayer of the Petition be Granted the said Margaret proving to the Satisfaction of His Majestys Council that she Enjoys no Land in right of the number of persons mentiond in the above Petition.

Read the Petition of John Dart, merchant in Charles Town, praying a warrant of Survey for 400 acres of Vacant Land out of the Townships, in Colleton County or elsewhere. Orderd That a Warrant of Survey do Issue to the Pet'r for 400 acres of Vacant Land prayed for.

Read the Petition of Thomas Smith praying a warrant of Survey for 250 acres of Land in virtue of His Family Right sworn to before His Maj'tys Attorney General. Orderd That a Warrant of Survey do Issue to the Pet'r pursuant to the Prayer of his Petition on any vacant Lands out of the Townships.

Read the Petition of Jacob Egler praying his Family right consisting of five persons Swore to. Orderd That a Warrant of Survey do Issue to the Pet'r for 250 acres on Vacant Lands out of the Townships.

Read the Petition of Will: Thomas praying his Family right consisting of six persons Sworn to. Orderd That a Warrant of Survey do Issue to the Pet'r for 300 acres on Vacant Lands out of the Townships.

Read the Petition of Will: Amey praying his Family right consisting of five persons in one of His Maj'tys Townships, sworn to. Orderd That a Warrant of Survey do Issue to the Pet'r for 250 acres in any of his Majestys Townships except Orangeburgh and the Townships on the South side of Santee River.

Read the Petition of Sam'l Dupree praying a Warrant for his Family Right consisting of 8 persons Sworn to. Orderd a Warrant of Survey do Issue to the Pet'r for 400 acres on Vacant Land out of the Townships.

Read the Petition of Joseph Edward Flower Esq'r praying his Family Right consisting of ten persons, in the Township of Purrisburgh. Orderd That a Warrant do Issue to the Pet'r for 500 acres of Land in the Township of Purisburgh, His Hon'r The Lieutenant Governor and His Majestys Hon'ble Council taking into Consideration, the Pet'r had been very Instrumental in the settling the said Township, and he was settled there before his Maj'tys Royal Instructions were signified that none but ____ Protestants should have Grants for Lands in that Township.

Read the Petition of Maurice Lewis praying a Warrant for 500 acres of Land in Some of His Majestys Townships having swore to his family right before the

Attorney Genl. Orderd That a Warrant do Issue to the Petitioner for 500 acres of Land in any of the Townships except Orangeburgh, and the Townships on the South side of Santee River.

Read the Petition of Nicolas Mattison and Henry Mews praying a Warrant may Issue to them for 500 acres of Land between them, the y having Ten persons in Family Sworn to. Ordered a Warrant of Survey do Issue to the Pet'rs for 500 acres of Vacant Land out of the Townships.

Read the Pet'n of James Crawford praying 300 acres of Land in any of his Majestys Townships he having six persons in family as sworn before the Attorney Genl. Orderd That a Warrant of Survey do Issue to the Pet'r for 300 acres of Vacant Land out of the Townships.

Read the Petition of John Fenn praying 550 acres of Land he having Eleven persons in family proved before the Attorney Genl. Orderd That a Warrant do Issue to the said John Fenn for 550 acres of vacant Land out of the Townships.

Meeting of Wednesday the 14'th of July 1736

Orderd That a Warrant of Survey do issue to Jermyn Wright Esq'r for 1000 of Vacant Land out of the Townships.

Read the Petition of Thos Cheeseman praying his Family Right of 30 persons sworn to in any of the Northern Townships. Orderd That a Warrant of Survey do Issue to the Pet'r for 1500 acres of Land in any Township except Orangeburgh and the Townships to the southward of Santee River.

Read the Petition of James Ripalt praying His Family right consisting of 17 persons Sworn to, on Vacant Land. Orderd. That a Warrant of Survey do Issue to the Pet'r for 850 acres of Vacant Land.

Read the Petition of James St. John Esq'r praying a family Right consisting of nine persons on Vacant Land. Orderd. That a Warrant of Survey do Issue to the Pet'r for 450 acres of Vacant Land out of the Townships.

Read the Petition of George and Mary Colleton, praying their Sev'l family Rights of 5 and 13 persons on Vacant Land. Orderd That warrants of Survey do Issue to the Pet'rs for 250 and 650 acres of vacant Land out of the Townships.

Read the Petition of George Douglas praying His Family Right of Ten persons on Vacant Land. Orderd That a warrant of Survey do Issue to the Pet'r for 500 acres of Land out of the Townships.

Read the Petition of John Dunn praying his Family right of ten persons on Vacant Land. Orderd That a warrant of Survey do Issue to the Pet'r for 500 acres of Land out of the Townships.

Read the Petition of Francis Baker praying his Family right consisting of 13 persons on Vacant Land. Orderd That a warrant of Survey do Issue to the Pet'r for 650 acres of Land out of the Townships.

Read the Petition of Sarah Johnson praying 550 acres of Vacant Land her Family right sworn to. Orderd That a warrant of Survey do Issue to the Pet'r for 550 acres of Land out of the Townships.

Read the Petition of John Lindar, John Rudoph Nettman, and John Alleman praying their family right in Purisburgh for 850 acres their family consisting of 17 persons Sworn to. Orderd That a warrant of Survey do Issue to the Pet'r accordingly.

Read the Petition of Wm Clarke praying for 500 acres of Land in Pedee, his family consisting of ten persons. Orderd That a warrant Issue to the Pet'r accordingly.

Read the Petition of Alex'r Nesbit praying 1300 acres of Vacant Land out of the Townships. Orderd That a warrant of Survey do Issue to the Pet'r for 1300 acres of Land out of the Townships.

Read the Petition of Peter Leger praying 600 acres of Vacant Land his family consisting of 12 persons Sworn to. Orderd That a warrant of Survey do Issue to the Pet'r for 600 acres of Vacant Land out of the Townships.

Read the Petition of Gabriel Marion praying 950 acres of Vacant Land his family consisting of 19 persons Sworn to. Orderd That a warrant of Survey do Issue to the Pet'r for 950 acres of Vacant Land out of the Townships.

Read the Petition of James Smalwood praying that he may be permitted to Surrender two Warrants Granted him one for 300 and the other for 1000 acres of Land and that in lieu of the said Warrants he may obtain one for 1300 acres in any of the Townships to the northward of Santee River. Orderd that a Warrant os Survey do Issue to the Pet'r for 1300 acres of Land in any of the townships except Orangeburgh, and the Townships to the Southward of Santee River.

Read the Petition of John Wallis Esq'r praying his Family Right consisting of 32 persons, sworn to in Pedee Township. Orderd That a warrant of Survey do Issue to the Pet'r for 1600 acres of Land vacant and out of the Townships.

Read the Petition of Moses Britten praying his Family Right consisting of 18 persons Sworn to in any one of his Maj'tys Townships. Orderd That a warrant do Issue to the Pet'r for 900 acres of Vacant Land out of the Townships.

Meeting of Friday the 16'th July 1736

Read the Petition of Thomas Ellery Gen't in behalf of himself and Anne his wife heir at Law to her late Brother Mr. William Moore deceased setting forth that the said Moore had Sev'l Tracts of Land layd out to him by virtue of His Family right and otherways, but died before Grants could pass to him for the same. Therefore prays that Grants may pass in the name of him the said Ellery for the said Sev'l Tracts of Land, the said Moore dying Intestate and the said Ann being his only sister and heir at Law. Orderd That Grants be prepared pursuant to the Prayer of the Pet'n.

Read the Petition of Nath: Wickham Setting forth that in the year 1734 he obtained a Warrant for 2050 acres of Land part of which has been since layd out and Granted to the Hon'ble James Kinloch Esq'r and praying he may have liberty to relinquish all his Right & Title to the said Warrant, surrender the same and in lieu thereof that a New Warrant may Issue to him for 2050 acres on any Vacant Land. Orderd That a warrant do Issue to the Pet'r pursuant to the Prayer of His Petition on his Surrendring the first Warrant.

Read the Petition of John Goodbee praying his Family right consisting of 26 persons Sworn to, on vacant land. Orderd That a Warrant do Issue to the Pet'r for 1300 acres of Vacant Land out of the Townships.

Read the Petition of James McElvy praying his Family right consisting of six persons Sworn to, on vacant land. Orderd That a Warrant do Issue to the Pet'r for 300 acres of Vacant Land out of the Townships.

Read the Petition of William Williamson praying his Family Right consisting of nine persons swore to, in the Township of Williamsburgh. Orderd That a Warrant of Survey do Issue to the Pet'r for 450 acres in any of the Townships except that Township of Orangeburgh and the Townships to the southward of Santee River.

Read the Petition of Ester Bate praying hers Family Right consisting of 15 persons sworn to, in the Township of Williamsburgh. Orderd That a Warrant of Survey do Issue to the Pet'r for 750 acres in any of the Townships except that Township of Orangeburgh and the Townships to the southward of Santee River.

Read the Petition of Alex'r Smith praying his Family right consisting of 14 persons Sworn to, he disclaiming a former survey made by virtue of a former warrant, the Land being already Granted to another persons. Orderd that the Surveyor Gen'l do grant the Pet'r a new precept.

Read the Petition of David Mongin praying his Family right consisting of five persons in the Township of Purisburgh. Orderd that a Warrant do Issue tot he Pet'r as prayed for.

Orderd That a Warrant do Issue to Mr. Henry Michael Cook for a Town Lott and 500 acres of Land in any of the Townships except Orangeburgh and the Townships on the South side of Santee River.

Meeting of Saturday the 17'th day of July 1736

The Hon'ble Joseph Wragg Esq'r layd before this Board a Grant for 4000 acres of Land on Pedee River passed to him the 25th of June last, also the Affidavit of Peter Lane Deputy surveyor for the Township of Queensborough, setting forth that he surveyd the same 4000 acres of Land on the said Wraggs warrant, but that being Informd and examining finds two Tracts of 250 acres each lying with the bounds of the said Lands has been granted prior to the said Wraggs Grant, vizt to James Gordon Esq'r 250 acres and 250 acres to Saml Baker. The Said Wragg therefore desires a warrant for 500 acres of Land in the Township of Queensborough in lieu of the 500 acres Granted as above prior to his. Orderd that the said Mr. Wragg have a Special Warrant for 500 acres of Land in the Township of Queensborough in lieu of so much within his Platt granted Prior to the above said Gordon and Baker.

Heard a Caveat Enterd by John Baxter against John Wilsons having a Tract of 500 acres of Land in the Township of Williamsburgh. And considering the arguments on both sides His Majestys Council are of Opinion y't it appears that the said Wilsons warrant was legally executed and that there was no prior survey made of said Land. Therefore Ordered that a Grant do pass to john Wilson for the s'd Tract of Land.

Read the Petition of John Edwards setting forth that he has never been possessed of any Lands in this Province, that he is very desirous of settling here and praying a warr't for so much Land in this Province in any of the Townships as to this Board shall seem meet. Orderd that a Warrant do Issue to the Pet'r for 500 acres of Land and a Town Lott, either in Queensborough or Kingston Township.

On Reading the Petition of Sebastian Zouberbulher, setting forth That by reason of His long Illness he has not been able to perform his Contract of bringing over 100 familys to settle in One of the New townships & C. and praying longer time for performing his said Contract. Ordered That the Prayer of the Petition be Granted, and as the Township of New Windsor is already run out, that ta Surveyor shall go upon their arrival to shew the spot and survey the Lands as prayd for, and that the time limited to bring over the People be one Year from Oct'r next which will be in the year 1737.

Meeting of Friday the 13'th day of August 1736

Read the Petition of David Lewis, Sam'l Wild, and Dan'l James setting forth that on proper encouragement from this Province they have positive Directions from Sev'l of their Country Men natives of the Principality of Wales or their descendents Inhabitants of the Province of Pensilvania to look out such Quantity of Land in this Province property for the raising and Cultivating Hemp, Flax; Wheat, Barley &c. and that on their favourable Report Sev'l Familys would Import themselves in order to settle some of His Maj'tys Vacant Lands, and the Pet'rs being of Opinion that the Land which lies of both sides of Pedee River to wit 8 miles deep on each side of the s'd River from the Township already run out as far up as where the two main branches unite, and Ten Thousand Acres of Vacant Land within the said Township on the north side of the said River is the soil that appears to them most proper for the purposes aforementioned and the Pet'rs praying also that the said Land as before described may be reserved and set a part for the use of the said Familys for the space of four years. orderd That the Prayer of y'e Petition be Granted except that the Land to be reserved be only for the Space of two years instead of the four prayed for.

Meeting of Saturday the 14'th day of August 1736

Read the Petition of Penelope Reynolds widdow praying a Warrant may Issue to her name for 750 acres of Land survyd on a warrant Issued to her late Husband who dyed before he could obtain a Grant for the same. Orderd that a Special Warrant Issue to the Pet'r for the said 750 acres .

Read the Petition of Andrew Monclar Darbalestior praying a warrant for 300 acres of Land to which he is Entitled to by his additional family Right sworn to. Orderd That a Warrant of Survey do Issue to the Pet'r for 300 acres of Vacant Land out of the Townships.

Read the Petition of Mary Verdily spinster praying her family Right of Eleven persons on vacant Lands. Orderd that a Warrant of Survey do Issue to the Pet'r for 550 acres of Vacant Land out of the Townships.

Read the Petition of Peter May praying his family Right consisting of Ten persons on vacant Lands. Orderd that a Warrant of Survey do Issue to the Pet'r for 500 acres of Vacant Land out of the Townships.

Read the Petition of James Coachman setting forth that he has 8 persons in Family and desiring a Warrant may Issue to him for 400 acres of Land Sworn to. Orderd that a Warrant Issue to the Pet'r for 400 acres of Vacant Land out of the Townships.

Read the Petition of William Whitesides praying 750 acres of Vacant Land he having 15 persons in Family Sworn to. Orderd that a Warrant of Survey do Issue to the Pet'r for 750 acres of Vacant Land out of the Townships.

Read the Petition of Benj'a Chiles praying a Warrant for his family Right consisting of fifteen persons sworn to. Orderd that a Warrant of Survey Issue to the Pet'r for 800 acres of Vacant Land out of the Townships.

Read the Petition of James Moore praying a Warrant for 600 acres of Land in virtue of his Family Right sworn to consisting of 12 persons. Orderd that a Warrant of Survey do Issue to the Pet'r for 600 acres of Vacant Land out of y'e townships.

Read the Petition of Isaac Chandler praying a Warrant for 450 acres of vacant Land his consisting of nine persons sworn to. Orderd that a Warrant of Survey do issue to the Pet'r for 450 acres of vacant land, his Family consisting as above.

Read the Petition of Joshua Snowden praying a Warrant for 500 acres of vacant Land in virtue of his family right consisting of ten persons sworn to. Orderd that a Warrant of Survey Issue to the Pet'r for 500 acres of vacant land out of the Townships.

Read the Petition of John Jelsey praying a Warrant for 200 acres of in Waccamaw Township he having of four persons in Family sworn to. Orderd that a Warrant of Survey do Issue to the Pet'r for 200 acres of land in the said Township.

Read a Certificate Sworn to by David Shehan before Dan'l Laroche Esq'r one of His Maj'tys Justices of the Peace of his Family Right consisting of 3 persons; the said Shehan praying a Warrant for 150 acres of Land. Orderd That a Warrant of Survey do Issue to the said David Shehan for 150 acres of Vacant Land out of the Townships.

Meeting of Friday the 27'th August 1736

Read the Petition of Michel Janes praying His Family Right consisting of nine persons sworn to on Vacant Land. Orderd That a Warrant of Survey do Issue to the Pet'r for 450 acres of Vacant Land out of the Townships.

Read the Petition of Sam'l Masters praying his Family Right consisting of 8 persons sworn to on Vacant Land. Orderd That a Warrant of Survey do Issue to the Pet'r for 400 acres of Vacant Land out of the Townships.

Read the Petition of Hezekiah Russ praying his Family Right consisting of Ten persons on Vacant Land sworn to. Orderd That a Warrant of Survey do Issue to the Pet'r for 500 acres of Vacant Land out of the Townships.

Read the Petition of Ralph Masson praying his Family Right consisting of six persons sworn to in Kingston Township. Orderd That a Warrant of Survey Issue to the Pet'r for 300 acres in Kingston Township.

Read the Petition of Sam'l Pickings praying his Family Right consisting of 7 persons sworn to on Vacant Land. Orderd That a Warrant of Survey Issue to the Pet'r for 350 acres of Vacant Land out of the Townships.

Read the Petition of John Otterson praying his Family Right consisting of four persons sworn to on Vacant Land. Orderd That a Warrant of Survey do Issue to the Petit'r for 200 acres of Vacant Land out of the Townships.

Read the Petition of Joseph Bugnion praying his Family Right for 750 acres of Vacant Land sworn to. Orderd That a Warrant of Survey do Issue to the Pet'r for 750 acres of Vacant Land out of the Townships.

Read the Petition of Joseph Child praying a Warrant for 800 acres of Vacant Land his Family Right sworn to. Orderd That a Warrant of Survey Issue to the Pet'r for 800 acres of Vacant Land out of the Townships.

Read the Petition of Col'o Prioleau praying a Warrant for 800 acres of Vacant Land his Family Right sworn to. Orderd That a Warrant of Survey Issue to the Pet'r for 800 acres of Vacant Land out of the Townships.

Read the Petition of Thomas Grange praying a Warrant may issue to him for 950 acres of Vacant Land his Family Right consisting of 19 persons sworn to. Orderd That a Warrant of Survey Issue to the Pet'r for 950 acres of Vacant Land out of the Townships.

Read the Petition of Will: Greenland praying 350 acres of Vacant Land his Family Right sworn to. Orderd That a Warrant of Survey Issue to the Pet'r for 350 acres of Vacant Land out of the Townships.

Read the Petition of Cornelius Sullivan praying a Warrant for 200 acres of Land his Family Right sworn to. Orderd That a Warrant of Survey Issue to the Pet'r for 200 acres of Vacant Land out of the Townships.

Read the Petition of Ann Baxter praying a Warrant may Issue to her in Trust for her son the same number of Acres having been run out to her late husband who dyed before he could obtain a Grant for the same. Orderd That the Prayer of the Pet'n be Granted in trust for the Pet'rs son as prayd for.

Read the Petition of Burnaby Bull praying a Warrant for 650 acres of vacant Land his Family Right sworn to. Orderd That a Warrant of Survey Issue to the Pet'r for 650 acres of Vacant Land out of the Townships.

Read the Petition of John Colleton Esq'r praying a Warrant for 450 acres of vacant Land his Family Right sworn to. Orderd That a Warrant of Survey Issue to the Pet'r for 450 acres of Vacant Land out of the Townships.

Read the Petition of John Leay praying a Warrt. for 200 acres of vacant Land his Family Right sworn to. Orderd That a Warrant of Survey Issue to the Pet'r for 200 acres of Vacant Land out of the Townships.

Read the Petition of Stephen Hartley praying a Warrant for 250 acres of Vacant land His Family right sworn to. Orderd That a Warrt. of Survey Issue to the Pet'r for 250 acres on vacant Land out of the Townships.

Read the Petition of Peter Benoist praying a Warrant for his Family Right consisting of 12 persons sworn to. Orderd That a Warrant of Survey Issue to the Pet'r for 600 acres on vacant Land out of the Townships.

Meeting of Thursday the 16'th September 1736

Read the Petition of Mr. John Thorpe praying a Warrant for 700 acres of Land his Family Right Sworn to, in any Township except Purisburgh. Orderd That a Warrant of Survey Issue to the Pet'r for 700 acres of Land in Kingston Township.

Read the Petition of John Pennefather praying a Town Lott and one hundred Acres of Land his Family right sworn to, in Williamsburgh. Orderd That a Warrant Issue to the Pet'r pursuant to the Prayer of his Petition.

Read the Petition of George Hamlin praying a Warrant for 800 acres of vacant Land, his Family right Sworn to. Ordered That a Warrant Issue to the Pet'r for 800 acres of vacant Land out of the Townships.

Read the Petition of John Spencer praying a Warrant for 1000 acres of vacant Land, his Family right consisting of 20 persons Sworn to. Ordered That a Warrant Issue to the Pet'r for 1000 acres of vacant Land out of the Townships.

Read the Petition of Patrick Danelle in behalf of himself and his Brother an Infant praying a Warrant for 100 acres of Land in Pedee Township. Ordered That a Warrant Issue to the Pet'r for according to the Prayer of his Petition.

Read the Petition of Henry Ferguson praying a Warrant for 350 acres of vacant Land in this Province being his Family right Sworn to. Ordered That a Warrant of Survey Issue to the Pet'r for 350 acres of vacant Land out of the Townships.

Read the Petition of Abraham Colson praying a Warrant for 600 acres of Land his Family right consisting of 12 persons. Ordered That a Warrant Issue to the Pet'r for 600 acres of Vacant Land out of the Townships.

Read the Petition of Thomas Burtin Janier praying a Warrant for 300 acres of vacant Land his Family right sworn to. Ordered That a Warrant Issue to the Pet'r for 300 acres of Vacant Land out of the Townships.

Read the Petition of Dorothy Webb praying a Warrant for 450 acres of vacant Land her Family right sworn to. Ordered That a Warrant Issue to the Pet'r for 450 acres of Vacant Land out of the Townships.

Read the Petition of Dan'l Pepper praying a Warrant for 350 acres of vacant Land his Family right sworn to. Ordered That a Warrant Issue to the Pet'r for 350 acres of Vacant Land out of the Townships.

Meeting of Friday the 17'th September 1736

Read The Petition of Joseph Mary praying his family right Sworn to in Amelia Township. Ordered That a Warrant os Survey do Issue to the Pet'r for 200 acres of Land in Amelia Township.

Meeting of Wednesday the 29'th September 1736

On motion of Mr. Whitaker in behalf of Cap't Dry, relating to a vacant Tract of Land between the s'd Cap't Dry and Cockfields Lands still in dispute and Claimd by Mr Elliot as having first run it out, which was resurveyd by Order of Council of the 29th May last and the Council being heard on both sides and platts of the Resurvey being produced and Examind. It was Resolved and Orderd That the said Tract in dispute be equally divided between the said Dry and Cockfield.

The Hon'ble Mr. Secretary Hammerton having represented to this Board, that he has a right to a Tract of Land of between five or six hundred Acres more or less on Pon Pon River in Colleton County bounded by Lands belonging to Mr. Champneys, Mr. William Browne, Mr. John Parker and Mr. James Ferguson, which s'd Tract or the greatest part thereof was surveyd and run to Robert Beeth by said Ferguson the 29th Janry 1733 and by him the said Beeth assignd over to him the said John Hammerton Esq'r for a valuable Consideration and that said Mr. Hammerton having produced to this Board a Platt of the said Tract and also a proper Instrument under the Hand of Rob't Hume Esq'r assignee and Attorney to James Maxwell, whereby the said Hume does renounce and disclaim all his benefit Right and demand to the said Tract by virtue of a Survey thereof made for him on a warrant of the said James Maxwell, and praying an order of Council do Issue to the Surveyor Gen'l to Certifie a Platt of the said Tract of Land which on a Survey thereof made to Benj'a Godfrey appears to contain 675 acres. Orderd That James St. John

Esq'r Surveyor Gen'l do forthwith Platt and Certify to the Board the said so made for the said Land to Benj'a Godfrey, Surveyd by Nath'l Deane then a Deputy Surveyor y'e 10th of this instant September.

Read the Petition of Andrew Broughton Esq'r praying his Family right and a Low Swamp fronting of His upland Tract, the said Tract lying on the East side of the West Branch of Cooper River the front of which has never been yet Surveyd to him and the Pet'r praying the same Indulgence as has been allowed to other his Majestys Subjects in the same Circumstances, together with his family Right. Orderd That a Warrant do Issue to the said Andrew Broughton Esq'r for 1550 acres of Land he having 31 persons in Family, and also for the Low Swamp fronting his Tract as prayed for and that Mr. Secretary Hammerton be served with a Copy of this Order.

Meeting of Thursday the 30'th September 1736

His Majestys Hon'ble Council took into Consideration the Motion made by Mrs. Whitaker and Capt. Charles Wyndham in behalf of John Roberts Esq'r concerning Lands convey'd by the Hon'ble the Lord Carteret to him the said Roberts in this Province. Resolved That the Motion is just and consonent to His Majestys Instructions and Orderd that Mr. Secretary Hammerton do prepare a Grant for the overplus of Land according to a Draught layd before this Board, which was approved of in order the same may be signd by the Honble the Lieutent. Governor.

Mr. Pinckney moved in the Case depending between Anthony White and William Scriven relating to a tract of Land adjoyning lands of the said Scrivens at Wyneau, and on producing the affidavit of Peter Lane a Deputy Surveyor taken before John Wallis Esqr. one of His Majestys Justices of the peace on y'e 11th of Sepr' inst. It is Orderd that a Grant do pass for the said Tract of Land to the said Anthony White.

Read the Petition of Peter Marion praying a new warrant for 1950 acres of Land in lieu of a Warrant dated the 5th of July 1733. Ordered That on Surrender of the said former warrant, a new warrant do Issue to the Pet'r for the Land he prays for.

Read the Petition of Marmaduke Ash, praying a Warrant for 200 acres of vacant land his family consisting of 4 persons sworn to. Orderd That a Warrant of Survey do Issue to the Pet'r for 200 acres of vacant Land out of the Townships.

Read the Petition of John Read Jun'r praying his Family Right consisting of Ten persons sworn to on vacant Lands. Orderd That a Warrant of Survey Issue to the Pet'r for 500 acres of vacant Lands out of the Townships.

Read the Petition of Charles Pinkney Esq. in behalf of James Hasel Esqr setting forth that the said Hasel on the 16th of March 1732 obtaind his Majestys Grant for 200 acres of Land in Granville County that some time in the year 1734 the said Hasel was obliged to go off this Province on his private affairs, and that by reason thereof he had not been able to settle the said Lands pursuant to the Conditions mentiond in the said Grant and therefore prayd that on his paying all the arrears of Quit Rents due to his Majesty for the said Lands the Term for settling the same might be further enlarged that no disadvantage might arrise by y'e s'd James Hasel on account of his not having settled the said Lands within the time prescribed by the said Grant. Ordered That the Prayer of the Petition be granted and that the time for settling the said Land be enlarged to the 29th day of September 1737.

Read the Petition of Geo: Hunter Gen't praying a Special Warrant for 1500 acres of Land on Ox Swamp already surveyed by him and lying with the Township of Williamsburgh. Orderd That the Pet'r have 1000 acres of the said Land.

Meeting of Friday the 1'st October 1736

Read the Petition of Thomas Corbet, Master of the Free School of Charles Town in this Province, praying a Warrant for 400 acres of Land his Family Right and Representing that as Master of the Free School he had used his best Endeavours in that Station to Educate and Instruct the youth of this Province and therefore humbly hoped this Board would take the same into Consideration and Grant him such a further Quantity of his Majestys Lands as their honours should think fit either in the Township of Queenburgh or that of Kingston. His Majestys Honble Council taking the same into Consideration and being convinced of the Truth of the Petitions allegations. Ordered that a Warrant do Issue to the said Corbet for One Thousand acres of Land in the Township of Kingston or Queenborough at the Option of the Petition'r.

Read the Petition of Robert Austin, merchant, praying a Special Warrant may Issue to him for the Lands surveyed by Mr. John Musgrove. Ordered That a Special Warrant do Issue to the said Austin for the same.

Read the Petition of Robert Hedger setting forth that as three Tracts of Land the One of 700 acres his Family Right the other of 650 and 600 acres which he purchased lye within Lines of Pedee Township tho' he was assured by the Surveyor who run the said Tracts that they were not in the said Township and being informed that being in a Township makes these Grants Voidable Therefore as he has been at very great Charge on that Account humbly prays that upon the Surrender of the three Voidable Grants aforesaid he may have three Grants pass to him for the said Lands in his own name. Ordered that upon the Petitioners Surrender of the three Grants afore mentioned he may have three Grants pass to him for the Lands aforesaid in his own Name according to the Prayer of his Petition. Read the Petition of James Akin of Berkley County Planter Setting forth That having bought one Tract of Five hundred acres of One Charles Codner and having one of his own of the same Quantity which both happen to be in Williamsburgh the said Lands being Granted as usual with a Provisoe that if they fell within a Township they should be deemed as vacant Lands, the Petit'r therefore prays that as he was not apprised of the same he may on the Surrender of these Grants have the said Lands Granted under Township Warrants and they he may have a Common Warrant for 1000 acres in Lieu of that for the 1000 acres so Surrendered. Ordered That the Prayer of the Petition be Granted.

Meeting of Wednesday the 13'th October 1736

Read the Petition of Elenor Frederick praying for 550 acres of Land and a Lot in the Township of Kingston the same being for her Family Right Sworn to and Ordered that the Prayer of the Petition be Granted.

Ordered that Warrants do issue to the following Persons for vacant Lands they having Sworn to their Family Right before Thomas Dale, Esquire, One of his Majesty's Justices of the Peace, vizt

To Abraham Vanbestall for 350 acres
To Johannes Mayer ... 350 ---
To Hans Amacher... 300 "
To Anna Maria Till... 250

Meeting of the 11'th November 1736

Read the Petition of Robert Wright Jun'r Esq'r praying his Family Right for Eighteen Persons which right was proved on Oath before his Majesty's General. Ordered That a Warrant do issue to the said Robert Wright pursuant to the prayer of his Petition on vacant Land.

Read the Petition of Albert Dynmager praying his Family Right consisting of Twelve persons on vacant Land. Ordered That the Prayer of the Petition be Granted and that a warrant do issue to the Peti'r for 600 acres on vacant Land.

Read the Petition of Joseph Cragg praying a Warrant for his Family Right consisting of twenty two persons on vacant land. Ordered that a warrant do Issue to the Petitioner for 550 acres of Land as prayed for.

Read the Petition of William Bellinger praying a Warrant for his Family Right consisting of Twenty Persons on vacant Land. Ordered That a Warrant do issue to the Petition for 1000 acres of Land as prayed for.

Read the Petition of Captain James Sutherland praying 1000 acres of Land and a Town Lot in a Township he being one of his Majestys Officers as Commander of Johnsons Fort. Ordered that a Warrant do issue to the Petitioner for 1000 acres and a Town Lot in Kingston Township on Waccamaw River.

Read the Petition of George Haddrell praying 700 acres of vacant Land his Family Right consisting of fourteen Persons. Ordered that a Warrant do issue to the said Haddrel pursuant to the prayer of his Petition.

Read the Petition of Collonel Thomas Lynch praying 3150 acres of vacant Land for his Family Right consisting of 63 persons. Ordered that a Warrant do issue to the said Coll'l Lynch pursuant to the prayer of his Petition.

Read the Petition of John Maccaw praying 550 acres of Vacant Land by Virtue of his Family Right consisting of Eleven Persons. Orderd That a Warrant do issue to the said John Maccaw for 550 acres of Land pursuant to the prayer of his Petition.

Meeting of Friday the 12'th November 1736

Read the Petition of Thomas Potts setting forth That he obtained a Warrant and Grant for 270 acres of Land which he has possessed built upon and Improved and that now he is threatned to be turned out of the same on pretence the said Tract is within the Lines of Williamsburgh and praying relief therein. Ordered That a Township Grant for Williamsburgh to the Petitioner for the said Tract on his surrendring the former Grant.

Read the Petition of Richard Hill, Merchant, signed on his behalf by Mr. Whitaker & Mr. Guerard praying leave to surrender a Grant he obtained for 700 acres of Land which he being informed lies within the bounds of Williamsburgh prays he may surrender the said grant and obtain a new one for that Quantity of Land of the same Date and Tener as the former except the Proviso concerning the said Lands being within the Township. Ordered That a Warrant issue to the Petitioner for a new Grant as prayed for on his surrendring the former Grant.

Read the Petition of Jasper King praying his Family Right consisting of fourteen persons in Craven County sworn to. Ordered That a Warrant of Survey issue to the Petitioner for 700 acres of Land according to the prayer of his Petition.

Read the Petition of Joseph Murray praying 500 acres in virtue of his Family Right consisting of Ten persons to. Ordered That a Warrant of Survey issue to the Petitioner for 500 acres of vacant Land according to the prayer of his Petition.

Read the Petition of John Brown praying 50 acres of Land his own Right. Orderd that a Warrant of Survey issue to the Petitioner for 50 acres of vacant Land.

Read the Petition of Charles Windon setting forth that he has Six persons in Family as appears on Oath and praying 300 acres of Land in a Township. Ordered that a Warrant of Survey issue to the Petitioner for 300 acres and a Town Lott in Kingston Township.

Read the Petition of John Snow setting forth that he has Six Slaves for which he has hitherto had no land as appears by his Oath and praying a Warrant of Survey for 300 acres on vacant Land. Ordered That a Warrant of Survey issue to the Petitioner accordingly.

Read the Petition of William Snow praying his Family Right consisting of six persons which he has proved on Oath. Ordered That a Warrant of Survey issue to the Petitioner for 300 acres of vacant Land.

Read the Petition of John Hale proving on Oath that he has Nine persons in Family and praying a Warrant of Survey may issue to him for 400 acres vacant Land. Ordered That a Warrant of Survey issue to the Petitioner according to the Prayer of Petition.

Read the Petition of William Hartman proving on Oath that he has 8 persons in Family and praying a Warrant of Survey may issue to him for 400 acres vacant Land. Ordered That a Warrant of Survey issue to the Petitioner for 400 acres of vacant Land.

Read the Petition of Edward Webb praying his Family Right consisting of Eight persons proved upon Oath. Ordered That a Warrant of Survey do issue to the Petitioner for 400 acres of vacant Land.

Read the Petition of John Johnson praying his family right consisting of Seven persons and also such an addition of Land as to this Honble Board shall seem most in consideration he is an Officer of the Customs and that the same may be laid out for him in one of the Townships. Ordered that a Warrant of Survey issue to the Petitioner for 600 acres of Land in Kingston Township.

Read the Petition of Thomas Weaver praying his Family Right consisting of Eight persons which right he has sworn to on vacant Lands. Ordered That a warrant of Survey issue to the Petitioner for 400 acres of vacant Land pursuant to the prayer of his Petition.

Read the Petition of George Holmes setting forth that he has 12 Persons in his Family as proved on Oath and praying a Warrant may issue to him for 600 acres of vacant land. Ordered that a Warrant of Survey issue to the Petitioner pursuant to the prayer of his Petition.

Read the Petition of Peter Oliver praying his Family Right Consisting of 10 persons as appears on Oath on vacant Land. Ordered that a Warrant of Survey issue to the Petitioner for 500 acres of Land on vacant Lands.

Read the Petition of Edward Keating praying his Family Right consisting of 13 persons sworn to. Ordered that a Warrant of Survey issue to the Petitioner for 650 acres on vacant Land.

Read the Petition of Ann Goodbee praying a Warrant for 734 acres the remaining part of a warrant for 1450 acres issue to her late Husband and also for the further Quantity of 1050 acres the Encrease of her Family Since the said Warrant was issued making in the whole 1784 acres. Ordered that a Warrant issue to the Pet'r according to the prayer of her Petition.

Read the Petition of James Singleton praying his Family Right of 22 persons Sworn to. Ordered that a Warrant of Survey issue to the Petition'r for 1400 acres of vacant Land pursuant to the Prayer of his Petition.

Read the Petition of John Welsted praying his Own Right to 50 acres of land. Ordered that a Warrant of Survey issue to the Petitioner according to the prayer of his Petition.

Read the Petition of Claudius Richburgh praying his Family Right of four persons sworn to. Ordered That a Warrant of Survey issue to the Pet'r for 200 acres of vacant Land.

Read the Petition of Robert Newman praying his Family Right consisting of two persons sworn to. Ordered That a Warrant of Survey issue to the Pet'r for 100 acres of Land as prayd for.

Read the Petition of George Pawley praying his Family Right consisting of Eleven Persons sworn to and also for an Overseer. Ordered that a warrant of Survey issue to the Petitioner for 550 acres of vacant land for his Family Right of 11 persons.

Read the Petition of Samuel Wells praying his Family Right of Eight persons sworn to. Ordered that a Warrant issue to the Pet'r for 400 acres on vacant Land.

Read the Petition of David Baldy setting forth that he has Eighteen Persons in his Family which he as sworn to and praying a Warrant for 900 acres of vacant Land. Ordered That a Warrant issue to the Pet'r pursuant to the prayer of his Petition.

Read the Petition of John Mackey praying his family Right consisting of fourteen persons sworn to, on vacant Land. Ordered That a Warrant of Survey Issue to the Pet'r for 700 acres Vacant Land.

Read the Petition of John Pettinger praying his Family Right consisting of Six Persons to which he has sworn on vacant Land. Ordered that a Warrant of Survey issue to the Pet'r for 300 acres of vacant Land as prayed for.

Read the Petition of Michael moore Setting forth that he has six persons in Family to which he has made Oath and praying a Warrant of Survey may issue to him for his said Family Right on vacant Lands. Ordered that a Warrant of Survey do issue to the Pet'r for 300 acres of vacant Land pursuant to the Prayer of his said Petition.

Read the Petition of William Field praying his Family Right consisting of Eleven persons which he has proved on Oath and praying a Warrant may issue to him in virtue of his said Family Right for 550 acres of vacant Land. Ordered That a Warrant of Survey issue to the Pet'r for 550 acres of Land as prayed for.

Read the Petition of David Crawford praying his family Right consisting of 11 persons Sworn to on vacant Land. Ordered that a Warrant of Survey issue to the said David Crawford for 550 acres of Vacant Land pursuant to the prayer of his Petition.

Read the Petition of John Piott setting forth that he has 11 Persons in his Family which Number he has Swore to and praying that a Warrant of Survey do issue to him for 700 acres of Land in one of the Townships. Ordered that a Warrant of Survey issue to the Pet'r for 700 acres of Land in any of the New Townships except in such Townships as are already excepted by order of Council.

Read the Petition of John Haydon praying his Family Right consisting of Eight persons to which he has made Oath on vacant Lands. Ordered that a Warrant of Survey issue to the Pet'r for 400 acres of vacant Land pursuant tot he prayer of his Petition.

Resolved that James St. John Esq'r his Majestys Surveyor General or some other proper persons be agreed with by this Board to Survey and mark out the Bounds or outlines of a certain Quantity of Land from the Township Line on Pedee River up to the place where the two main Branches unite eight miles back on both sides from the River and that the said Land be Reserved according to the prayer of the Petition of David Lewis, Samuel Wild, and Dan'l James for the Welsh Families therein mentioned to be Imported into this Province and that all the Lands not run out within the Line as above mentioned at the time of marking out the same be reserved for settling the said Welsh Familys.

Meeting of Saturday the 13'th November 1736

Read the Petition of William Snow setting forth that he had a Grant of 1800 acres of Land in August 1736 which land was Surveyd and run out before the Township of Williamsburgh was fixed and ascertain that he has built a House and barn on the said Land and planted the same and praying on his surrendring the said Grant he may obtain a Special Warrant of Survey for the said Land in the Township of Williamsburgh.

Upon reading the Petition of John James, Robert Witherspoon, William Maccormick, James McCuley, John Bernes, and Henry Megumery complaining that Mr. George Hunter has run out some of the Lands admeasurd to them by Mr. Williams Deputy Surveyor on Ox swamp and representing they had built hutts and cleared Six acres of Land for Provisions &C and praying an Order may pass that they may Enjoy the said Lands The said George Hunter and James McCuley were Ordered to attend this Board and they attended accordingly. This Board took into Consideration the said Petition and heard what Mr. Hunter had to say in Support of his Survey and it appearing to this Board that the said Hunter is entitled to 1000 acres on the said Swamp by virtue of a Patent Surveyed in 1723 and has paid Taxes for the same, It was Ordered and his Honor the Lieutenant Governor Signd a Special Warrant to James St. John Esq'r his Majestys Surveyor General to admeasure or cause to be admeasured to the said George hunter 1000 acres of Land on the said Swamp as delineated in a Plat annexed to the said Warrant in order a Grant may pass to him for the Same.

On Reading the Petition of James Akin setting forth amongst other things that Sundry persons had begun to survey and make settlement on 1000 acres of Land situate on Black River in Craven County in the Township of Williamsburgh formerly Granted to himself and praying a Special Warrant for Resurveying the same in order to have a proper Grant passed for the said Lands on surrendring to his Majesty his former Grant.

Meeting of Wednesday the 1'st December 1736

Read the Petition of Nehemiah Duncombe praying his Family Right consisting of five persons Sworn to in a Township. Ordered that a Warrant issue to the Petitioner for 250 acres of Land in the Township of Kingston or Queensborough at the Pet'rs Option.

Read the Petition of Thomas Monck Esq'r praying his Family Right consisting of Ten Persons on vacant Land. Ordered That a Warrant of survey Issue to the Petitioner for 500 acres of Vacant Land pursuant to the prayer of the Petition.

Meeting of Thursday the 2'd December 1736

On motion of Mr. Grame on behalf of Capt. James Akin relating to a Petition which was read in Council the 13th of November last setting forth that he had a Warrant for 1000 acres of Land as mentioned in the Petitioner aforesaid, and that apprehending his Right tot he Same was invaded by one or more persons, humbly prays relief from this Board. His Majesty's Honble Council taking the same into Consideration and having heard the merit thereof and also Council on both sides, It was Ordered That the Honble Mr. Secretary Hammerton do forthwith prepare a Special Warrant in the Name of the said James Akin for the Land aforesaid in order to be signed by his Honour the Lieut. Governor.

Read the Petition of William Baker setting forth that he has thirty two persons in Family for which he hitherto has had no land as Sworn to and praying a warrant may Issue to him for surveying 1600 acres of Land on vacant Land. Ordered That a Warrant of Survey Issue to the Pet'r pursuant to the Prayer of his Petition.

Read the Petition of Thomas Elliot, son of William Elliot, setting forth That he has an additional Family Right of fourty nine persons for which he has hitherto had no Land as sworn to by him and praying a Warrant may Issue to him for 2450 acres of Vacant Land. Ordered That a Warrant of Survey do Issue to the Pet'r for the Quantity of Land he prays for in his said Petition.

Read the Petition of Archibald Neal setting forth That he has Thirteen persons in his Family for which Number he has never had any Land as appears by his Oath and praying a warrant may issue to him for 650 acres in virtue of his said family Right. Ordered That a Warrant of Survey issue to the Petitioner for 650 acres of Land on vacant Land, according to the prayer of his Petition.

Read the Petition of Peter De St. Julien setting forth that he has twelve persons in his family for which he has had no Land as appears on Oath by him taken and praying a warrant do issue to him for 600 acres of vacant Land. Ordered That a Warrant of Survey do issue to the Pet'r for 600 acres of Vacant Land as prayd for.

Meeting of Friday the 3'd December 1736

Read the Petition of Moses Martin setting forth that he has Six persons in family for which he hitherto has had no Land as appears on Oath and praying a Warrant do issue to him for surveying 300 acres of vacant Land. Ordered that a Warrant of Survey do issue to the Pet'r for 300 acres of vacant Land as pray'd for by the Petition.

Read the Petition of Alexander Smith praying a Warrant of Survey may issue to him for his additional family Right consisting of ______ Persons. Ordered that a Warrant of Survey issue to the Petitioner according to the prayer of his Petition.

Read the Petition of James Grame Esq'r setting forth that he has Ten persons in Family for which he has no Land and praying a Warrant of Survey may issue to him for 500 acres on vacant Land. Ordered that a Warrant of Survey issue to the Petitioner for 500 acres of vacant Land pursuant to the prayer of his Petition.

Meeting of Friday the 3'd December 1736 P. M.

Read the Petition of John Chevillete and Sarah his Wife praying that the Land his late father in law Francis Yanam had a Warrant for a Town Lott and 500 acres of Land in the Township of Purisburg which were accordingly admeasured and surveyed to him but he the said Yanam dying before the Grant could pass to him for the same. The Petitioners therefore pray a warrant may pass to them for the said Lott and 500 acres of Land as mentioned in the Petition in order it may be Granted to the Pet'r and his wife. Ordered that a Warrant do pass to the Pet'rs as prayd for.

Read the Petition of Abraham Croft setting forth that he has ten persons in family for which he never has yet had any Land and praying a Warrant of survey may issue to him for 500 acres of Land in Williamsburgh Township he having Sworn to his said Family Right. Ordered that a Warrant of Survey issue to the Petitioner for 500 acres of Land in any of the Northern Townships not excepted.

Read the Petition of William May praying his Family Right of three persons Sworn to for which he hitherto has had no Land. Ordered That a Warrant of Survey issue to the Petitioner for 150 acres of Land in Waccamaw Township.

Read the Petition of Paul Bruneau setting forth that he has four persons in Family for which he has never yet had any Land as appears by his Oath and praying a warrant of Survey may issue to him for 200 acres of vacant Land. Ordered that a Warrant of Survey issue to the said Pet'r for 200 acres of vacant Land as prayd for.

Read the Petition of Daniell Mooney setting forth that he has six persons in his Family for which he has never had any Land as appears on Oath and praying a Warrant do issue to him for 300 acres of vacant Land. Ordered that a Warrant of Survey issue to the said Pet'r for 300 acres of vacant Land as prayd for.

Read the Petition of John Brunson praying his Family Right Consisting of ten persons for which he has never had any Land as appears by his Oath in

Craven County. Ordered that a Warrant of Survey issue to the said Pet'r for 500 acres of Land as prayd for.

Read the Petition of William Rumsey Setting forth that he has Seven Persons in family for which he has never had any Land as appears on Oath and praying a Warrant of Survey may issue to him for 350 acres of vacant Land. Ordered That a Warrant of Survey do issue to the Pet'r for 350 acres of vacant Land as prayd for.

Read the Petition of Richard Parry Setting forth that he has twenty Persons in Family for which he has hitherto had no Land as appears on Oath and praying a Warrant of survey may issue to him for 1000 acres of vacant Land. Ordered that a Warrant of Survey do issue to the Pet'r for 1000 acres of vacant Land as pray'd for.

Read the Petition of Valentine Hordman setting forth that he has eight Persons in his Family for which he has never had any Land as appears on Oath and praying a Warrant of Survey issue to him for 400 acres of vacant Land. Ordered that a Warrant of Survey issue to the Pet'r for 400 acres of vacant Land as pray'd for.

Read the Petition of Thomas Skipper praying his family Right consisting of Eight persons as Sworn to by him, on vacant land. Ordered that a Warrant of Survey issue to the Pet'r for 400 acres of vacant Land pursuant to the prayer of his Petition.

Read the Petition of Richard Bartlet praying a Warrant of Survey may issue to him for 300 acres of Land, he having Swore to his family Right consisting of five persons. Ordered that a Warrant of Survey issue to the Pet'r for 300 acres of vacant Land pursuant to the prayer of his Petition.

Read the Petition of Nicholas Burnham setting forth that he has thirty Eight persons in Family for which he has never yet had any Land as appears by his Oath and praying a warrant may issue to him for 1900 acres of vacant Land. Ordered that a Warrant issue to the Pet'r for 1900 acres of vacant Land as prayd for.

Read the Petition of Benjamin Tucker setting forth that he has twelve Persons in family for which he has hitherto had no Land and praying a warrant of Survey may issue to him for 600 acres of vacant Land and a Town Lott either in the Township of Kingston or that of Queensborough and also that he may receive his Majesty's Bounty of Provision and Tools &c. Ordered that a Warrant of survey issue to the Pet'r for 600 acres of Land in either of the Townships above mentioned together with a Town Lot, but that part of his Petition relating to the Provisions and Tools be rejected.

Meeting of Saturday the 4th December 1736

On application of the Reverend Mr. John Fordree minister of Prince Frederic Parish praying a Warrant for Such a Quantity of Land as this Board shall judge proper and has been allowed to other ministers of the Church of England in this Province. Ordered That a Warrant of Survey issue to the said Fordrie for 1000 acres of Land out of the townships.

Read the Petition of William Wilsford praying his Family Right of four persons proved on oath in any of his Majestys new Townships with the same indulgence as is granted to other New Comers. Ordered that a Warrant of Survey issue to the Pet'r for 200 acres of Land in any of the Townships not excepted.

Read the Petition of William Brisbane setting forth that he has fourteen persons in Family and praying a warrant may issue to him for Seven hundred acres of Land in any of the New Townships. Ordered that the Prayer of the Petition be granted his proving his said Family Right.

Read the Petition of Elizabeth Miller setting forth that She has Nine persons in family and praying a warrant may issue to her for 450 acres of vacant Land. Granted provided the Petitioner prove and make it appear her husband was not possessed of any Lands by virtue of the said Family Right.

Read the Petition of Crafton Carvon praying his Family Right consisting of Nine persons and that a Warrant of Survey may issue to him for 450 acres of Land and a Town Lott in Williamsburgh. Ordered that a Warrant of Survey issue to the Pet'r for 450 acres of Land and a Town Lott in Williamsburgh.

Meeting of Monday the 6th December 1736

Ordered That Alexander Arbuthnot have a Warrant for 50 acres and a Lott in the Township of Williamsburgh with Provisions Tools &c.

Read the Petition of Coll. George Lucus setting forth that he is desirous to Cultivate and Settle Two thousand acres of Land in this Province and praying a Warrant for the same. Ordered That a Warrant of Survey issue to the Petitioner for 2000 acres of vacant Land.

Read the Petition of James Seaman Esq'r praying a Warrant for 200 acres of Land he being desirous to settle and Cultivate the same. Ordered That a Warrant of Survey issue to the Petitioner for One Thousand Acres of vacant Land.

Read the Petition of William Morgan praying 50 acres of Land and a Town Lott in the township of Williamsburgh together with Provisions Tools &C. Ordered That the prayer of the Petition be Granted.

Read the Petition of Margaret Morgan praying 50 acres of Land and a Town Lott in the township of Williamsburgh together with Provisions Tools &C she being a New Comer. Ordered That the prayer of the Petition be Granted.

Read the Petition of Dennis Doyle Setting that he is in family himself his wife and two Children and praying a Warrant of Survey may issue to him for 200 acres of Land and a Town Lott in some of the Northern Townships and that he may be allow'd his Majesty's Bounty of Provisions Tools &c. Ordered that a Warrant of Survey issue to the Petition and that he be allow'd Tools and Provisions as pray'd for.

Read the Petition of Nath: McMullen praying 200 acres and a Town Lot tin one of his Majesty's Townships to the Northward he having four persons in Family and being lately come in from Ireland also prays for Tools Provisions &c. Ordered that a Warrant of Survey issue to the Petitioner and that he be allowed Tools and Provisions &c as pray'd for.

Read the Petition of Gideon Ellis setting forth that he has twelve Persons in family for which he has not as yet had any Land as appears upon oath, and praying a Warrant of Survey may issue to him for 600 acres of vacant Land. Ordered that a Warrant of Survey do issue to the Pet'r for 600 acres of Vacant Land as pray'd for in the said Petition.

Read the Petition of Bartholomew Ball setting forth that he has an addition of Eight Persons in his Family for which additional Number he prays a Warrant of Survey may issue to him for 400 acres of Vacant Land, he having Sworn to his said Right before Justice Wallis. Ordered that a Warrant issue to the Pet'r for 400 acres of Land as pray'd for.

Meeting of Tuesday the 7th December 1736

Read the Petition of Richard Middleton setting forth that he has twelve persons in his Family for which he has not yet had any Land to which he has swore and Praying a Warrant of Survey may issue to him for 600 acres of Vacant Land. ordered That a Warrant of Survey do issue to the Petitioner for 600 acres of vacant Land as pray'd for.

Read the Petition of Col. William Waties setting forth that he has an additional Family Right of Forteen persons for which he has not as yet had any Land as sworn to before the Attorney General and praying a Warrant of Survey may issue to him for 700 acres of Vacant Land. Ordered That a Warrant of Survey do issue to the Pet'r for 700 acres of Vacant Land as prayed for.

Meeting of Wednesday the 8th December 1736

On hearing the Caveat Entred by Mr. Breton against Pierce Pawley it appeared to this Board that the said Pawley first run out the Land and that he applyed to the Surveyor General to Certify his Platt before any other person run the same or applyd to this Board for a Warrant so to do. Therefore this Board is of Opinion that the Surveying and running out of the said Land by Breton without a Special Warrant from this Board and without Notice first given to the said Pawley was irregular and Contrary to the Rules and Orders of this Board and therefore It is Ordered that a Grant be passed for the said Pawley for the said Land and that the Surveyor General do certify the said Platt in order thereto.

Read the Petition of Mr. John Chevillette setting forth that William Staples a Deputy Surveyor run out a Town Lot No. 5 for Mr. Francis Yanam deceased but the said Staples dying before he had Certify'd the Platt of the said Lott the Surveyor General refuses to Certify the same Altho' there is a platt and Certificate of said Lott writ in the said Staples hand tho' not signd as aforesaid and the Pet'r praying relief on the premises. His Majestys' Honble Council taking the same into Consideration It was Ordered that the Surveyor General do Certify the said Platt.

Read the Petition of John Basnett setting forth that he is settling & Cultivating 400 acres of Land and a Town Lott in the Townsh'p of Williamsburg and that he has built a house upon the said Lott That he finds by his Grant for the said Lott and Land That his Majestys Quit Rent becomes payable from the date of the said Grant and therefore prays that on Surrendring the aforesaid Grant he may obtain another Grant for the said Lott and Land free of Quit Rent for the Term of Ten years next after the date of said Grant. Ordered That a Grant do pass to the Pet'r as pray'd for.

Read the Petition of John Basnett setting forth that he has a family Right additional of five persons which he has sworn to before his Majestys Attorney General and praying a Warrant of Survey may issue to him for 250 acres of Land in the Township of Williamsburgh. Ordered That a Warrant of Survey do issue to the said Basnett for 250 acres in the Township of Williamsburg has prayd for.

Read the Petition of Francis Cordes praying his family Right of Five persons on vacant Land he having swore the said Right. Ordered That a Warrant of Survey issue to the Pet'r for 250 acres of vacant Land in this Province.

Read the Petition of James Smith setting forth that he has eight persons in family sworn to by him and praying a warrant may issue to him for 400 acres of vacant Land. Ordered that a Warrant of Survey issue to the Pet'r for 400 acres of Land as prayd for.

Read the Petition of Elias Horry of Craven county praying he may be appointed Coroner for the said county the said office being vacant by the death of Elias Horry his late father. Ordered that a Commission be prepared by the Secretary of this Province for appointing the said Horry coroner of Craven County according to the prayer of the Petition.

Meeting of Thursday the 9th December 1736

Read the Petition of Captain Edward Fennel praying One Thousand acres of Land and a Lott in the Township of Williamsburgh, Kingston, or Queensborough, being desirous to Cultivate the same and settle it. Ordered That the said Fennel have a Common Warrant issue to him for 1000 acres of vacant Land.

Read the Petition of Daniel James setting forth that his Family Consists of Seven persons for which he has not as yet had any Land as appear on his oath and praying a warrant may issue to him for 350 acres of Land to be laid out in the Township of Queenbro' or in the Land set apart for the Welch people expected from Pensilvania. Ordered that a Warrant of Survey do issue to the Petition pursuant to the prayer of his Petition.

Read the Petition of Thomas Goodman setting forth that he has seven persons in his family for which he has had no lands and praying a Common warrant may issue to him for 350 acres of Land he having Sworn to his said family right. Ordered that a Common Warrant do issue to the Pet'r for 350 acres of Land as pray'd for.

Read the Petition of Charles Filbin setting forth That he has Twenty Persons in Family for which he has hitherto had no Land as appears upon Oath, and praying a Common Warrant may issue to him for 1000 acres of vacant Land. Ordered That a Warrant issue to the Petition'r for 1000 acres of vacant Land as pray'd for.

Meeting of Friday the 10th December 1736

Read the Petition of Joseph Izard setting forth that his Family consists of Twenty Five persons that he is not possessed of any Land in this Province as may appear by the Oath he has taken and therefore praying a Warrant may issue to him for 1250 acres of Land in one of the Northern Townships. Ordered that a Warrant of Survey do issue to the Pet'r for 1250 acres of Land as prayed for.

On reading the Petition of William Cattell Esq'r praying a Resurvey of certain vacant Land lying contiguous to a plantation belonging to the said William Cattell on long Savannah in Berkley County formerly survey'd for the Petitioner by Robert Godfray, a Deputy Surveyor. it is Ordered that his Majestys Surveyor General do Cause the said Land to be Resurveyed and that he return a platt thereof to this Board and it is further Ordered that the said William Cattel do give Notice to Mr. Isaac Nichols of the time when the said Resurvey shall be made and that he also give notice to the said Nichols to attend this Board at the time of the Return of the said Resurvey and of the time the said Resurvey shall be Returned to shew cause if any he can why the aforesaid Land should not be Granted to the said William Cattel.

Meeting of Tuesday the 14th December 1736

Whereas the Hon'ble Arthur Middleton Esq'r hat made Complaint unto me that he hat a Tract of Land of 4705 acres to the Southward granted to him about two years ago but upon a Search made into the Survey of the said Land it appears that the said Land doth not answer to the Survey nor the Survey to the Platt as it is laid out and the said Middleton desiring that a Resurvey may be made of the said Land that the Platt and the Land may agree, all which being made appear before me to be true, These are therefore to desire and Direct you to Order some of your Deputys to make a just and true survey of the said Land that the platt of the said Land may be made to agree with the Land so resurveyed and a Certificate with the Platt thereof to be returned into the Secret'ys office that the said Mr. Middleton may have a new Grant for the Same. To James St. John, Esqr, Surveyor General.

Read the Petition of Mary Stevenson setting forth that she has twelve persons in her Family for which she never has as yet had any Land and praying a Warrant may issue to her for 600 acres of vacant Land having Sworn to her said Right before the Attorney General. Ordered That a Warrant of Survey issue to the Pet'r for 600 acres of Vacant Land pursuant to the prayer of her Petition.

Meeting of Wednesday the 15th December 1736

Whereas Andrew Broughton Esq'r hath made complaint unto me that he has a tract of Land of Four thousand One Hundred and fifty acres to the Southward survey'd to him to Mr. Hugh Brian who having not return'd a Platt thereof unto your Office. These are therefore to desire and direct you to Cause a platt of the said Land to be returnd into your Office by the said Hugh Brian that the same may be Certified by you in order it may be Returned into the Secretarys Office that he may prepare a Grant for the same. Which said Order was Signed by the honble the Lieu't Governor and directed and sent to the Surveyor General.

Read the Petition of Mr. William Bruce praying a Warrant of Survey for 1650 acres of Land in one of his Majestys Townships his family consisting of thirty three persons viz't himself, wife, three Children, one Servant and 27 slaves all in his own Right and for which he never has had any Land. On Examining the said Petition It is Ordered that a Warrant do issue to him for 800 acres of

Land in the Townships of Kingston and Queenborough and that a Common Warrant issue to him for the remaining 850 on vacant Land.

Read the Petition of Mr. Arthur Foster praying a Common Warrant for One Thousand acres of Land in Consideration of his Services and great Losses and Discouragements he hath had in serving the Publick. Ordered That a Warrant of Survey issue to the Pet'r for 1000 acres of Land pursuant to the prayer of the Petition.

Read the Petition of John Newton praying a Warrant of Survey for 250 acres of vacant land his Family Consisting of five persons sworn to before the Hon'ble Mr. Secretary Hammerton. Ordered That a Warrant of Survey do issue to the Petitioner for 250 acres pursuant to the Prayer of his Petition.

Read the Petition of Mr. James Kelly praying his Family Right of 21 persons on vacant land. Ordered that a Common Warrant issue to the Petitioner for 800 acres of vacant Land his Father having already had a warrant of survey for the right of five of the 21.

Meeting of Thursday the 16th December 1736

Read the Petition of William Marten praying a warrant may issue to him for a Town Lott and two hundred acres of Land in the Township of Amelia and also the same Indulgence as Granted to other New Comers. Ordered that the Prayer of the Petition be Granted.

Read the Petition of William Pool Esq'r praying 700 acres of vacant land in this Province he having a Family Right of Fourteen Slaves. Ordered That a Warrant of Survey issue to the Pet'r for 700 acres of vacant Land as prayd for in his Petition.

Mr. Secretary Hammerton having acquainted this Board that a Fait was this day delivered him to make out a Special Grant by on Order of this Board to Capt. James Akin for One Thousand Acres of Land in Williamsburgh Township with a Remittance of the Quit Rent for ten years. On Considering the Matter Ordered that the said Grant for 1000 acres of Land be made for the payment of the Quit Rent from the date of the said Grant the said Grant being at first run out on a Common Warrant before the Boundary Lines of the s'd Township were ascertained.

Meeting of Friday the 17th December 1736

Read the Petition of James Richbourgh praying a Common Warrant may Issue to him for 200 acres of Land his Family Consisting of four persons. Ordered That a Warrant of survey issue to the Petitioner for 200 acres of vacant land pursuant to the prayer of his Petition.

Read the Petition of Stephen Fogartie praying a Common Warrant may Issue to him for 400 acres of Land he having Eight persons in Family. Ordered That a Warrant of survey issue to the Petitioner for 400 acres of vacant land pursuant to the prayer of his Petition.

Read the Petition of John Dutarque setting forth That he had two Grants one for 618 acres and the other for 400 acres that the said Lands were before Granted to Capt. Thomas Hening and Mr. Henry Lewis, and therefore prays he may upon the surrender of those two Grants obtain a Warrant for 1018 acres of Vacant Land in this Province. Ordered that the Prayer of the Petition be Granted, the Petitioner proving his allegations.

Read the Petition of Richard Marten praying a Warrant for 400 acres in one of the Townships having Eight Persons in Family and never was possessed of any Lands in this Province. Ordered that a Warrant of Survey issue to the Petitioner for 400 acres in one of the New Townships pursuant to the prayer of his Petition.

Read the Petition of Philip Massey setting forth that he being administrator to his Brother Joseph Massey and finding that the said Joseph Massey's estate is not sufficient to pay the debts the Pet'r therefore prays that as the said Joseph Massey had Surveyd to him 500 acres of Land but dying before a Grant could be obtained for the same, he may have a Grant for the said Land in Trust for the use of the said Joseph Massey's Estate to Enable him to pay off the Debts of the said Joseph. Ordered That a Special Warrant do issue to the Surveyor General in the Name of the said Philip Massey as Administrator of Joseph Massey for the Land mentioned in the said Petition in Order that the Platts of the said Land of 500 acres now in the Surveyor Generals Office in the Name of Joseph Massey deceased be Certifyed in the name of the said Philip Massy that a Grant may pass for the same according to the Prayer of the said Petition in Trust to be Sold and applyed towards payment of the Debts of Joseph Massey. But it is further Ordered that before the Grant shall pass the said Philip Massey shall enter into Bond with Sufficient Security for that purpose.

Meeting of Wednesday the 12 January 1736/7

Read the Petition of John Dunlay praying a Warrant of Survey may issue to him for 300 acres of Land and a Town Lott in the Township of Queenborough and also the Bounty of Provisions he having five persons in Family. Ordered That a Warrant of Survey issue to the Pet'r for 250 acres and a Town Lott in the Township of Queenborough.

Read the Petition of Frederick Boshan praying a Warrant of Survey may issue to him for 150 acres of Land and a Town Lott in the Township of Williamsburgh together with Provision &c his family consisting of three persons.

Ordered that a Warrant issue to the Petitioner for a Town Lott and 150 acres of Land in Williamsburgh but that he be allowed no provisions.

Read the Petition of Isaac Porcher praying a warrant of Survey may issue to him for 800 acres of Land in this Province he having Sixteen Persons in Family. Ordered that a Warrant of Survey issue to the Pet'r for 800 acres of vacant land as prayed for.

Read the Petition of Benjamin Child setting forth that he obtained a warrant from his Late Excellency Governor Johnson for 1850 acres of Land which said Warrant was Executed for the Petitioner and now the Petitioner finds that 602 acres of said Land was run out before for another person and therefore prays that he may have a Warrant for 602 acres of Land the remainder of his former Warrant and an Order for his platt for the same quantity formerly laid out to him, and now of no value to be given up. Ordered that the prayer of the Petition be Granted the Petitioner proving the allegations in his Petition.

Meeting of Thursday the 13th January 1736/7

Read the Petition of Matthew Crease praying a warrant of survey for 500 acres of Land in this Province having swore to his Family Right before the Attorney Gen'l. Ordered That a Warrant of Survey do issue to the Pet'r for 500 acres of Land vacant.

Meeting of Friday the 14th January 1736/7

Ordered that Cap't John Cleland's Grants for Lands in Townships be altered and put in the same Form as Township grants are now in.

Ordered that the Lands by a former Order of this Board adjudged to William Dry and John Cockfield Esq'r be Certifyed by his Majesty's Surveyor General in one Platt that a Grant may pass for the same to the said Dry and Cockfield.

On reading the Petition of Joshua Saunders setting forth that his Brother William Saunders died Intestate and that he as nearest of Kin and heir at Law took out Letters of Administration That there is a Platt belonging to his said Brother for 314 acres of Land and therefore most humbly prays that he may have a rant made out to him for the said Land. Ordered that the Attorney General make out a special Fiat for the said Land in order that the Pet'r may have a Grant for the same.

Meeting of Saturday the 15th January 1736/7

Whereas Twenty acres of vacant land lying between a tract of land heretofore Granted to Barnaby Bull deceased and another Tract of Land belonging to William Dry Esq'r was Ordered by this Board to be laid out by the said William Dry and john Cockfield and whereas the said Land has been since surveyed in pursuance of the said Order by Hugh Rose a Lawful Deputy Surveyor. It is therefore Ordered that his Majesty's Surveyor General Do Certify that platt of the said Land surveyed as aforesaid by the said Hugh Rose for the said William Dry Esq'r and John Cockfield in one Platt.

Meeting of Monday the 19th January 1736/7

Read the Petition of John Knox Sen'r praying a warrant of Survey and a Town Lott in the Township of Williamsburgh for 300 acres of Land he having swore to his Family Right before John Cleland Esq'r. Ordered that a Warrant of Survey do issue to the Petitioner for 300 acres of Land and a Town Lott either in the Township of Williamsburgh or that of Kingston.

Read a Petition of Cap't William Pinckney praying a warrant of Survey amy issue to him for 900 acres of vacant Land in this Province he having swore to his Family Right for that Quantity before the Attorney General. Ordered that a Warrant of Survey do issue to the Pet'r as pray'd for.

It appearing to this Board that several persons have bought Negroes Imported into this Province with an Intent to sell them again and before such sale have sworn and taken out warrants for fifty acres a head as their Family Right upon the said Negroes and immediately after have sold or Transfered such Slaves to others who also have taken out Land on the said Slaves. It is ordered That no person for the future shall have any Warrant for Lands until oath made before a Magistrate that the Number of Slaves Sworn to is Bonafide of his Family and that he had no Intention at the time of buying the said Slaves to sell them again with a Twelve months after his taking out such Warrant and that the same be mentioned in the Certificate accordingly.

In pursuance of an Order of Council passed the 13th of August last James St. John Esq'r Surveyor General was agreed with to survey and Sett apart a Certain Quantity of Land on Pedee River for the use of a Considerable Number of Welch People agreeable to the Petition of David Lewis, Samuel Wild and Dan'l James and accordingly Hugh Rose a Deputy Surveyor appointed for that purpose laid before this Board a Plan of 17840 acres lying on each side of Great Pedee River But as this Board is now informed That the has been Some mistake in Setting forth the Lands desir'd by the Pet'r in their Petition and that the same lies more in little Pedee River and may be ascertained and markd off to prevent any Incroachments without any great Expence. Therefore it is now Ordered that the Lands be Reserved for the said Welsh People shall include 10,000 acres on the North East Corner of the Reserved Land in Queenborough Township running from Great Pedee River and so to Continue that Course of Lands to Little Pedee River and from thence up the said Pedee River so far as the Same divides into two Branches and so far as the Province Line is now mark'd running over from thence to Great Pedee River by a Parallel line to the said Township which Land lying between the said Two Rivers and bounded as aforesaid as to the said 10,000 acres shall be reserved for the said Welsh people for the time mentioned in said Order of the 13th August last....

Meeting of Tuesday the 8th February 1736/7

Read the Petition of William Porter praying Land for four Slaves he is possessed of. Ordered That a Warrant of Survey issue to the Pet'r for 200 acres of vacant Land as pray'd for.

Meeting of Wednesday the 9th February 1736/7

Read the Petition of John McAlexander praying a Warrant of Survey may issue to him for 200 acres of Land and a Town Lott in Kingston Township he having four persons in his Family. Ordered a Warrant of Survey issue to the Pet'r for 200 acres of Land in Kingston or Queenborough Township at his Option.

Meeting of Friday the 18th February 1736/7

Whereas Daniel James has personally appeared before this Board and Informed his Majesty's Council that the Lands which David Lewis, Saml Wild and himself prayed for in their petition of the 13th August last to be set apart for the Welch Familys mentioned therein were the vacant Lands they had viewed and desired might be Reserved for them lying eight miles on each side of Great Pedee River and up to the two main Branches thereof and that the Lands Set forth and prescribed in the order of Council of the 21st January last are not the Lands they desired and were Design'd them agreeable to the said Petition as this Board was informed nor wills these Lands suit their Intention of planting Hemp and Flax and the said James also informing this Board that several of the said Familys on the Encouragement they had from the first Order of Council have sold their Possession in Pensilvania Some being arrived and others on their way to this Province, These are therefore to Reverse the said Order of council of the 21st January last and to confirm the said 1st Order of the 13 August the Lines to run parallel as near as may be with the course of Great Pedee River and the Surveyor General is Ordered and Directed particularly to instruct his Deputys not to Survey (for any other persons than the said Welsh people) any more of the said Lands above Pedee Township lying with 8 miles on each thereof and so up to the aforesaid Main Branches and that the Surveyor General be Served with a Copy of this Order there being a Proclamation already issued to give publick Notice of the same.

Read the Petition of John Rowland praying a warrant of Survey may issue to him for 600 acres of Land and a Town Lott in the Township of Queenborough, he having five Children besides himself in family. Ordered That a Warrant of Survey issue to the Pet'r for 300 acres of Land only and a Town Lot in the Township of Queenborough.

Ordered that James St. John Esq'r Survey'r General Do Certify Immediately a Platt of 3249 acres of Land in Craven county being part of a Tract of Land containing 4649 acres surveyed by John Gough a Deputy Surveyor in the month of January 1732 by virtue of a warrant Directed to him and Dated Decemb'r 18th 1731 for the survey of 9150 acres for the honble James Kinloch Esq'r being the Quantity of Land Ordered to the said John Gough the 9th of Septemb'r 1736 being part of the said Tract of 4649 acres of Land agreeable to the former order of Council March 26th 1736.

Meeting of Thursday the 3d March 1736/7

Read the Petition of Mrs Eliz'a Hayes widow setting forth that she has Ten Persons in Family which she has Sworn to before the Attorney General and having no Land in this Province humbly prays She may obtain a Warrant of Survey for 500 acres of Land either in the Township of Williamsburgh Queenborough or Kingston. Ordered that the Prayer of the Petition be Granted and that a Warrant of Survey issue to her in either of the aforementioned Townships at her Option.

Read the Petition of George Lucas Esq'r setting forth that he has Imported Four white Indented Servants and Thirty One Slaves for which he prays such a Quantity of Land as he is entitled to by his Majestys Instructions in One of the New Townships. Ordered that a Warrant of Survey issue to the Pet'r for 1800 acres of Land in any one of the Townships not Excepted.

Meeting of Friday the 4th March 1736/7

Read the Petition of Jane Johnson Sen'r and Jane Johnson Jun'r praying a Warrant of Survey for 100 acres of Land and a Town Lot in the Township of Williamsburgh in their own Right. Ordered that a Warrant of Survey issue to the Pet'r pursuant to the Prayer of their Petition.

Read the Petition of Rachel White praying a warrant a Warrant of Survey may issue to her for her Family Right consisting of Six persons on vacant Land. Ordered that a Warrant of Survey issue to the Pet'r for 300 acres of vacant Land as prayed for.

Read the Petition of John Jenkins praying a warrant of Survey may issue to him for 150 acres and a Town Lott in the Township of Queenborough, he having three persons in family. Ordered that a Warrant of Survey issue to the Pet'r pursuant to the prayer of his Petition.

Read the Petition of Archer Smith praying his Family Right consisting of 26 persons on vacant Land. Ordered that a Warrant of Survey issue to the Pet'r for 1300 acres of vacant Land as prayed for.

Read the Petition of William Bryan praying his Family Right consisting of Two persons and a Town Lot in Kingston Township. Ordered that a Warrant of Survey issue to the Pet'r for a Town Lot and 100 acres of vacant Land as pray'd for.

Read the Petition of Richard Cradle praying a warrant may issue to him for his Family Right consisting of two persons in the Township of Williamsburgh. Ordered That a Warrant issue to the Pet'r for 100 acres of Land as prayd for in his petition.

Read the Petition of William Thomas praying a Warrant of Survey may issue to him for his Family Right consisting of Six persons on vacant Land. Ordered that a Warrant of Survey issue to the Pet'r for 300 acres of Land as pray'd for.

Read the Petition of Meimus Gaillard praying his Family Right consisting of twelve persons on vacant Land. Ordered that a Warrant of Survey issue to the Pet'r for 600 acres of vacant land pursuant to the prayer of his Petition.

Read the Petition of Marmaduke Ash praying a Warrant of survey may issue to him for 450 acres of Land in Kingston Township being entitled thereto by his Family Right. Ordered that a Warrant of Survey issue to the Pet'r pursuant to the Prayer of his Petition.

Read the Petition of Duncan McQuin praying a Warrant of Survey may issue to him for his Family Right consisting of 17 persons on vacant Land. Ordered that a Warrant of Survey issue to the Petition for 850 acres of vacant Land as pray'd for.

Read the Petition of Judith Lewis praying her Family Right consisting of three persons on vacant Land. Ordered that a warrant of Survey for 150 acres of Land as pray'd for.

Read the Petition of Thomas Blith setting forth that he has Seven persons in his Family and praying a Warrant of Survey may issue to him for 350 acres of vacant Land. Ordered that a Warrant of survey issue to the Pet'r for 350 acres of vacant Land as pray'd for.

Read the Petition of William Stephens setting forth that he has three persons in Family for which he has never yet had any Land and praying a Warrant of Survey for 150 acres of Vacant Land. Ordered that a Warrant of Survey issue to the Pet'r for 150 acres of vacant Land as pray'd for.

Read the Petition of Gaven Witherspoon praying a Warrant of Survey may issue to him for 50 acres of Land in the Township of Williamsburgh. Ordered that a Warrant of Survey issue to the Pet'r as pray'd for.

Read the Petition of Abraham Staples praying a warrant may issue to him for 150 acres of Land in virtue of his Family Right on vacant Lands. Ordered that a Warrant of Survey issue to the Pet'r for 150 acres of vacant Land as pray'd for.

Read the Petition of David Deleseure praying a warrant of Survey may issue to him for 150 acres of Land in virtue of his Family Right in one of the New Townships. Ordered that a Warrant of Survey issue to the Pet'r pursuant to the Prayer of his Petition.

Read the Petition of David Dalbiat praying a warrant of Survey for 200 acres of Land in one of the New Townships His Family consisting of 4 Persons. Ordered that a Warrant of Survey issue to the Pet'r for 200 acres of Land as prayd for in any Township not excepted.

Read the Petition of William Boldue praying a warrant of Survey may issue to him for 50 acres of Land in the Township of Williamsburgh. Ordered That a Warrant of Survey issue to the Pet'r as pray'd for.

Read the Petition of John Carrol praying a Warrant of Survey may issue to him for 300 acres of Land on the Township of Williamsburgh he having six Persons in Family. Ordered that a Warrant of Survey issue to the Pet'r for 300 acres of Land in the Township of Williamsburgh as pray'd for.

Read the Petition of Mr. John Watson setting forth that he has 16 persons in Family and praying that in their Right a Warrant of Survey may issue to him for 800 acres of vacant land. Ordered that a Warrant of Survey issue to the Pet'r for 800 cares of vacant Land as pray'd for.

Read the Petition of Blanch McKey praying a warrant of Survey may issue to her for 200 acres of Land and a Lott in the Township of Williamsburgh her Family Consisting of 4 Persons. Ordered that a Warrant of Survey issue to the Pet'r for 200 acres of Land in the Township of Williamsburgh has pray'd for.

Read the Petition of George Hall setting forth that he has Eleven Persons in his family and praying that in right of the same he may have a Warrant of Survey Issue to him for 550 acres of Land. Ordered that a Warrant of Survey issue to the Pet'r for 500 acres of vacant Land as pray'd for.

Read the Petition of Rob't Fladger praying his Family Right consisting of 12 persons on vacant Land. Ordered that a Warrant of Survey do issue to the Pet'r for 600 acres of vacant Land as pray'd for in the Petition.

Read the Petition of William Hendrick setting forth that he has 26 persons in Family and praying a Warrant of Survey may issue to him for 1300 acres of vacant Land. Ordered that a Warrant of Survey do issue to the Pet'r for 1300 acres of vacant Land as prayed for.

HEMPSTEAD COUNTY LIBRARY
HOPE, ARKANSAS

Read the Petition of William Poole setting forth that he has 16 persons in Family in right of which he prayeth that a Warrant of Survey may issue to him for 800 acres of vacant Land. Ordered that a Warrant of Survey do issue to the Pet'r for 800 acres of Land on vacant Land pursuant to the Prayer of his Petition.

Read the Petition of John Dicks praying a warrant of survey may issue to him for 50 acres of Land in the Township of Williamsburgh. Ordered that a Warrant of Survey issue to the Pet'r for 50 acres of Land in the Township of Williamsburgh as prayed for.

Read the Petition of John Rodass praying a Warrant of Survey issue to him for 300 acres of Land in the Township of Williamsburgh his Family consisting of Six persons. Ordered that a Warrant of Survey do issue to the Petitioner for 300 acres of vacant Land in the Township of Williamsburgh as pray'd for.

Read the Petition of Charles Filbin praying a Warrant of Survey may issue to him for 200 acres of vacant land his Family consisting of four persons. Ordered that a Warrant of Survey issue to the Pet'r for 200 acres of land as pray'd for.

Read the Petition of William Smith setting forth that he has five persons in Family and praying that in right of them a warrant of Survey may issue to him for 250 acres of Land in one of the new Townships. Ordered that a Warrant of Survey do issue to the Pet'r for 250 acres of Land in any of the New Townships.

Read the Petition of the Reverend Mr. Nathan Bassett setting forth that he has nineteen persons in Family and praying that in right of them a Warrant of survey may issue to him for 950 acres of vacant land. Ordered that a Warrant of Survey do issue to the Pet'r for 950 acres of vacant land pursuant to the prayer of his Petition.

Read the Petition of the John Dutarque praying that a Special Warrant may issue to him for 350 acres of vacant Land in right of his Family which consists of seven persons. Ordered that a Warrant of Survey do issue to the Pet'r for 350 acres of Land as prayed for in said Petition.

Read the Petition of William Cashpull praying a Warrant of Survey may issue to the Pet'r for 100 acres of Land in Kingston Township in virtue of his Family Right. Ordered that a Warrant of Survey do issue to the Pet'r for 100 acres of Land in Kingston Township pursuant to the Prayer of his Petition.

Read the Petition of Esau Ourry praying a Warrant of Survey may issue to him for 100 acres of Land in the Township of Purysburgh in virtue of his Family Right. Ordered That a Warrant of Survey do issue to the said ourry for 100 acres of Land in Purysburgh Township as pray'd for.

Read the Petition of William Gascoign setting forth that he has 12 persons in Family and praying a Warrant of Survey may issue to him for 600 acres of Land in one of the New Townships. Ordered That a Warrant of Survey issue to the Petitioner for 600 acres of Land in any of the Townships not excepted.

Read the Petition of Thomas Elliot son of Wm. Elliot Sen'r praying that a Special Warrant may issue to him for a Platt returnd in the Secretary's Office of the Overplus Lands lying within the mark'd Tress buttings and Boundings of Two Tracts of Land granted at 12 P hundred acres and further prays that a Grant may be made out agreeable to the old Quit Rent Law. Ordered that the Prayer of the Petition be Granted the Petitioner proving the allegations in his Petition set forth.

Meeting of Saturday the 5th March 1736/7

For as much as it appears absolutely necessary to this Board That a discreet Vigilant and Understanding person should reside in or near the Township of Orangeburgh Amelia and Saxe Gotha now Inhabited by Swiss Protestants who being unacquainted with the English Tongue Labour under difficulties for what of a person that speaks their Language and Christian Motte having offered his Service to this Board and being well recommended and Qualifyd for that Service, It was ordered that the said Christian Motte have a Warrant for 100 acres and a Town Lott in such of the aforesaid Townships as he small make Choice of and that he be allowed out of the Sinking fund the sum of £200 currency for one Year from the date of this Order as a Reward for his Service for Superintending, advising and directing the Swiss and other Inhabitants in the said Townships and the better so to Enable him to Execute the same that he be put into the Commission of the Peace and have a Majors Commission for that District.

Meeting of Tuesday the 15th March 1736/7

Read the Petition of William Jackson setting forth that he had a Warrant for 100 acres of Land which he run out and settled and being now found to lye within the Line of Williamsburgh Township and praying a Warrant to run out the same on Surrendring the first Warrant. Ordered that a Warrant of Resurvey do issue to the Petition for the said Land on his Surrender of the former warrant as prayd for.

Read the Petition of William Elvis praying a Warrant of survey may issue to him for 300 acres of vacant Land his Family Consisting of Six persons. Ordered That a Warrant of survey do issue to the Pet'r for 300 acres of vacant Land pursuant to the Prayer of his Petition.

Read the Petition of William Kempt setting forth that he has an additional Family Right of One White Servant and One Negro for which he prays a Warrant of survey may issue to him for 100 acres of Vacant Land. Ordered that a Warrant of Survey issue to the Pet'r for 50 acres of vacant Land in right of the Negro only.

Meeting of Wednesday the 23d March 1736/7

Read the Petition of Robert Thorpe Esq'r setting forth That he has 37 persons in his Family and praying a Warrant of Survey may issue to him for 1850 acres of vacant Land in right of his family. Ordered that a Warrant do issue to the Pet'r for 1850 acres of Land to be laid out in one tract except for Marshes front Lands or surplus Lands.

Read the Petition of Thomas Orchard praying a Warrant of Survey for his family Right consisting of Six persons on vacant Land. Ordered That a Warrant of Survey issue to the Pet'r for 300 acres of Land as prayd for.

Read the Petition of James Craige praying a Warrant of Survey may issue to him for his Family Right consisting of four persons on vacant Land. Ordered That a Warrant of Survey issue to the Pet'r for 200 acres of Land as prayd for.

Read the Petition of James Lemming praying his Family Right consisting of Seven persons on vacant Land. Ordered That a Warrant of Survey issue to the Pet'r for 350 acres of Land as prayd for.

Read the Petition of Thomas Robert praying his Family Right consisting of 7 persons on vacant Land. Ordered That a Warrant of Survey issue to the Pet'r for 500 acres of vacant Land pursuant to the prayer of his Petition.

Meeting of Friday the 25th March 1737

Read the Petition of John Ioor praying a Warrant of Survey for his Family Right consisting of three persons on vacant Land. Ordered That a Warrant of Survey issue to the Pet'r for 150 acres of Land pursuant to the prayer of the Petition.

Read the Petition of Benjamin Perry praying a Warrant of Survey may issue to him for his Family Right consisting of 38 slaves. Ordered That a Warrant of Survey issue to the Pet'r for 1900 acres of vacant land pursuant to the prayer of the Petition.

Read the Petition of Sam'l Elmes praying a Warrant of Survey may issue to him for his Family Right consisting of nine Persons on vacant Land. Ordered That a Warrant of Survey issue to the Pet'r for 450 ares of vacant Land pursuant to the prayer of his Petition.

Read the Petition of Emanuel Smith praying a Warrant of Survey may issue to him for his Family Right consisting of 7 persons on vacant Land. Ordered that a Warrant of Survey may issue to the Pet'r for 350 acres of vacant Land as prayd for in his Petition.

Read the Petition of Daniel Bourget praying a Warrant of Survey may issue to him for his Family Right consisting of five persons on vacant Land. Ordered that a Warrant of Survey issue to the Pet'r for 250 acres of vacant Land as prayd for in his Petition.

Read the Petition of John Dennon praying a Warrant may issue to him for 100 acres of Land and a Town Lott in the Township of Williamsb'g he having Two persons in his Family and further praying his Majestys allowance of Provisions. Ordered that a Warrant of Survey issue to the Pet'r for 100 acres of Land and a Town Lott in the Township of Williamsb'g but no allowance of Provisions.

Meeting of Thursday the 31st March 1737

On Reading the Petition of Johannes Tobler setting forth that being an Inhabitant of the Canton of Appenzell and hearing of the Encouragement which this Government gives to New Comers that have a mind to settle in the Townships in this Province took a Resolution to leave his Native Country and to come to his place where the Pet'r has been informed that a Tract of Land is given as a Reward or Gratuity to any Persons that undertakes to settle one of the said Townships and the Pet'r having brought over with him One hundred and Seventy Persons for that purpose humbly prays for the Benefit of the said Encouragement. It is Ordered that the People above mentioned be deemed as part of Mr. Zouberbuhler's People but that the said Tobler have 550 acres as a Gratuity added to 950 acres he had Warrants for to make up in the whole 1500 acres.

It is likewise Ordered that Mr. Zouberbuhler for his Care and Trouble in bringing over the People and being their Minister have 900 acres added to the 600 acres he had for his Family Right to make up in the whole 1500 acres.

Meeting of Friday the 8th April 1737

Complaint being made to this Board by Maurice[?] Lewis Esq'r on behalf of the Welsh Families lately arrived from Pensilvania in order to Settle the Lands on Pedee River pursuant to an Order of this Board on the 13th August last That notwithstanding the aforesaid order and the several Orders made by this Board Since, for setting a part and Surveying Lands for the said Welsh Families already arrived no Land is yet Surveyed for those People but that the Persons appointed for that service have neglected to pursue the Order of this board whereby those People are Deprived of Lands to Settle upon to their very great Prejudice if not ruin. Having therefore taken the premises under Consideration and to prevent the Like abuse and Delay for the Future. It is Ordered That John Ouldfield Jun'r Esq'r be the person appointed immediately to survey to all the Welsh People, now arrived so much Land as each of them are Intitled unto by their Family Right on such part of Great Pedee River agreeable to the Orders of this board of the 13 August and the 18th February last past as the said Welsh People shall make choice of and return Platts thereof to the Clerk of this Board in order that the said Surveys may pas Regularly thro' the Office of his Majestys Surveyor General and also that the said Oldfield do perform and mark out the Lands intended to be Reserved for the Welsh People according to the directions of the above said Orders of Council of the 13th August and 18th February and return a Platt thereof to the Clerk of the council in order to be laid before this board for which service due care shall be taken to make him all reasonable Satisfaction.

Read the Petition of Kennedy Obrian praying a warrant of survey may issue to him for his Family Right Consisting of thirteen Persons on vacant Lands. Ordered that a Warrant of Survey issue to the said OBrian for 650 acres of vacant Land but that due care be taken that the same be not Run out on the Lands Granted to the Chickesaws.

A Certificate on Oath taken before H. Berenger de Beaufin Esq'r one of his Majesty's Justices of the Peace for Granville County being produced at this Board proving an Additional Family Right of 16 persons belonging to Samuel Mountagut Esq'r of the Township of Purysburgh for which he prays Land. Ordered that a Warrant of Survey issue to the said Mountagut for 800 acres of vacant Land.

Read the Petition of William Trueman praying a Warrant for 500 acres of Land in this Province. Ordered That a Warrant of Survey issue to the Petit'r for 500 acres of vacant Land.

Read the petition of Francis Parrot praying a warrant may issue to him for two Persons he has in Family on vacant Land. Ordered that a Warrant of Survey issue to the Petitioner for 100 acres of vacant Land.

Read the Petition of Joseph Horsey praying a Warrant of Survey may issue to him for 50 acres of Land and a Town Lott in the Township of Williamsburgh together with the Kings Bounty of Provisions. Ordered That a Warrant of Survey issue to the Petitioner for 50 acres of Land and a Town Lot in the Township of Williamsburgh as prayd for But that the Petitioner be not allow'd the Kings Bounty.

Read the Petition of Daniel Smart praying a Warrant of Survey issue to him for 50 acres of Land and a Town Lot in the Township of Purisburgh. Ordered That a Warrant of Survey issue to the Petitioner for 50 acres of Land as prayed for.

Read the Petition of John Bedon praying a warrant of survey may issue to him for his Family Right consisting of Fourteen Persons on vacant Land. Ordered that a Warrant of Survey issue to the Pet'r for 700 acres of vacant Land as prayd for.

Read the Petition of Isaac Motte setting forth that being a New Settler in the Township of New Windsor likewise being appointed by Mr. Commissary Taylor to give out the provisions to the New Settlers in the said Township and being in hopes to Encrease his Family there desires he may obtain a Lott and some Lands in said Township. Ordered That a Warrant of Survey issue to the Pet'r for a Town Lott and 200 acres of Land in the Township of new Windsor.

Meeting of Thursday the 21 April 1737

Read the Petition of Hugh Rose praying a Warrant of Survey for 150 acres of Land in the Township of Purisburgh he having three persons in Family. Ordered that a Warrant of Survey issue to the Pet'r for 150 acres of Land as pray'd for.

Read the Petition of John Henry Mayerhoof praying his Family Right of two persons in the Township of Purysburgh. Ordered that a Warrant of Survey issue to the Pet'r for One hundred acres of Land as prayd for.

Read the Petition of Henry Mayerhoof Long Andrews praying a Warrant of Survey may issue to him for his Family Right consisting of Two persons in the Township of Purisburgh. Ordered that a Warrant of Survey issue to the Pet'r for 100 acres of Land in the Township of Purysburgh as pray'd for.

Read the Petition of John Grob praying a Warrant of Survey may issue to him for his Additional Family Right of One Person in the Township of Purysburgh. Ordered that a Warrant of Survey issue to the Pet'r for 50 acres of Land in the Township of Purysburgh as pray'd for.

Read the Petition of Joseph Elliot praying his Family Right consisting of 50 persons on vacant Land. Ordered that a Warrant of Survey issue to the said Elliot for 2500 acres of vacant Land as pray'd for.

Read the Petition of Joseph Hunt [Hurst?] praying a Warrant of Survey may issue to him for 400 acres of vacant Land he having 8 persons in family. Ordered that a Warrant of Survey be issued to the Pet'r for 400 acres of vacant land as pray'd for.

Read the Petition of Blanch McKey widow praying a Warrant may issue to her for 200 acres of Land and a Town Lott in Williamsburgh Township together with the Allowance of Provisions &c. Ordered that a Warrant do issue to the Petitioner pursuant to the Prayer of his Petition and also the Allowance of Provisions &C pray'd for as is Granted to New Settlers in the Townships.

Read the Petition of Edward Stephens praying a warrant may issue to him for his Family Right Consisting of Six Persons in Pedee Township. Ordered that a Warrant of Survey do issue to the Pet'r for 300 acres of Land in the Township of Pedee, as pray'd for.

Read the Petition of Thomas Russell praying a Warrant of Survey may issue to him for his Family Right Consisting of four Persons on vacant Land. Ordered That a Warrant of Survey do issue to the Pet'r for 200 acres of vacant Land as prayd for.

Meeting of Wednesday the 4th May 1737

Read the Petition of Thomas Goodman praying a Town Lott and 200 acres of Land in the Township of Queenborough the Petitioner being well skilled in the Method of raising hemp and Flax, and ready to Communicate his knowledge therein for the Benefit of the Publick &ca. It was Ordered that a Warrant of Survey issue to the said Goodman pursuant to the Prayer of his Petition he surrendring a Former Warrant issue to him for 350 acres of Land.

Read the Petition of William Grislo praying a warrant of Survey may issue to him for his Family Right Consisting of 8 Persons on vacant Land. Ordered that a Warrant of Survey issue to the Petition'r for 400 acres of vacant Land as prayd for.

Read the Petition of Alexander Campbell praying a Warrant of Survey may issue to him for his Family Right consisting of five Persons on vacant Land. Ordered That a Warrant of Survey issue to the Pet'r for 250 acres of Vacant Lands as pray'd for in his Petition.

Meeting of Thursday the 5th May 1737

Read the Petition of William Hamilton, Messenger of this Board, praying for a Quantity of Land in Pedee Township as to this Board shall seem meet in consideration of his Services &c. Ordered that a Warrant of Survey issue to the Pet'r for 500 acres of Land in Pedee Township.

Read the Petition of Archibald Lamont praying a Warrant of Survey may issue to him for his Family Right consisting of two persons for 100 acres and a Town Lott in the Township of Williamsburgh. Ordered That a Warrant of Survey issue to the Pet'r for a Town Lott and 100 acres of Land in the Township of Williamsburgh.

Read the Petition of Thomas Tew praying a Warrant of Survey for his Family Right consisting of five persons. Ordered That a Warrant of Survey issue to the Pet'r for 250 acres of Land in Pedee Township.

Read the Petition of joseph Robinson praying a Warrant of Survey for his Family Right consisting of 7 Persons on vacant Land. Ordered that a Warrant of Survey issue to the Pet'r for 350 acres of vacant Land as prayd for.

Read the Petition of Albert Dedman praying his Family Right consisting of five persons on vacant Land. Ordered that a Warrant of Survey issue to the Pet'r for 250 acres of vacant Land as prayd for.

Meeting of Tuesday the 28th June 1737

Read the Petition of William McDaniel praying a Warrant of Survey may issue to him for his Family Right Consisting of four Persons. Ordered That a Warrant of Survey issue to the Pet'r for 200 acres of Land and a Town Lott in the Township of Williamsburgh.

Read the Petition of Elias Foissin Esq'r praying a Warrant of Survey may issue to him for his Family Right consisting of Twenty four Persons on vacant Land. Ordered that a Warrant of Survey issue to the Pet'r for 1200 acres of vacant Land as prayd for.

Read the Petition of Thomas Maccully praying his own Right of 50 acres and a Town Lott in Kingston Township and his Majesty's Bounty of Provisions &c. Ordered that a Warrant of Survey issue to the Pet'r for 50 acres and a Town Lott in Kingston Township but that he be allowd no provisions.

Read the Petition of Saml Mountagut Esq'r praying a warrant may issue to him for his Additional Family Right consisting of 16 persons within the Limits of Purisburgh Town'p where he is now Settled he having had no Land as yet for the said Number of Persons. Ordered that a Warrant of Survey issue to the Pet'r for 800 acres of vacant Land in the Limits of Purysburgh Township the Pet'r returning a former warrant issue to him for the same number of persons on vacant Land.

Read a Certificate taken on oath before James Wright Esq'r Attorney Gen'l praying the Right of Samuel Margill by a Daughter being born to him. Ordered that a Warrant issue to the Petitioner for 50 acres of Land for said additional Family Right as pray'd for.

Meeting of Wednesday the 29th June 1737

Read the Petition of Isaac Dumont praying his Family Right consisting of Four persons on vacant Land. Ordered that a Warrant of Survey issue to the Pet'r for 200 acres of vacant Land as prayd for.

Meeting of Friday the 1st July 1737

Upon Reading the Memorial of Anthony Williams, Deputy Surveyor for the Township of Williamsburgh, setting forth that by several surveys and Encroachments on the Lands intended for the Town Glebe and Common there was not more than 400 acres but what was the Property of Private Persons That there was a large Tract of Land not more than one quarter of a Mile from the Town Line over a Small Swamp which he apprehended may in all Respects answer the Purposes for the Glebe and Common the Following Order was directed to the said Anthony Williams vizt.

You the said Anthony Williams are hereby Ordered and Required to lay out the said 400 acres mentioned in the Memorial into Town Lotts agreeable to the Order of Council of the 8th August 1735 and that you immediately survey 300 acres of vacant Land over the Swamp for a Glebe the most Convenient for that purpose and most Contiguous to the to the Town.

Read the Petition of Robert Williams merchant praying a warrant of Survey may issue to him for his Family Right consisting of 26 Persons viz 24 whites and 2 Negroes in the Township of Purysburgh Sworn to before H. Bereger de Beaufin Esq'r One of his Majesty's Justice of the Peace for Granville County. Ordered That a Warrant of Survey Issue to the Pet'r for 1300 acres of Land in the Township of Purysburgh, pursuant to the Prayer of the Petition.

Read the Petition of William Roberts on a Dispute him and Mr. Albergotty. Ordered that the said Petition do lye upon the Table until further Order, and that in the meantime, each of the Contending Parties keep what they are in possession of.

Read also the Petition of Ulysses Anthony Albergotty Esq'r relating to the said and Ordered as above.

Ordered that James St. John Esq'r Surveyor Do immediately Certify to the Honble James Kinloch Esq'r a Platt of 3249 Acres of Land in Craven County as he was directed by an Order of Council of the 18th February last an attested Copy of which Order was yesterday delivered to him by Mr. George Hunter, and that if the said Surveyor General has any just Objection against Signing the said Platt That he appear at this Board this afternoon and represent the same to his Honour the Lieut. Governor and his Majesty's Honble Council.

Read the Petition of Joseph Tedler Setting forth that he paid a valuable Consideration for 650 acres of Land which Land was Surveyd and laid out and a Platt thereof returned into the Surveyor General's Office in the name of Ann Lowry the Person he purchased the said Land of. That the said Land so run was taken in and included in a parcel of Land afterwards run out for Coll. Lucas so that he cannot receive any Benefit from the first Survey, notwithstanding his paying a Valuable Consideration and likewise Tax for the same and therefore prays a Warrant may issue to him for Surveying 650 acres of Vacant Land in his own Name in Order a Grant may pass to him for the same. Ordered that a Warrant of Survey do issue to the Pet'r as pray'd for in his Petition.

Read the Petition of John Horskens praying a Warrant of survey may issue to him for his Family Right consisting of two persons on vacant Land. Ordered that a warr't of Survey issue to the Pet'r for 100 acres vacant land as pray'd for.

Read the Petition of Constance Fitch Praying a Warrant of Survey for her Family Right consisting of 41 Persons for 2050 acres of vacant Land. Ordered That the said Petition do Lye upon the Table until it is made appear that no warrant has been Granted in right of said Family to Joseph Fitch or Manley Williamson.

Read the Petition of Daniel Townsend praying a Warrant of Survey may issue to him for his Family Right consisting of 18 Persons on vacant Land. Ordered That a Warrant of Survey do issue to the Pet'r for 900 acres of Land vacant as pray'd for.

Read the Petition of Jonathan Wood praying a Warrant of Survey for his Family Right consisting of eight persons on vacant Land. Ordered that a Warrant of Survey issue to the Pet'r for 400 acres of vacant Land as prayd for.

Read the Petition of John Delagaye praying his Family Right consisting of five persons on vacant Land. Ordered that a Warrant of Survey issue to the Pet'r for 250 acres of vacant Land as prayd for.

Read the Petition of Joseph Mitchell praying a Warrant of Survey may issue to him for his Family Right consisting of 19 Persons in the Township of Amelia. Ordered That a Warrant of Survey do issue to the Pet'r for 950 acres of vacant Land as prayed for in the Township of Amelia.

Read the Petition of Kenneth McKenzie praying a Warrant of Survey may issue to him for his Family Right consisting of Ten Persons in one of the Townships. Ordered That on the Petitioners making oath he intends to settle the Land prayd for with the Servants mentioned in his Petition.

Read the Petition of Thomas McCulloch relating to a Caveat Entred by Tho's Potts and Ribton Hutchinson mercht against his having a Grant for 800 acres of Land in the Township of Williamsburgh. Ordered that the said Petition do lie for further Consideration.

Read the Petition of Nicholas Roche praying his Family Right Consisting of Ten Persons in the Township of New Windsor. Ordered that the said Petition do lie upon the Table for further consideration.

Read the Petition of June Servant setting forth that she has 13 Persons in Family and praying a Warrant of Survey may issue to her for 650 acres of Land in one of the Townships. Ordered That a Warrant of Survey do issue to the Pet'r for 650 acres of Land in any of the Townships not excepted.

Read the Petition of James Postell praying a Warrant of Survey may issue to him for his Family Right consisting of 16 persons on vacant Land. Ordered that the Prayer of the Petition be Granted.

James St. John Esq'r Surveyor General appear at this Board pursuant to the Order of this Morning and agreed to sign the Platt in said Order mentioned for the Honble James Kinloch Esq'r the beginning of next week.

Meeting of Tuesday the 5th July 1737

Read the Petition of Thomas Bolton setting forth that he has Sixteen Persons in family for which he has never yet has any Land and praying a Warrant of Survey may issue to him for 800 acres of vacant land. Ordered That a Warrant of Survey issue to the Petitioner for 800 acres of vacant Land pursuant to the prayer of the Petition.

Read the Petition of the Widow Jenneret setting forth That she has obtained a Warrant of Survey for 300 acres of Land and the Deputy Surveyor she Employed has admeasured and Return'd a Platt of only 150 acres and praying an order may issue to her for admeasuring the remaining 50 acres. Ordered That the said Petition be sett aside The Pet'r having a Right by her warrant to run the remaining 50 acres.

Read the Petition of Anne Howard praying a Warrant of Survey may issue to her for her Family Right Consisting of 12 Persons on vacant Land. Ordered That a Warrant of Survey issue to the Petitioner for 600 acres of vacant Land as pray'd for.

Read the Petition of John Spencer praying a Warrant of Survey may issue to him for his Family Right Consisting of 12 Persons on vacant Land. Ordered That a Warrant of Survey issue to the Petitioner for 600 acres of vacant Land as pray'd for.

Read the Petition of Mary Vernod praying that the warrant for 1000 acres of Land issued to her late Husband the Rev'd Mr. Vernod may be Surrendered and That a Warrant for a like Number of acres may issue in her Name in the Township of purysburgh or New Windsor. Ordered That the Prayer of the Petition be Granted.

Read the Petition of Lewis Bignon praying a Warrant may issue to him for his Family Right Consisting of eight Persons for Surveying 400 acres of Land in the Township of New Windsor. Ordered That the Pet'r do on Oath prove that he has not any Land in the Province.

Read the Petition of Mr. John Baxter setting forth That he had Imported 30 Persons into this Province agreeable to his Obligation for that purpose on Granting him a Warrant for 1500 acres of Land in the Township of ________ and also praying a Warrant for 650 acres for 13 Persons in the Township of Williamsburgh, Queenborough, or Kingston which Number he also Imported with the above 30 persons in the Ship John and Edmond, John Coffin Comander from Belfast as appears by a Certificate from Mrss's John and Edmund Atkins, Owners of the said Ship. It is therefore Ordered That the said John Baxter have a warrant for 650 acres of Land and three Town Lotts in the Townships of Williamsburgh or Kingston, and also that the said John Baxter's Obligation be Delivered up to him, he having Complied with the Conditions thereof.

Meeting of Tuesday the 12th July 1737

Upon Reading the Petition of the Scotch Servants lately arrived in this Province from Scotland, Setting forth That they came over Indented Servants to Kenneth McKenzie or his Assigns on board Captain Urquhart where they have been already Six weeks in Port, and having Expended all their Provisions, and that said Captain Declaring he can supply them no longer, and therefore praying Relief of this Board. his Majesty's Council taking the same into Consideration, and also that the Captain who brought over the said Servants having been six weeks in this Port and the Provisions already Expended besides some fresh Provisions provided by the said Captain Since his arrival for the said servants, and the said Capt. having Represented That he is no longer able to Subsist them and several of the said servants being already fallen sick, and it being to be feared that many more may become so this violent hot season, by being continued on board the vessell which may occasion a Contagious Distemper, the ill Consequence of which is to be dreaded It is therefore the Opinion of his Majesty's Council That it is for the Interest of the Persons Concerned that the said Servants be immediately disposed of to the best advantage and to preserve the Lives or the said People as well as to prevent a general Infection which may arise from Sickness or want of wholsom Provisions.

Meeting of Wednesday the 13th July 1737

Read the Petition of Thomas Wiggan praying a Warrant of Survey may issue to him for his Family Right consisting of Ten Persons on vacant Land. Ordered That a Warrant of Survey do issue to the Pet'r for 500 acres of vacant Land as pray'd for.

Read the Petition of George Haig praying his Additional Family Right of four Persons in Amelia Township where he has lands already. Ordered That a Warrant of Survey issue to the Pet'r for 200 acres of vacant Land in Amelia Township as pray'd for.

Read the Petition of Mary Hugget praying a Warrant of Survey may issue to her for her Family Right Consisting of Two Persons. Ordered that a Warrant of Survey issue to the Pet'r for One Hundred Acres of Land in Amelia Township as pray'd for.

Read the Petition of Lewis Bignon praying his Family Right Consisting of Eight Persons in the Township of New Windsor. Ordered to lie on the Table.

Read the Petition of Robert Perryman praying a Warrant of Survey may issue to him for his Family Right consisting of Ten Persons on vacant Land. Ordered that a Warrant of Survey issue to the Petitioner for 500 acres of vacant Land as prayd for.

Meeting of Friday the 29th July 1737

Read the Petition of John Linning praying his additional Family Right of two Slaves. Ordered that a Warrant of Survey Issue to the Pet'r for 100 acres.

Read the Petition of William Grace praying his Family Right consisting of three Persons on vacant Land. Ordered that a Warrant of Survey Issue to the Petition'r for 150 acres as pray'd for.

His Hon'r the Lieu't Governor Sign'd a Warrant directed to James St. John Esq'r Survey'r General for laying out of Lands within the Township of Queenborough Or in any place within Eight Miles above the said Township reserved for the Welch Protestants vizt

To Jeremiah Rowell 150 acres
To Samuel Soranny 100 ditto
To Thomas Bowen 150 ditto
To Evan Vaughan 350 ditto
To Saml Evans 500 ditto
To Evan Davis 50 ditto.

Meeting of Saturday the 30th July 1737

Read the Petition of Eliz Singleton Setting forth that she has 12 persons in Family for which she has never had any Land and praying a Warrant of Survey may issue to her for 600 acres of vacant Land. Ordered That a Warrant of Survey issue to the Pet'r for 600 acres of vacant Land as pray'd for.

Read the Petition of Thomas Lainee setting forth That he has Seven Persons in Family for which he has never had any Land and praying a Warrant of Survey may issue to him for 350 acres of vacant Land. Ordered that a Warrant of Survey issue to the Pet'r for 350 acres of vacant Land as pray'd for.

Read the Petition of Jonathan Wood praying a Warrant of Survey may issue to him for his Family Right consisting of two persons on vacant Land. Ordered That a Warrant of Survey issue to the Pet'r for 100 acres of Land.

Meeting of Thursday the 11th August 1737

Upon application to this Board of Benjamin Waring Esq'r praying a Warrant of Resurvey for a Tract of Land of 500 acres upon Sawkee Bluff on Pedee River conveyd and made over to him by Landgrave Thomas Smith. Orderd That a Warrant of Resurvey do issue to the Surveyor Gen'l accordingly.

Meeting of Friday the 12th August 1737

Read the Petition of Wm Guy Jun'r praying a Warrant of Survey for a Tract of Land as to this Hon'ble Board shall seem meet in Consideration of his being a Clerk in the Secretarys Office. Ordered That a Warrant of Survey issue to the Pet'r for 500 acres of vacant Land, not on account of his being a Clerk in the Secretary's Office but in Consideration of his having been extremely diligent and of great Service to the Publick at the time this Province was alarmed and threatned with a Spanish Invasion.

Read the Petition of Jonathan Bryan setting forth that he run out a Warrant of 1200 acres of Land which Land happened to fall within the Limits of Purysburgh and therefore praying a New Warrant may issue to him for 1200 acres on vacant Land and that the Platt formerly returnd may be delivered to him. Ordered That a Warrant of Survey issue to the Petitioner for 1200 acres on vacant land and that the Plat formerly returned be cancelled.

The said Jonathan Brian further prays a warrant of Survey for his Family Right consisting of thirty three persons on vacant Land. Ordered that a Warrant of Survey issue to the Pet'r for 1650 acres of vacant Land on his making oath he is intitled to that Quantity of acres by the Number of Persons in his Family as usual.

Read the Petition of John Summers praying a Warrant of Survey may issue to him for his Family Right Consisting of Six Persons on vacant Land. Ordered That a Warrant of Survey issue to the said Pet'r for 300 acres of vacant Land as prayd for.

Read the Petition of John Summers praying a Warrant of Survey may issue to him for his Family Right Consisting of Nine Persons on vacant Land.

Ordered That a Warrant of Survey issue to the said Pet'r John Summers for 450 acres of vacant Land as prayd for.

Read the Petition of Dan'l Shaw setting forth that he purchased a Warr't for 482 acres of Land from Archibald Hamilton who died before Grant could pass to him the said Hamilton for the same and praying a Grant for the Said 482 acres in his own name. Ordered that a Grant do pass to the Pet'r as prayd for.

Read the petition of Dan'l Horry praying a Warrant of Survey may issue to him for his Family Right Consisting of 22 persons. Order'd That a Warrant of Survey do issue to the Petitioner for 1100 acres of Land vacant.

Meeting of Wednesday the 21st September 1737

Read the Petition of John McElveny setting forth that the Dep'y Surveyor had made a Mistake in the Survey of his Land and returnd his Platt 450 acres (now in the Surveyor Generals Office) Short of his Warrant and praying that the Surveyor General be directed to Order one of his Deputys to Compleat the said Survey pursuant to the said Warrant. Ordered That the Surveyor General do accordingly direct one of his Deputys to Compleat the said Survey agreeable to the said Warrant.

Read the Petition of John Leavy setting forth that he had in Family Seven persons and praying a Warrant of Survey may issue to him for 350 acres of Land. But is appearing to this Board that the Petitioner had not mentioned in his said Petition or proved by the Certificate thereunto annexed that no Land had been hitherto run out for the said Seven Persons. Resolved That the said Petition is therefore Defective. Resolved that the said Petition be Rejected.

Read the Petition of Wm. Mitchell, Master of the Hopewell Brigantine, praying a Warrant may issue to him for 1000 acres of Land in any of the Townships of Kingston, Queenborough, or Williamsburgh. And Rejected the Same.

Read the Petition of Martin Campbell of New Windsor setting forth that he has Six persons in Family and praying a Warrant of Survey for 300 acres of Land in the Township of New Windsor and also a Town Lot. Ordered That a Warrant of Survey do issue to the Pet'r for 300 acres and a Town Lott in New Windsor as prayd for.

Read the Petition of John Lindar Setting forth that he had settled a Tract of Land by agreement with William Roberts, That sometime afterwards it appeared the said Roberts had no Title to the said Land and the petitioner thereupon apprehending it to be vacant bought a warrant of survey in order to lay it thereon. That he had the said Land accordingly Surveyed and a Plat thereof returned but that the said Roberts opposes a Grant should pass to the Pet'r for the said Land and praying this board will Releive him in the Premisses So that a Grant may pass to him for the Land pursuant to the said Return. Ordered That the said Roberts do attend this Board To morrow morning to Shew Cause why a Grant may not pass to John Lindar according to the Prayer of the said Petition, That the said Roberts have Notice thereof this Evening and that he have a Copy of the said Petition if he desires it.

Read the Petition of Thomas Smith of New Windsor Setting forth that he had heretofore run out 250 acres of Land for which he has a Grant That the Chickesaw Indians have Since Settled thereon, and praying in lieu thereof he may obtain a Warrant of Survey for the like Quantity of Land and Lott in the Township of New Windsor. Ordered That a Warrant of Survey do issue for 250 acres of Land and a Town Lott in the Township of New Windsor according to the Prayer of his Petition upon the Petitioners Surrendering the Grant therein mentioned.

Meeting of Thursday the 22d September 1737

Will: Roberts attended this Board pursuant to the Order of yesterday and it appearing that the Land pray'd for by John Lindar in his Petition Read at this board Yesterday belongs to Coll. Rycroft both Partys were dismissed.

Read the Petition of Rebecca Ridgill praying a Warrant of Survey for 300 acres of Land in Kingston Township her Family consisting of Six persons. Ordered that a Warrant of Survey issue to the Pet'r for 300 acres of Land in Kingston Township as prayd for.

Read the Petition of Richard Smith praying a Warrant of Survey may issue to him for a Town Lott and 50 acres of Land in Kingston Townsh'p. Ordered That a Warrant of Survey issue to the Petitioner for a Town Lott and 50 acres of Land pursuant to the Prayer of the Petition.

Read the Petition of John Leavy setting forth that he has Seven Persons in Family for whom he had hitherto had no Land as appears by his Oath and praying a Warrant of Survey may issue to him for 350 acres of Land for his said Family Right. Ordered that a Warrant of Survey do issue to the Pet'r for the Number of acres prayd for in his said Petition.

Meeting of Friday the 23d September 1737

Read the Petition of Coll. Samuel Prioleau setting forth that by the last will and testament of Coll. Gabriel Bernard, late Ingineer, he is appointed Sole Heir and Executor of the Deceased. That the said Bernard is Indebted both here and in England, and that the said Deceased had built a House on a Lott in Purisburgh Township which cost him One hundred Pounds currency for which the said Deceased had no Grant and therefore the said Prioleau prays for a Title to the said Lott and as much Land as this Board shall think proper to Enable him to pay the Deceased's Debts. Ordered That the Pet'r as Executor to the said coll. Bernard Deceased have a Grant for the Lott mentioned in the Petition and One hundred acres of Land.

Read the Petition of Stephen Cabanis setting forth that he has five Persons in Family for which he has not yet had any Land and praying a Warrant of Survey may issue to him for 250 acres of Land. Ordered that a Warrant of Survey issue to the Pet'r as pray'd for.

Read the Petition of Thomas Smith setting forth that he has Eleven persons in Family for which he has had no Land and praying a Warrant of Survey may issue to him for 550 acres of Land in the Township of new Windsor. Ordered That a Warrant of Survey for 500 acres of Land do issue to the Petitioner in the Township of New windsor as pray'd for.

Read the Petition of Peter Johnson setting forth that Joseph Johnson decd had admeasured and laid out to him a Tract of Land of 500 acres in Craven county in his life time pursuant to a Warrant issued to him for that purpose but died before a Grant could pass to him for the same. That this Board had formerly Orderd a Grant to pass to William Brockington Grandfather by the mothers side to Sarah Johnson daughter of the said Johnson deceased an infant and in Trust for her the said Sarah That the said Child is since dead and that the Pet'r is heir at Law to the said Infant decd and therefore prays a Grant may issue to him as heir at Law for the said Land and it appearing to this Board that no Grant had been heretofore issue to Brockington for the use of the said Infant. Ordered that a Grant do pass to the said Peter Johnson as prayd for.

On Reading the Petition of Gabriel Escott one of the Executors named in the last will and testament of Paul Jenys Esq'r decd It is Ordered that the Original Will of the said Paul Jenys be brought in before the Ordinary and proved on Wednesday the 5th October next.

Read the Petition of Coll. John Palmer setting forth that he has twenty Persons in Family and praying a warrant of Survey may issue to him for 1000 acres of Land and it appearing by the attorney Generals Certificate the Petitioner had no land hitherto run out by virtue of the said Family Right. Ordered That a Warrant of Survey do issue to the Petitioner for the Quantity of Land prayd for.

Meeting of Wednesday the 5th October 1737

Read the Petition of Coll. William Waties setting forth that he has 13 persons in Family in this Province for which he has not hitherto had any Land and praying a warrant of Survey may issue to him For Nine hundred acres of Land in Right of his said Family. Ordered That a Warrant of Survey do issue to the said Coll. Waties for 900 acres of land as prayed for.

Read the Petition of Thomas Lynch setting forth That he has 21 Persons in Family for which number no Land has been hitherto run, and praying a Warrant of Survey may issue to him for 1050 acres of Land in this Province. Ordered that a Warrant of Survey issue to the Pet'r for 1050 acres of Land as pray'd for.

Read the Petition of Thomas Forrest setting forth that he has 6 persons in Family now in this Province and intends to Import more to intitle him to 1000 acres of Land in any of his Majesty's Townships and praying a warrant of Survey may issue to him for the same. Resolved that the said Petition be rejected.

Mr. Gabriel Escot appearing at this Board by his Proctor and praying That a Citation may issue to Eliz'a Jenys one of the Executri'x of the said Last Will and Testament of her late Husband Paul Jenys Esq'r to bring in and prove the will of her said Husband.

Read the Petition of Joseph Panton praying a Warrant of Survey may issue to him for 250 acres of Land in either Saxe Gotha or Williamsburgh and a Town Lott as also his Majestys Bounty.

Read also the Petition of John Wilson praying a Warrant of Survey for 100 acres of Land and a Town Lott in the Townsh'p of Williamsburgh as also his Majesty's Bounty.

Ordered that the Prayer of the Petitions above mentioned be granted excepting his Majesty's Bounty.

Read the Petition of Thomas Forrest praying a Warrant of Survey for 300 acres of Land in any of the Townships his Family Consisting of Six persons. Ordered that a Warrant of Survey do issue to the Petitioner for 300 acres of Land as prayd for.

Read the Petition of Brian Kennedy praying a Warrant of Survey for 200 acres of Land in any of his Majestys Townships. Ordered that a Warrant of Survey do issue to the Pet'r for 200 acres of Land as prayd for.

Read the Petition of Jeremiah Knoll praying a Warrant of Survey may issue to him for 50 acres of Land and a Town Lott i new Windsor. Ordered that a Warrant of Survey do issue to the Pet'r as prayd for.

Meeting of Friday the 7th October 1737

It appearing to this Board that one Staples a Deputy Surveyor had run out 350 acres of Land for John Cripps in the Township of Purisburgh and that the said Staples dying some time after the said Survey another surveyor by a subsequent survey run out 200 acres part of the said Three Hundred and fifty acres, It is therefore ordered that the Surveyor General do issue a special Precept directing the present Dep. Surveyor of the Township of purisburgh to run out the said 350 acres of Land for the said John Cripps and return the Platt thereof Immediately.

Read the Petition of Wm. Hoggatt praying a Warrant of Survey for 550 acres of Land in the Township of Pedee as his Family Right as also his Majestys Bounty. Ordered That a Warrant of Survey do issue to the Pet'r for the Land and Bounty prayd for.

Meeting of Wednesday the 7th December 1737

Read the Petition of Abraham Colson praying a Warrant of Survey may issue to him for his Family Right consisting of Sixteen Persons. Ordered That a Warrant of Survey issue to the Pet'r for 800 acres for his said Family Right.

Read the Petition of Robert Mckee praying 50 acres of Land in the Township of Williamsb'g. Ordered That the Prayer of the Petition be Granted.

Read the Petition of John Gibson praying for 100 acres in the Township of Saxe gotha. Ordered that the Prayer of the Petition be Granted.

Read the Petition of John Davis praying 100 acres of Land in Amelia Township. Ordered that the prayer of the Petition be Granted.

Read the Petition of Mary Broadway praying 100 acres of land in Amelia Township. Ordered that the prayer of the Petition be Granted.

Read the Petition of Mary Osgood widow praying a Warrant of Survey may issue to her for her Family Right Consisting of Twenty Persons. Ordered that a Warrant of Survey issue to the Pet'r for 1000 acres of Land as prayd for.

Read the Petition of Patrick Brown praying for 150 acres of Land in the Township of Saxegotha. Ordered that the Prayer of the Petition be Granted.

Read the Petition of Jerome LeBeuf praying for 100 acres of Land in Amelia township. Ordered that the Prayer of the Petition be Granted.

Read the Petition of John and Robert Akels brothers praying for 50 acres of Land each in the Township of Williamsburgh together with his Majestys

County. Ordered that a Warrant Issue to the Pet'r for the Land Prayed for but without being allowd the Kings Bounty.

Read the Petition of John McLleween praying a Warrant of Survey may issue to him for 200 acres of Land his Family Consisting of four Persons. Ordered that a Warrant of Survey issue to the Pet'r for 200 acres of Land as pray'd for.

Read the Petition of Arch'd Mackee praying 300 acres of Land for his Family Right Consisting of 6 persons. Order'd That a Warrant of Survey Issue to the Pet'r for 300 acres of Land as prayd for.

Read the Petition of Rob't Boyers praying for 350 acres of Land his Family Right consisting of Seven Persons. Ordered That a Warrant of Survey issue to the Pet'r for 350 acres of Land for his Family Right as pray'd for.

Meeting of Friday the 9th Decem'r 1737

Read the Petition of Coll. John Palmer Setting forth That in the year 1716 he obtaind a Grant from the Lords Proprietors for a Tract of Land of 300 acres being part of the Yamase Lands, That by accident the Grant was Lost out of the Secretary's Office, and therefore humbly prays That as he has pay'd Quit Rent and Taxes ever Since he had the Land, he may have a New Grant for the Same under the same Quit Rents for Lands formerly Granted by the Lords Proprietors as the Quit Rent Law directs. Ordered That a Special Warrant do issue to the Pet'r directed to the Survey'r General for the Resurvey of the said Land.

Read the Petition of Robert Sams praying he may have a Warrant of Resurvey for a Tact of 200 acres purchased by him of Richard Freeman, The Grant of which was tore and obliterated. Ordered that a Warrant of Resurvey do issue to the Pet'r for the said Land.

Read the Petition of Susanna Beldwin praying a warrant of Survey may issue to her for her Family Right consisting of five persons for 250 acres of Land either out of or in one of the Townships. Ordered That a Common Warrant Issue to the Pet'r for 250 acres of Land vacant.

Read the Petition of Robert Hyat praying a Warrant may issue to him for his Family Right for 2500 acres of Land his Family Consisting of thirty Persons. Orderd That a Warrant Issue to the Pet'r for 1500 acres of Land as prayd for.

Read the Petition of James Berry praying a Warrant of Survey for 1400 acres of Land his Family Consisting of twenty Eight persons. Ordered That a Warrant of Survey issue to the Pet'r as prayd for.

Read the Petition of Paul Trapier praying a warrant of Survey do issue to him for his Family Right Consisting of Eight Persons. Ordered that a Warrant of

Survey do issue to the Pet'r for 400 acres of Land being intitled thereto by his Family Right.

Read the Petition of Eliz'a Croxton praying a Warrant of Survey may issue to her for 350 acres of Land for her Family Right consisting of Seven persons. Ordered That a Warrant of Survey Issue to the Pet'r for 350 acres of Land for her Family Right as prayd for.

Read the Petition of John Alstone praying a Warrant of Survey may issue to him for 350 acres of Land his Family Right consisting of Seven Persons. Ordered That a Warrant of Survey do issue to the Pet'r for 350 acres of Land as prayd for.

Meeting of Tuesday the 13th Decem'r 1737

Read The Memorial of ____ Devald and Jacob Keuffer praying they may have the Liberty to Surrender their Right to two hundred acres of Swamp land and also for 50 acres of Land in Purisburgh Township and that in Lieu thereof a Warrant of Survey may issue to them for 250 acres in the s'd Township. Ordered that a Warrant of Survey do issue to the Pet'r for 250 acres of Land in the Township of Purisburgh as prayed for, they the Pet'rs Surrendring their Former Warrants for the like Quantity of Land.

Meeting of Wednesday the 14th Decem'r 1737

Read the Petition of Jeremiah Rowell, Evan Vaughan, Evan Davis, Sampson Thomas, Samuel Sorоncy, Thomas Bowen and Samuel Evans setting forth that about Seven Months ago they Transported themselves and their Familys from Pensilvania into this Province in order to settle upon the Tract allotted for the Welch and Pensilvanians and having not lands yet laid out are almost Starved for want of Provisions and therefore pray that an Order may pass to the Commissary Genl to Supply them with Such Provisions as may be thought proper by their Honors. Ordered That the Commissary Genl do provide Six Bushels of Corn and One Bushel of Salt for every head of the Familys pray'd for who have not already receiv'd any publick Bounty.

Meeting of Thursday the 15th Decem'r 1737

Read the Petition of James Atherton lately arriv'd in this Province with four Children and praying 250 acres as his Family Right and also his Maj'tys Bounty of Provisions. Ordered That a Warrant do issue to the Pet'r for 250 acres in the Township of Queenborough and that the Commissary General provide Six Bushels of Corn P head and two Bushels of Salt for this Family with two Hoes and two axes.

Read the Petition of Joseph and Samuel Smith brothers praying a warrant of survey may issue to them for 100 acres of Land together with his Majesty's

Bounty. Orderd That Warrants do issue to the Pet'rs for 50 acres of Land each in Pedee Township and that the Commissary Genl do provide Six Bushels of Corn, One Bushel of Salt, one axe and one hoe for each.

Read the Petition of Thomas Groome praying a Warrant of Survey may issue to him for 200 acres of Land his Family Consisting of four Persons. Ordered that a Warrant of Survey do issue to the Pet'r for 200 acres of Land as pray'd for.

Read the Petition of Wm Crofts praying a Warrant of Survey may issue to him for 350 acres of Land in virtue of his Family Right of Seven Persons. Order'd That a Warrant of Survey issue to the Pet'r for 350 acres of Land as pray'd for.

Meeting of Friday the 16th Decem'r 1737

Read the Petition of James McGirt praying a Warrant may issue to him for 250 acres of Land for his Family Right he having five Persons in Family. Orderd That a Warrant of Survey Issue to the Pet'r for 250 acres of Land as prayd for.

Upon Reading the Petition of Mr. Zouberbulher dated London July 12th 1737 setting forth the Reason that disabled him from performing his Engagement to bring over a certain Number of Swiss Familys to settle in the Township of New Windsor within the time therein mentioned, and praying that the time may be prolonged for two years. This Board having full Considered that same and Examined into the State of the Sinking Fund do find the Settlers already arrived and the Several Engagements entred into for Settling the several Townships in this Province will Amount to more than the Produce of that Fund. It is therefore the Unanimous Opinion of this Board That they cannot Engage to furnish the Familys Mr. Zouberbulher proposes to Import with any Bounty of Provisions, Tools &C Notwithstanding which all poor Protestants who arrive in this Province will be Intitled to fifty acres P head granted to them and their Heirs forever in the Several Townships in this Province free of Quit Rents for Ten years and all proper Countenance and Incouragement from this Board.

Read the Petition of Thomas McCree Setting forth That his Father who arrived here in June last after viewing the Lands at Williamsburgh came to Town in order to procure a Warrant of Survey and his Majesty's Bounty but during the said application he dyed, and therefore the Pet'r prays a Warrant may issue to the said Family and that the Bounty may be allowed. Ordered that a Warrant do Issue to the Pet'r for so many as their Family shall appear to Consist of but, as the Sinking Fund falls very Short, the Bounty cannot be Granted.

Meeting of Saturday the 17th Decem'r 1737

Read the Petition of John Brown praying a Warrant of Survey may issue to him for his Family Right consisting of Six persons either in or out the Townships. Order'd that a Warrant of Survey issue to the Petitioner for 300 acres of Land in any of the northern Townships or on vacant Land without the Bounty.

Read the Petition of Jacob Newberry praying a Warrant of Survey may issue to him for 150 acres of Land he having three persons in Family in or out of One of the Townships.Order'd that a Warrant of Survey issue to the Petitioner for 150 acres of Land in any of the northern Townships or on vacant Land without the Bounty.

Read the Petition of Henry Oldacre praying a Warrant of Survey may issue to him for 50 acres of Land in or out of the Townships. Orderd That a warrant of Survey issue to the Pet'r as pray'd for, but not to have the King's Bounty.

Read the Petition of John Newberry praying a Warrant of Survey may issue to him for his Family Right Consisting of Seven persons in or out of the Townships. Orderd That a Warrant of Survey do issue to the Pet'r for 350 acres of Land within any of the Northern Townships or on vacant Land without allowance of the Kings Bounty.

Read the Petition of Hasker Newberry Setting forth that he has Six persons in Family and praying a Warrant of Survey may issue to him for 300 acres of Land in or out of the Townships. Orderd That a Warrant of Survey issue to the Pet'r for 300 acres of Land as pray'd for in any of the Townships or on vacant Land without the Bounty.

Meeting of Wednesday the 11th January 1737/8

Read the Petition of Alex'r Steward praying that on his Surrendring a Grant pass'd to him for 500 acres of Land in the Township of Queensborough, he may Obtain another for the said Quantity Free of Quit Rent for Ten years. Order'd the Said Petition to lye on the Table.

Read the Petition of Tho's Bennet praying his Family Right consisting of Seventeen persons in Amelia Township. Order'd That a Common Warrant Issue to the Pet'r for 850 acres.

Read the Petition of John Tabian praying his Family Right consisting of Twenty persons Granted on Vacant Land.

Read the Petition of Arthur Bull praying his Family Right consisting of nine persons Granted on Vacant Land.

Read the Petition of Capt. Tho's Gates praying his Family Right consisting of Eight persons Granted on Vacant Land.

Read the Petition of Frederick Grimke merchant praying his Family Right consisting of 18 persons Granted on Vacant Land.

Read the Petition of Tho's Witten praying his Family Right consisting of Eight persons Granted on Vacant Land.

Read the Petition of Edward Broughton praying his Family Right consisting of 4 persons Granted on Vacant Land.

Read the Petition of Rob't McMurdy praying his Family Right of Ten persons & a Town Lott in the Township of New Windsor.

Granted as prayd for.

Read the Petition of Stephen Crell a Settler in Saxe Gotha Township praying his Majestys Bounty of Provisions &ca. Order'd the said Petition be Refferd to the Commissary General.

Read the Petition of Rob't Vaughan praying his Family Right of nine persons in New Windsor. Granted.

Read the Petition of John Gray praying his Family Right of 4 persons and a Town Lot in New Windsor. Granted.

Read the Petition of Several Swiss lately arrived in this Province praying His Majestys Bounty of Provisions &ca. Ordered That Said Petition be Refferd to the Commissary General.

The Commissary General Attended this Board and made his Report on the Petition of Stephen Crell to him Referr'd in the forenoon that the said Creel had his Proportion of Provisions and Tools. Order'd That the said Crell's Petition is therefore Dismiss'd.

The said Commissary General also made his Report on the Petition Reffer'd this Morning to him of Several Swissers lately arrived in this Province. Order'd That the said Petition be Sent to the Commons House when they next meet.

Meeting of Thursday the 12th January 1737/8

Read the Petition of John Woods praying his Family Right Consisting of five persons and also His Majesty's Bounty of Provisions. Order'd a Warrant to Issue for the Land pray'd for but no Provisions.

Read the Petition of Allen Wells for his Own Right. Granted fifty acres Vacant Land.

Read the Petition of Joseph Harley praying his Family Right Consisting of fifteen persons. Granted vacant Land.

Read the Petition of Tho's Way praying his Family Right consisting of 13 persons. Granted 650 acres Vacant Land.

Read the Petition of Rob't Quarterman praying his Family Right Consisting of 12 persons. granted 600 acres vacant Land.

Read the Petition of Maj'r James Richard of Purrisburgh praying his Family Right of Eight persons. Granted vacant Land.

Read the Petition of Tho's Baker praying his Family Right of 16 persons. Granted on vacant land.

Read the Petition of James Michie Esq'r praying his Family Right of 33 persons. Granted 1650 acres Vacant Land.

On application of Frederick Grimke merchant praying the Warrant he yesterday obtain'd for 190 acres of Land his Family Right may be alter'd thus viz't instead of a Tract, a tract or tracts and that the same alteration be made in the Surveyor Generals Precept to His Deputy and that the Secry of this Province do make that alteration in the Original Warrant Lodged in his Office and that the said Secry and Surveyor General be Servd with an Attested copy of this minute.

Whereas the Honourable William Bull Esq'r President &ca. had a Warrant Issue to him for a Tract of Land Amounting to 352 acres in Virtue of which Warrant a Grant was prepared to be Sign'd by the late Lieut't Governour by whose Death the Administration came to the said William Bull as Eldest Councillor and it not being proper he should sign a Grant to himself. Resolved and Order'd That the Said Grant by Sign'd by the Hon'ble Alex'r Skene, Esq'r.

Meeting of Thursday the 19th January 1737/8

Read the Petition of Mr. John Atchison praying a Warrant for One thousand three hundred Acres of Land having Twenty Six persons in Family Sworn to before the Attorney General. And Granted.

Read the Petition of Margarett Hessen praying She may have her Right of fifty Acres of Land in the Township of Orangeburgh. Granted.

Meeting of Friday the 20th January 1737/8

Read the Petition of William little praying a Warrant for Six hundred acres of Land he having twelve persons in Family Sworn to before the Attorney General. Granted.

Read the Petition of Rob't Pringle merchant, who having Six persons in his Family and never had no Land therefore prays he may have a Warrant for three hundred acres of Land Within any one of the three Northern Townships. Granted.

Read the Petition of the following Welch persons viz't

Abel James	6 persons in Family
Thomas James	13 persons in family
Daniel Davenal	4 Do
Griffith James	6 Do
James David	4 Do
Sam'l Greenwood	7 Do
Griffith John	2 Do
Johanah Rolp	13 Do
James Rowland	3 Do
William Eynon	10 Do
Dan'l James	2 Do
Evan Harry	2 Do
David James	8 Do

praying they may have Warrants for their Several Family Rights layd out either in the Welch Lands or in the Township of Queensborough as will best Sute their Conveniency. Orderd. That Warrants do Issue according to the Prayer of their Petition.

Meeting of Saturday the 21st January 1737/8

On Application of Mr. Edward Broughton Ordered That on Surrendring his Warrant for two hundred acres of Land a Warrant for the same Quantity of Land may Issue to him in One of the Townships he paying his Fees.

Read the Petition of John Bonneau praying a Warrant for four hundred acres of Land having Eight in Family Sworn to before the Attorney General. Granted.

Read the Petition of Miles Godment who having himself, wife, two children & Two Servants in Family prays he may have a Warrant for three hundred acres of Land in the Township of New Windsor. Granted.

Read the Petition of James Smith praying a Warrant for a Lott and four hundred acres of Land in Williamsburgh having Eight persons in Family Vizt his Wife & Children. Granted.

Meeting of Thursday the 26th January 1737/8

Read the Petition of Danl Welshysen Esq'r praying a Warrant for four hundred and fifty Acres of Land having nine Persons in Family Sworn to before the Attorney General. Granted.

Read the Petition of Mr. Tho's Cooper Setting forth that he had obtaind a Warr't for Gov'r Johnson in the year 1731; But the said Warrant for 650 acres was run out on Lands of Mr. Trewin, and therefore praying (as he has never Since layd out any Lands by Virtue of the said Warrant and has an Increase of twenty three slaves and One Indented Servant) for a Warrant of nineteen hundred and fifty acres, having Sworn to his Family before the Attorney General.

Read the Petition of John Hautt praying a Warrant for 150 acres having three persons in Family Sworn to. Granted.

Read the Petition of Mich'l Christopher Row, praying a Warrant for One hundred Acres of Land in Orangeburgh Township he having Sworn to his Right. Granted.

Read the Petition of Eliz'a Perriman praying a Warrant for four hundred acres of Land having Sworn to her Right. Granted.

Read the Petition of Eliz'a Stanley widow praying a Warrant for Eight hundred Acres of Land having Sworn to her Right. Granted.

Read the Petition of John Robinson praying a Warrant for three hundred acres of Land Either in the Township of Queensborough or the Welch Lands having Sworn to his Right. Granted in the Township of Queensborough.

Read the Petition of Richard Mason praying a warrant for Seven hundred acres of Land having Sworn to his Right. Granted.

Read the Petition of Denis McKelvin praying a Warrant for four hundred acres of Land in Amelia Township having Sworn to his Right and likewise for His Majestys Bounty of Provisions. Granted the Land in Amelia Township as pray'd for but no Provisions.

The Hon'ble Mr. Kinloch having produced to this Board a Platt of five hundred acres of Land layd out in Craven County Certifyed by Fracis [sic] Younge, Esq'r then Surveyor General together with a Certificate of Secry Harts Acknowledging there was a purchased Received for the said Land. It is

Order'd that a special Warrant do issue to the Hon'ble James Kinloch Esq'r for the Resurvey of the said Land that a Grant may pass to him for the Same.

Read the Petition of Tho's Mackee praying a Warrant for five hundred and fifty acres of Land having in Family himself Wife and Nine Children Sworn to before the Attorney General. Granted.

Read the Petition of Philip James praying a Warrant for two hundred and fifty acres of Land in Queensborough or the Welch Tract having Sworn to his Family Right.

Read the Petition of William Terrell praying a Warrant for two hundred acres of Land in Queensborough or the Welch Tract having Sworn to his Right. Granted.

His Majestys Council Agreed. To Enquire whats become of the Platt Returned of the Land Run for the Use of the Garrison of Rangers at Saltketche That the Line from the N. W. Corner of New Windsor Township to run N. W. 13½ Degrees to Horse Creek the Lands lying between that Line and Savanna River e Reserved for the Use of the Garrison at Fort. That the Tract of Land lately Run out by Order of the Government Containing 21574 acres be properly Granted for Such Uses as the Government Shall think proper (but however Intended at present for the Use of the Chickasaw Indians now living there).

Meeting of Wednesday the 1st February 1737/8

Mr Isaac Maziick Enter'd a Caveat against Mr. Joseph Spencer having a Grant for a Certain Tract of Land Containing 66 Acres in Craven county. Mr. Graham of Council for Mr. Spencer Moved that an Order of Council might be Sent to John Spencer Evidence for the said Joseph Spencer to appear in Council Immediately that he shall be protected from all writs Executions &ca during his Attendance on this Court and Until his Return home. And Accordingly Such an Order was Sent to him.

Mr. Whitaker Moved that Mr. Sere and Mr. Horry might be Sworn as Evidences for Mr. Maziick. And Mr. Graham moved that Mr. John Spencer should be Sworn as Evidence for Mr. Joseph Spencer.

After Council was hear on both sides it appear'd to His Hon'r the President and His Majesty's Hon'ble Council that the 66 acres was run out by Mr. Spencer before his Sale of the 500 acres and lay without the lines of the said Platt, and at the time of Spencers Running out the said 66 acres it was the Front of his own Land. Therefore it was Orderd that a Grant do pass to the said Joseph Spencer for the said Tract of 66 acres of Land.

HEMPSTEAD COUNTY LIBRARY
HOPE, ARKANSAS

Meeting of Thursday the 2d February 1737/8

Read the Petition of John Linder praying a Warrant for one hundred and fifty acres of Land in Purrisburgh having 3 persons in family Sworn to. Granted.

Read the Petition of Daniel Couturier praying a Warrant of Survey for two hundred acres of Land having four persons in Family for which he has had no Land Sworn to before Mr. St. Julien.

Read the Petition of Damaris Elizabeth Ravenel widow praying a Warr't for four thousand Acres of Land and having Eighty persons in Family for which there never has been any Land Granted Sworn to before Mr. St. Julien. Granted.

Read the Petition of Capt. Stephen Beauchamp praying a Warrant for four hundred acres of Land and a Lott in Williamsburgh having no Lands in this Province. Granted.

Read the Petition of Methringham praying a Warrant for three hundred and fifty acres of Land & Lott in Williamsburgh Township he having no Lands in the Province. Granted.

Read the Petition of James Bullock praying a Warrant for Eight hundred acres of Land having Sixteen persons in Family Sworn to. Granted.

Read the Petition of Hugh Bryan praying a Warrant for thirteen hundred acres of Land having twenty seven persons in Family Sworn to. Granted.

Read the Petition of Anthony Saxby praying a Warrant for four hundred and fifty acres of Land in New Windsor having no Lands in this Province and nine persons in Family Sworn to. Granted.

Read the Petition of James Hall praying fifty acres & Lott in Kingston having no Lands in the Province. Granted.

Read the Petition of John Dexter praying four hundred & fifty acres and Lott in Williamsburgh having no Lands in this Province. Granted.

Read the Petition of Nath'l Drew praying a Warrant for five hundred Acres of Land Sworn having Sworn to his Family Right. Granted.

Read the Petition of John Jones praying a Warrant for three hundred and fifty Acres of Land. Granted.

Read the Petition of Sarah Bosher praying a Warrant for three hundred and fifty Acres of Land having Sworn to her Right. Granted.

Read the Petition of John Cox praying a Warrant for One thousand Acres of Land in one of the Townships to be Run in a Tract or Tracts having Sworn to his Right. Granted a Warrant in a Township to be Run in one Tract.

Read the Petition of William Lang praying a Warrant for three hundred acres of Land in a Township having Sworn to his Right. Granted.

Read the Petition of Edmond Cousins praying a Warrant for four hundred and fifty acres of Land and a Lot in New Windsor having Sworn to his Family Right and that he has no Lands. Granted.

Read the Petition of Several Poor Protestants lately arrived to settle and Cultivate Lands in this Province according to His Majestys instructions and therefore praying Lotts and Lands according to their Several Familys in the Township of Kingston and his Majesty's Bounty of Provisions. Granted the Lands but no Bounty.

Meeting of Friday the 3d February 1737/8

As it has been thought proper by a former Resolution that none but His Majesty's Council should have Lands in Townships Except Such as are Intitled to it that upon Such a Warrant His Hon'r the late Lieut't Governour had a Tract of Land run out which happens to be within and without the Township Line of Purrisburgh and as the said Lieu't Gov'r did not think proper to Grant Land to himself he made over his Right to his son Andrew Broughton Esq'r But his Death prevented the said Grant being Signed. It is therefore the Opinion of His Majestys Council that the President do Sign the said Grant.

Meeting of Saturday the 4th February 1737/8

Read the Petition of Ann McCullough widow setting forth that he husband had obtain'd a Warrant of Eight hundred acres of Land to be layd out in Williamsburgh but the said Land has since been Granted to another and as she has added two Negroes to her Family She therefore prays a Warrant for Nine hundred acres in the Township of Kingston and a Lott in her own name. Granted the Prayer of the Petition on her surrendring the former Warrant of Eight hundred acres.

Read the Petition of Jean McQueen praying a Warrant for one thousand Acres of Land having Sworn to her Family Right. Granted.

Read the Petition of Elias Horry praying a Warrant for nine hundred Acres of Land having Sworn to his Family Right. Granted.

Read the Petition of Tho's Crow praying a Warrant for five hundred acres of Land having Sworn to his Family Right. Granted.

Read the Petition if Nicholas Roche praying a Warrant for Six hundred and fifty acres & lott in the Township of New Windsor he having no Lands in this Province and having Sworn to his Family Right. Granted.

Read the Petition of Tho's Forrest praying a Warrant for two hundred Acres of Land in a Township having Sworn to his Family Right. Granted a Common Warrant.

Meeting of Thursday the 23d February 1737/8

The Hon'ble Joseph Wragg Esq'r Attorney for Samuel Wragg Esq'r of London, Laid before this Board two Platts and Grants for Five hundred acres of Land Each granted to the said Samuel Wragg and Jacob Satur by the late Lords Proprietors the 15th day of May 1714, both situate lying and being on the west side of Pedee River and hath such marck'd Trees and bounds as appears by the Respective platts annexed to the Grants, which Lands the said Joseph Wragg hath not bee able to find, altho' dilligent search hath been made by persons Employ'd by him for that purpose and the said Wragg being advised that the Act for Limitation may be a Barr if longer Delayed to be found. He therefore desires a Special Order of this board Directed to John ouldfield and George Pawley Esq'rs or either of them to make dilligent search and enquiry for the said two tracts of Land and to authorize and Empower them or either of them to Enter upon and Survey any Lands that was Vacant at the passing of the said Grants and which in their or either of their opinion bears a likeness or similitude thereto; in order to Discover the marked trees and Real Bounds of the said Two Tracts of Land and make a Return thereof to this Board or the said Wragg. Resolved That an Order do Issue accordingly Directed to the said Ouldfield and Pawley or either of them.

Meeting of Friday the 24th February 1737/8

Read the Petition of John Harris praying a Warrant for five hundred acres of Land having Sworn to his Right. granted.

Read the Petition of William Swinton and James Exors of the last Will and Testament of James Futhey setting forth the said Futhey had obtained a Warrant for his Excy Govern'r Johnson by which he had run out two Tracts of 250 acres of Land Each in Craven County and as the said Futhey did by his will bequeath the said lands to his only son Robert Futhey and there being as yet not Grants for the same they therefore pray that Grants may pass to the said Rob't Futhey for the Said Lands. Order'd that a proper Grant do pass to the said Robert Futhey for the said Lands.

Read the Petition of Henry Sheriff praying a Warrant for two hundred acres of Land having Sworn to his right. Granted.

Read the Petition of Bartholomew Ball praying a Warrant for three hundred and fifty acres of Land having Sworn to his right. Granted.

Read the Petition of John Baxter praying a Thousand acres of Land having Sworn to his right. Granted a common Warrant for a thousand acres.

Read the Petition of John Stephens praying a Warrant for Six hundred and fifty acres of Land having in Family a Child a Servant Maid and Six Slaves and also 5 hired Slaves and praying that he may have a Warrant to take up the said Lands where he can find them. Granted a Warrant for the Child and the Six Slaves only.

Read the Petition of Alex'r Tate praying a Warrant for two hundred Acres of Land in Amelia Township having no Lands in the Province and having Sworn to his Right. Granted.

Meeting of Saturday the 25th February 1737/8

Read the Petition of Lt. Colo. William Sanders praying a Warrant for Eight hundred Acres of Land having Sworn to his Right. Granted.

The Hon'ble Tho's Waring Esq'r informed this board that he had Ten Slaves in Family for which he never has had any Land and therefore praying a Warrant for five hundred acres of Land. Order'd that a Warrant do Issue to the Hon'ble Tho's Waring Esq'r for five hundred acres accordingly.

Meeting of Saturday the 28th February 1737/8

Read the Petition of William Whippy praying a Warrant for Seven hundred and fifty acres of Land having Sworn to his Right before the Attorney General. Granted.

Read the Petition of John Whippy praying a Warrant for four hundred and fifty acres of Land having Sworn to his Right before the Attorney General. Granted.

Read the Petition of Joseph Whippy praying a Warrant for four hundred acres of Land having Sworn to his Right before the Attorney General. Granted.

Read the Petition of James Kerr praying a Warrant for five hundred acres of Land having Sworn to his Right before the Attorney General. Granted.

Read the Petition of Sam'l Edgar praying a Warrant for two hundred acres of Land having Sworn to his Right before the Attorney General. Granted.

Read the Petition of Thomas Early praying a Warrant for Six hundred acres of Land having Sworn to his Right before the Attorney General. Granted.

Read the Petition of Edward North praying a Warrant for nine hundred acres of Land having Sworn to his Right before the Attorney General. Granted.

Read the Petition of William Buchannan praying a Warrant for two hundred and fifty acres of Land having Sworn to his Right before the Attorney General. Granted.

Read the Petition of James Finlay praying a Warrant for a Lott and two hundred and fifty acres of Land in Williamsburgh Township having Sworn to his Right before the Attorney General. Granted.

Meeting of Wednesday the 1st March 1737/8

Read the Petition of Florence Mahoney praying a Warrant for five hundred fifty acres of Land having Sworn to his Family Right. Granted.

Meeting of Friday the 3d March 1737/8

Read the Petition of Jacob Brown praying a Warrant for four hundred and fifty acres of Land having Sworn to his Right. Granted.

Read the Petition of Peter Tage praying a Warrant and a Lott in Purrisburgh having no Lands in this Province and having Sworn to his Right. Granted.

Read the Petition of William Nichols praying a Warrant for three hundred acres of Land having Sworn to his Right. Granted.

Read the Petition of John Ashee lately Arrived from Pennsilvania praying a Warrant for one hundred and fifty acres of Land and a Lott in the Welch Tract or Queensborough Township having Sworn to his Right. Order'd that a Warrant do Issue for the Petitioner in the Township of Queensborough.

Read the Petition of Tho's Polk praying a Warrant for two hundred and fifty acres and a Lott in Queensborough of the Welch Tract. Order'd that a Warrant do Issue for the Township of Queensborough.

Meeting of Tuesday the 7th March 1737/8

Read the Petition of James Maxwell Esq'r praying a Warrant for Sixteen hundred Acres of Land having Sworn to his Right. Granted.

Read the Petition of Tho's McClelland praying a Warrant for three hundred Acres of Land having Sworn to his Right. Granted.

Meeting of Wednesday the 8th March 1737/8

Read the Petition of William Dalton praying a Warrant for twelve hundred and fifty Acres of Land having Sworn to his Right. Granted.

Read the Petition of John Sich[?] Sietz[?] praying a Warrant for two hundred Acres of Land in Orangeburg having Sworn to his Right. Granted.

Read the Petition of William James praying a Warrant for One hundred and fifty Acres of Land having Sworn to his Right. Granted.

Read the Petition of David Wilson praying a Warrant for One hundred Acres of Land having Sworn to his Right. Granted.

Meeting of Thursday the 9th March 1737/8

Read the Petition of Thomas Bartlet praying a Warrant for Eight hundred and fifty acres of Land having Sworn to his Right. Granted.

Read the Petition of Obediah Allen praying a Warrant for two hundred ares of Land having Sworn to his Right. Granted.

Read the Petition of Mr. Arthur Baxter praying a Warrant for three hundred acres of Land and a Lott in one of the Townships of Queensborough, Kingston or Williamsburgh having no Lands in this Province and having Sworn to his right. Granted.

Read the Petition of Peter Warnor who having married a Widdow that had a Child prays he may have a Warrant in Right of them to be layd out in the Township of Purrisburgh. Ordered have a Warrant for 50 acres in Right of his wife in Orangeburgh.

Meeting of Saturday the 11th March 1737/8

Read the Petition of William Tihude praying a Warrant for three hundred acres of Land in Orangeburgh having Sworn to his Right. Granted.

Read the Petition of William James praying a Warrant for four hundred acres and a Lott in One of the Northern Townships having Sworn to his Right. Granted.

Read the Petition of Charles Hope praying a Warrant for four hundred acres & Lott in One of the Northern Townships having Sworn to his Right. Granted.

Read the Petition of George Austin setting forth that he took out a Mediterranean Pass in March 1736 but by the neglect of the Gentleman the vessell was Consign'd to has not yet Received a Certificate & praying to have a longer time allowed. Ordered that there shall be Six months time allowed.

Meeting of Thursday the 23d March 1737/8

Read the Petition of Rev'd Joseph Bugnion praying a Warrant for thirteen hundred acres of Land and a Lott in Queensborough having Sworn to his Family Right. Ordered that a Common Warrant do Issue to the Petit'r for thirteen hundred acres of Land.

Read the Petition of Elihu Baker Sen'r praying a Warrant for twelve hundred and fifty acres of Land having Sworn to his Right. Granted.

Read the Petition of Joseph Brunson Sen'r praying a Warrant for Eight hundred acres of Land having Sworn to his Right. Granted.

Read the Petition of Thomas Read praying a Warrant for 300 acres of Land having Sworn to his Right. Granted.

Read the Petition of Tho's Hogg praying a Warrant for a Lott and two hundred acres of Land in one of the Townships except Purisburgh having Sworn to his right.

Meeting of Friday the 24th March 1737/8

Read the Petition of Mrs. Ann Gibbes widow setting forth that her late husband Mr. John Gibbes had Survey'd and lay'd out three Tracts of Land two of them Containing five hundred acres of Land Each and the other thirty five Acres But he Dyed before Grants passd to him for the said Lands and Praying that the Attorney General may be orderd to prepare Special Fiats for the said Lands the Platts lying in the Surveyor Generals Office that Grants may pass to her for the same. Orderd That Mr. Attorney General do prepare Special Fiats for the said Lands according to the Prayer of the Petitioner that Grants may pass to her for the Same.

Read the petition of Peter Taylor Esq'r praying a Warrant may Issue to him in the name and for the use of Elizabeth Gibbes a minor for twelve hundred acres of Land She having twenty four persons in Family. Orderd that a Warrant do Issue according to the Prayer of the Petition.

Meeting of Tuesday the 28th March 1738

Read the Petition of William Hamilton praying a Warrant for two hundred acres of Land having Sworn to his Right. Granted.

Read the Petition of Francis Piercy praying a Warrant for a Lott and two hund. acres of Land in New Windsor having no Land in this Province and having Sworn to his Right. Granted.

Read the Petition of Peter Marion praying a Warrant for two hundred and fifty acres of Land having Sworn to his Right. Granted.

Read the Petition of Peter Porcher praying a Warrant for five hundred acres of Land having Sworn to his Right. Granted.

Read the Petition of Richard Baylis praying a Warrant for two hundred and fifty acres of Land having Sworn to his Right. Granted.

Meeting of Thursday the 1st June 1738

"At a Council held in the house of Mr. Francis Sureau at Ashley Ferry...."

Read the Petition of Henry Dawbuz praying a Warrant for three hundred and fifty acres of Land having Sworn to his Right. Granted.

Read the Petition of Dan'l and Tho's Laroche praying a Warrant for four thousand One hundred and fifty acres of Land having Sixty Eight slaves and thirteen White persons in family having Sworn to their right before the Attorney General. Granted.

Meeting of Thursday the 8th June 1738

Read the Petition of John and Edm'd Atkin praying a Warrant for One thousand acres of Land having twenty persons in Family two of them without the Bounds of the Province at Present. Order'd a Warrant for 850 acres of Land.

Read the Petition of Job Rothmahler praying a Warrant for Six hundred Acres of Land having Sworn to his Right. Granted.

Read the Petition of John Linter praying a Warrant for four hundred acres and Lot of Land in Queensborough having Sworn to his right. Granted.

Read the Petition of James Gordon praying a Warrant for fifteen hundred and fifty acres of Land within Queensborough having Sworn to his right. Granted.

Read the Petition of Mr. Alex'r Nesbit praying a Warrant for Seven hundred and fifty Acres of Land having Sworn to his Right. Granted.

Read the Petition of the Rev'd Tho's Morrit praying a Warrant for Seven hundred and fifty Acres of Land having Sworn to his Right. Granted.

Read the Petition of Joseph Chamberlain praying a Warrant for four hundred Acres of Land having Sworn to his Right. Granted.

Read the Petition of John Roberts praying a Warrant for one thousand and fifty Acres of Land having Sworn to his Right. Granted.

Read the Petition of Joseph Hasfort praying a Warrant for Seven hundred Acres of Land having Sworn to his Right. Granted.

Read the Petition of Hannah Brazitt praying a Warrant for Eleven hundred Acres of Land having Sworn to his Right. Granted.

Read the Petition of John Baxter praying a Warrant for two hundred Acres of Land and the Remission of his Fees. Order'd that a Warr't do Issue having his Fees.

Upon Reading the Petition of Edm'd Bellinger Esq'r Setting forth his Claim to Several Tracts of Land therein mention'd. It was Order'd the Surveyor General do Certify the Platts Returned into his Office on the Several Family Warrant Mention'd in the Petitio of the said Bellinger Except such as ly within the Lines or Bounds of two Barroneys or Tracts of Land containing Twelve thousand Acres each Run out of Survey'd on the Yamasee Land by John Fripp, Deputy Surveyor, by Virtue of a Certain Grant Patent or Power from the late Lords Proprietors to John Danson Esq'r.

Meeting of Wednesday the 19th June 1738

Read the Petition of John Craig praying his Family Right of twenty persons. Granted.

Read the Petition of Dan'l Moloy praying his Family Right of 3 persons. Granted.

Read the Petition of Rice Price praying his Family Right of Six persons. Granted.

Read the Petition of Thomas Powell praying his Family Right of Ten persons. Granted.

Read the Petition of the Welch and Pensilvanians Settled in Queensborough Township and Welch Tract praying the Time Pmitted by an Order of Council on the 13th August 1736 for those people Settling the Welch Tract may be prolonged. Orderd that the Term prescribed by the Order of Council of the 13th August 1736 which Expires on the 13th August ensuing be prolonged to the 13th of August 1739.

Read the Petition of Rob't McKehan praying his Family Right of Six persons. Granted.

Read the Petition of James Frazer praying his Family Right of 8 persons. Granted.

Read the Petition of John McPherson praying his Family Right of Seven persons. Order'd to lye on the Table til the Pet'r appears before the council. Read the Petition of Tho's Harry, Joshua Wills, John Jones and James Rogers praying their Family Rights Consisting in all of thirteen persons. Granted.

Read the Petition of John Green praying Land for his two Slaves. Granted.

Read the Petition of Alex'r Moore praying his Family Right of Twenty One persons. Granted.

On Motion of Mr. Whitaker in behalf of Alex'r Hume Esq'r Devisee of Rob't Hume Esq'r Deceased for leave an appeal against an Order made the 8th June last in favour of Edm'd Bellinger Esq'r and that he has time to enter his Reasons at large against the said order and that he have copys of the Proceedings allowed paying Fees for the Same. Ordered that the Same be Granted Accordingly.

Meeting of the 8th August 1738

Read the Petition of Nicholas Jones praying His Family Right consisting of four persons for 200 acres and a Town Lott in the Township of Orangeburgh together with His Majestys Bounty. Ordered That the Prayer of the Petition be Granted and that the Commissary General Pay him the bounty.

Meeting of the 8th August 1738

Read the Petition of Nicholas Jones praying His Family Right consisting of four persons for 200 acres and a Town Lott in the Township of Orangeburgh together with His Majesty's Bounty. Ordered That the Prayer of the Petition be Granted and that the Commissary General Pays him the Bounty.

Meeting of Wednesday the 30th August 1738

Ordered that Hugh Bryan do attend the Council on the 14th of September next at Ashley Ferry to shew cause for his Entring a Caveat in behalf of General Oglethorpe against Mr. James Bullock for 866 acres of Land in Granville County on Savanna River.

Read the Petition of Lewis Timothy praying his additional family wright of Six slaves and Two white Children on vacant Land out of the Townships.

Ordered that a Warrant Issue to the Petitioner for 400 acres of Vacant Land he swearing to his said family Right.

Read the Petition of Nathaniel Ford praying his Family right Consisting of Six persons on Vacant Land. Granted.

Read the Petition of John McPherson praying his family Right of Seven persons in the Township of New Windsor. Ordered that a Warrant Issue to the Petitioner for three hundred and fifty acres and a Town Lott in New Windsor.

Meeting of Tuesday the 12th September 1738

On Motion of the Hon'ble Mr. Wragg for 2500 acres of Land being thereto intituled by His family Right. Ordered that a Warrant Issue to the said Mr. Wragg for 2500 acres of Land Vacant and that Mr. Secretary or his Deputy prepare the Same.

Meeting of Tuesday the 16th September 1738

Read the Petition of Major Christian Mote praying a Warrant for 500 acres of Land in Consideration of his Services as Major and a Magistrate in the Township of Orangeburgh, SaxeGotha, and Amelia. Ordered that a Warrant do Issue according to the prayer thereof.

Read the Petition of Mary Larrimore Setting forth that She has ten persons in family for which she has hitherto had no Land and therefore praying a Warrant of survey may Issue to her for 500 acres of Vacant Land. Ordered That a Warrant do Issue to the Petitioner according to the prayer of her Petition.

Read the Petition of William Anderson Setting forth that he has Eight persons in his family for which hitherto he has had no Land & therefore praying a Warrant of Survey may Issue to him for 400 acres of Vacant Land.

Read the Petition of Kenneth Mackenzie setting forth that he hath nine Slaves and three White Servants in his family for which he had hitherto had no Land and therefore praying a Warrant of Survey may Issue to him for 600 acres of vacant Land. Ordered that a Warrant of Survey do Issue to the Petitioner pursuant to the prayer of his Petition.

Meeting of Thursday the 16th November 1738

Read a Certificate Signed by Major Christian Mote in favor of Herman Geager of SaxeGotha who had two Sons born at one time and therefore prayes for a warrant of one hundred Acres of Land without any Charges. Granted.

Ordered That whereas a Grant of Seven hundred Acres of Land in Craven County passed the 19th of Feby 1738 to Martha wife of John Goodwin by the name of Martha Bell her former husbands name through a Mistake. That the Minutes of Council relating thereto & the Grant shall be altered accordingly.

The Hon'ble Joseph Wragg Esq'r a member of this Board desireing a Special Warrant to Survey the Marsh on Land fronting or lying before the Land Granted to said Wragg & Paul Jenys Esq'r on the head of Chehaw River so Farr as the Said River or the Run that leads to the same, and the said request appearing just and reasonable, It is orderd that a Special Warrant do Issue to the said Wragg according to his Desire.

Meeting of Thursday the 17th November 1738

The Hon'ble Joseph Wragg Esq'r in behalf of his brother Samuel Wragg Esq'r of London, applyed to this Board by his Memorial of the 23d day of February last to grant him on Order of Council for John Ouldfield & George Pawley Esq'rs or either of them to make diligent search and Inquiry for two Tracts of five hundred acres of Land each granted by the late Lords Proprietors to the said Samuel Wragg and Jacob Satur in the year 1714 as appears P said Grants and the said memorial of the said Joseph Wragg and of the 7th Day of March following, an order of Council passed to Empower the said John Ouldfield and George Pawley or either of them to put the said order in Execution but as no Return hath yet been made by either of them, and the said Wragg being desirous that Cap't Meredeth Hughes be added to the said Ouldfield & Pawley to perform the said Order. It is therefore Ordered that Cap't Meredeth Hughes be added to the said John Ouldfield and George Pawley Esq'rs and he is hereby authorized & empowered to put the said Order of the 7th March last in Execution Joyntly with the said John Ouldfield & George Pawley or either of them or separatly by himself exclusive of said Ouldfield and Pawley.

Read the Petition of Randal Varley praying a Warrant for one hundred acres of Land having Sworn to his family Right. Granted.

Read the Petition of Mr. Paul De St. Julien praying a Warrant for Eleven hundred acres of Land having Sworn to his family Right. Granted.

Read the Petition of Mr. Benjamin Mazyck praying a Warrant for five hundred acres of Land having Sworn to his Right. Granted.

Read the Petition of Abiah Small, widow, praying a Warrant for three hundred acres of Land having Sworn to her Right. Granted.

Read the Petition of Mr. Jerome LeBeuf praying a Warrant for one hundred acres of Land having Sworn to his Right. Granted.

Read the Petition of John Shauvereau praying a Warrant for Eight hundred acres of Land having Sworn to his Right. Granted.

Read the Petition of Frederick DeJean praying a Warrant for one hundred and fifty acres of Land having Sworn to his Right. Granted.

Read the Petition of Ditto praying a Warrant for four hundred and fifty acres of Land having Sworn to his Right. Granted.

Read the Petition of Willm. Bradley praying a Warrant for thirteen hundred acres of Land having Sworn to his Right. Granted.

Read the Petition of John Amory praying a Warrant for five hundred acres in the Township of Purrisburgh having Sworn to his Right. Granted.

Read the Petition of Gasper Meyer praying a Warrant for fifty acres in the Township of Purrisburgh having Sworn to his Right. Granted.

Read the Petition of Elizabeth and Thomas Jenys Executrix and Executor to Paul Jenys Esq'r deceased setting forth that the late Paul Jenys had Obtained a Warrant for two thousand acres of Land from the late Lieut. Governor Colo. Broughton But the said Jenys dying before the Land could be run out, therefore the Petitioners pray that as Trustees to the said Paul Jenys Children they may Obtain a new warrant for the like quantity of Land that a grant may pass in their names in Trust for the said Children. Granted on Surrendring the former Warrant.

Meeting of Thursday the 14th December 1738

Read the Petition of Patrick Bird praying a warrant for two hundred acres of Land in one of the Townships having Sworn to his Right and having no Land in this Province. Granted.

Read the Petition of David Hulonbert praying a warrant for two hundred acres & Lott in Purrisburgh having Sworn to his Right. Granted.

Read the Petition of John Taylor praying a Warrant for two hundred Acres of Land having sworn to his Right. Granted.

On motion of James Michie in behalf of Isaac Mazyck Esq'r of Charles Town, setting forth and shewing that Catherine Renie late of Charles Town widow deced obtained from the late Lieutenant Governor and his Majestys Hon'ble Council a warrant for admeasuring and Setting out unto the said Catharine Renie Five hundred Acres of Land in the Township of Williamsburgh or Queensborough and that the said Catherine Rainey in her life time assigned, Transferrd & Sett over unto the said Isaac Mazyck all her Right, Title and Interest in & to the said Warrant, but in the meantime before a grant might pass to the said Isaac Mazyck his heirs and assigns for the said five hundred acres of Land as assignee to the said Catherine and that the attorney general be ordered to prepare the Fiat. Ordered that a Special Grant do pass to the said Isaac Mazyck for the said five hundred acres of Land and that the Attorney General do prepare the Fiat accordingly.

Meeting of the 16th December 1738

Read the Petition of the Rever'd Francis Guichard praying a Warrant for one thousand five hundred and fifty acres of Land having sworn to his family Right. Granted.

Read the Petition of Mr. Zachariah Villepontoux praying a Warrant for one thousand three hundred acres of Land having Sworn to his family Right. Granted.

Read the Petition of Mr. John Steel praying a Warrant for four hundred acres of Land and a town lott in the Township of Orangeburgh having Sworn to his family Right and that he has no Lands in this Province. Granted.

Meeting of the 4th January 1738/9

Read the Petition of Jonathan Scott praying a warrant for five hundred acres of Land and a Lot in New Windsor having sworn to his family Right. Ordered that the prayer of the Petition be granted.

Meeting of the 17th January 1738/9

Read the Petition of Mr. Isaac Dubose praying a warrant for one thousand acres of Land having Sworn to his family Right. Ordered that the prayer of the petitioner be Granted.

Read the Petition of Mr. James Stewart praying a warrant for four hundred and fifty acres of Land having Sworn to his family Right. Ordered that the prayer of the petitioner be Granted.

Read the Petition of Mr. William McCullough setting forth that his father John McCullough had obtained a Warrant for Running out his five hundred acres of Land and a Lot on his Majestys Bounty in Kingston Township for his family Right and hath sealed the same agreable to his Majesty's Instructions but before the same could be Granted he dyed leaving behind Eight Orphan Children. The Petitioner therefore prays that as the Eldest Son and having the Care and charge of providing and Bringing up the family he may have a Grant for the said Lands and Lot for the use of the children and to enable him to bring them up. Granted and orderd that a Grant may be made out to him accordingly.

Read a Certificate signed by Major Christian Mote setting forth that Jacob Christaler an Inhabitant of Orangeburgh came into this province with his wife about Two years ago, Soon after went to serve this Country as a Soldier at Port Royal but being Honourably discharged the said Service and having a mind to settle in Orangeburgh he went to Peter Taylor, Esquire, commissary General to receive his half Years Bounty of Provision who gave him Twenty Three pounds four shillings Currency and afterwards eight pounds more from Major Mote by order of the said commissary and as the said Jacob Christaler hath been an Inhabitant of Orangeburgh about a Twelve month past with his wife and has been for the most part afflicted with Sickness which has reduced him very much He therefore prays that he may be Enabled to purchase necessarys. Ordered that if the Petitioner has not had his full Bounty as his ship mates have had he have the Remainder allowed him.

Meeting of the 20th January 1738/9

Read the Petition of John Mackey praying a Warr't for One hundred acres of Land having Sworn to his family Right. Ordered that the prayer of the Petition be granted.

Meeting of the 23rd January 1738/9

Read the Petition of James Law setting forth that he had obtained a Warrant for One hundred and fifty acres of Land in Williamsburgh That your Petitioner Immediately settled upon a Tract containing one hundred acres and he being poor and having made treat Improvements upon it he could not leave it but he intended to run out the said tract of one hundred acres as soon as his family should Increase, that his family is now Increased by the birth of two children but he is now informed that the said Land has been run out for one Hopkins for the use of one Stubbs or some other person who purchased the said Hopkins Warrant. The Petitioner therefore humbly prays that he may have a special warrant for the said hundred cares. Ordered that the Petitioner have a Special Warrant Issue to him according to the prayer of the petition.

Read the Petition of John Mathews praying a Warrant for Two hundred acres of Land and a Lot in Williamsburgh having Sworn to his family Right and also prays for his Majestys Bounty. Ordered that the Petitioner have a Warrant for Two hundred acres of Land in Williamsburgh and a Lot but no Bounty.

Read the Petition of James Pogue praying a warrant for five hundred acres of Land and a Lot in one of the northern Townships he Expecting his family over in a short time and also prays for his Majestys Bounty Ordered that the petitioner have a Warrant for a Lot and one hundred acres of Land in one of the northern Townships only having but himself and wife in family now in this province but no Bounty allowed.

Meeting of the 24th January 1738/9

Read the Certificate of Major Christian Mote in favour of George Shooler, John Happersizel, Jacob Bruck and John Weitstein setting forth that they have had but one half Years Provision Bounty and that they are in Great want and therefore pray that they may have the other half Years Provision Bounty allowed them to Enable them to buy necessary for their familys. George Shooler family himself, wife, one daughter fourteen years old, one thirteen, one twelve, one son Eight, one Daughter vie and one four years of age.
John Happersizel in family himself and his wife.
Jacob Brucks family himself and wife, one son Ten years old, one Nine and Two men servants.
John Weitsteins family himself and wife and Two children.

Ordered that the commissary do furnish the above named persons with half Years Provision as they had before.

Read the Certificate of Major Mote in favour of Bernard Snell setting forth that he had been in this province for some years and went into service by which he has as yet been deprived of his Majestys Provision of Bounty and he being now out of service humbly prays he may have one half Years Provision and money allowed him to buy necessarys. Ordered that the Commissary do furnish him with the like half Years provisions as others in his Circumstances have had.

Meeting of the 26th January 1738/9

Read the Petition of Henry Ferguson praying a Warrant for three hundred acres of Land having Sworn to his family Right. Ordered that the Prayer of the Petition be Granted.

Read the Petition of John Skinner praying a Warrant for Two hundred acres of Land having Sworn to his family Right. Ordered that the prayer of the Petition be Granted.

Meeting of the 27th January 1738/9

Read the Petition of Maria Hanshaw praying a Warrant for fifty acres of Land in Orangeburgh Township having Sworn to her family Right. Ordered that the prayer of the Petition be Granted.

Meeting of the 6th February 1738/9

Read the Petition of John Godbold setting forth that he had obtained a Warrant for Two hundred and Fifty acres of Land in the Year 1732 that the Secretary in filling up the said Warrant made a mistake and wrote James instead of John so that the Petitioner can't get his Platt out of the Surveyor

Generals Office till the mistake be rectifyed He therefore Humbly prays that the said Mistake be rectifyed that he may have a Grant for the said Land. Ordered that the said mistake be rectifyed accordingly.

Meeting of the 8th February 1738/9

Read the Petition of John Scott and Wm. Scott praying a Warrant for five hundred acres of Land being willing to become Joint Tennants to the King and having Sworn to their family Right. Ordered that the Prayer of the Petition be Granted.

Read the Petition of James Boggs praying a warrant for two hundred and fifty acres of Land having sworn to his [family right]. Ordered that the Prayer of the Petition be Granted.

Meeting of the 9th February 1738/9

Read the Petition of Mr. John Roberts praying a Warrant for one Hundred and fifty acres of Land having Sworn to his family Right. Ordered that the Prayer of the Petition be Granted.

Read the Petition of Moses Crausby[?] praying a Warrant for one Hundred and fifty acres of Land in the Township of Queensborough having Sworn to his family Right. Ordered that the Prayer of the Petition be Granted.

It is Ordered that the Reverend Mr. Joseph Bugnion have a Common Warrant Issue to him for thirteen hundred acres of Land on his returning a former Warrant which he obtained the 12th day of May 1738 for the like Quantity of Land in the Township of Queensborough and paying his fees.

Meeting of the 15th February 1738/9

Read the Petition of Richard Godfrey praying a Warrant for One thousand Six hundred and fifty acres of Land in this Province having Sworn to his family Right. Ordered that the Prayer of the Petition be Granted.

Meeting of the 21st February 1738/9

Read the Certificate of Major Mote in favour of Peter Hubert of Orangeburgh the said Peter Hubert praying for half Years Bounty having received one half Years Provision already.

Read the said Major Certificate for Margarett Shooler widow of Jacob Shooler Deceased she praying for one Half years Provision having received the other half Years already her family consists of herself and six Daughters the Younger being Eleven Years of Age.

Read the Certificate of the said Major in favour of Hans Early praying for such Allowance of Provisions as others his fellow Inhabitants having yet Received none and having been a Souldier at Port Royal himself only in family.

Read the Petition of Nicholas Jones, Christian Jones, Grace Jones, and Susanna Jones praying one Half years Provision having received one half Years already.

Ordered that the Commissary do furnish all the above persons which such quantity of Provisions as is usually allowed or that they are Intitled to.

Read the Petition of William Guy Jun'r praying a Warrant for one thousand and fifty acres of Land having sworn to his family Right. Ordered that the prayer of the petition be Granted.

Read the Petition of Benjamin Smith praying a Warrant for six hundred and fifty acres of Land having sworn to his family Right. Ordered that the prayer of the petition be Granted.

Meeting of the 22nd February 1738/9

Read the Certificate of Major Christian Mote in favour of Isabella Hotto setting forth that the said Hotto is now out of Servitude and prays for a warrant in Orangeburgh Township for three hundred and fifty acres of Land and his Majestys Bounty of Provisions for himself [sic] and family consisting of himself, his wife, and a son 15 years old, Daughter 16, daughter 13, one son 12, and one Son Two years of Age. Ordered that the Petitioner have a Warrant for Three hundred and fifty acres of Land in Orangeburgh and that the Commissary do furnish the Petitioner and his family with the usual Bounty of Provisions.

Meeting of the 23d February 1738/9

Read the Petition of William Jackson praying a Warrant for Seven hundred acres of Land having sworn to his family Right. Ordered that the prayer of the petition be Granted.

Read the Petition of Captain John Jackson praying a Warrant for Seven hundred acres of Land having sworn to his family Right. Ordered that the prayer of the petition be Granted.

Meeting of the 24th February 1738/9

Read the Petition of Thomas Collier praying a Warrant for Two hundred and fifty acres of Land having Sworn to his family Right. Ordered that the Prayer of the Petition be Granted.

Read the Petition of Frederick DeJean praying a Warrant for One hundred and fifty acres of Land in Purrisburgh having Sworn to his family Right. Ordered that the Prayer of the Petition be Granted.

Meeting of the 28th February 1738/9

Read the Petition of William Brockington praying a Warrant for four hundred acres of Land having eight persons in family one of which is a hired Servant for one Year and having sworn to his family Right. Ordered that the petitioner have a Warrant for three hundred and fifty acres of land only.

Read the Petition of Samuel Bacon praying a Warrant for two hundred and fifty acres of Land having Sworn to his family Right. Ordered that the Prayer of the Petition be Granted.

Read the Petition of John Gorton praying a Warrant for four hundred and fifty acres of Land having Sworn to his family Right. Ordered that the Prayer of the Petition be Granted.

Read the Petition of Samuel Stevens praying a Warrant for five hundred acres of Land having Sworn to his family Right. Ordered that the Prayer of the Petition be Granted.

Meeting of the 4th April 1739

Read the Petition of Mathias Caler praying a Warrant for one hundred and fifty acres of Land and a Lot in Orangeburgh having three persons in family and his Majestys Bounty. Ordered that the Prayer of the Petition be Granted.

Read the Petition of Hans Towmen praying a Warrant for one hundred and fifty acres of Land and a Lot in Orangeburgh and his Majestys Bounty of Provisions. Ordered that the Prayer of the Petition be Granted.

Meeting of the 5th April 1739

Read the Petition of John George Kirk praying a Warrant for One hundred acres of Land in the Township of Orangeburgh and for his Majesty's Bounty of Provisions having in family himself and wife. Ordered that the Land be Granted and Six months provisions.

Read the Petition of George Haig praying a Warrant for one hundred acres of Land in the Township of Saxe Gotha having Sworn to his family Right. Ordered that the prayer of the Petition be Granted.

Read the Petition of Christopher Bearman praying a Warrant for three hundred and fifty acres of Land having Sworn to his family Right. Ordered that the prayer of the Petition be Granted.

[Meeting of the 5th April 1739]

Read the Petition of John Reed praying a Warrant for four hundred and fifty acres of Land having Sworn to his family Right. Ordered that the prayer of the Petition be Granted.

Read the Petition of Peter Pearce praying a Warrant for one hundred and fifty acres of Land having Sworn to his family Right. Ordered that the prayer of the Petition be Granted.

Read the Petition of Hugh Murphey praying a Warrant for one hundred and fifty acres of Land having Sworn to his family Right. Ordered that the prayer of the Petition be Granted.

Read the Petition of Philip Jackson praying a Warrant for Two hundred and fifty acres of Land having Sworn to his family Right. Ordered that the prayer of the Petition be Granted.

Read the Petition of John Minson praying a Warrant for a Lot and one hundred acres of Land in Orangeburgh having Sworn to his family Right. Ordered that the prayer of the Petition be Granted.

Read the Petition of William Gardner praying a Warrant for three hundred acres of Land having Sworn to his family Right. Ordered that the prayer of the Petition be Granted.

Read the Petition of William Hughes praying a Warrant for fifty acres of Land in Queensborough having Sworn to his family Right. Ordered that the prayer of the Petition be Granted.

Read the Petition of Duggle McKeithon praying a Warrant for five hundred and fifty acres of Land having Sworn to his family Right. Ordered that the prayer of the Petition be Granted.

Read the Petition of Magdelaine Boulay praying a Warrant for four hundred acres of Land and a Lot in Orangeburgh having Sworn to his family Right. Ordered that the prayer of the Petition be Granted.

Read the Petition of John Cooke praying a Warrant for four hundred and fifty acres of Land having sworn to his family Right. Ordered that the prayer of the Petition be Granted.

Read the Petition of Alexander McCants setting forth that his father had obtained a Warrant for Two hundred and fifty acres in Williamsburgh which was run out and a Platt returned into the Surveyor Generals Office; that a little time after his father dyed and left him the said Land by will, that the said Platt still lyes in the Surveyors Office and therefore he prays that a Grant may pass to him for the said Land in his own name. Ordered that the prayer of the Petition be Granted.

Read the Petition of Mary Russel widow setting forth her husband Charles Russel had obtained a Warrant from the late Excellency Governor Johnson which was never Executed as appears by the Precept annext to the Petition and therefore prays a warrant in her own name for the same Quantity of Land in Trust for her children as her husband Desired in his Will. Ordered that a Warrant do pass to the Petitioner in trust for the children of Charles Russel deceased pursuant to his will.

Meeting of the 6th April 1739

On Reading the Petition of Jane Erwin widow and Relict of Robert Erwin deceased, Ordered that provided Mr. William James do sent down a proper Conveyance of that tract of Two hundred and fifty acres of Land in Williamsburgh which the widow Erwin now lives upon to her and her heirs and deposite it in the hands of the Clerk of the council he shall have a Grant pass to him for that Tract of three hundred acres of Land mentioned in the Petition in his own name.

Meeting of the 12th April 1739

Read the Petition of John Bryant praying a warr't for fifty acres of Land in Williamsburgh having Sworn to his family Right and also prays for his Majestys Bounty of Provision. Ordered that the prayer of the Petition be Granted.

Meeting of the 13th April 1739

A Caveat was Read and enter'd by Benjamin Whitaker Esq'r in behalf of Frederick French of the City of Dublin in the Kingdom of ireland Esq'r that no Grant may pass to Peter De St. Julien Esq'r for any Lands lying within the Barony Commonly called Taphoe on Santee River lately in the possession of Alexander French Esquire deceased and is Butting and partly bound on Santee River and lands of James Kinloch Esquire called Eutaw Spring for that the said Lands were Surveyed by the said De. St. Julien are part of the Baroney, which Baroney or any part thereof not in his Majestys Power to dispose, for that the same became vested in John Bayly of the Kingdom of Ireland Esq'r by virtue of a Patent from the late Lords Proprietors and by mesne Conveyance from the said John Bayly became vested in the said Alexander French Deceased who devised the Same to his only son and heir at Law Frederick French the younger who is now dead and upon whose death the said Barony Legally Descended to the aforesaid Frederick French his unkle and heir at Law. Benjamin Whitaker of Council with the Complainant.

[Meeting of the 13th April 1739]

Read the Petition of Hugh Rose Deputy Surveyor praying that as he is not allowed the full of his account for running the Welch Tract he may have a Warrant for five hundred acres of Land and a Lot in the Township of Purrisburgh and that the Commissary do furnish him and his two Servants with one years Provisions.

Read the Petition of Andrew Monclair Darbalestier praying a warrant for five hundred acres of Land having never had any Lands surveyed to him by virtue of a warrant obtained by him for three hundred acres of Land and which warrant is annexed to the Petition and also having sworn to his family Right. Ordered that on Surrendring the above mentioned Warrant for three hundred acres of land to the Secretary the petition have a Warrant to issue to him for five hundred acres of land.

Read the Petition of Thomas Harrington praying a Warrant for three hundred and fifty acres of Land having Sworn to his family Right. Ordered that the prayer of the Petition be Granted.

Read the Petition of William Metcalf praying a warrant four hundred and fifty acres of Land having Sworn to his Family Right. Ordered that the prayer of the Petition be Granted.

Read the Petition of the Rev'd Mr. Thomas Bearett [?] praying a warrant for five hundred acres of Land having sworn to his family Right. Ordered that the prayer of the Petition be Granted.

Read the Petition of Josiah Collings praying a warrant for five hundred acres of Land having sworn to his family Right. Ordered that the prayer of the Petition be Granted.

Read the Petition of Jacob Rooch praying a Warrant for fifty acres of Land in Purrisburgh having sworn to his family Right. Ordered that the prayer of the Petition be Granted.

Read the Petition of the same for one hundred acres in Purrisburgh and ordered to be granted.

Read the Petition of Andrew Winkler praying a Warr't for one hundred acres of land in Purrisburgh having Sworn to his family Right. Ordered that the prayer of the Petition be Granted.

Read the Petition of Johanas Wanderliek praying a warrant for one hundred acres of land in Purrisburgh having Sworn to his family Right. Ordered that the prayer of the Petition be Granted.

[Meeting of the 13th April 1739]

Read the Petition of Martin Lasman praying a warrant for two hundred and fifty acres of land having Sworn to his family Right. Ordered that the prayer of the Petition be Granted.

Read the Petition of Peter Laffitte praying a warrant for one hundred and fifty acres of land having Sworn to his family Right. Ordered that the prayer of the Petition be Granted.

Read the Petition of Peter Laffitte praying a warrant for two hundred acres of land in Purrisburgh having Sworn to his family Right. Ordered that the prayer of the Petition be Granted.

Read the Petition of Peter Laffitte praying a warrant for one hundred acres of land having Sworn to his family Right in Purrisburgh. Ordered that the prayer of the Petition be Granted.

Read the Petition of Lodwick Kails praying a warrant for one hundred acres of land having Sworn to his family Right. Ordered that the prayer of the Petition be Granted.

Read the Petition of David Kulmbert praying a warrant for one hundred acres of land in Purrisburgh having Sworn to his family Right. Ordered that the prayer of the Petition be Granted.

Read the Petition of Michael Rohr praying a warrant for one hundred and fifty acres of land in Purrisburgh having Sworn to his family Right. Ordered that the prayer of the Petition be Granted.

Read the Petition of Mr. Henry Chiffelle praying a warrant for four hundred and fifty acres of land having Sworn to his family Right. Ordered that the prayer of the Petition be Granted.

Read the Petition of Francis Delgres praying a warrant for two hundred and fifty acres of land having Sworn to his family Right. Ordered that the prayer of the Petition be Granted.

Read the Petition of John Linder praying a warrant for one hundred acres of land having Sworn to his family Right in Purrisburgh. Ordered that the prayer of the Petition be Granted.

Mr. Linder laid before this Board a List of Several Platts of Land belonging to the Inhabitants of Purrisburgh now lying in the Several Officers of the Surveyor General Attorney General and Secretary and prayed that he might have an order to the said Officers to deliver the same to him in behalf of the Inhabitants. Accordingly the order was delivered to him.

On Reading the Petition of John Linder in behalf of himself and the rest of the poor Protestants now settled in Purrisburgh setting forth some apprehentions they are under of being now obliged to pay the fees in the Several offices in taking out their several Platts and Grants and therefore praying to have such relief as may prevent delay in obtaining their Grants. It is therefore ordered that the Surveyor General, Attorney General and the Secretary do forthwith lay before the Board an Exact List of all the Platts now lying in the Respective officers belonging to such of the Inhabitants in the Several Townships as have been allowed his Majestys Bounty of Land Gratis and which came into this offices before the 24th March past.

Meeting of the 9th May 1739

Benjamin Whitaker Esq'r enters a Caveat on behalf of John Roberts in the Kingdom of Great Britain, Esquire, against any grant passing to any person or persons and particularly against the heirs of assigns of Colo Purry deceased for any Lands within the supposed lines of the Township of Purrisburgh, the said Lands having been laid out to the Right Hon. the Lord Carteret whose assignee the said John Roberts, before the Township of Purrisburgh was laid out or ascertained. 7 May 1739. Benjamin Whitaker.

On reading the petition of Mr. Charles Peter Purry and the above Caveat Enterd by Mr. Whitaker, it is ordered that Mr. Whitaker do attend tomorrow at three o'clock precisely to give his reasons why Grants should not pass to the said Charles Purry for the Land he claims.

Meeting of the 10th May 1739

Read the Petition of George Haddrell praying a warrant for Six hundred acres of Land having Sworn to his family Right. Ordered that the prayer of the Petition be Granted.

Read the Petition of Philip Ayton praying a warrant for five hundred acres of Land having Sworn to his family Right. Ordered that the prayer of the Petition be Granted.

Read the Petition of Adam Frolig praying a warrant for fifty acres of Land on his own head in the Township of Orangeburgh pursuant to his Majestys Instructions. Ordered that the prayer of the Petition be Granted.

Read the Petition of John Newberry praying a warrant for one hundred acres of Land having Sworn to his family Right. Ordered that the prayer of the Petition be Granted.

Read the Petition of Thomas Moses praying a warrant for two hundred and fifty acres of Land to be lay'd out in the Welch Tract having come over on purpose to Settle there from Philadelphia and having Sworn to his family Right. Ordered that the prayer of the Petition be Granted.

Read the Petition of William Evans praying a warrant for fifty acres of Land to be lay'd out in the Welch Tract he having Sworn that he has no land in this province. Ordered that the prayer of the Petition be Granted.

Read the Petition of Martin Fridig praying a warrant for one hundred and fifty acres of Land in the Township of Saxe Gotha having Sworn to his family Right. Granted and ordered accordingly.

Read the Petition of John Newberry setting forth that he is a Carpenter and proposes to build a Good Corn mill on the Welch Tract for the use of the Inhabitants there as well as those in Williamsburgh and to compleat the same in a Twelve month, and the said Petitioner further setts forth that he proposes afterwards to build a saw mill the petitioner therefore humbly prays that he may obtain a warrant for one hundred acres to build the corn mill on and five hundred acres of Land for the Saw mill either within or without the Township of Williamsburgh where he may meet with Convenient Land and hopes to meet with Encouragement and assistance from the Board on his Labourious undertaking for the Publick Good.

On Reading the above petition his Honour the Lieutenant Governour gave the above petitioner Six hundred acres to encourage his undertaking out of his own warrant not being willing to Grant any of the Kings Lands But according to his Majestys Instructions that is to say for family right.

Mr. Whitaker having been heard in relation to the Caveat entered by him yesterday, It was ordered that he attend again tomorrow nine oclock with what papers and Platts he has relating to this Dispute with Mr. Purry.

Meeting of the 11th May 1739

Mary Phinlander appeared at this Board and produced and surrendred a warrant which her late husband Frederick Phinlander had obtained from the late Governour Johnson for four hundred acres and a Lot in Purrisburgh and prayed at the same time she might have a new warrant for the like quantity of Land and Lot in the aforesaid Township in her own name and her children now living vizt Christian and Martin her sons and Mary her daughter and prays also for the Bounty not having had any yet. The same appearing Reasonable to this Board, It is ordered that a Warrant do issue as prayd for, and that the Bounty be allowed for four together with the charges of Running out the Land.

Read the Petition of Colo. William Waties praying a warrant for five hundred acres of Land having sworn to his family right. Ordered that the prayer of the petition be Granted.

Read the Petition of Colo. William Hazzard praying a warrant for eleven hundred acres of Land having sworn to his family right. Ordered that the prayer of the petition be Granted.

Read the Petition of William McPherson praying a warrant for six hundred acres of Land having sworn to his family right. Ordered that the prayer of the petition be Granted.

Read the Petition of George Stahley setting forth that he obtained a Warrant for Two hundred acres of Land in Orangeburgh and had the same Lay'd out but the same proving bad he humbly prays he may have a warrant Issue to him for the like quantity in the said Township and is willing to pay the charges. Ordered that a Warrant do issue to the Petitioner as prayd for on his surrendring the former warrant and Platt.

Read the Petition of Daniel James setting forth that the order of this Honourable Board for the Reservation of the Welch Tract upon Peede River for the sole benefit of such Welch Pensilvanians as shall come over with an Intent to settle in this Province expires in the beginning or the month of August next. That several Deputy Surveyors are at Present very busy in purchasing and collecting of warrants to lay out considerable Quantitys of Land in the said Tract Immediately upon determination of the said order. That several familys in Pensylvania are determined to remove themselves into this Colony provided this Board will prolong the time of Reservation. That the Petitioner sails for Pensilvania next week and that the Removal of the said familys will in a great measure depend upon the Petitioner Representation of this Board's prolonging the time. The petitioner therefore humbly prays that the Reservation may be prolonged for two years more from the month of August next that he may be Enabled to give the said familys encouragement to come over. Ordered that the time be prolonged according to the prayer of the petition for two years from the month of August next and that the surveyor general be directed to acquaint his Deputys therewith.

Read the Petition of William Peter setting forth that he had purchased from the late Charles Hart Esquire for a valuable consideration all his the said Charles Harts Rights and title to one thousand acres of Land intended to be surveyed by virtue of a warrant and precept granted to the said Charles Hart for that purpose and bearing date the Tenth day of April 1736 which appears by said Precept annexed to this Petitio that no Survey as yet been made of the same, and that Mr. Ellery administrator disclaimed all manner of Right thereto the assignment having been produced to him which is now layd before this Board. The petitioner therefore humbly prays he may have a warrant in Lieut of the former Warrant so Surrendred for the same quantity of Land in his own name. Ordered that the Petitioner have a Warrant Issued to him for one thousand acres of Land upon the Surrender of the former warrant.

[Meeting of the 11th May 1739]

Read the Petition of Major Christian Mote praying a warrant for an additional family Right of Two hundred acres of Land and Lot in Orangeburgh and for his Majestys Bounty. Granted the said Land only.

Read the Petition of Mr. John Fordice Clark praying a warrant for five hundred acres of Land either within or without the Township of Queensborough having no Land in this Province and having sworn to his Right. Granted without the Township of Queensborough.

Read the Petition of George Chicken praying a warrant for five hundred acres of Land having sworn to his family Right. Ordered that the prayer of the petition be granted.

Read the Petition of Richard Miller praying a warrant for Two hundred and fifty acres of Land having sworn to his family Right. Ordered that the prayer of the petition be granted.

His Majestys Council taking under consideration Mr. Charles Purry Petition Setting forth that his Majesty by his Instruction had given orders that Colonel John Peter Purry the Petitioner father should have 48,000 acres of Land free from Quit Rents for Ten years upon condition that the Same should be cultivated within Ten years from the date of the Grant That his Majesty also ordered that the said Land should be laid out within the Six mile Line to be run round the Township of Purrisburgh That 18,650 acres of the aforesaid 48,000 acres was Granted to the Petitioner's father in his life time but by a mistake subject to the payment of Quit Rents from the date of said Grant. The Petition therefore prays that he may surrender the said Grant of 18,650 acres made to the petitioners father, and that this Honble Board would order his Majesty's Surveyor General to Certifye the Platts Returned into his Office for 29,350 acres remainder of the said 48,000 as well for the said 18,650 acres to be surendered in order that Grants be prepared for the Same in the name of the petitioner Son and heir at Law of the said Colonel John Peter Purry deced free of Quit Rents for the space of Ten Years pursuant to the Intent of his Majestys Instructions.
His Majestys Council taking under consideration Mr. Whitaker Reasons against the said Grants passing to the said Purry are of opinion that Grants do pass to the Petitioner for the said Lands according to his Majestys Instructions for that purpose that is to say for the 29,650 not yet granted.

Meeting of the 31st May 1739

Read the Petition of John Eberley praying a warrant for 200 acres of Land in Orangeburgh having sworn to his family Right. Ordered that the prayer of the Petition be Granted.

On motion of Mr. Graeme in behalf of Judith Peyre and Abraham Crouch praying an order to Mr. Mickie to bring into Council a Grant for one thousand & sixty acres of Land granted by mistake to Hugh Butler Esquire in order to have the same vacated having been unduly obtained. Ordered accordingly and that Mr. Hugh Butler Jun'r or the attorney of said Hugh Butler Esquire have notice thereof some time this afternoon and that the said Grant be vacated unless cause be shewn to the contrary by Ten of the Clock tomorrow morning.

Meeting of the 1st June 1739

Pursuant to the order of yesterday the grant of Hugh Butler Esquire for One thousand and sixty acres of Land was brought into Council and canceled.

Read the Petition of Jacob Buckolt praying a warrant for Two hundred and fifty acres of Land to be run out on the Welch Tract he being a Pensilvanian and having sworn to his family right. Ordered that the prayer of the Petition be Granted.

Read the Petition of Mary Christiana Frank praying a warrant for one hundred acres of Land and a Lot in Orangeburgh Township for herself and her son together with his Majestys Bounty of Provisions. Ordered that the prayer of the Petition be Granted.

Meeting of the 2nd June 1739

Read the petition of Thomas Elerbee praying a warrant for five hundred acres of Land having Sworn to his family Right. Ordered that the prayer of the Petition be Granted.

Read the petition of Wm. Heatly praying a warrant for three hundred and fifty acres of Land having Sworn to his family Right. Ordered that the prayer of the Petition be Granted.

Read the petition of Francis Young praying a warrant for seven hundred acres of Land having Sworn to his family Right. Ordered that the prayer of the Petition be Granted.

Meeting of the 5th June 1739

Read the Petition of Elias Snell praying a warrant for one hundred acres of Land having Sworn to his family Right and that it may be layd out in the Township of Orangeburgh. Ordered that the prayer of the Petition be Granted.

Meeting of the 6th June 1739

Read the Petition of Doc'r George Dicks praying a warrant for five hundred and fifty acres of Land having Sworn to his family Right and. Ordered that the prayer of the Petition be Granted.

Read the Petition of Thomas Evans setting forth that he came from Pensilvania about Eighteen months ago with his wife and Six children that he has had his Land in the Welch Tract but has yet received no Bounty and therefore prays for the Same. Ordered that the Petitioner leave the Same Bounty allowed him and his family as was allowed to them that came in when he came in, when he did.

Read the Petition of Hans Jacob Miers praying (as he is now out of this time) a Warrant for fifty acres of Land in Orangeburgh and his Majesty Bounty of Provisions having Sworn to his family Right. Ordered that the prayer of the Petition be Granted.

Read the Petition of John Francis Henry praying a warrant for one hundred acres of Land in Purrisburgh and his Majesty's Bounty having Sworn that he hath his wife and child come over. Ordered that the prayer of the Petition be Granted.

On motion of Mr. Graeme that a Grant might pass to the Rever'd Mr. Francis Guillard for Two hundred and five acres of Marsh Land situate in Berkley County on the north side of Fausters Creek butting and bounding as in the platt thereof is mentioned, Ordered that a Grant for the said Lands do pass to Mrs. Isabeau Guichard wife of the said Francis the same being the Marsh adjacent to a tract of Land now in her possessio by virtue of the last will and testament of Levy Guillhard her late husband deceased.

Read the Petition of Daniel Pepper praying a Warrant for two hundred and fifty acres of Land in New Windsor having sworn to his family Right. Ordered that the prayer of the Petition be Granted.

Meeting of the 15th June 1739

Mr. Thompson appeared at this Board and surrendred two conveyances from the Charraw Indians of their Lands on Peede River the one fort the north east side and the other for the south west side of the said River signed by Robert Huir, King and fourteen of the head men dated 4th day of August 1737 for the consideration of three hundred heavy buck skins, the said Thompson and the same time layd before this Board a more particular account of the whole expence he had been at in the purchase of the said lands.... It was ordered at the same time that John Thompson should have two warrants for five hundred acres of Land each to be run in the Welch Tract as a further Consideration given him for the aforesaid Land.

Read the Petition of Elizabeth Kese one of those who first came in with Captain Purry praying a warrant for fifty acres of Land and Lot in Orangeburgh as also his Majesty Bounty being now out of her time. Granted and allowed the same provision the others had who came in with her.

Meeting of the 20th June 1739

Read the Petition of William McNaught praying for his Majestys Bounty of Provisions being come over in Captain Adams in February 1737 with his family consisting of nine persons vizt himself wife and seven children as follows John 21, Alexander 16, Thomas 14, Joseph 10, Robert 7, Richard 4 and Jane 6 years of age and having sworn to the Truth of his Petition. Ordered that the commissary General do furnish the said William McNaught and his family with the usual Bounty of Provisions.

Read the petition of Piere Maille praying a warrant for Two hundred acres of Land in Purrisburgh having Sworn to his additional family Right. Ordered that the prayer of the Petition be Granted.

Meeting of the 6th July 1739

His Honour the Lieutenant Governor having informed the Board that there were Several persons had already Built good dwelling Houses upon vacant Lots in Beaufort Port Royal and were desirous of having grants for the Same, It is the opinion of this Board that such persons as have or shall build Houses of the Dimentions of fifteen feet by thirty shall have grants for the same.

Read the Petition of John Evans praying a warrant for three hundred acres of Land having Sworn to his family Right. Ordered that the prayer of the Petition be Granted.

Read the Petition of James Rickson praying a warrant for two hundred and fifty acres of Land having Sworn to his family Right. Ordered that the prayer of the Petition be Granted.

Read the Petition of Alexander Rattery praying a warrant for five hundred acres of Land having Sworn to his family Right. Ordered that the prayer of the Petition be Granted.

Read the Petition of Samuel Williams praying a warrant for three hundred acres of Land having Sworn to his family Right. Ordered that the prayer of the Petition be Granted.

Read the Petition of John Martin Lasman praying a warrant for two hundred and fifty acres of Land in Purrisburgh with a Lot and also his Majestys Bounty of Provisions having Sworn that he has five persons in family and being now out of his time. Ordered that the prayer of the Petition be Granted with the usual Bounty of Provisions that others have had who came with him.

Read the Petition of William Hamilton, messenger to this Board, praying to have a Warrant for five hundred acres of Land in this province in Lieu of a warrant he had obtained for laying out the like quantity of Land in Queensborough. Ordered that the petitioner have a warrant for five hundred acres as prayd for his surrendring his former warrant.

On Mr. Joseph Izard's surrendring a warrant he had formerly obtained for Twelve hundred and fifty acres of Land in the Township of Kingston of Queensborough dated the 16th December 1736. Ordered that the said Joseph Izard have a Warrant Issue to him for Twelve hundred and fifty acres of Land.

Meeting of the 7th July 1739

Read the Petition of James Michie, Esquire, praying a Warrant for Eight hundred acres of Land having sworn to his family Right. Ordered that the prayer of the Petition be Granted.

Read the Petition of John Mckenzie, Esquire, praying a Warrant for Eight hundred and fifty acres of Land having sworn to his family Right. Ordered that the prayer of the Petition be Granted.

The Petition of the Welch and Pensilvanians settled upon Peede River humbly sheweth that in the month of August 1736 an order of this Hon'ble Board was obtained to appropriate the Land lying for eight miles of each side of Peede River up from Queensborough Township to the Fork to the Sole use of the said Welch and their Descendants the Pensilvanians who should come over to this province for the space of two years that Immediately after the passing of the said order Several thousand acres of Land were run out by Inhabitants of this Province within the said Bounds for all or most of which Grants are now obtained to the great disapointment of your petitioners and the prevention of many Industrious familys removing themselves into this Colony. However that your petitioners were not absolutely discouraged by this Disappointment but went high up the River and upon Search discovered very large quantitys of good land, proper for the production of Hemp, Flax and European Grain, and suitable to their Intentions of planting within the Bounds aforesaid But that your petitioners have not been able to sitt down upon the said Land untill very lately and after they had consumed the little substance they had brought with them from their native country, that an applicant was thereupon made to your Honours to enlarge the Term of appropriation which was granted for the Term of one year and was afterwards upon a second application prolonged for two years more that notwithstanding such your Honors orders Two Deputy Surveyors (to wit) Blythe and Gallispie have layd out considerable quantitys of Land within the appropriated Limits some by virtue of General Warrants and others as your Petitioners are Informed without any warrants at all that they have Industriously given out for their own Lucre and gain that the aforementioned orders are void, Your Honours power in the Desposition of his Majestys Land being .merely executive and no Judicial or Discretonary, Your Petitioners further Complain that several Out Laws and Fugitives from the Colonies of Virginia and North Carolina most of whom are Mullatoes or of a mixt Blood, have thrust themselves amongst your Petitioners to their great annoyance and Disturbance which said persons pay no Quit Rents to his Majesty nor Contribute towards the Publick Taxes and charges of this Government But for the most part live in defyance of all Laws and are a Pest & Nuisance to the adjacent Inhabitants, That if your Petitioners could give assureances of your Honours orders being faithfully carried into Execution and these Settlers being undisturbed in their plantations by any Fugitives of Renagaddes Several Industrious persons would come over as well from the Colony of Pensilvania as the principality of Wales under these Circumstances your Petitioners humbly throw themselves upon your Honours Mercy praying that you would be pleasd to take their Case into Consideration and give them such relief in the Premises as to your Honours wisdom and goodness Shall Seem most fitting. Maurice Lewis, William James, on behalf of the Petitioners.

On Read the above Petition, Maurice Lewis, Esquire, one of the Petitioners was Directed to attend this Board as Soon as he can conveniently in order to make appear the Allegations contained therein relating to Blythe and Gallaspie. [order to the surveyor general and proclamation follow]

Meeting of the 2d August 1739

Read the Petition of Thomas Lloyd, Gentleman, setting forth that he in the Year 1717 had purchased a Tract of three hundred acres of Land of the Lords Proprietors for which he now produces the purchase Receipt, That the said land was surveyed by Francis Young, Esquire, the Surveyor General as appears by the Platt thereof Certifyed by him, that a Grant was also prepared for the same which was never Signed and therefore praying he may obtain a special Grant for the said Land with the Platt annexed pursuant to the quit Rent Law he having payd Tax for the Same for the Space of Twelve Years. Ordered that the Attorney General do prepare a Special Grant for the said Land according to the prayer of the Petition.

Read the Petition of James Berrie setting forth that William Hendrick in his life time had layd out unto him Two Tracts of Land in Colleton County in this province the one containing 192 acres the other 458, Platts of which were returned in the Secretarys office certifyed by James St. John Esq'r, Surveyor General, that before Grants could pass the said Hendrick dyed that the petitioner married the said Hendricks Daughter heir at law to her father, that the said Grants were lately signed in a mistake the Petitioner therefore humbly prays that he may have a Special Grant pass to him in his name and his assigns for the said Land. Ordered that the Attorney General do prepare Special Grants according to the prayer of the Petition.

Read the Petition of Peter Benoist of Craven County planter only Surviving Executor of the last Will of Samuel Benoist late of this province deceased setting forth that the said Samuel Benoist in his life time and layd out to him a Tract of Land containing four hundred acres as by the said Platt produced appears that the said Platt was Certifyed by the Surveyor General James St. John Esquire and returned into the Secretarys office that before a Grant could pass for the said Land to the said Samuel Benoist he dyed, and that platt has remained in the Secretarys office together with the Attorney Generals Fiat and now ready to be prepared That there are two children of the said Samuel alive and in the care of the petitioner That your Petitioner is Constituted and appointed Executor of the last will of the said Samuel by which will the said Samuel bequeathed a third part of his estate real and personal to each of his said children, the Petitioner therefore prays that a Special Grant may be made out to him of the Tract of Land aforesaid in Trust for the said orphan children their Heirs and assigns. Ordered that the Attorney General do prepare a Special Grant according to the prayer of the Petition.

<u>Meeting of the 3d August 1739</u>

Read the Petition of Walter Augustine praying a Warrant for three hundred acres his family Right being to [sic]. Ordered that the prayer of the Petition be Granted.

Read the Petition of James St. John, Esquire, praying a Warrant for nine hundred acres of Land having Sworn to his family Right. Ordered that the prayer of the Petition be Granted.

Read the Petition of John Daniel praying a Warrant for two hundred acres of Land having Sworn to his family Right. Ordered that the prayer of the Petition be Granted.

Read the Petition of Lewis Lormier praying a Warrant for three hundred acres of Land having Sworn to his family Right. Ordered that the prayer of the Petition be Granted.

<u>Meeting of the 4th August 1739</u>

On Reading the Petition of Francis Roche seting forth that Christopher Arthur late of this Province deceasd did by his last will and testament devise and bequeath a considerable large Tract of Land lying in St. Thomas's Parish to his nephew Bartholomew Arthur who is still alive and his kinsman Patrick Roche deceasd whose son and heir at law your petitioner is to be equally divided between them, that no dividing line has as yet been Regularly Run through the said Lands agreable to the will of the said Devisor, but the said Bartholomew Arthur has during the minority of your petitioner disposed of not only one moiety of the Lands in quantity or value but of some hundred acres over and above such a moiety to the Great Injury and Damage of the

Petitioner. He therefore prays that an order be given by this Board to two Deputy Surveyors to run out a Dividing Line of the said Tract as aforesaid, So that he may bring his Action at Law, or other Legal Remedy for the Recovery of the premises.

Ordered that John Hentie and Isaac Porcher Jun'r, Two Deputy Surveyors, do run the Dividing Line on the Lands of Christopher Arthur deceasd situate in St. Thomas Parish, and by him devised to Bartolomew Arthur and Patrick Roche deceasd between the heirs and assigns of the said Devisees, and to Return a Plan thereof as Soon as possible to this Board.

Meeting of the 17th August 1739

Read the Petition of William Eliott praying a warrant for one hundred acres and a Town Lot in New Windsor having Sworn to his Family Right. Ordered that the prayer of the Petition be Granted.

Read the Petition of William Day praying a warrant for Four hundred acres and a Town Lot in New Windsor having Sworn to his Family Right. Ordered that the prayer of the Petition be Granted.

Read the Petition of Richard Perry praying a warrant for Twelve hundred and fifty acres of Land having Sworn to his Family Right. Ordered that the prayer of the Petition be Granted.

Read the Petition of John Neilson praying a warr't for Twelve hundred and fifty acres of Land having Sworn to his Family Right. Ordered that the prayer of the Petition be Granted.

Read the Petition of John Laeing praying a warrant for four hundred and fifty acres of Land having Sworn to his Family Right. Ordered that the prayer of the Petition be Granted.

Read the Petition of John Trobeville praying a warrant for three hundred and fifty acres of Land having Sworn to his Family Right. Ordered that the prayer of the Petition be Granted.

Read the Petition of the Reverend Samuel Hunter praying a warrant for five hundred and fifty acres of Land having Sworn to his Family Right. Ordered that the prayer of the Petition be Granted.

Read the Petition of Margaret Stehili praying a warrant for fifty acres of Land having Sworn to her Family Right and also praying for his Majesty's Bounty. Ordered that the prayer of the Petition be Granted.

Read the Petition of John Welfe praying a warrant for two hundred acres of Land in Orangeburgh having Sworn to his Family Right. Ordered that the prayer of the Petition be Granted.

Read the Petition of Alexander McCants seting forth that his father had obtained a warrant for Two hundred and fifty acres of Land in Williamsburgh, that his father dyed before a Grant was Signed for the said Land, that some time after the Petitioner obtained an order of this Honourable Board for the said Grants passing to him in his name, But the Petitioner being very poor, therefore humbly prays that the Charges of taking out the said Grant may be payd. Ordered that the prayer of the Petition be Granted.

Page 5: Meeting of 7 April 1742

A Petition of William Gardner was laid before the Board shewing that he having his Family encreased with 4 white and 2 Black servants, for whom he as yet has had no Land assign'd him, humbly prayed their Honours to grant him 300 Acres of land in Prince Frederick Parish, Winiaw, near the head of Black-mingo Creek, on the north side, that a Warrant be made out to him for admeasuring the same by virtue of his Family right. Which petition being considered was Granted.

Pp. 5-6: The Petition of Thomas Greenwood was also read shewing that about 6 years agoe he came into this Province in order to settle himself and Family that soon after his arrival he applyed to one Mr. Gillespy a deputy Survey'r to procure him a warrant in right of his Family which then consisted of four persons according to an affidavit then made before Mr. Wallis.

That y'r s'd Gillespy disappointed the Petitioner which oblig'd him to come afterwards to Town, but y'r Council was then not sitting. That the Petitioner so far as his Circumstances would allow of has improved a Tract of land containing about 300 acres up Pedee 6 miles from said river upon the swamp of Jeffrey's Creek and has built a House for the Conveniency of himself and Family but it appears, that y'e s'd tract is now taken within the Land set apart and run out for the Welch. The Petitioner nevertheless in Consideration of his having no other land in the Province, and his having Settled that Tract long before the Land was run out for the Welch & being poor and unable to make any other Settlement, in the Province except whereon he now lives, and as his not having procured a Warrant to Secure the said Land, before now was not owing to any neglect but his Poverty, therefore prayed that their Honours would grant him a Warrant to Secure the said Tract containing 300 acres agreeably to his Family right consisting of Six Persons. This Petition being duly considered was granted....

Page 6: The Petition of John Mayers was also Read humbly shewing that he having five white Persons in Family and having as yet had no lands granted him, but being willing to Cultivate and Improve two hundred and fifty acres prays that their Honours would according to his Majestys Instructions grant him a Warrant for admeasuring y'e Same, on the north side of Lynches Creek near Queensborough in Craven County. The above Petition having duly considered was granted....

Pp. 6-7: The Petition of Jane Sinklair [Sinclair] shewing that she has a Family consisting of twenty three persons for whom she as yet hath not obtained any Grant of Land in this Province nor in the time of her deceased Husband James Sinkler wherefor she humbly prays their Honours to grant her according to the tenore of his Majestys gracious Instructions a Warrant for admeasuring out to her land on the south side of Santee River in the Parish of St. James's Santee in Craven County near the Plantation of Coll. Waities.

It was the opinion of his Majestys Council that y'r consideration of y'e said Petition be postponed till tomorrow.

Page 7: Read the Petition of George Hamlin, Robt. Miller, Jo. Kinnson, Samuel Way, Mathew Beard shewing that they Labour under very great Inconveniencys for want of having a regular survey made on their several Tracts of land whereby they might be able to knew each others boundaries & present trespasses, wch other ways they apprehend they may be liable to, therefore they humbly pray their Hon'rs to take the same into consideration and to order two proper surveyors to settle the Boundaries of each Persons's tract, thereby prevent future disputes. Ordered That the said Petition do ly on the Table.

Read the Petition of Ann Masters, setting forth that Whereas y'e Petitioners husband Samuel Masters of this Province Planter by virtue of a Warrant bearing date y'e 27th of August 1736, had admeasured and laid out to him a Certain Tract of Land containing 300 acres commonly called Star Bluff, Situated in Craven County and bordering on Wacomaw River as by the plat thereof returned and now recorded in y'e Surveyor General's Office of this province may appear and whereas the said Land has been so surveyed & set apart the s'd Samuel Masters is dead, without first having obtained a Grant of the same, and whereas the Petitioner widdow of y'e said Samuel Masters has the said Tract devised to her & her Heirs by the last will & Testam't of her said deceased husband bearing date the 12th day of May 1739, she therefore prays that their Honours would take y'e premises under their Consideration and grant her the free possession of the said 400 acres of Land on Star Bluff on Wacomaw River &c. Which Petition being examined and duly Considered was Granted upon the Allegations appearing by y'e will referred to.

Page 8: Meeting of April 8th Thursday morning 1742

Read again y'e Petition of Ann Masters, mentioned in the minutes of yesterday, whereupon Ordered that his Majesty's attorney General do prepare a special fiat for y'e above mentioned Tract of 300 acres of Land at the Star Bluff in Craven County in order that a grant may pass to the said Ann Masters for the same pursuant to the prayer of her Petition.

Read the Petition of William Miles, Setting forth that he has now in this Province a Family of thirty Persons for whom he as yet hath not obtained any Lands, but being desirous to Improve and Cultivate a Settlement, prays for one thousand five hundred acres of land to be admeasured out to him, pursuant to his Majesty's Instructions, as to Family right, and that y'e s'd Warrant & grant be for land in Colleton County joining to land already possessed by the Petitioner, viz upon Domny hills near Ashepoo River. It was agreed that the consideration of ye said petition de deferred till next meeting of his Majesty's Council.

Page 9: The Petition of Jane Sincklair having according to a resolution of the Board in the minutes of Yesterday been taken into Consideration it was Ordered That a Warrant be prepared by y'e Secretary according to y'e prayer of y'e Petition and the petition....

The Petition also of William Miles was according to a minute of y'e last meeting of y'e Council reconsidered, and Ordered that it be brought before the Board when the Petitioner shall there attend in person.

Friday morning April the 9th 1742.

The Petition of William Miles was According to a Resolution at the Last meeting of Council considered, whereupon it was ranted &c. Ordered that the Secretary do prepare a warrant....

Pp. 11-12: Meeting of Saturday morning April 10th 1742

Read the Petition of Mathew [British copy has Martyn Lyons] Lyons setting forth That he came into this Province from Virginia about one Year and a half agoe with an Intention to Cultivate and Settle some of his majesty's vacant lands in this Province; that he has a Family of twelve persons but that Eleven of them are an yet not arrived in this Province, tho the Petitioner offers to be bound for their coming hither wherefore as he is desirous to settle Six hundred Acres of Land without the Township of New Windsor desires their Honours would be pleased to Grant him a Warrant for admeasuring the said 600 Acres within the said Township, at a place called Beach Island, where he has already built a House & made some improvements and has a Stock of Cattle thereon.

The Prayer of this Petition was granted as to fifty acres of Land for the Petitioner himself, and a warrant for 50 acres Ordered to issue accordingly and for an Ancouragement to the Petitioner to bring in the other Persons of his Family be came settlers in this Province it is ordered that Five hundred & fifty acres of Land lying Contiguous to the 50 Acres hereby ordered to be granted shall be reserved for the Petitioner for a twelve month from this date.

Page 17: Meeting of Monday morning the 12th day of April 1742

Read the Petition of William Sym, praying that a Warrant be granted him of Survey for four hundred and fifty acres of the adjacent land situated without the six miles adjoining upon the Township line of Williamsbourgh in Craven County. Which petition being considered was granted....

Page 24: Meeting of Wednesday morning April 28th 1742

The humble Petition of John James sheweth That about two years last past Y'r Petitioner had a Tract of About two hundred Acres of land surveyed to him by Anthony Williams, Deputy Survey'r, by virtue of special orders issue for that purpose by y'r Honors, That your Petitioner has several times made application to y'e s'd Williams, as likewise to one ... Smith who as the said Williams informed y'r Petitioner had y'r plat, but could not or any time present or either of them to deliver the same whereby your Petitioner is prevented from having a Grant. That y'r Petitioners warrant of Survey contains 400 Acres of Land which could not be fully executed on Ox Swamp in Williamsbourgh Township, the place where the said deputy ran the 200 Acres Tract. That Y'r Petitioner has in his Custody as Trustee for Samuel Delap a warrant of Survey belonging to said Delap for

[Pages 25-28 are missing in the South Carolina copy; the British copy has, as follows:] 150 acres of Land as yet unexecuted. That y'r Pet'r is Informed Y'r Hon'rs were pleased to order a special warrant of Survey to issue for One Robert Byers to resurvey a Tract of Land belonging to Rich'd Hall deceased and to Lay the s'd Byers' Familly right on the Surplus land if any be found within the said Hall lines. That Y'r Pet'r is credibly informed there are upwards of 1500 acres of land within the said Halls lines and that after the said Halls right of 500 acres, and that said Byers right of 500 acres are set apart and fixed that there will be a surplus of Land within the s'd Lines sufficient for Y'r Pet'r. Yo'r Pet'r therefore most humbly prays Y'r Hon'rs will direct that the s'd Deputy Survey'r or the s'd Smith may deliver the s'd Plat to yo'r Pet'r or return the same into the Survey'r Generals Office and that y'r Hon'rs will be pleased to order a Special Warrant of Survey for the remainder of the Land not yet run out for y'r Pet'r as also for the 150 acres of Land to Samuel Delap to be laid on the surplus land within the said Richard Halls Lines. John James. Order'd that a Copy of the above Petition be served on his Majesty's Surveyor General and that he do Enquire into and Certify to the Board the Conduct of his Deputy in the Particulars complained of in the Petition, and also whether any and what quantity of Surplus Land be contained within the lines of the said Richard Hall.

Meeting of Friday morning 4th of May 1742

Read the Petition of Eliz'a Newberry praying for the renewal of a Warrant of 150 acres of Land on Pedee river about 150 miles from Winyaw w'ch had been formerly granted to her husband and on Order to the Survey'r General to admeasure the same, but has as yet not been deliver'd her.

[South Carolina copy resumes here]

Page 29: This Petition being read, his Hon'r the Liut. Govr. shewed a letter he had received from Coll. George Pauly a deputy Survey'r acknowledging that he the said Pauly did survey 150 acres up Pedee in the Welch Tract in behalf of the said Petitioner's husband Jacob Newberry & returned y'e Plat into the Surveyor's office. The whole of the Petition being taken into Consideration Ordered that his majesty's attorney General do issue out a

Special Fiat for the said land prayer for to be conveyed to the said Elizabeth Newbery and her Heirs.

Read the Petition of John Lynder shewing that he had in the year 1737 run out a tract of 200 acres of land in Oaktree Creek w'ch being the remaining part by the Towns'p line of Purisburgh, of a Tract of 2200 acres laid out by Colonel Rycroft in the year 1732 but not granted to him and that one Albergotti has since obtain'd a grant for 50 acres of land being a part of the said Colonel Rycroft's Tract. The Petitioner therefore pray'd that in consideration of his having built a small house and planted many mulberry and other tress bearing fruit upon the said Tract of y'e 200 acres That their Honours would give him a Grant of the same. On reading which Petition and finding that y'e said John Linder had not any Family right to the whole of y'e Land prayd for, it was therefore not granted.

Pp. 43-44: Meeting of Wednesday PM the 19th day of May 1742

James St. John Esqr. survey. General of this Province according to an Order of Council of april 28th did lay before the Board the order he had sent to Mr. Peter Lane his Deputy for resurveying the Plat of land belonging to Richd. Hall of Craven County, deceased, as also Mr. Lane's answer, and the Plats resurveyed, on Mr. Hall's lines, w'ch was Ordered that a letter be forthwith sent to y'e Survey'r General to acquaint him That y'e Council are at a loss to understand the Platts he sent by Mr. Lane in y'e said resurvey untill they see the original Plat or survey given to Mr. Hall & that he lay y'e same immediately before this Board.

Pp. 44-45: Meeting of Thursday morning the 20th day of May 1742

Read the Petition of Grace Hall shewing that she had entered a Caveat at y'e Secretary's office, against one Crafton Korawen and Anthony Williams who pretended a right to land in the Township of Williamsbourgh, wherefore she humbly desires their Honours would be pleased to postpone the hearing, until Mr. William Cattell come to Town, who she says knows y't she has y'e best right to administer and is nearly concerned in y'e affair. That she being in trust for a Tract of Land in y'e Township of Williamsbourgh, and as she apprehends all Lands there are to be resurveyed, She humbly desires their Hon'rs will give her the preference if any found more than what is specified in the Plat, and grant as she has some rights not yet run out and a large Family to support. On reading this Petition it was Ordered to ly upon the Table.

A caveat having been entered by Robert Byers against any grant of survey for the lines of Richard Hall deceased in the Township of Williamsbourgh. After this was read it was Resolved That upon considering the return & resurvey made by John Lane deputy survey'r according to the direction of James St. John Esqr. Survey'r General of certain lands in the Township of Williamsbourgh claim by the representatives of Rich'd Hall containing 1418 acres of land & hearing what was alledged by the Partys entering Caveats against a Grant of 350 acres of land within the said resurvey being passd to Robt. Biers, It was the Opinion of the Board that a grant of the said 350 acres of Land the Plats whereof were returned by y'e said Peter Lane Deputy Survey'r be prepared in order to be past to y'e s'd Robt Biers in the usual manner. Ordered that a Certified Copy of this be sent to the Survey'r General also the Plat for 350 acres and they were then sent accordingly.

Pp. 45-46: Meeting of Thursday PM the 20th day of May 1742

Read the Petition of the Rev'd John Baxter setting for[th] that the Petitioner being possessed of a Warrant of Survey for 650 acres within some of y'e Townships and having one white person and five negroes in family for which he never has had any warrant of surveyed he therefore in consideration of said warrant and of y'e s'd six persons of his family prayed for a common warrant of survey for 950 acres of land within Craven County nigh to black mingo Swamp and to y'e lands now possessed by the Petitioner that is to say that the s'd Warrant or Grant be in lieu of his former warrant of land granted by Govr Broughton dated the 12th day of August 1737. The Petitioner at y'e same time begd leave to represent to their hon'rs that y'e Warrant which he now lays before them to be granted him is purely and solely for his own use and purpose. Which petition being read and Considered and also the Warrant by Gov. Broughton exhibited and read at y'e Board, tit was granted according to y'e prayer thereof....

Pp. 49-50: Meeting of Saturday PM the 22d day of May 1742

Read the Petition of Anthony Kaufman setting forth that he arrived in this Province about six years ago with his family in order to better himself but coming in with little or no money was sold servant to Coll. Vanderdussen for three years, w'ch time was expired almost three Years ago, who after that lived in lower Settlements, and is now desirous to settle in Orangeburgh. Therefore humbly prays their Honours that a Warrant be Issued for allowing him his Family right in the said Township lands and his Majesty's most gracious bounty. On reading and considering the said Petition it was Ordered that the same be reconsidered when the Petition shall next attend.

Read also the Petition of Crafton Karwon setting forth that as a Grant of Lands had formerly been issued forth to him, by the Board in Williamsburgh Township the which he is willing to certify if required, and whereas there is arisen no small difficulty as y'e Pet'r is informed with regard to y'e Grants of Lands in that Towns'p. He humbly prays their Hon'r that he may have the liberty to have a resurvey of his lands w'ch have been already granted him, so as that he may have the preference of obtaining a Special Warrant for running them same. Ordered that y'e said Petition do ly on y'e Table.

Page 51: Meeting of Tuesday PM the 25th day of May 1742

Read the Petition of Abraham Paxton setting forth that Whereas he had four Persons in Family, he prayed their Hon's would be pleased to grant him a Warrant of survey for 200 acres of Land between Mrs. Smith's plantation and Ashley river about near two miles from Charles Town that Tract being marsh land. Which petition being considered was rejected.

Read also the Petition of Rene Gegye setting forth that as he had a Family of three persons, prayed that their Hon'rs would be pleased to grant him a right for one hundred and fifty acres of marsh land behind the Work house of Charles Town. Which Petition being read and Considered was rejected.

Pp. 68-69: Meeting of Friday morning the 28th day of May 1742

Read the Petition of Henry Lockly & his wife, Jacob Rincher, George Burchard, Jacob Burchard, Anna Maria Burchard, John Togeley, Brian Burchard, Jacob Burchard, Anna Maria Longin, Anna Maria Deitchwiler, Elizabeth Warley, John Ulrich Hogen, Michael Hogen, Anna Maria Hogen, Frena Hogen, J'o Ulrich Volger, Anna Maria Volger, praying that in Consideration of their having rece'd the Kings Provision Bounty They may have a Warrant & Grants unto each of them, who are mentioned with a Lot in the Town. Which Petition being taken into Consideration, it was Ordered That the prayer thereof be Granted, viz to the three first named, and that the orphans have the land when they shall come of age.

Read the Petition of John Gaspar Gallier & Family, John Gasper Giger & family, John Snalling & Family, Abram Giger & family, Jacob Liver & family, Julius Gredig & family, Casper Gray & Family, Cunrad and Casper Cuntsler, Jo Jacob Biemen & Family, Herman Giger & Family, Eliz: Shalling & family, shewing that as they are arrived & settled in his Majesty's Township of SaxGotha ever since the year 1737 and received his majesty's most gracious Bounty of provision and warrants for lands, in SaxGotha Township but that they could not find in what Office they are, Therefore they humbly pray his Honr the Liet. Govr. and his Majesty's honble Council that they would be pleased to order that Search May be made in the proper officers for y'e s'd Warrants to prevent their future attendence and expences. Whereupon it was ordered that the Commissary do mark search in the several offices after the said warrants & y'e returned Plats and that he pay the Charges of the Grants.

Pp. 69-70: Read the Petition of Hans Jacob Reimanspergar Setting forth the Expenses he had been at in carrying several German Orphans in Carts to Sax Gotha Township and all the Sick Children into his house to nurse &c. & desiring the whole provision bounty w'ch had been alotted to them, that he may have an Allowance of so much p'r week for having maintained them, being willing to return the orphans the rest. Which Petition being read & Considered It was ordered that the said Reimansperger do accompt with the

Orphans for the sum of £71-5-0 as y'e remainder of seventeen guineas that the four Orphans who lived with him five weeks in their Sickness do pay him at the rate of twenty shill's p'r week, for the same out of the bounty money w'ch was allowed to them.

The Petition of Anthony Kaufman mentioned in the minutes of the 22d Instant and read at this Board was again Considered, praying for a Warrant for Land at the Towns'h of Orangebourgh, and also for his Majesty's provision bounty, W'ch Petition was according to y'e prayer thereof Granted and Mr. Secret'y ordered to prepare a Warrant accordingly.

Page 97: <u>Meeting of Monday PM the 5th day of July 1742</u>

Read the Petition of Thomas Elerbee setting forth that he and his family consisting of Eleven persons came from Virginia about 5 years past & settled and Cleared Lands near Pedee River and obtained a warrant for his Family right but which happened to be within the Limits of the Welsh Tract and a Convenient place to fix a Water mill, When the Welch Inhabitants came to settle above 4 years past one Daniel James persuaded the petitioner to remove peaceably from that place by the run of water and gave the Petitioner and his family liberty to Settle and Cultivate any other Vacant Land which he should find within the Limits of the Welsh Tract and did also himself get a Special Warrant for 250 acres of land which is run out for the Petitioner and returned Wherefore begs for a Grant for the same he having lived ever since thereon and now wants more land on the same Tract or adjoyning thereto to Cultivate and Settle his Family being increased to 20 and 2 persons, he having six persons lately purchased or born for which as yet he has had no warrant he therefore prays for a Warrant of Survey for laying out Three hundred Acres of Vacant land and a special warrant of survey for running out 550 acres of Vaccant Land more within the Limits of the said Welch Tract in the Lieu of his Common Warrant. Resolved that the Consideration of the said Petition be posponed untill the Petitioner appear personally before the Board.

Read the Petition of John Robertson, Commander of the Brigg Henry and Mary, setting forth That being bound on a Voyage from Antigua to Virginia he came into this Port only to Land William Boone, Esqr., and his family and relations with their goods the better for strengthen this Province that the Petitioner had no other Business here and was ready to depart, Therefore desires leave to depart and be free of the duty of Gun Powder and the Duty for Beacon and Buoys or to give him such relief as shall seem meet. Ordered that this Petition do ly on the Table.

Page 98: Read the Petition of William Boone setting forth that he with his Wife a large family of Children and a considerable number of Slaves arrived a few days agoe from Antigua on John Robinsons Brigantine with design to settle in this Province that he had been at very heavy Charges in transporting so large a family and is obliged by Articles of Agreement with the said

Captain to pay all Port Charges his Vessel may be subjected to. That Captain Robinson was bound from Antigua to Virginia and only stoped here to land the petitioner & family who is also further Obliged in case of my Extraordinary Detention to an additional Charge of Demurrage. Therefore he humbly Prays to remit the said Port Charges and Suffer Cap: Robinson to proceed in his Voyage. The council were of opinion that the said Petition Be amended by being directed to both houses of assembly.

Page 177-178: Meeting of Friday PM the 6th day of August 1742

The following Petition of John Fairchild was read. The Humble Petition of John Fairchild Sheweth That your Petitioners family consists of Eight persons for whom he has never as yet had any Warrant. Your Petitioner therefore humbly Prays your honours will be pleased to grant him a Warrant of Survey for four hundred acres of Land on the north side of Santee River before Jack's Creek....

Page 186: Meeting of Tuesday PM the 10 day of August 1742

The Petition of Mr. John Fairchild was read praying for 400 acres of land on the north side of Santee River below Jacks Creek which was accordingly granted.

Pp. 225-226: Meeting of Friday Morning the 27th day of August 1742

The humble Petition of Peter Roth of Orangeburgh sheweth That whereas some People of the said Township of Orangeburgh had some years ago undertaken to build a Mill for the benefitt of the said Township but having found it impossible to perform it in their way have now left it off, and entirely abandoned this s'd undertaking, and Whereas a Mill would be very beneficial to all the Inhabitants and much contribute to the improvement of the said Township, yo'r humble Petitioner proposes to build a Mill at his own Expences, tho' he does not expect that the Emoluments will entirely answer the Charges, but to ascertain to him the property of the said Mill to be built he humbly desires that yo'r Honours would be pleased to grant him One Acre of Land, Scituate upon Edisto River and joyning the town place of Orangeburgh being vacant land for to build the Mill upon.... Charles Town the 1st Septr 1742. Peter Roth. The Petition being Considered by his Majesty's honb'le Council was accordingly granted.

Page 229: Meeting of Tuesday Morning the 31st day of August 1742

Read the following Petition of Gabriel Manigualt [sic], Esqr., Praying that the Petitioner as Executor of Gov. Johnsons will might have a Grant past for 8000 acres of Land in Granville County.

Page 231: Meeting of Tuesday PM the 31st day of August 1742

The Humble Petition of Hugh Rose, Surveyor at Purysburgh, Sheweth that yo'r Petitioner obtained a Warrant for 50 Acres of Land in Purysburgh and a Town Lott bearing date the 16th of April 1739 as his own personal right, and w'ch yet remains unexecuted; and since w'ch time he has purchased two Slaves which are now his property for w'ch he hat taken up no Land. And Whereas by a certain Instrument in writing singed by Col. John Pury yo'r petitioner became Intitled to a right to three hundred acres of Land in the Township of Purysburgh pursuant to a power grantd to him by his Majesty for that purpose, and which writing yo'r Pet'r deliver'd to James Abercromby Esqr. his Majesty's Attorney General sometime in the year 1736 and soon after the date &signed thereof to the best of yo'r Petitioners remembrance; which said writing is lost or mislaid as yo'r Petition'r is information by the said James Abercromby. And Whereas yo'r Petitioner is desirous to Cultivate his said Family right of one hundred & fifty cares as also the said 300 acres pursuant to his Majesty's instructions to yo'r Honor, May it therefore pleas yo'r Honour to grant him a Warrant of survey for the said one hundred & fifty acres and three hundred ares on his Majesty's Bounty... Hugh Rose. Revolved that Mr. Rose's Petition & the Consideration of his acompt be deferred to a further meeting.

Page 232: Meeting of Wednesday Morning Sept. the 1st 1742

The Petition of Hugh Rose mentioned in the former minutes & the accompt he gave in were again read... it was agreed that a Warrant be granted to him for the same accordingly upon his Majesty's
Bounty and Mr. Commissary Dart was directed to defray the Charges thereof out of the Towns'p fund.

Pp. 247-248: Meeting of Tuesday Morning the 7th day of Sept. 1742

Read the following Petition of John Frasher also an attestation from the Rever'd Mr. Christian Theus[?] at Mr. Frasher's marriage with Elizabeth Remisperger...

The humble Petition of John Frasher Sheweth That your Petitioner has been arrived in this County about 18 months ago and now hapned to marry John Jacob ReimsSperger's daughter, so I humbly pray your Honours that a Warrant may be given unto me for myself & my wife- Likewise his Majesty's most gracious Provision Bounty for my Self... P. S. Please your Hon'rs that the Warrant may be made out for the Township of Saxagotha because my desire is to settle myself there. Charles Town the 7th Septr 1742. John Frasher. Resolved that a Warrant for One hundred Acres in the Township of Saxgotha be Issued forth to the said John Frasher but in consideration of his not coming from Europe but form Georgia to settle in this Country his Majesty's Bounty was not allowed the Petitioner.

Page 260: Meeting of Friday PM the 17th day of Sept. 1742

Read the Petition of Peter Delmestre... sheweth that he having a Family and 4 White people and 4 Negroes for whom he never applied for taking up his family right Prays an Ord'r for a Warr't for 400 acres in the township of Purisbourgh in Granville County. Resolv'd that the same be granted.

Read again the Petition of Gabriel Manigault Esqr. Ord'd that a Grant be prepared according to the tenure of the petition.

Read the Petition of James Brozet setting forth that he had been resident in the province about 5 years but has not taken up his family right that his family consists of 49 Persons including 42 Slaves in Consideration whereof he prays an ord'r for a warr't for 2450 acres of Land upon Chehaw River in Colleton County where he Intends w'th his said Family to settle, which being considered of was granted....

Pp. 294-295: Meeting of Wednesday PM the 6th of Octob'r 1742

Peter Negerlei w'th his wife & 4 Children as also Peter Huber w'th two Children hav'g arrived from Holland by way of Philadelphia in order to settle in this Province who having been admitted before the board took the oaths in order to their being naturalized & accordingly signed the usual Declaration and having also been sworn as to their family right, Order'd that a Warrant of three hund'd acres of Land be prepared for the s'd Peter Negerlei as his family right in Orangeburgh Township..

Order'd also that a Warrant of One hundred Acres be prepared for peter Huber, as his family right in the said Township. That both the Petitioners be Entitled to his Majesty's gracious Bounty....

Read the Petition of John Gardner praying Five hundred fifty acres of Land in behalf of himself, his wife, & 9 slaves as Family right vizt 400 acres in Amelia Township and 150 acres near the Widdow Russells in Craven County.

Page 295: Meeting of Monday [sic] Morning the 7th of Octob'r 1742

Anna Negerlei with four Children and Barbara Horger w'th One Child, having arrived from Holland by way of Philadelphia in order to settle in this Province having been brought before the board, & having swore to their Family right, Ordered that a Warrant for two hundred & fifty acres in the township of Orangeburgh be prepared for the s'd Anna Negerlei as her said right. That a Warrant be also prepared for the s'd Barbara horger for one Hund'd acres in the sd. Township of Orangeburgh as her family right and that both receive his Majesty's Gracious Bounty....

Page 305: Meeting of Saturday Morn'g the 9th of Octob'r 1742

Read the Petition of Edward Rouse who appearing swore to his Family right. Praying that in consideration of having 11 persons six whites the rest Negroes that their Hon'rs wo'd grant the Petition'r 550 acres upon Black River joyning to land called Raggs Barony. Which Petition being considered was accordingly granted....

Page 312: Meeting of Friday Morn: the 15th of Octob'r 1742

Read again the Petition of Edward Rouse and the Secretary direct'd to make out the warrant for 550 acres accordingly.

Read the Petition of Penelope Davis widow setting forth That she has four Children & that her husband was One of the poor Welsh men that was Settled on the Welsh Tract on Pedee River but not hav'g a Grant she had been turned out & the s'd Land run out for one David Lewis and praying a warrant of survey for Two hundred & fifty acres within the s'd Welsh Tract on his Majesty's Bounty in behalf of her self and her four children. Ordered That the Secretary do prepare a Warrant for 250 acres in the said Welsh Tract accordingly and that the Comissary do pay the same out of the Township Fund.

Page 313: Read the Petition of Frenetta Cast setting forth That she was a Single woman a Swiss Protestant and been in the County some time but that neither she nor her Father & Mother & 6 Children that came also here had every any Land or Warr't granted them and praying a warr't for 50 acres in the Towns'p of Purysburgh & the usual bounty. The Petition was granted.

Read the Petition of William Carey, Setting forth That he has six white people in family & lives on the Welsh Tract upon 300 acres of Land there by Consent of the welsh family's as by the Certificate hereto annex'd appears & Came from Pensilvania 10th on Intent to settle here That he hath already built a House & made other improvem't there & prays a Survey warr't for the said Tract in order to obtain a Grant. The Certificate set forth That it was by desire of the Inhabitants of the s'd Welsh Tract & signed by 14 of them he being an honest man & a peaceable good neighbour. Grant'd the 300 acres but not the bounty.

Page 316: Meeting of Saturday Morning the 16th of Octob'r 1742

Read the Petition of William Guy setting forth That he has Ten in family for w'ch he has hitherto had no Land & praying a Warrant of survey for 500 Acres of Land on the Township of New Windsor. Which Petition being read was not granted by reason of his being an Inhabitant and having other Lands in the province.

Pp. 337-338: Meeting of Tuesday afternoon the 2'd of Nov'r 1742

Read the Petition of Thomas Walleson, Setting forth That he arriv'd in this Province ab't twelve months ago with his wife & two Children: That he was desirous of settling in the Town of Saxa Gotha & Praying a warr't of survey for Land there as also his Majesty's Bounty. Ordered That the Secretary do prepare a Warrant for two hundred Acres in the said Township of Saxa Gotha, but his Majesty's Bounty was not allowed him.

Read the Petition of Michael Rorore praying for 350 Acres in the Township of Purisburgh by virtue of his family right, and also for his Majestys bounty... Ordered That the Secretary do prepare a Warrant for three hundred and fifty acres of Land in the Township of Purisburgh to the said Michael Rorore, and that the Comissary do defray the charges and pay the usual fees he having the kings bounty also granted him.

Read the Petition of Oliver Allison, Setting forth That he had obtained a Warrant for 300 acres upon his arrival in the Province abo't a Twelve month ago but on account of his bad state of health had not run out the same, and praying a warr't in exchange for the like number of acres in Queensborough Township as also his Majesty's Bounty. Which Petition being considered the Council did not think fitt to grant the same.

Pp. 352-353: Meeting of Thursday the 18th Novemb'r 1742

Read the Petition of John Jervey praying that a Warrant be Issued to him for 400 Acres of Land to be laid out upon Folly Creek in Colleton County by virtue of his Family right having eight Persons therein. The Land he Purposes to have a Grant of he says is bounded on William Cockrams Land on One side and ____ Atkins on the other side. On Considering the same It was the Opinion of his Majesty's Council that it be granted him....

Pp. 360-361: Meeting of Thursday morning the 25th day of Nov'r 1742

The humble Petition of John Cleland, Esqr., Sheweth, That the Lords Proprietors of this Province in & by their severall Grants bearing date the 15th day of Sept'r 1705 all signed by Nathaniel Johnson, James Moore & Nicholas Trott & duly recorded in the Secretary's Office, did give & grant unto the following Persons their heirs & assigns sundry Tracts of Land in Craven county vizt.

To John Perry 500 Acres bounding on the north on Wahaw River, to the East on Weenea River to the South on Edward Perrys land, and to the west on Elizabeth Elliots Land at the yearly rent of Five shillings.

To Edward Perry 500 Acres bounding to the north on John Perrys land, at y'e yearly rent of Five shillings.

To John Perry 200 Acres of Land bounding on the south on Sampeet Creek and to the East & West on Edward Perrys Land at the yearly Rent of two shillings.

To Edward Perry 100 Acres bounding to the south on Sampeet Creek, to the east & west on ____ John Perry's land and on the north on Elizabeth Elliots Land, at the yearly Rent of one shilling.

To John Perry 100 Acres of Land, bounding on the south on Sampeet Creek, To the West on John Abraham Mottes Land, to the north on Elizabeth Elliotts land, and to the east on Edward Perrys Land at the yearly Rent of one shilling.

To Elizabeth Elliot one thous'd nine hundred Acres of Land, bounding to the south on John & Edward Perry's & John Abraham Motte's their land, to the east on Edward Perrys Land, to the North on John Abraham Motte's land: and to the west on Land now laid out at the yearly Rent of nineteen shillings...

That the said Six Tracts of Land by virtue of diverse mesne assignments & conveyances re become vested in yo'r Petitioner And that your Pet'r being apprehensive that there may be a greater Quantity of acres containing with the bounds as described in the above mentioned grants, that in comprised & mentioned to be granted by the said Grants, and he being willing& Desirous if any such surplus should be found to be within the said bounds on Resurvey of the same, to pay to his Majesty such Quit Rents as ought to be paid, for the same, upon the granting of such Surplus Lands (if any) to your Petitioner his heirs & assigns. Charles Town, 25th Novem'r 1742.
Ordered that the Prayer of the said Petition be granted....

Page 369: Meeting of Wednesday Morning the 1st Decemb'r 1742

Read the Petition of James Mackpherson [McPherson] setting forth That he having 26 Persons in Family for whom he has as yet no warrant for running out land, prays that by virtue of such his Family right 500 acres may be alloted him in Granville County, St. Hellenas parish, bordering on the lands already possessed by the Petitioner, and the remaining 800 as soon as the Pet'r can find out an unoccupied Tract of Land. On Considering the said Petition it was resoldv'd that Mr. Secretary do Issue out a Warrant for 1300 acres--whereof 500 to be contiguous to the Lands already possessed by the Petitioner.

Page 370: Read the Petition of William Coram setting forth that he having Six in family for whom as yet he had no land in their right prays that 100 acres be admeasured to him in the parish of St. James's Goose Creek belonging to the Petitioner, and 200 more acres butting & bounding on the Widdow Brunstons land in the same Parish. Which being Considered was granted.....

Pp. 391-392: Meeting of Wednesday Morning the 15th Decemb'r 1742

Read the following Petition of Francis Young & James Jones setting forth That they were both Inhabitants of the Welsh Tract That Mr. Gelaspi on the 7th of Nov'r 1740 procured a War't for James Jones for running out 350 acres in his family right in South Carolina But begs that the s'd war't be exchanged for a war't amongst his old Neighbours in the Welsh Tract on the South Side of Pedee River.

Francis Young having likewise obtained a Warr't for 700 Acres of Land by the s'd Gelaspi humbly Begs his Hon'r to Exchange the said Warrant for another Warrant to be run out for him on the Vacant Land on the South Side of Pedee River in the Welsh Tract that they might continue to live amongst their Old Neighbours. The said Petitions being duly Considered Resolved That the Prayer of their Petitions be granted whenever they shall send hither, or produce a Certificate from some Magistrate living with the said Welsh Tract that the allegations exhibited in their said Petitions are just and that they are desirous that the said Petitioners should return to live among them.

Pp. 410-412: Meeting of Friday PM the 14th day of Janry 1742/43

The humble Petition of Thomas McCree, James McNeely, Alexander McCree and William dobbin sheweth that your Petitioners arrived into this Province sometime in the year 1736 with purpose to settle some of his Majestys Townships Encouraged thereto by the bounty given to those Protestants as Settled therein That your Petitioners obtained warrants of survey to run Land in proportion to their respective family rights in the Township of Williamsburgh viz. The said Thomas McCree 650 acres, James McNeely 600 Acres, Alexander McCree 150 Acres, and William Dobbin 250 Acres, that in pursuance of the said Warrants your Petitioners applyed to Anthony Williams Deputy Surveyor to run the lands assigned to them who accordingly directed your Petitioners to settle on the Lands, whereon they now severally reside and who Informed your Petitioners at the same time that whither that Land was Vacant or run out by a Common Warrant he had sufficient authority to settle them thereon by virtue of a Letter form the Honble Thomas Broughton Esquire, Then Lieut. Gov'r to him directed to that purpose.

That your Petitioners accordingly settled on the said lands under the Authority of the said Deputys directions Expecting that he would from time to time Survey the same for your Petitioners but under some pretence or other the said Deputy delayed Executing the said Warrants.

That sometime after your Petitioners had considerably Improved their respective Tracts of land, that they were Informed that the said Land belonged to James Akins Esqr. and soon after had warning given them to withdraw, which so alarmed and intimidated some of your Petitioners that they submitted, only Thomas McCree who believed his right good was sued in an

Action of Trespass at the sute of the said Mr. Akkins and Cost in Considerable damage which would have reduced the said Mccree and his family to great want and misery, had not your Honours in your great goodness paid the Costs of Suit and Damages.

That there are now no good and fertile lands in the said Township vacant, and your Petitioners having some reason to hope your Honours purpose to purchase a quantity of land in the said Township for the use of your Petitioners, Your Petitioners therefore most humbly take leave to represent to your Honours the great loss and almost insurmountable difficulties that will attend their removale from their present dwellings and clearing new Ground. Some of your Petitioners are old and all poor exhausted in spirits and in pursue and therefore unable to undergo the fatigue and Charge. That your Petitioners beleive the said James Aikins Esqr. will dispose of the Considerable value (exclusive of the Improvements) in Compassion to your Petitioners Circumstances.... October 18th 1740. Agreed that the said Petition be Considered tomorrow.

Page 414: Meeting of Tuesday Morning the 18th January 1742/43

Read the Petition of Ann Rothmahler... shewing that Robert Rothmahler obtained from the Honble Thomas Broughton Esqr., late Lieut. Gov'r of this Province, a Warrant for 300 acres of land in Craven county. That pursuant to the said Warrant there was a Tract of 400 Acres of Land laid out to the said Robert Rothmahler in Craven County afors'd but before the said Robert Rothmahler had obtained a Grant for the same he dyed without making any Disposition of the same either by his Last Will and Testament or otherwise. Wherefore the said Pet'r humbly prays that a Grant of the said 400 acres of land may be passed to her in Trust for the several Children of the said Robt Rothmahler. Ordered that the prayer of the Petition be granted....

Pp. 414-415: The Petition of George Hunter humbly sheweth That your Petitioner is appointed as an Attorney by Frederick French Esqr. of Dublin and thereupon thinks himself obliged to act in relation to his Lands in this Province as much as may be to his Interest Your Petitioner by Letters from said French understands that James St. John Esq'r. Surveyor General Informed the said French /heir at law to Col. Alexander French late of this Province deceased/ that over and above the lands held by his Brothers Patent, he was very well Intitled to 500 and odd acres in Granvil County which was worth one hundred pounds Sterling That in pursuance of Mr. Frenches desire application was made to the said St. John who answered he knows nothing about the Land &C Since which time your Petitioner on good reasons believes that the said St. John has run out the same Tract of Land by his family warrant the Plat whereof with a grant annexed now being in the Secretarys Office to be passed against the passing thereof your Petitioners Entered a Caveat on the 15th day of Decem'r last Your Petitioner therefore Prays that your Honours will order a warrant of Survey directed to the said James St.

John for the Survey thereof that a grant thereunto may pass to the said Frederick French Esquire.... George Hunter. Janry 13th 1742/3 Charles Town. Which being read, Ordered that a Copy of said Petition be sent to Mr. St. John and that the Clerk of this Board acquaint Mr. St. John that his Honr. the Lieut. Gov. and council have appointed Thursday morning for the hearing the Claim of the said Mr. French, Mr. George Hunter the Petitioner having Entered a Caveat.

Pp. 415-416: The Petition of Joseph Edward Flower Sheweth That your Petitioner has been an Inhabitant in Beaufort Town on Port Royal Island above Eight years past at which time lay many vacant Lotts unimproved but no opportunity then of getting his Majestys Grants for any. That your Petitioner having settled here, Did then fence & build several houses on two vacant Lotts known in the grant plat of said Town by the numbers (337) and (338) and a presumption of Obtaining the preference of a grant for them when it should be his Majestys pleasure to give directions for granting them away and have been adding to the building on the said Lots Ever since first settling of them. Your Petitioner therefore humbly begs that your Honours will Consider the premises and grant them a warrant directing his Majestys Surveyor General to Survey and lay out the afores'd Lotts... Jos: Edw'd Flower. Beaufort, Port Royal, Jan'ry 1st 1742/3.

Page 421: Meeting of Tuesday PM the 18th day of January 1742/43

Alexander Hall humbly sheweth and declareth That I the Exhibitor and writer hereof have taken up a Residence in this Province in the Township of Emelia or Saxagotha I cannot be positive which and have resided thereupon vaccant land lying between the Plantation of Mr. George Haige, Justice of the Peace & the plantation of One Daniel Cydar, both on the west and east granted contiguous to the River Santee southward near a twelve month preceding this time and have built an house and raised some provisions by the advice of some men of Note in this Province, and am certanly informed that the Right Honble the Gov'r and council of this Province have some years preceding this Enacted and determined in Council for the Encouragement and support of any person or persons that shall take up a habitation in the uppermost and remote parts of this Province that every such person persons or family shall of the Governm't have 50 acres of unmanured land Some money & Instruments of Tillage or Plantation tools a piece and for every one such Individual gratis on all Considerations during the time of his or their abode in the place taken up... Alexander Hall. Ordered that 50 acres of land be granted him in Emelia Township that the Comissary furnish him with 10 bushels of Corn an Axe and how and that he defray all Charges relating to his Petition and Grant.

Page 422: Read the following Petition of Joackim Ballis... that he came from Switzerland to settle here that he and his family were Servants to the Honble. John Colleton, Esqr., and that having been sometime out of his servitude is now desirous to have his family right of land in Orangeburgh his family consists of himself, wife and three children and one man servant for whom he prayeth he may also have the usual bounty... Joachim Ballis (X).

Decem'r 2d 1742. Joackim Ballis the Petitioner declareth before me upon oath that he hath six persons in family for whom he never has received any Land or bounty. J. Colleton. Ordered that the said Petition do lye on the table untill his family right can be proved before the Board.

Page 441: Meeting of Wednesday PM the 19th day of Janry 1742/43

The humble Petition of John Delagage most humbly sheweth that the said poor Petitioner being an Inhabitant of Purrsyburgh and being Informed that there were a Parcel of good Land without the Lines of the said Township the 1st day of July 1737 the late Governour Broughton was pleased to grant him a Common warrant for admeasured and laying out to him two hundred and fifty acres of the said good Land but before the warrant came to hand the said Good land was run out to other persons and now your Honours poor petitioner most humbly beggs that your Honours will be pleased to exchange that common warrant for a Township warrant that he may lay out the same on the vacant land within the Township of Purrysburgh... John Delagagge. Ordered that the prayer of the above Petitioner be granted.

Page 444: Meeting of Thursday morning the 20th day of January 1742/43

The Humble Petition of John Alston of Craven county, Planter, sheweth That your Petitioner by virtue of diverse mesne conveyances is seized and possessed of a certain Tract of land derived from and under Landgrave Daniels Patent on Waccamaw Neck in Craven County afores'd and butting easterly on the sea & westerly on Waccamaw River That your Petitioner is apprehensive that within the boundary Lines of the said Tract there may be contained a great quantity of land than is specified in his said conveyance and willing to become tennant to his Majesty for the same. Your Petitioner therefore humbly prays your Hon'rs that on Order may Issue to his Majestys Surveyor Genl to give Directions for the resurveying of his Lands to the Intent that if there shall be found a greater quantity within his lines than is mentioned with in his conveyance the same may be granted to him upon the same quit rents as are reserved on the said Landgrave daniels Patent... T. Pinckney for Alston. And upon reading and Considering whereof it is ordered that James St. John Esq'r Surveyor General by himself or any of his Lawfull Deputys cause the said Land of said John Allston.... to be resurveyed....

Page 445: Mr. George Hunter who Exhibited a Petition to this board as mentioned int he minutes of Tuesday the 18th Instant attended the council together with Hugh Rose the Deputy Surveyor of the land in Question between Mr. French and Mr. St. John as mentioned in the same Petition when the Letter of Attorney to the said George Hunter from Frederick French attested by Richard Prest, Notary Publick, was read dated at Dublin Anno

Domini 1741. At the same time, Mr. St. John Surveyor General to whom according to order in the said minutes of the 18th Instant a Copy of the said minutes & petition were sent, Returned to the board the following verbal message viz: That he did not care to concern himself any further in the affair that if the Gov'r thought proper to grant a warrant to Mr. Hunter in behalf of Mr. French he was well satisfied. Thereupon on considering the same the Prayer of Mr. Hunter's Petition was granted.

Page 448: Meeting of Friday morning the 21st day of Janry 1742/43

The Petition of Jacob Bonet Humbly Sheweth That your Petitioner is desirous to have a Town Lot in Beaufort. Your Petitioner therefore humbly prays a grant of a warrant for a Lot No. (203) whereon he has built a house in the aforesaid Town.... Which Petition being read and considered was granted.

Upon considering the Petition of Joseph Edward Flower Exhibited at this Board on the 18th Instant
was ordered by his Majestys Council that the prayer of the said Petition be not granted untill the heirs of the late John Woodward Esqr. to whom the said Lots of land were Ordered consent thereto.

Page 449: Meeting of Saturday morning the 22d day of Janry 1742/43

The humble Petition of John Phipps sheweth That your Petitioner having Eight persons in his family for whom as yet has he not Claimed any family right Prays your Honors to allow him a warrant to be issued for admeasuring 400 acres of vacant land lying on the north side of Santee River over against Mr. Welchhausen adjoining to land already possesd by your Petitioner near Murrays Ferry, Craven county. Janry 21 1742/43. John Phipps.

Pp. 449-450: The Humble Petition of Mary Bedon wife of Stephen Bedon surviving daughter of Danl. Callahan Senr. decd and also sister to Danl Callahan Junr. likewise dec'd as supposed. Sheweth That your Petitioners said Father in his lifetime had duly survey'd to him on 21st of Septr 1717 One Town Lot in the Town of Beaufort known by the number (100) and certified by Francis Yonge Esqr. late Surveyor Gen'l to the Lords Proprietors. That your Petrs said Brother had also at the same time a Lot survey'd to him known by the number (101) Certified in like manner That before grants could be obtained for the said Lots the land office was shut up by the said Lords Proprietors. That the said Surveyor Generals Certificates for the said Lots were burnt in the late dreadfull fire in Charles Town but your Petition is ready if requested by your Honours to make proof of there having been such certificates in your Petitioners custody. That your Petitioners said father dyed in the 1718 leaving behind him one son (the above named David [sic]) and another Daughter besides your Petitioner. That your Petitioners Father by his last will now in record in the Secretarys office bequeathed the said Two Lotts in the words following viz. I give and bequeath unto my Loving son Daniel

Callahan & his heirs and assigns forever Two Lotts int he Town of Beaufort upon Prot Royal Island which also in default of Issue are to revert to my two daughters above named their heirs or assigns. That your Petitioners Brother went off this Province in the year 1718 also about a month before his Fathers death and according to advice from the late Mr. Speaker Lloyd who undertook to Enquire after him in England (which Letters were also burnt in the said fire) he sailed up the Mediterranean the said year on a Vessle belonging to Mr. Jeffreis of Bristol which Vessel was never heard of after. And that your Petitioners said sister die din the year 1732. Your Petitioner therefore humbly Prays (as she is Informed your Honors are about passing grants of the Town Lotts in Beaufort) that Your Honours will be pleased to order grants of the said two Lotts to be passed to your Petitioner. Mary Bedon. Whereupon it appearing that the allegations Exhibited in the said Petition were true, the Prayer thereof was granted.

Pp. 455-456: Meeting of Wednesday morning Janry the 26th 1742/43

The Petition of Samuel Sorency Humbly Sheweth That your Petitioner at his first Arrival into this Province obtained a warrant for 100 acres of land to be laid out in the Welsh Tract whereon I now live, That your Petitioner hath since two Children come from Pensilvania to this place which I have made oath of before William James, Esqr., who Informes that it will not do without my proving my rights in the Council Chamber but as I am but low in the world and live at so great a distance from Charles Town and not having a horse to ride nor money to bear my Expences and the Bearer Thomas Bowen can prove if need by that I have such Children, Your Petitioner therefore humbly prays your Hon. to take my Case into Consideration and grant me a warrant for 100 acres of his Majestys land to be laid out in the Welsh tract... Samuel Sorency. The above said Samuel James swore to his family right before William ares Esqr. one of his Majestys Justices assigned to keep the peace in Craven County in the Province aforesaid, The prayer of which said Petition was granted....

The Humble Petition of Daniel McDaniel Sheweth that your Petitioner humbly Prayeth that your Hon. and Honours will grant me a warrant of one hundred acres that is for me and my Wife to be laid in the Welsh Tract for which Encouragem't your Honours have been pleased to rant for Welsh and Pensilvanians have transported my self into South Carolina... Daniel McDaniel. The above mentioned Daniel McDaniel swore to his family Right before Alexander Gordon, Esqr., Clerk of his Majestys Council. The Prayer of said Petition was granted.

Pp. 456-458: Read also the Petition of several other Inhabitants of the Welsh Tract...

That we have left Pensilvania and have transported ourselves over to this Province by the Encouragement given to Settle this afores'd Tract of land but as some of us had our lands run out and the Plats put in the Surveyor Generals Office four years ago and as well are so poor that we can't get money to pay the charge of surveying and granting Has discouraged many from coming over and we are afraid the discouragement being so great we not being sure of our grants by reason of our Poverty that some that has come over will return from us again So we your Humble Petitioners hope your Honour and Honours will take it into your serious Consideration what satisfaction it is to Every man to have his titles to lands secure....

Philip James
Abel James
Thomas Evans
Philip Douglas
Nicholas Roger
John Evans
David Harry
David Lewis
Willm. Kerby
Thomas Mosses
William Terrell
Mary Evans
John Jones
Walter Dowen
Abel Evans
Nathanl. Evans
David James
William Jones
Peter Roblyn
Jeremiah Rowell
Creen Vaughan
John Evans
Daniel Devonald
Simon Parson
John Carter
Thomas Evans
Saml Surancy
Griffith John
Danl Honahorn
Tobe Edward

Whereupon it having been represented to his Honr. the Lt. Govr. in Council that several familys of Welch that had intended to become settlers in the whole tract on Peedee River in this Province have as it was apprehended been prevented from coming into this Province by the dangers arising from the present War with Spain and that by the Advice recd. from Pensilvania several of the said Welch familys were Expected to arrive here the next year, but as the time for reserving the Welsh Tract would expire in the month of August next it was prayed that the said Term might be further Enlarged, the same was considered and it was ordered by the Lt. Gov. that the said Term be Enlarged for two years from the Expiration of the said present term... and upon reading and considering the Petition of Philip James, Abel James, Thos Joans and other settlers... it was the opinion of the Board that they had desired only the lands to be reserved for a term to them which was accordingly done and which term had been further Enlarged for their benefit but not to have their surveys of land carryed through the offices at the Publick Expence that being only for such Welsh as should come from the Principality of Wales... it was the opinion of the Board and so ordered that for the first 20 Barrells of good and merchantable white flower of 200 weight neat each which shall be made in the said Tract and brought to the markets in Chas. Town there shall be paid to the makers thereof upon proof of its being bone fide the produce of the said Tract a bounty of £5 currency for each Barrell.

Page 459: Meeting of Thursday Morning the 27th day of Janry 1742/43

Read and considered the Petition of Joakim Baltis Exhibited to this Board on the 28th of this Instant January and the Allegations thereof being proved by the oaths. The Honble John Colleton Esquire/ the prayer thereof was granted.

Page 481: Meeting of Wednesday Morning the 16th day of February 1742/43

Read the Petition of Dr. John Martine shewing that he hath hitherto taken up no Land and being desirous to Cultivate & Settle 1000 acres of Land pursuant to his Majestys Instructions to your Honours for That purpose. Prays Their Honours to grant him a warrant of Survey for the said 100 acres of Land in Tract or Tracts on or near Goose Creek, in the Parish of St. James Goose Creek and bounding on Captain Hugh Granges Land in the afs'd Province, Which Petition being considered the prayer thereof was granted.

The Petition of Wm. Lyford sheweth That your Petitioner has been an Inhabitant in Beaufort Town on Port Royal Island above Eleven Years with my family w'ch time lay many unimproved Lotts but no opportunity then of getting his Majestys Grant... did build on two vacant lots, numbers three hundred fifteen and three hundred sixteen. Beaufort Town, January the 11th 1742/3. William Lyford. Which being read and Considered the prayer of the Petitioner was Granted.

Page 482: Read the Petition of Captain David Cuttler Braddock most humbly sheweth That your Petitioner had a mind to settle in Beaufort Town in Port Royal Island. I did purchase a Lot of Mr. James Hustane who has made Emprovements on the said Lott known in the Grand Plott of the said Town by the number Three hundred and fourteen on a presumption of obtaining the preference of a Grant for it... Beaufort Town, January the 15th 1742/3. David Cuttler Braddock. On considering the said petition it appeared that the said Lot prayed for had been granted in the Year 1718 to one Thomas Domingo.

Page 483: Read the Petition of Benjamin Lloyd Sheweth That your Petitioner hat been a liver in the Town of Beaufort upwards of Nine Years as The Lott Number (29) in the Said Town Lays Vacant He most humbly prays your Honours would be pleased to Grant him a warrant for the Survey of the Same... Ben Lloyd. Which being read and Considered it appear That in the Year 1717 July 29th It was Surveyed by Andrew Polevan.

Page 485: Meeting of 15th Feb'ry 1742/3

Read the Petition of Andrew Waltzer and his wife Barbara with Two Children John and Martin Sheweth That your Petitioners having been arrived in this province some time ago in Captain _____ and lived with Doct'r Holzendorf upon his Plantation but are waiting now to take up Lands to become our own Therefore we humbly pray your Honours that a warrant may be given for 200 acres and admeasured in the Township of Pourrisburgh Likewise we humbly address our Selves to Your Honours That his Majesty's most Gracious Provision may be allowed to us for the better Emprovement of the said Land. Andras Walser, his wife Barbara with 2 Children John and Martin. Which petition being considered and he having produced certificate of his having been a Neufchatel in Swizerland Engaged to Serve Colonel Purry for four Years in Carolina in Quality of Servants and That in the said Quality They did serve first in Carolina before They went to Georgia the Prayer of his Petition both with regard to the Land and his Majestys Bounty was granted.

Pp. 485-486: Read also the Petition of John Harkey praying for fifty acres of Land and a Lott in Purrisburgh to be admeasured to him by virtue of his family right and also his Majestys Bounty and having produced his certificate the prayer of the said petition was also granted.

Pp. 511-512: Meeting of Friday Morning the 18th February 1742/3

Read the Petition of Leonard Rochler and Catherina his wife praying for 100 acres of Land in the Township of Orangeburgh by virtue of his Family right w'ch Petition being considered and the petitioner having proved their right. It was agreed that the Petition be granted and that they do received his Majestys bounty.

Read the Petition of Ezechiel Stoll and his wife with two children praying for Land by virtue of his Family right in Orangeburgh Township which Petition being considered and the Partys having proved their rights upon oath.... The prayer of the Petition was granted and also his Majestys bounty.

Read the Petition of Anna Engel Baber shewing that she obtained her lands pursuant to her family right in the Townsh'p of Orangeburgh but as her family is increas'd to five persons is Informed she is intitled to a Cow and a Calf and a hog and prays their Hon'rs to grant her the same. Which petition being considered the same was rejected not being intitled to any other bounty than what she hath already received.

Page 513: Read the Petition of John Baker shewing That he hath a family of Six persons in this Province for w'ch he hath hitherto take up no Land prays Three hun'd acres on Santee River near the Sea. w'ch Petition being considered that the party having proved his right the prayer thereof was granted.

Page 17: Meeting of 26th February 1742/3

Read the Petition of Richard Spencer shewing that he has 14 people in family for whom as yet he hath not obtained the grant of any Lands, and being desirous to Cultivate a tract of Land on Combee River of 700 acres in St. Bartholom's Parish within two miles of the said River not far from Mr. Goddin's plantation prayed that a Warrant might be issued for admeasuring the Same. The Petitioner having proved the allegations in this Petition, the prayer thereof was granted and y'e Secretary Ordered to prepare a Warrant accordingly.

Page 33: Meeting of 2d March 1742/3

Read the Petition of Jacob Spouler praying for a Warrant to be issued to him for admeasuring land in Saxegotha Township as the Family right of three Children born in this Province and also for his Majestys most gracious bounty, which Petition being considered, and he having proved his family right for two Children, one hundred acres, were accordingly granted him in the said Township of Saxgotha and the Secretary ordered to prepare a warrant accordingly.

Pp. 43-44: Meeting of 4th March 1742/3

The Petition of Thomas McCree, James McNeely, Alex'r McCree, and William Dobbin as mentioned in the minutes of the 14 Jan'ry was read again at this Board, whereupon James Aiken Esq'r Complained of, in the said petition was sent for, who attending accordingly, his Hon'r the Lieu't Gov'r and the members of his majesty's Council Expostulated with the said Gentleman, concerning the hard Case of the Petitioners, that he may amicably be induced to give a reasonable satisfaction to them, the Suffering Petitioners as to permit particularly, that at least Thomas McCree shall possess the Lands in dispute, they which, he has already Cultivated, and improved for his own use; After several replys of Mr. Aiken about the nature of his right, it was resolved, that he take the matter into further Consideration and return an answer some time to morrow to this Board.

Page 169: Meeting of 16th April 1743

Read the Petition of Capt. Frederick Dejean Humbly Shewing That the Pet'r by virtue of a family right as a forreign Protestant, residenter in this Province was possessed of two Tracts of land consisting of 600 acres Each, in the Township of Purisbourgh, but for which, he never obtained a grant but w'ch land, has by the Inundations of the river Savannah, been overflowed, so as not to admit of Culture, or to build upon, as this, has occasioned the loss of three different Crops of grain to the Peti'r he humbly prayed their Hon'rs to order a Grant and a Warrant for admeasuring to him 600 acres in lieu of the land w'ch has been overflowed, near to Mr. Kenah's Land, at a place called

Altamaha, granted to Mr. Robert Johnson in Granville County. April 26, 1743. Ordered, That Mr. Secretary Search in his office, fit here be any Grant of the said land and report the same at the next meeting of the Council.

Pp. 179-180: Meeting of 28th April 1743

Read the Petition of William James shewing That whereas the late Mr. Daniel James on the Encouragement given by this Board, for building Grist mills, in the Welch Tract, received one hundred pounds with intent to build one of the said Mills, the which would have entitled him to the like Sum, when perfected, viz within two years, That the Pet'r has since the death of the s'd Daniel James, built a Compleat Grist mill on the said Tract in expectation of receiving £200 before mentioned, tho not within the time limited. That the Charge of building the said Mill has been more than was expected, the Pet'r therefor pay's that the Hon'ble Board would take his case into Consideration, and order him what Encouragem't they should Judge meet. Whereupon it appearing that the said Daniel James, having died before the time, in w'ch he Contracted to make the said Mill was expired, and without having finished the Same or done any thing towards effecting thereof, and that the Petitioner who is guardian of his Children, did in Compliance with the foresaid Contract, compleat y'e same after the sd. Daniel James's death, he therefore pray'd to have liberty to take up the bond given by Daniel James on receiving the first hundred pounds towards compleating the said Mill, and the remaining £100 as the Encouragement Stipulated, in the minutes of Council of y'e 7th July 1739, and which was ordered accordingly and an order drawn on the Treas'r for £100 payable to William James.

Pp. 204-205: Meeting of 7th May 1743

Read the Petition of Capt. James Stewart shewing that as he hat an increase of Eleven black servants in his Family for which hither to he has not had any land assigned him, prays that a warrant be Issued for admeasuring to him 550 Acres, at 4 holes Swamp near the division line between Goose reek, and Dorchest'r parishes. The Said Petition being Considered, and the Petitioner having swore to have family right, the prayer thereof was granted, and the Secretary Ordered to prepare a Warrant for admeasuring the same.

Read the Petition of David Montague in behalf of his Father in law Mr. Patrick MackCay shewing that the latter had obtained a Warrant for 2600 Acres of land, near the Six mile line, at Purisburgh, that the petitioner had begun, but was obliged to brake of y'e Survey in the time of the alarm and not being Able to have a Surveyor to lay out the same according to the time limited, in the said warrant prayed for a fresh warrant to be issued. Mr. Montague appearing and an authentic Copy of the said warrant being produced under y'e hand of Mr. St. John, Survey'r General, the pray'r of the Petitioner was accordingly ordered to be granted, when he Petitioner should deliver up, and make a Surrender of his original Warrant.

Page 217: Meeting of 13th May 1743

Captain William Scott appeared before his Hon'r the Lieu't Gov'r with his title to a Lot in that part of Beaufort Town, w'ch is reserved to his Majesty's house, and offered to Surrender of Convey the same to his Majesty, upon having a grant for the Lot No. 135, or Lot 169 granted to him.

Pp. 217-218: Read the Petition of Richard Woodward the only surviving son of John Woodward the Elder deceased shewing that the petitioners said Brother John Woodward obtained an order from their Honors and a Fiat for a Grant from his Majesty's attorney General, on the 20th day of April 1741 for the five following Lots in Beaufort Town, Port royal, viz: No. 337, 338, 340, & 341, also the Lot 336, which being Considered, it was the opinion of his Majesty's Council, that a Warrant do issue for Surveying the same, to the said Richard woodward.

Ordered that a Warrant be Issued directing the Survey'r General to Survey in the Town of Beaufort Port Royal the Lots no: 317, 318, 321, & 322 to the Reverend Lewis Jones, Rector of the Parish of St. Helena and his Successors, Rectors of the said Parish, for the time being, for the use of y'e Church and Church yard, of the said Parish.

Read the Petition of William Orr praying for the lots in Beaufort Town, No. 323 & 324 also the Lot 320. Ordered That the prayer of the Petition be granted, and That a warrant be Issued to the Survey'r General for admeasuring the Lots 323 & 329 for the use of the meeting house and burying Ground, and 320, for the use of the minister thereof, and his Successors in the said meeting house for the time being.

Pp. 218-219: Read the Petition of Robert Williams shewing That the Petitioner arrivd in this Province in the month of Jan'ry with nineteen White persons in family including Servants and brought a Considerable Cargo to Beaufort Port Royal where intending to Settle, humbly prays a Warrant for two lots to be granted him there viz No. 307 & 308, that he may be able to build & improve y's sd Lotts. Upon Considering the same it was Ordered That the pray'r of the said Petition be granted, and that a Warrant for Surveying the Same be Issued accordingly.

Page 219: Read the Petition of Thomas Beswicke praying for the Lotts No. 171 & 172 in Beaufort Town. The Pray'r of which Petition was granted and a Warrant ordered to be Issued for Surveying the said Two Lots to Thomas Beswick.

Read the Petition of Allan Macklane praying for the lot 347 in Beaufort Town. The Pray'r of the said Petition was granted and a Warrant ordered to be Issued for Surveying the same to y'e s'd Allan Macklane.

Read the Petition of Thomas Burton praying for the lot in Beaufort Town, No. 309. The Prayer of the said Petition was granted and a Warrant ordered to be Issued for admeasuring lot 309 to him Accordingly.

Page 220: Meeting of 14th May 1743

Read the Petition of Nicholas Haynes praying to have a Grant to the Lotts in Beaufort Town No. 167 & 169, but those lots being in the reserved lands for his Majesty's use, It was Ordered, that in stead of those lots, the lots No. 166 & 167 in the other part called the new Town be granted to him, and that a Warrant do Issue accordingly.

Page 233: Meeting of 8th June 1743

Read the Petition of Jacob Young humbly shewing That he hath a family of four persons for whom he as yet has not any lands assigned him, as Family Right therefore prays That a warrant be Issued for admeasuring to him 200 acres of land on Santee River, in Berkely County in the Township of the Congrees, where he intends to settle with his Family and to Cultivate y'e said Land. The Petitioner having proved his Family right before the Board, the prayer thereof was granted and the Secret'ry ordered to Issue a Warrant for admeasuring 200 acres accordingly.

Page 237: Meeting of 10th June 1743

Jacob Young who exhibited a Petition to this Board last Wednesday prayed that he be permitted to amend the said Petition in order to obtain his Majesty's bounty, in Consideration that he is to reside in the Congree Township, Who being called upon, was desired to produce a certificate from Doctor Moultrie with whom he had lived as a servant, of his service.

Jacob Young according to a minute of this morning, brought a Certificate from Doctor Moultrie, of his having served the said Gentleman three years in this Province, the which expired last April, whereupon the Petitioner having been Swore that he intends forthwith to go and reside at the said Township of the Congrees, it was the opinion of his Majesty's Council that he be allowed his Majesty's bounty for himself, his wife, and two children under 12 years of age.

Pp. 284-285: Meeting of 20th August 1743

Read the following Petition of James Maxwell of Goose-creek... That the Petitioner hath 20 Persons in family for whom he has not yet had any land granted unto him, and the peti'r being desirous to become his Majesty's Tennant within this Province humbly prays y'r Hon'rs to grant him a warrant directed to his Majesty's Survey'r General to admeasure or cause to be admeasured and laid out to y'r Petitioner one thousand acres of land in this

Province, situate lying and being between the Congress and a Place called Seluda and that your Peti'r may in due time have a Grant for the same... James Maxwell. The Petitioner having appeared before his Hon'r the Lie't Gov'r and council and proved the allegations of his Petition upon oath, the said tract of Land was accordingly granted him and the Secretary ordered to prepare a Warrant for y'e Same.

Page 334: Meeting of 9th September 1743

Read the Petition of John Hunt praying that in Consideration of having 14 Persons in Family for whom he as yet has not received any land, but being desirous to Cultivate 700 acres in St. Bartholomew's Parish, Colleton County near to certain lands possessed already by y'r Petit'r and the rest where he can find vacant land &c. Which Petition being Considered and the Petitioner having upon oath proved his Family right the 300 acres mentioned in the s'd county and parish were Granted.

Page 339: Meeting of 15th September 1743

Read the Petition of John Luke shewing That the Peti'r arrived from Philadelphia in this Province, wife a wife and Six children, in order to settle in the Welch Tract, and therefore prays that y'r Honours would be pleased to grant him a Warrant for 400 acres of land, and his Majesty's most gracious Bounty. The Peti'r appearing before the Board & Swearing to his s'd family right, their Hon'rs in Consideration of his numerous family of Children ordered That the said 400 acres be granted, and the Fees of survey, petition, grant & c be defrayed out of the moneys of the Township fund and that the Secret'ry prepare a Warrant for the said Land accordingly.

Pp. 339-340: Read the Petition of George Livingstone shewing That the Peti'r is possessed in his own right of a tract of 1500 acres of land on Port Royal Island and is very much interested in the success of the Settlements of the Souther parts of this Province and that having no Lot in Beaufort Town prays that Lot 346 may be given him under such Rents, Covenants and restrictions as are Usual in the Grants of y'e s'd Town lots, Etc. Ordered that this Petition do ly on y'e Table.

Pp. 342-343: Meeting of 5th October 1743

Read the Petition of Charles Radcliffe shewing that the Peti'r is an Inhabitant of Fredericksbourgh, having an Intent to build a Water mill as well for the well settling of the Place &c as for Public utility. Therefore prays that the same encouragem't and bounty may be granted him by their Honors as is given to others who Contrive and make such mills. The above Petition being Considered It was agreed by his Majesty's Council, that Twenty pounds Currency be advanced him by the Commissary in Part, and one hundred pounds more on his compleating the said mill, and that he give security to return the said twenty pounds in case within two years after the present date, the said mill is not compleated.

Read the Petition of Mark Cattertell humbly shewing That he having four in Family for whom he has not had any lands prays that Their Hon's would grant him 200 acres of Land and a Town lot as also the bounty allowed to such as settle in y'e said Township. Which Petition being Considered, and the Petitioner having proved his Family right, the land & Lot were granted, and the Secret'ry ordered the prepare a Warrant accordingly.

Pp. 343-344: Read the Petition of Thomas Bryan humbly shewing That the Petit'r having two Persons in Family for whom he has not had any Lands assigned him, and being desirous to Settle in the Wateree Township, viz Fredericksbourgh, humbly prays their Hon'rs would grant him 100 acres and the bounty allowed to Such as Settle in the said Township. The Petitioner appearing before the Board and proving his Family right, It was ordered that a Warrant be Issue for the land prayd for, that he be allowed a Town lot and the charge of his, as well as Mark Cattertells Petitions, Warrants Grants &c be defrayed them out of the Township fund.

Pp. 349-350: Meeting of 8th October 1743

Read the Memorial of the Executor of the last will & Testament of John Girardeau deceased shewing that The memorialist had obtained his Majestys Grants for two Tracts of Land in Granville County in the names of Richard Girardeau, James, and Isaac Girardeau, the three youngest sons. That the said Grants being in possession of the memorialist were by some accident separated from the Plats, and are either lost or mislaid. That as the said Grants are upon record in the Secret'rys office, he prays the Secretary may be directed to make authentic copies of y'e said Grants, that they may be annexed to the Plats in lieu of the original Grants. Signed Wm Bull. Ordered That y'e said Petition be considered on another occasion.

Pp. 360-361: Meeting of 11th October 1743

Read the Petition of John Granget, who lately arrived in this Province with his daughter, who having married Mary Burchard one of the Swiss orphans lately arrived, intends to settle in Saxgotha and therefore prays that his Majesty's bounty of one Years provision, be granted him, and 150 acres of land in the said Township and a Town lot. The Petitioner having proved his Family right, the 150 acres of Land and the Town lot prayed for and all the charges of his Petition, Warrant & C was ordered to be allowed him by y'e Commissary out of the Township fund.

Page 362: Meeting of 12th October 1743

Read again the memorial of the executor of y'e last will and testam't of John Girardeau, the prayer of the petition was granted and the Secret'ry ordered to make out authentic copies accordingly.

Reconsidered the Petition of John Granget mentioned in the minutes of yesterday and due Information being had the said Petitioner did originally before his leaving Europe to settle in this Province and having bee landed in Pensilvania by the Conveyance of a ship bound from holland therewith intention to come and settle here the Board ordered that he have his Majesty's bounty.

Page 393: Meeting of 9th November 1743

Read the Petition of Frederick Arnold shewing that the Pet'r being newly come in to y'e province w'th intent to settle in one of the Township, humbly prays for his Majesty's Gracious bounty of one year's provisions & 150 acres of land and a lot in SaxGotha Towns'p by virtue of his Family Right. The Pet'r appearing before his Hon'r and his Majesty's Council, and having proved the allegations of his Petition upon oath to be true, It was ordered that y'e said Pet'r have the 150 acres of land and a y'e Town lot prayed for, and that the King's bounty of provision be granted to him only.

Page 394: Read the Petition of Francis Young shewing That he having three persons in family for whom he has not had any land assigned him, prays That 150 acres of land be granted him on Pedee River in the Welch Tract, upon the So side of that river bounding between Jo: Thomas's line, and one Vaghan's land, the Pet'r at the same time produced a certificate of his having lived there before the Settlem't of the Welch, signed by two Justices of the Peace in that place. The Pet'r having appeared before his Hon'r ye Lieu't Gov'r and Council, and proved the allegations of his Petition upon oath, it was Ordered that the prayer thereof be granted.

Read the Peti'n of James Galespy shewing That the Petito'r having Six persons in Family for whom he has not as yet had any land assigned him humbly prays that a Warrant of Survey for 300 acres be granted him, in the Welch Tract. The Pet'r not appearing to Swear to his Family right, his petit'n was ordered to Lye on y'e Table.

Pp. 394-395: Read the Petition of Henry Roach shewing That the Petitioner being an Inhabitant of this Province prays that by virtue of his Family right 100 acres of land in the Welch Tract may be granted him. It appearing that the Petitioner not being a Welchman, or of Welch extract, the prayer of his Petition was not granted but ordered that it do lye on the Table.

Pp. 395-396: Read the Petition of Bartholomew Zouberbhuler shewing that there are a Great many Germans at Orangebourgh Santee and thereabouts who are very desirous to have the word of God preached to them, and their children, and who desire to be instructed in the True Religion, humbly prays that he may be sent to serve in one or two places to preach to them and to be supported with a Competent Salary until he shall be able to take a Voyage to England to be ordained by the Bishop of London, and at the same time proposes to bring over with him a number of Germans w'ch he thinks may be as great a umber as ever was brought at any time into this Province it being a Great Encouragem't to them when they find that they may have the Gosple not only in their voyage, but also after their arrival in this Province, preached to them &C. Upon reading the said Petition it was the opinion of his Majesty's Council, that providing the Petit'r do produce a Certificate from the Inhabitants of Orangeburgh of their desire to receive him as a preacher among them, and also a Certificate from the Ecclesiastical Commissary Mr. Garden of his qualifications to receive orders in the Church of England, and his engaging to go home to London to receive ordination and after that, to go to Germany to procure others of his Countrymen to Come over to Settle in this Province That the sum of 500 pounds Currency be advanced him out of the Township fund, in order to enable him to perform the same.

Pp. 398-399: Read the Petition of James Gamble shewing that he having nine years agoe obtained a Grant for 250 acres of land in Williamsbourgh Township w'ch proved so extreamly barren that Three of his best Crops did not exceed ten Bushels of rough rice, The Pet'r having now five persons more in family for whom no lands have been assigned, prays that two hundred and fifty acres being part of nine hundred acres of Land in the said Township surveyed for Culketh Golightly Esq'r and by him disclaimed in favour of the Petitioner as appears upon the back of the said Plat, date the 14th of October 1743 and also a Town lot number 29 be Granted him and that a Warrant of Survey for y'e 250 acres and the Town lot above mentioned may be directed to the Surveyor General for his Executing the same, and that a Grant may be accordingly prepared for him and the Charges thereon remitted. The Pray'r of the said Petition was granted, except that part relating to y'e remitting of the Fees & accordingly a Warrant was ordered to be directed to the Survey'r General that he may return a Plat of the 250 acres prayed for and mark out the same within the old containing 900 acres aforesaid. Ordered That Mr. Golightly's Plat be returned to y'e Survey'r General's office.

Page 399: Meeting of 10th November 1743

Ordered that a Warrant be issued for the Lot 135 in Beaufort Town Pt Royal to Cap't William Scot, in lieu of the Lot 114 which he engaged to surrender to his Majesty, pursuant to a minute of Council date y'e 13th of May 1743.

HEMPSTEAD COUNTY LIBRARY
HOPE, ARKANSAS

Page 400: Ordered that the Lots No 366, 367, 368, 369 in Beaufort Port Royal be granted to Thomas and Richard Wigg, and that a Warrant do issue to them accordingly.

Ordered that the Lot 314 in Beaufort Port Royal be granted to David Culter Braddock, and that a Warrant do issue accordingly.

Page 413: Meeting of 11th November 1743

Read the Petition of Paul Grimbol praying for a lot in Beaufort Town P't Royal No. 78. Ordered that the prayer of y'e foresaid Petition be granted, and that y'e said Lot 78 be admeasured out to him.

Read the Petition of Andrew Hogg praying for two lots in Beaufort Town P't Royal number 344 & 29. Ordered that the pray'r of y'e said Petition be granted, and a Warrant for those two lots be prepared accordingly.

Read the Petition of Dorothy Jones widdow praying for two lots in Beaufort Town P't Royal viz No. 120 & 124. Ordered That the said lots be granted to Thomas Jones son of Dorathy Jones and That a Warrant do issue accordingly.

Page 414: Read the Petition of Mr. John Thorpe for the Lots no. 174, 176 in Beaufort Town Port Royal. Ordered, That y'e Lot No. 175 be granted him only, and a Warrant to Issue accordingly.

Read the Petition of Thomas Grimbol for y'e Lots 373 & 374 in Beaufort Town Port Royal. Ordered, That the Lot No. 374 be granted him only, and a Warrant to Issue accordingly.

Read the Petition of Captain William Pinckney praying for the Lots No. 127 & 128 in Beaufort Town Port Royal. It appearing that y'e Lot No. 128 is granted to Mr. William Scott, Ordered, That the Lot No. 127 be granted to the Petitioner, and That a Warrant to Issue accordingly.

Read the Petition of Wm Lyford for the Lots No. 315 & 316 in Beaufort Town Port Royal against the Granting of which, there had been a Caveat Lodged but w'ch having been withdrawn, the said Lots were granted to Mr. Lyford 28 is granted to Mr. William Scott, Ordered, That the Lot No. 127 be granted to the Petitioner, and That a Warrant to Issue accordingly.

Read the Petition of Sarah Woodward & Isaac Chardon for the Lots No. 361, 362, 363. The prayer of the said Petition was in part granted viz for no. 361 to Sarah Woodward & 362 to Mary Hudson.

Pp. 414-415: Read the Petition of George Hunter in behalf of Frederick French, Esq'r, with Certificates of two Lots in Beaufort Town P't Royal viz No. 69 & 74. Lot 69 appeared to have been surveyed prior in Time to Ichabod

Winburn, but nor prior Claim appearing for Lot 74, Ordered that the pray'r of y'e said Petition be granted as to y'e Lot 74.

Page 415: Read the Petition of Joseph Edward Flower for two lots in Beaufort Town Port Royal, viz No. 115 & 116 when it appearing that no. 116 was Surveyed to Edward Ellis July 2d 1717. The Lot 115 was only Ordered to be granted him and a Warrant do Issue accordingly.

Read the petition of George Livingston praying for the Lot 311 in Beaufort Town Port Royal. Ordered, That y'e pray'r of y'e s'd Petition be granted and that a Warrant do issue accordingly.

Read a Letter from Colonel William Hazzard praying for the Lot either No 345 or 349 or 350 in Beaufort Town P't Royal. Whereupon it was Ordered that the o. 345 be granted him and that a Warrant do issue accordingly.

Pp. 415-416: Meeting of 12th November 1743

Certificates having been produced to the Board Dated 21st Dec'r 1717 under the hand of Francis Young then Survey'r General, of his Having laid out in Beaufort town P't Royal the Lot No. 100 to Daniel Callahan Senior, and anther Lot No. 101 to Daniel Calahan Jun'r with a Grant annexed to Each under the great seal of Robert Johnson Esq'r then Governor of this Province. It was Ordered, that the Special Fiat be Cancelled w'ch was ordered by the minutes of Council date y'e 22d of Jan'ry last, to be prepared in order for passing a Grant of the said two lots unto Mary Bedon wife of Stephen Bedon, surviving Daughter of Daniel Callahan Sen'r and Surviving Sister also of Daniel Callahan Junior.

Page 416: Read the Petition of Alex'r Gordon, Clerk of y'e Commis'y praying for a lot in Port Royal No 31, or any other lot in Beaufort Town, but it appearing as if 31 had been already Granted It was Ordered, that the Lot in Beaufort Town No. 310 be granted the Petitioner, and that a Warrant do issue to him accordingly.

Pp. 416-417: On motion it was Ordered That Warrants be Issued for laying out the following Lots in Beaufort Town to the Members of this Board, in order to promote the setting the same to
the Hon'ble James Kinloch Esq'r no. 328, 387 being back lots.
to Coll. Fenwick No. 370
to Joseph Wragg No. 239
to John Hammerton 112
to John Colleton 106
to Edmond Atkin No. 364
to Joseph Blake No. 363
to Wm Middleton 313
to John Cleland 105

to Colonel Ch's Pinckney 238
to Richard Hill 109

Page 417: Janet Fleming wife of John Fleming of the Town'p of Williamsbourgh attended his Hon'r and his Majesty's Council with a piece of fine white holland containing 27 yards w'ch by a Certificate under the hand of John Basnet Esq'r one of his majesty's Justices of y'e Peace for Craven County appeared to be made with Flax the Growth of the said Flemings Plantation and was spun by the said Jannet his wife and wove by David Witherspoon of the same Township, Weaver. And thereupon it was Considered that a proper Gratuity should be made the said Jannet Fleming for having Set so laudable an Exemple of Care & Industry, in producing and manufacturing the first piece of fine Holland in the said Township, and the Sum of fifty pounds was ordered to be payed her out of y'e part of the Township fund arising by y'e late duty law by public Treasurer accordingly.

Page 422: Meeting of 19th November 1743

Mr. Peter Negorly having this day informed the board that his warrant dated in Oct'r 1742 had not yet been executed and that the time was almost elapsed, It was Ordered that the said Warrant should be executed within three months from this day.

Page 435: Meeting of 13th December 1743

Read the Petition of Ursula Annerhausley shewing That she being arrived from Switzerland in Sep'r 1736 in Expectation of his Majesty's bounty in order to settle in one of the Townships, intends to reside in SaxGotha therefore humbly prays for his majesty's bounty & 50 acres of land and a Town lot in that Township. Whereupon it was agreed by the Board that the pray'r of her Petition be granted, and y'e Commiss'ry directed to pay her his majesty's bounty and y'e Charges of her Petition, Warrant &C.

Pp. 438-439: Meeting of 14th December 1743

Read the following Petition of Benjamin Loyd shewing That he ab't 8 years ago prayed for a warrant for a lot in Beaufort P't Royal No 29 and applied again last month of June when y'e Clerk of this Board informed him that y'e said lot had by warrant been granted to Andrew Hogg, planter, of Portroyal. The Peti'r begs leave to inform the Board that the said Andrew Hogg has been dead near 7 years agoe, that the s'd warrant was granted on a petition of the s'd Hogg lodged in the council Chamber in his lifetime, and the said warrant passed about one month since whereupon the Pet'r apprehending the warrant being made out to one not in being is void, prays therefore that the warrant for y'e said lot be made out in y'e name of y'e Pet'r. Ordered, that this Petition be reconsidered.

Pp. 453-456: Meeting of 16th December 1743

Read the following letter from the Rev'd Mr. John Fordice to the Hon'ble John Cleland Esq'r dated the 15th November 1743.

Sr, in my Journey lately to Pedee I had an opportunity of Seeing some of the Welsh Settlem'ts on that tract of land commonly called the Welsh neck w'ch in general is as good land as ever was plowed and capable of great improvements but ill bestowed on a people who will never answer the Intention of the Governm'ts Indulgence to them.... The following information I received Oct'r 15th 1743 from Sampson Thomas whom you know as he told me and will give oath to y'e same if called,

Imprimis, Job Edwards borrowed Samuel and Abel Wilds children of Samuel Wilds by way of Indented apprentices to Increase his Family by which means he obtained land and Bounty, for them, both, and afterwards cancelled the pretended Indenture, when his business was done, altho Land & bounty had been obtained before, for said children and Edwards.

2dly, David James obtained land & bounty for three children yet in Pensilvania.

3ly Thomas Evans obtained Land and bounty for two children let in Pensilvania arrived here since who no doubt will receive bounty in their own names.

4ly James James obtained land & bounty for Sampson Thomas's wife and two children in name of his own Family, who were neither Servants nor apprentices to the said James, and the said Sampson Thomas who is my Informer obtained land and bounty for four in Family as his right.

5ly Daniel James obtained land for Lamuel Greenwoods and David James's Familys in name of his own, and these Familys afterwards received land and bounty in their own names. Thus they borrowed from one another to serve their fraudulent ends....

6ly Daniel Oenvenald settled on vacant land joyning his own already run out in order to prevent others settling the same claiming it as his own property & thereby the longer deprives the King of Quit Rents and the Country of Taxes.... John Fordyce

[new volume]

Pp. 48-49: Meeting of 17th January 1743/4

Read the Petition of William Jones praying that in Consideration of his having been three Years settler in y'e Welch Tract without having had his Majesty's bounty That the same may be granted him & the Warrant and Grant for 400 acres of land in the Welch Tract may be delivered him. The same being Considered his Majesty's Bounty was not granted because the Pet'r had not applied for the same according to the Terms prescribed by law, but in Consideration of the sickness which had been in his Family, That y'e Charges of his petition, warrant & C be defrayed by the commissary out of the Township Fund.

Page 49: Read the Petition of John Jervey humbly shewing that he had obtained an order and Warrant the last of which was produced at the Board for 400 acres of land on Folley Creek, Colleton County but on acc't of sickness was unable to run out the Land at the time assigned by Law, therefore prayed that another warrant be granted. The Peti'r appearing before the Board and Swearing to his Family right the prayer thereof was granted.

Read the Petition of William Carey praying That in Consideration of the increase of one in his Family 50 acres of Land in the Welch Tract be granted him. The Petit'r having appeared before the Board and made affidavit of the Truth of his prayer the Same was Granted.

Page 63: Meeting of 24th January 1743/4

Read the Petition of Joseph Mills shewing that an The Pet'r with his son came into this Province w'th an intention to Settle and Cultivate what land may be alotted him by virtue of Family right, and having only two Persons in Family as yet viz. himself and son as above mentioned Humbly prays y'r Excellency and Honors that 100 acres of Land may be assigned him in Queensborough Township on Pedee river in Craven County, and the Pet'r also prays That his Majesty's Gracious bounty may be allowed him in Consideration of his not only Settling on the Land above prayed for but in being dayly in Expectation of the arrival of more of his children & others in this Province all with the Same Intention of Settling here &c. Joseph Mills. Which Petition being Considered & the Petitioner appearing before the Board and Swearing to his Family right the pray'r thereof was Granted, and the Secret'ry ordered to prepare a Warrant accordingly.

Page 64: Read the Petition of Robert Jordan inhabitant of the Towns'p of Kingston on Wacomaw River, shewing That the Pet'r by Virtue of Family right, had obtained a Warrant for five hundred and fifty acres of land in Kingston Town'p which by experience in his Endeavors to Cultivate y'e Same, the Ground has proved so barren that he can not by labour nor Industry get a Living thereby, Wherefore he Humbly prays his Excellency and their Honors, That he may be allowed to Exchange his Warrant for five hundred acres in the s'd Town'p or Land not occupied, but run out for Col. Waitis. He also prays That one hundred and fifty acres more may be granted him there on account of Increase of Family and the same be upon little Pedee near Mr. Francis Britain's Estate &c. Robert Jordan. Which Petition being Considered the Petitioner was desired to send down the Plat of the Land mentioned of 500 acres, from the s'd Townsh'p to the Clerk of this Board, and as to that part of the Petition w'ch prays for 150 acres on acc't of Family right The Petitioner appearing before the Board, he proved the Same upon Oath, Wherefore the Council were of opinion That when the Plat mentioned is returned, they will proceed upon the said Petition at the same time....

Pp. 71-72: Meeting of 24th January 1743/4

Read the Petition of James Lesesne shewing That the Petitioner has 14 Persons in Family for whom he as yet has not obtain'd any Lands as his Family right, but being desirous to Cultivate land in this Province, Prays his Excell'cy and their Hon'rs would be pleased to grant that a Warrant be Issued for admeasuring 700 acres of Land in Berkley County near the Parish Church in St. Thomas's Parish and w'ch is contiguous to the Plantation of Isaac Lesesne deceased &c. Chas Town. Janry 17th 1743. The Petitioner appearing before his Excellency in Council and Swearing to his said Family Right namely of his having at pres't in the Province but four Persons in Family, two hundred acres were granted him only, of the Lands prayed for and the Deputy Secret'ry was ordered to prepare a Warrant for measuring the Same.

Pp. 74-76: Meeting of 13th February 1743/4

Reconsidered the Petition of the Rev'd Mr. Bartholomew Zouberbhuler w'ch had been exhibited at this Board on 10th day of Nov'r 1743 praying that in Consideration of the Earnest desire of the Inhabitants of Orangeburgh Santee to have a Person to preach the Gosple to Them, in their own language, he is willing to perform that pastoral duty but being as yet unordained desires to be support with a Competent Salary until he shall be able to take a Voyage to England to be ordained at w'ch time he proposes to bring over a number of Forreign Protestants to Settle in this Province who are unwilling to Come over for want of having the Gosple preached to them in their voyage here. Whereupon, It appearing by a former minute of Council on the 20th of Nov'r last that provided the Pet'r shall produce a Certificate from the Inhabitants or Orangeburg of their desire to receive him as a Preacher among them, and also a Certificate from the Rever'd Mr. Garden of his qualification to receive orders, That then the sum of five hundred pounds current money be advanced to him out of the Township fund, in order to enable him to perform his voyage and bring over the Protestants to settle here as he mentions. Whereupon the Petit'r produced the following Certificate....

These are to Certify whom it may concern and in particular the Rt. Rev'd the Lord Bishop of London, that the Bearer Bartholomew Zouberbhuler, a native of Apenzel in Swisserland, appears to me on Credible testimony to have resided in this province for the space of 7 years last past, and ruing that time to have been of good Life & behaviour as becometh a Candidate for holy orders &c. Signed Alex'r Garden. Febry 13th 1743.

Pp. 84-85: Meeting of 22d February 1743/4

Read the Petition of Samuel de Surrency shewing That having obtained from this Hon'ble Board an order for a Warrant dated 27th day of January 1742 for the having admeasured to the Petitioner one hundred acres of Land in the Welch Tract. And whereas it is Expressed in the s'd Warrant that it shall be returnable within 12 months after the said date, your Pet'r humbly begs Leave to remonstrate to y'r Excellcy and y'r Honours that after receiving the aforesaid Warrant Mr. St. John the Survey'r General dyed, and his Deputy to whom it was directed would not act any more on acc't of his said death, the Warrant therefore could not be returned according to the Tenure thereof. the Pet'r therefore Humbly prays that a fresh Warrant may be issued to him for admeasuring the said 100 acres in the Welch Tract and the Pet'r as in Duty &c. Samuel de Saurency. The above Petition being read and Considered and the Pet'r appearing before the Board with his former Warrant, the same was Cancell'd and the Prayer of his Petition granted and Mr. Secre'try ordered to prepare a Fresh Warrant accordingly the Pet'r praying y'e Fees.

Page 85: Read the Petition of Donald McDonald humbly Setting forth That the Pet'r having obtained from their Hon'rs a Warrant dated the 27th of Jan'ry 1742 for admeasuring to him one hundred acres of land in the Welch Tract, and whereas it is expressed in the said Warrant that it shall be returnable within 12 months after its s'd date, The Pet'r humbly begs Leave to remonstrate to his Excellcy and their Honours, That after receiving the foresaid Warrant Mr. St. John the Survey'r General dyed, and his Deputy would not survey the same until a new survey should be appointed. The Peti'r therefore prays that a fresh Warrant be issued for admeasuring the s'd 100 acres. The former Warrant being produced, was cancell'd and the Pray'r of the Petition granted and Mr. Secre'try ordered to prepare a Warrant accordingly.

Pp. 85-86: Read the Petition of Jane David humbly Setting forth that when she came from Pensilvania she proved her Family right, and left her Certificate with the attorney General w'ch being now lost or mislaid as she has five Persons in Family at Present Prays that she may have two hundred and fifty acres of land assigned her in the Welch Tract. The Petitioner not appearing to Swear to her Family right the Pray'r of Her petition was not granted.

Pp. 91-93: Meeting of 24th February 1743/4

Read the Petition of Jean Rudolph Grand humbly shewing that the Petitioner on acc't of the Encouragem't granted by his Majesty for all poor Protestant Familys, who would come over and settle in his Majesty's Province of South Carolina should receive all the benefits granted by his Majesty, the Pet'r on the said Encouragem't having come over the Seas with his Family & run three hundred and fifty acres of Land in Purysburg Township, but y'r Petitioner never could obtain a Grant for the same. Your Petit'r further sheweth, that there was Provisions granted to the first Settlers of the said Towns'p and Your Petitioner being one of the first, has however not received the benefit of the said bounty, your Petitioner humbly prays y'r Excellency to see him righted both in giving him a Grant for said Land, and Seeing he has allowance of Provisions as was Granted to others and your poor Petitioner shall ever &c.

At the same time his Excell'cy produced the following attestation concerning the Peti'r form Hector Beringer de Beaufain Esq'r his Majesty's Colle'r of the Customers at this Port viz. Sr, Rodolph Grand having applied to your Excell'cy for a Grant of his Land desired me to Certify to y'r Excell'cy what I know concerning the same, I therefore beg Leave to inform y'r Excell'cy that the Grant of Lots and Lands in Purysbourgh were transmitted to me 5 or 6 years ago, and that I did not receive any for the said Grand's Plantation, This I have occasion to remember, because the man being anxious about his Grant, made me search for it more than once. I have looked over the List of Grants, in the Secretary's Office, and have not found the s'd Grand's name there, but for his Lot in the Town. i beg leave to inform y'r Excell'cy that Rodolph Grand is one of the first Settlers in the said Town'p where he lived till within these Ten months last past that he had a good character there and that he was settled upon the Land... 25 Feb 1743/4.

The Pet'r at the same time laid before the Board the duplicate of a Plat in Purysburg Town'p for the 350 acres of Land in that Town'p with an Indorcem't by which it appeared that the original Plat was delivered into the Secretary's Office, in order for a Grant to be annexed thereto. Whereupon it was ordered that Mr. Grand's petitio so far as it relates to the bounty be rejected but then as it appears that the original plat for the said land was lodged in the Secretary's office in order to have a Grant, that the commiss'ry be directed to search, and produce the same in order that if it is granted it be delivered up to the Petitioner.

Page 142: Meeting of 6th March 1743/4

Read the Petition of James Shelton shewing That he has four Persons in family for whom as Yet he hath not obtained any Land, and therefore prays a Warrant for admeasuring to him, Two hundred acres of Land in the Wateree Township, which he designs forthwith to Settle & Cultivate and being poor humbly begs that the Expenses of his Petition and Warrant may be allowed him. James Shelton. March 6th 1743. To ly on the Table.

Pp. 142-143: Read the Petition of Tulliz Senid of Switzerland humbly shewing That he and his wife with one child now upwards of 13 Years old came here from Switzerland by the Way of Holland, in order to settle in this Province upon the Encouragem't of his Majesty's Bounty, ever some time the year 1752 but have not as yet receive either land or bounty; for that they being poor were obliged to be servants to Mr. David Hunt[?], lately deceased, of whose executors they have since obtained their discharge. Your Petitioner therefore humbly prays y'r Excellency and honors That they may have a Warrant granted them for one hundred & fifty acres of Land in SaxGotha Township, and the better to enable them to Cultivate the Same, that his Majesty's said Bounty be allowed to them &c., March y'e 6th 1743. The Pet'r appearing before the Board and proving upon oath the allegations of his Petition, the prayer thereof was Granted, and the Secret'ry ordered to prepare a Warrant accordingly, and the Commissary to pay him his Majesty's bounty.

Pp. 147-148: Meeting of 8th March 1743/4

Reconsidered the Petition of James Shelton as mentioned in the minutes of the 6'h inst: praying that in Consideration of his Great poverty he may have the Expences of his Petition Warrant & Grant defrayed by the Public, Whereupon the Peti'r appearing before his Excell'cy in Council and making affidavit of his inability to pay the Expences aforesaid, The Pray'r of his Petition was Granted and the Commissary ordered to defray the Same.

Page 152: Meeting of 9th March 1743/4

Bartholomew Zouberbhuler attended his Excellency the Gov'r in Council, according to order, when the Gov'r gave to understand that he had not acted well in the Exhibiting a Certificate from the Township of Orangeburgh, read at this board on November the 13th 1742 seeing that under the notion of having an Invitation to the ministry by the majority of that Township, there was on the Contrary a latter memorial laid before the Board signed by near ninety of the Inhabitants and by far the majority of that Township, praying that Mr. Gissendanner their present minister might be continued to preach among them and that Mr. Zouberbhuler going to preach in the s'd Township and his design to be settled there as a Minister was not be their desire, on the Contrary had occasioned no small disturbance in the said Township. That his proceedings with the Lt. Gov and Council in y'e s'd affair had not been with that Candor that might have been Expected from one who designed to take on him Holy Orders & that therefore he ought to be contented with at Least one half of what had been payed him by y'e Treasurer, and return the other 250£ or at any rate to procure a Joynt Security of one residing in Charlestown, that he would return the money in case he did not being over the Forreign Protestants mentioned... whereupon Mr. Zouberbhuler withdrew.

Page 196: Meeting of 13th April 1744

Read the Humble Petition of Lewis Linder a German, That he Came over from Germany in order to settle here, in the year 17345, upon the Encourage-m't of his Majesty's bounty, but that he hat not receive any part thereof. That ab:t 4 Years ago he obtained a Grant of two hundred acres of land in Orangeburgh Township but the land proves very indifferent and puts him to great Expence in the Cultivation thereof, therefore humbly prays an allowance of the s'd Bounty the better to enable him to clear the same. That the Pet'r having an Encrease of Eight Persons in his Family and designing to settle some of them on vacant land near or adjoining to Capt. Debong's Land and also Land belonging to one Goatsman in four hole Swamp Berkley County likewise prays a Swamp for four hundred acres there in right of the same &c. Ludwig Linder. On reading the above Petition and the Petitioner appearing and swearing to his Family right, It was ordered That the prayer thereof with regard to the Land be granted, he paying the fees for y'e Same but not the Bounty, and that Mr. Secretary be ordered to prepare a Warrant accordingly.

Pp. 196-197: Read the petition of Jacob Bridge shewing That he Came over from Germany in the Year 1737 in order to settle and Cultivate lands here, That he hath Six persons in Family for whom he hath not received any Land. That he is desirous of Settling and Cultivating a piece of vacant land in the four holes, Berkley County, near or adjoining to Capt. DeBongs land and one Goatsman along with y'r Pet'r Lewis Linder's family and humbly prays his Excell'cy and Their Honors would grant him a Warrant for running out his said right there, and also allow him the Charges of his Petition and warrant. April 13, 1755. Jacob Bridge. The Pet'r appearing before the Board, and swearing to his s'd Family Right, It was ordered That the three hundred acres of Land be granted him, but that he pay the Charges of his warrant and Grant. petition &c.

Pp. 197-198: Read the petition of Michael Murphy an Inhabitant of the Welch Tract, shewing that about nine years ago before the Settling of the Welch he purchased part of a Warrant of one Howard since dead for 300 acres of Land on the Welch Tract but the said Warrant for running out the same being afterwards lost, or mislaid, never was returned into the Office, not withstanding which, he built a house on the same, settled there, and made other Considerable Improvements and clear above 40 acres thereof and is well liked as a neighbour by all the Welch Familys there. That the pet'r having Since a Considerable increase of fourteen Persons in his Family for whom he hath not as Yet obtained any Land, or hath he any other land than as above said within the said Province. Prays a Warrant of Survey for Seven hundred acres in a Tract of Tracts of Vacant land, and that the s'd tract of Land whereupon the Petitioner is Settled as above or so much thereof as shall appear upon a resurvey to be Vacant to be part of the Same which land is butting on or near Colonel Pawly's land and to the west of John Brown. Michael Murphee. The Petit'r appearing and Swearing to the allegations of his said Petition, It was ordered that 500 acres of land only be Granted him and the secretary was accordingly ordered to prepare a Warrant for y'e Same.

Page 198-199: <u>Meeting of 14th April 1744</u>

Read the Pet'n of John Wessingher a German humbly shewing That the Petitioner having about two Years ago come into this Province with an Intention to Settle among his Countrymen having two in family viz himself and wife, humbly prays that one hundred acres of Land may With his Majestys

Bounty be granted him in Sax Gotha Township and the Pet'r shall &c. John Wessinger. Which Petition being Considered and the Petitioner appearing and Swearing to the s'd Family right, the pray'r thereof was Granted and the Commissary Gen'l to pay him the Bounty and the Secretary to prepare a Warrant accordingly.

Page 208-209: Meeting of 18th April 1744

Read the Petition of the Hon'ble Richard Hill Esq'r Shewing That the Petitioner is possessed of a part of a Lot in Charlestown No. 77 Situated on the north side of Vanderhorsts Creek. That he has been informed and verily believes that one half of the Marsh of the s'd Creek on the north side of the same allowing 30 feet in Breadth for a passage for Boats is now Vacant. The Peti'r therefore humbly prays That he may have a Warrant to the Survey'r General to run out as much of the said march from east to west, as runs paralel to the said part of the Lot No. 77 which by Estimation may be 170 or 180 foot in order to have a Grant for the same by which he will be enabled to fill up & improve his land now very Low & Subject to be overflowed and will also be of great Service in rendering the Navigation of the said Creek more commodious to those who have lands above him. In considered which Petition, It was ordered that the survey'r General be desired to lay before this Board a book of the Several Lots in Charlestown and also the Plat of Charles Town.

Page 209-210: The Surveyor General according to a minute of this morning having by order laid before the Board the Book w'ch ascertains the Buttings & Boundings of the Several Lots in Charlestown, and also the Plat of the same, as it did not appear that the marsh petitioned for, in the Petition of the Hon'ble Richard Hill Esq'r did belong to any person. It was agreed that the Prayer of the s'd Petition be granted and that the Secretary be ordered to prepare a Warrant accordingly.

Page 210-211: Read the Petition of Johannes Tobler shewing that the petitioner when he was in Europe was then informed that whoever had an Inclination to Settle in his Majesty's Province of South Carolina and spare y'e money It would be the best way to take some of their poor Country people with them, w'ch would much please the Governm't and that the Lands which would be admeasured to them if they died would be assigned to those who payed their passage, on that account the Pet'r payed the passage for Several poor people, whom he brought on his own expenses to this Province, but now finds the Contrary for one Conrade Augsler & John Shaffer with their familys having died, & whom on his first coming into y'e Province he might have made servants but did not, thinking if they should die before they could pay him, that their Lands would fall to him. Therefore humbly prays That as these above mentioned Persons lands are already admeasured & Joyns with the Petit'rs Land, that they may be granted to him, or be part of that warrant for y'e 600 acres which the Board granted him in the month of March 1737. and that he may obtain plats and Grants for the land admeasured to him some years ago. The Peti'r also humbly sheweth that his constant study for some years past was for making and inventing machins for the Easey and quick dispatch in pounding & Beating Rife, a thing very necessary in this Province, and as he was Informed that he would meet with very good Encourgem't from y'e Board if he could bring any such thing to perfection. He thinks proper to acquaint them that he was finished one at Peach Hill, different from all the others he has already made, it having a dreading Wheel, tryed and approved of by all the Planters that have seen the work, hopes therefore the Board would take the same into their Consideration &Ca. Johannes Tobler. Whereupon it was ordered That the Commiss'ry General do make a Search in the offices to see whether there are any Warrants or Grants as mentioned, and That He be aiding and assisting to the Petitioner therein.

Pp. 232-233: Meeting of 21st April 1744

Read the Petition of Robert Rouse an Irishman Shewing that in the year 1742 he came from Ireland in order to Settle in this Province, at which time he obtained a Grant for five hundred and fifty acres of land on Black River But that between the time of Granting the said Warrant, and the running out of the said land, some other person had run out y'e same, whereby ever since he has remained defeated of his Family right. Therefore prays his Excell'cy and Their Honors that upon Surrendering up his said warrant he may have another warrant for running out y'e said quantity of land on a Vacant Tract, adjoining to Col. Lucas's Land on Waccamaw River in Kingston Town'p. The above Petition being Considered the prayer thereof was Granted, and Mr. Secret'ry ordered to prepare a Warrant accordingly.

Page 233: Read the Petition of Robert Orr dissenting minister at Port Royal, shewing that the Petitioner having been possess of two lots at Beaufort viz Lot. No. 319, 320, which had been admeasured to him, by Colonel John Barnwel, and that two other Lots had been assigned for the meeting House and burying Ground of the disenters there, Prayed that a Grant may be Issued out for the two lots for the meeting House and buryal Ground be Secured for the purposes Intended &c. On reading the Petition of the said Robert Orr, that in the name of William Orr, was referred to for Beaufort Lots, and it appearing that y'e Petition in the name of William Orr was founded on a mistake, the same was ordered to be vacated, and the prayer of the foresaid Robert Orr granted.

Page 257: Meeting of 8th May 1744

Read the Petition of George Haig shewing That as he has an Encrease of six persons in his family for whom he hath not obtained any Land by virtue of said Family right, Prays for a Warrant for Surveying him three hundred ares of land in Amelia Township. The Board having Considered the said Petition and the Pet'r proved the allegations thereof upon oath and also that the Pet'r had heretofore obtained a Tract in Amelia Township as a new settler, was thereof of opinion that the prayer thereof be granted. Whereupon Mr. Deputy Secretary was ordered to prepare a Warrant for y'e Same accordingly.

Pp. 263-264: Meeting of 23d May 1744

Read the Petition of Isaac Hickman shewing that the Peti'r has been upwards of two Years a residenter in this Province, and Lived in the Welch Tract, that he has brought in ten people in Family from Pensilvania, in order to settle in the said Township and to Cultivate land there, Therefore he humbly prays his Excellency and their honors, to order a Warrant to be Issued to him, for admeasuring 500 acres of land in the said Tract, by virtue of his Family right and that in Consideration of the Great Expence he has been at, in bringing into the said Province his said Family, and that he may be y'e more Effectually Enabled to make a Settlement in the Province his money being quite exhausted, he Humbly prays his Excell'cy and Honors to order him his Majestys most Gracious Bounty &C. Chas Town May 9th 1744. Isaac Hickman. Inclose in the said Petition was the following declaration of Mr. James, Justice of y'e Peace in the Welch Tract, direct to his Excell'cy the Govr, and members of the council.

I, the subscriber, at the request of the Bearer, Isaac Hickman, do certify that the said Hickman has been some time an Inhabitant on or near the Welch Tract, and to the best of my knowledge has behaved himself like an honest man... Wm. James.

The Pet'r having appeared before y'e Board and swore to his Family right, the five hundred acres of Land were granted him on the Proviso that Mr. William James justice of y'e Peace aforesaid, shall send another certificate that the Petition he y'e same number in his Family mentioned in the Petition.

Read the Petition of Samuel Buxton shewing that he came from Pensilvania and has settled above 3 years in the Welch Tract and built there, upon a Tract called the naked Creek Swamp, on this side of the Gun Swamp adjoining to the lands of Mr. Dee Rush containing in the whole about 500 acres, that he has 10 in Family for whom he has had no land assigned him & prays for a Warrant for y'e s'd 500 acres. The Pet'r appearing and bringing with him a Certificate from Wm. James, Justice of the Peace in the Welch Tract , and that Pet'r swearing that he has nine Persons in Family, It was ordered that the Secret'ry do prepare a Warrant for admeasuring to him 450 acres accordingly.

Pp. 273-274: Meeting of 25th May 1744

Read the Petition of Robert Newman, together with the copy of a paragraph of the will and testament of William Newman, attested by John Champneys, Esq'r, Deputy Secretary, humbly shewing That the Petitioner's father William Newman deceased having obtained a Warrant of Survey from his late

Excellency Governor Johnson and in pursuance thereof had a Tract of land surveyed on the 20th of May 1733 in Craven County containing 211 acres the Survey being at present in the Surveyor's office. The Petitioner therefore as son and heir to William Newman prays that his Excell'cy and their Honors will accordingly grant the same, pursuant to the Directions of the last will and Testament of the Testator William Newman aforesaid...

William Newman's will dated 27th December 1739 "After giving or reserving one hundred acres already Granted he Gives the rest of his lands to be divided equally between Rob't Newman and Thomas Newman as they and the executors shall agree... Tis my will that y'e 100 acres of land at Okakoone or Coach whip hill, shall be Equally divided between Samuel Newman and Thomas Newman, and Robert Newman.... Deliverance Newman executrix, John Jones, Samuel Newman, and Rob't Newman, executors...." The Prayer of the Petition was Granted.

Page 297: Meeting of 30th May 1744

The Petition of Alexander Gordon, Clerk of this Board, shewing that since his arrival, not having applied for his Family right but being desirous of Settling part of his s'd Family in Business at Beaufort Port Royal prays his Excell'cy and their Honors that Lot No. 328 be given him in said Town. Ordered that the prayer of the s'd Petition be granted and that the Secretary do prepare a Warrant accordingly.

Page 298: Read the Petition of John Stone most humbly shewing That the Pet'r having an intention to Settle & build a house in the Town of Beaufort & wanting a proper place for so doing Humbly prays that the Board would be pleased to grant him a Warrant ... for Lot No. 129. The s'd Petition being considered that prayer of y'e same was granted and the Secret'ry ordered to prepare a Warrant accordingly.

Captain William Scott having petitioned for a Lot in Beaufort Town P't Royal the s'd lot petitioner for was allotted for the King, wherefore the Board assigned over to him the Lot No. 135 and the Secretary ordered to prepare a Warrant accordingly.

Pp. 298-299: Read the Petition of Stephen Bull Jun'r Esq'r humbly Shewing That he has been an Inhabitant near the Town of Beaufort many Years and having no lands in the Town and being desirous to build a house and Improve a Lot therein, Therefore prays... a warrant for one Lot in the said Town of Beaufort Number 356. This Petition was opposed by his Hon'r the Lieu't Gov'r the Petitioner having already a Lot in the said Township.

Page 299: Read the Petition of Joseph Bryan most humbly Shewing That he has been an Inhabitant near the Town of Beaufort many Years and having no lands therein, therefore prays... a warrant for one Lot in the said Town of

Beaufort Number 325. The prayer of the s'd Petition was granted and the Secret'ry ordered to prepare a Warrant for admeasuring the Same to Joseph Bryan accordingly.

Read the Petition of Thomas Christie shewing That he arrived in this Province directly from England with design to Settle in some of the Southernmost parts thereof in order to Carry on a Sturgeon fishery, above 12 months ago, but has not as yet a foot of land in this Province, Wherefore he prays his Excell'cy and their Honors, to grant him Lot No. 349, or 350, or 121 at Beaufort Town. the Secret'ry ordered to prepare for the Petit'r Thos Christy a Warrant for y'e Lot No. 121.

Pp. 300-301: Read the Petition of Jonathan Brian most humbly Shewing That the Pet'r has been an Inhabitant near the Town of Beaufort many Years, and at a Considerable Expence towards the Charges of a Pilot and Boat for the Encouragem't of Ships and Trade there, and having no lands in the town... wishes two lots of land Numbers 178 & 332 ... and whereas the Peti'r is possessed of fifty nine persons i Family and has not as yet obtained more than 2500 acres of land of his majesty's bounty, he therefore further prays that his Excell'cy would be pleased also to grant him in the Same warrant directions to admeasure and mark out to y'e Petitioner 450 acres of vacant land... the said Petition having been considered the Lot No. 178 was granted him and the Secretary ordered to prepare a Warrant for y'e same to Mr. Jonathan Brian accordingly.

Page 301: Read the petition of Hugh Bryan most humbly Shewing That the petitioner has been an Inhabitant near the Beaufort Town many Years .... having no lands in the Town ... wishes two lots of land Numbers 121 & 319. This Petition being Considered it was found upon Enquiry that both the lots petitioned for had been granted away to other people.

Pp. 301-302: Read the Petition of Robert Williams most humbly Shewing That the Peti'r is now building a Ware house on his lot No. 307 in Beaufort town and has occasion for a Warf to land and ship off his Goods, Therefore prays that the Board would be pleased to Grant him a Warrant directing his Majesty's Survey'r General to survey him out the water Tract, facing Church Street... facing a small tract reserved for a Fish market. The above Petition being considered, the same was rejected.

Page 302: Read the Petition of John Mulryne most humbly Shewing That the Petit'r as resided in Granville County for nine years past, and now intends to carry on Trade in the Town of Beaufort on Port Royal Island, but not being possessed of a Lot in the said Town, prays that the Board would be pleased to grant him a Warrant or Warrants during his Majesty's Survey'r Gen'l to Survey him out a Lot no 330... also the front of Charles Street from the Bluff or high water mark... to build a warf on... the said Petition being considered, the prayer thereof was Granted and the Secretary ordered to prepare a Warrant accordingly.

Page 303: Read the Petition of the Rev'd Wm Guy minister of St. Andrew humbly shewing That the Petitioner is possessed of one thousand acres of land in Granville County he therefore prays y'e Board to Grant him a lot in the Town of Beaufort Port Royal for building of a house &c. The Petition being read and Considered, the Lot no. 350 in Beaufort Town was Granted to him and Mr. Secretary ordered to prepare a Warrant accordingly.

Read the Petition of the William Lyford son of Capt. William Lyford, master of the Charles town Galley most humbly shewing That the Peti'r being a Carpenter and having a Great desire to make a Settlement at Beaufort Port Royal, where he was brought up and intends to Live... to permit him to build two houses and make a settlement on two lots in the new Town, being distinguished or known by the numbers 327 & 328... the s'd Petition being Considered the board upon Enquiry found that y'e said Lots prayed for had been already granted away to others.

Pp. 303-304: Read the humble Petition of Wm Bull Jun'r shewing That the Pet'r hath obtained a Grant for the Lot No 44 in Beaufort, but that the Peti'r hath since been informed that the said Lot was laid out to Mrs. Sarah Rhett about the year of our Lord 1718, Wherefore the Peti'r prays that a Warrant may be granted him to direct the lot number 327 to be ascertained and laid out in the s'd town of Beaufort for the Petitioner &c. On considering the above Petition, the Lot 327 was reserved to be granted until the Lott 44 mentioned be enquired into.

Page 304: Read the humble Petition of Thomas Drayton shewing That the Petitioner being possessed of several tracts of land in Granville County is desirous of having a Town lot in Beaufort, and therefore prays that the Board would be pleased to order a Warrant to lay out and ascertain the lot No. 325 in the s'd Town to the Petitioner &c. The said petition being considered that y'e lot 325 petitioned for had already been granted to another, the Board granted him the Lot No. 123 in lieu thereof, and Mr. Secretary ordered to prepare a Warrant for the same accordingly.

Pp. 304-305: Read the humble Petition of Daniel Pepper comm'r of Fort Moor, shewing that he having two sons by name Daniel and Gilbert whom he is willing to settle in business in Beaufort Port Royal, humbly prays the Board that two vacant lots in the said Town may be granted them, in consideration of his two sons being natives of this Province, his Intention being forthwith to build in the said Town and improve the said lots &c. Ordered that the Lots prayed for be specified by the Petitioner and that they be vacant.

Page 305: Read the Petition of James Williams most humbly shewing That the Peti'r being master & partly owner of the Defiance, arrived with her at Port

Royal, the beginning of this month Oct'r that he intending to carry off trade there, shall have occasion to build there a dwelling house and stores. Therefore humbly prays that the Board would order the Surveyor Gen'l to admeasure out to him a Lot in the Town of Beaufort No 240, in order to obtain a Grant for the same &c. The Petitioner having prayed for Lot 240, the same being Inquired into, it was found to have been granted away to another viz to Capt. Ashby Atkin[?].

Pp. 305-306: Read the Petition of Patrick Taisler[?] humbly shewing That the Peti'r having settled in this Province with his Family upwards of 4 Years, and having not hitherto petitioned y'r Honors for any land in the said Province, and being now inclinable to build upon and settle a Lot in the Town of Beaufort in the Island of Port Royal known by No. 364, he therefore prays that the Board would order the Survey'r Genl to admeasure out to him the s'd Lot in order to obtain a Grant for the same. On considering the Lot prayed for, it was found upon enquiry to have been Granted to another, but the Peti'r was directed by the Board to prefer another Petition for a Lot that is vacant.

Page 306: Read the Petition of John Chapman most humbly shewing that the Pet'r having been bound an apprentice to Mr. Robert Williams late of the Island of St. Christophers, merchant, but now of Port Royal, and the Pet'rs time being near expired and he intending to follow business him self and settle in the time of Beaufort, He therefore humbly prays that the Board would order the Surveyor Genl to admeasure out to him a Lot known by the No. 362 in order to obtain a Grant for the same &c. The number prayed for in the above Petition being enquired into was found to have ben granted away to another person.

Read the Petition of Andrew Bell, Blacksmith, humbly shewing that the Pet'r has for some time past been Inhabitant of the Town of Beaufort & as he has never Yet had any lands granted him, Therefore humbly prays y'r Hon'rs would be pleased to order the Lot known No. 121 of the Town of Beaufort to be laid out to him as it is now Vacant &c. The number prayed for in the above Petition being enquired into was found to have been granted away to another.

Pp. 306-307: Read the Petition of Tho's Bowman shewing that the Petitioner being informed that y'e Board intends to grant Lots of land in the Town of Beaufort and the Peti'r having land on Port Royal Island, therefore most humbly desires that y'e Board would be pleased to Grant him a Warrant for the running out of a Lot in the said Town of Beaufort known by the No. 125 and now vacant &c. The said Petition being Considered the prayer thereof was Granted, and Mr. Secret'ry ordered to prepare a Warrant accordingly.

Page 307: Read the Petition of John Yarwoth Jun'r humbly shewing That the Pet'r having resolved to Carry on Traffic in the Town of Beaufort Port Royal humbly prays that the Board would be pleased to grant him any vacant Lot in the said Town, in Consideration That the Pet'r is determined forthwith to build and improve the said Lot, and to Commence y'e Traffic he proposes to Carry on there without delay &C. As the Petr had prayed for a Lot without specifying the number, he as directed to ascertain y'e number in order that if vacant he may obtain y'e Same.

Pp. 307-308: Read the Petition of Hugh Anderson master of the Free school in Charleston shewing That whereas the Pet'r has a Family of Children and sons here, whom intends to settle in Mercantile business humbly prays Y'e Hon'rs that he may have Lot No. 363 in the Township of Beaufort where he Intends forthwith to build and Carry on the Same &c. The number prayed for having been enquired into it was found to have been granted away to y'e Hon'ble Joseph Blake.

Page 308: Read the Petition of Colonel Samuel Prioleau shewing That as the Petitioner is a Native of this Province and has a Plantation settled above twenty years at Port Royal as he has a numerous Family, some of whom he intends to Settle forthwith at that place in Business and to build there, Prays that their Honours would be pleased to grant him the Lot in Beaufort Town Number 31 for which no Grant has hitherto been Issued, the S'd Lot Joyning one already Purchaced by the Peti'r on both w'ch he intends immediately to build &c. Enquiry being made as to the number prayed for, it was found by y'e Board to have been Granted to another.

Pp. 308-309: Read the Petition of George Ducat inhabitant of Chas Town humbly Shewing that some years before the Indian War the Pet'r had admeasured and laid out to him a Town lot in Beaufort, No. 111 by virtue of a Warrant from the late Lords Proprietors under the hand & seal of the Hon'ble Charles Craven Esq're the then Gov'r by Col. John Barnwell who at that time surveyed most of y'e Lots in y'e s'd Town for wch warrants were Issued. That ye plat of the sd lot with a Great many other valuable papers & houshold furniture belonging to y'e Pet'r were taken away by the Indians in the sd War and by them burnt and destroyd. That the said office after that was shut up for a Considerable time and since the said lot was taken in among the King's land there, whereby the Pet'r is entirely defeated of the same. Therefore in consideration of the Premises the Pet'r prays a Grant for Lot No. 346 &c. The Petition being Considered that prayer thereof was Granted and Mr. Secretary ordered to prepare a Warrant for y'e Same Accordingly.

Pp. 371-372: <u>Meeting of 29th June 1744</u>

Read the most humble Petition of John Wolf a poor protestant Swisser lately arrived in this Province shewing That one Peter Indornpoint from Orange-burgh in this Province being come over to Switzerland with leave as it was said from this Government to Encourage poor people there to Settle in this Province, giving them hopes that they should have their passage payed, and bounty allowed for one Year's provision &c: several of his relations and acquaintenses took it into Consideration, but were in doubt about it because they had received no advice from their Friends who went over with Reimanspergher, tho they had promised it whereupon the humble Petitioner resolve to go before and to send them over a true account of the matter, But that he being arrived here with Capt. Charles Stedman, from Rotterdam hath been forced to bind himself and his Wife servants for three Years, unto Anthony Stack of SaxGotha for the Sum of £77 currency, payed by y'e s'd Anthony Stack to the said Capt Stedman for his passage whereby the humble Pet'r not only finds himself entirely disappointed in his Expectation but hath also the mortification to see his wife whch is big with Child subjected to hard Labour and often times to the ill humor of her master and mistress who for years before were but their Equals, and to see his children born in Slavery when he expected to enjoy greater Liberty, than he had at home. Wherefore he most humbly prays that it may please y'r Excell'cy and Your Honors to take his said Condition into merciful Consideration and the humble Pet'r that &c. John Wolf. Which Petition being Considered, was rejected.

Pp. 433-434: Meeting of 28th July 1744

Read the Petition of John Field praying for an Exchange of warrant for 1000 acres of Land on Brians neck upon Combee river contiguous to y'e Land of... which petition being considered that prayer of the Same was Granted and an order that y'e Deputy Secretary prepare a new warrant accordingly.

Pp. 439-440: Meeting of 3 August 1744

Read the Petition of the Widow Gebhard & 5 Children directed to his Excell'cy and y'e Board Shewing That her late Husband arrived in this Province some time in July 1742 in the time of the alarm, for which reason he could not then obtain his Grant for his Family right, nor his Majesty's Bounty, but was abliged to go down to the Country to seek Subsistance where he since died, as appears by y'e Certificate hereunto annexed. Therefore humbly prays y'r Excell'cy and Honors will grant her a Warrant in her name for the said right in the Township of Purysbourgh together with his Majesty's bounty &c. Maria Catherin Gebhard.

South Carolina, Granville County. This is to Certifie that Jacob Gebhard came to this Province in the time of y'e Spanish alarm with his wife and five children where he died, his widow and children desire to run land in the Township of Purysbourgh, and to live there, and as the People of a Good behaviour, I have granted them this certificate given the 11th June 1755 under my hand & Seal. John Linder, J.P.

Order that y's s'd Petition do ly on the Table.

Page 440: Read the Petition of Peter Rote of y'e Township of Orangeburgh, shewing That the Inhabitants of y'e said Township being favoured with a very plentiful Crop of wheat for Three Years Successively, and believing If there was a Water mill near to grind the Grain, it might probably enable them in time to furnish the Greatest part if not all the Province with wheat Flower, as Good and at a much cheaper rate, than that which is imported here, from New England, Philadelphia &C, and the s'd People of Orangeburgh knowing y'r said Petitioner to be Capable of Erecting such a Mill did a long time since solicit him to use his dexterity therein and y'r s'd Peti'r imagening it might be profitable to him self as well as Extreamly serviceable to his neighbors, did at last undertake and Employ himself in the said work, and after much care and industry hath built a mill and brought it to a degree of grinding, but not to perfecting, for y'r said Pet'r being an infirm man, has spent a great dale of money in Physick and is not yet Entirely restored to his former state of health, and is not able to proceed in finishing the said mill without some assistance and y'r said Petitioner being informed that when the Dutch People of Orangeburgh first arrived in this Province, the Late Lieut Govern'r the Hon'ble Thos Broughton, Esq'r and his Majestys Hon'ble Council did promise that if any artificer or man of Ingenuity among them would excercise himself in order to be Serviceable to his neighbours, or to the Province, he should now want money to Encourage or to help his proceedings, and your said Petitioner having used his utmost skill in the above mentioned work which is very manifest and visible to all the Inhabitants of Orangeburgh aforesaid, most humbly begs that your Excellency will be pleased Charitably to Consider the Case and to Consult with his Majesty's Hon'ble Council on the said Occasion, that a Small sum of the Publick may be granted to him for the purpose aforesaid. The above Petition being considered It was the opinion of his Majesty's Council that one hundred pounds Currency be given the Petitioner, in order to enable him to finish the said Mill, wch is so much for the Public Good in those Parts.

Pp. 478-479: Meeting of 5 October 1744

Read the Petition of James Reid and Henry Kennan humbly shewing That in Consequence of a Petition from the Settlers on the Welch Tract an order was Issued from the Council Chamber the 26th day of January 1742/3 to the Commissary to pay to the makers of the first 20 barrels of Good & mercantable white flour, each barrel weighing 200 weight upon proof of its being bona fide the produce of the said Tract, has been sent to us by Colonel George Pawley as his Factors, we have applied accordingly to John Dart Esq'r Commissary for the bounty, who notwithstanding the order of Council, refuses us payment. They therefore beg Leave to lay the aforesaid Case before his Excellency and his Majesty's Hon'ble Council, praying such relief in behalf of the said Col. George Pawley as in his wisdom shall seem meet &c. Ordered that y'e said Petition lye on the Table.

Page 479: Read the petition of John Hamilton Purdy shewing that the Pet'r has a Family of six persons viz himself, wife, three children & one negroe in this Province and has had no lands hitherto. Prays for a Warrant of survey for land in the Fork of Wateree river in proportion thereto. which being considered the Prayer thereof was Granted and the Dep'ty Secret'ry ordered to prepare a warrant accordingly on his swearing to his Family right.

Read the Petition of John Black humbly shewing That the Petitioner is lately arrived in this Province with his Family having right for four hundred acres of Land, Prays a Warrant for y'e same in the Wateree Township viz Fredericksburgh &c. The Peti'r appearing and Swearing to his said Family right the pray'r thereof was granted on his paying the usual Fees and the Dep'ty Secret'ry ordered to prepare a Warrant accordingly.

Pp. 479-480: Read the Petition of William Gray shewing that the Petitioner lately arrived in this Province with his Family, having Family right for three hundred and fifty acres of land, prays that a Warrant may be issued for running the same in Fredericksburgh Township and his Majesty's Bounty &C. Which Petition being considered and the Petitioner appearing before his Excell'cy in Council and swearing to his said right it was ordered that the Pray'r of the Petition with regard to the Land be granted, but not the Bounty on his paying the Fees and the Deputy Secretary do prepare a Warrant for the land accordingly.

Page 480: Read the Petition of Margaret ONeal widdow shewing that the Petr is desirous to take up land for herself and child, her deceased husband nor herself, having never taken up any in the Province, therefore prays for a warrant for surveying to her one hundred acres of land where she now lives in Berkley County adjoining to some lands of Mr. Daniel Horry in the uppermost settlement of Wampee. The Petit'r appearing and proving upon Oath y'e allegations of her said Petition, the prayer thereof was granted.

Pp. 480-481: Read the Petition of Gilbert Gibson of SaxGotha humbly Shewing That he having to maintain his old mother with four children under age in his Family and having no Land either left him by his Father deceased, or taken up any in his own right, humbly prays his Excell'cy and their Honors That Three hundred acres of Land be admeas'd to him on the northeastward of Santee river over against the Township of SaxGotha, or part whereof he now liveth &c. which Peti'n being Considered and the Petitioner appearing and proving the allegations of his s'd Petition upon Oath, the prayer thereof was Granted provided it is in Trust for the Petitioner, his mother, Elizabeth his sisters Sarah, Thene, Hannah & Jane Gibson.

Page 481: Read the Petition of John Lessly a poor Protestant Palatine shewing that he being lately arrived in the Province with his wife and nine children, whereof six are under 12 years of age, with an Intent to settle in one of the Townships upon the Encouragement of his Majesty's Bounty, humbly prays that the said Bounty of one Year's provision for him and his Family may be Granted to him as also for their further maintenance five hundred and fifty acres of Land in the Township of Fredericksburg at Pine tree Creek with a

Town Lot in the s'd Town. This Petition being Considered and the Petit'r appearing before his Excell'cy in Council and searing to y'e truth of y'e allegations of the said Petition the pray'r of y'e Same with regard to y'e land, the Lot and Bounty were granted and Mr. Commiss. ordered to pay the Bounty and y'e Dep'ty Secretary to prepare a Warrant accordingly.

Pp. 481-482: Read the Petition of Michael Brannom humbly shewing That the Petitioner is lately arrived in this Province with his family having right for two hundred acres of Land, therefore humbly prays that a warrant be Issued for running the same in the Wateree viz Frederickburg Township on his Majesty's Bounty &c. Which petition being Considered and the Petit'r appearing and Swearing to the Truth of his allegations therein mentioned, the Prayer thereof with regard to the land was granted, also the charges of his Peti'n, warrant, Grant &C. to be defrayed him by the Publick, but not y'e Bounty and the Commissary Gener'l was ordered to pay his charges, and the Dep'ty Secretary to prepare a Warrant for the land accordingly.

Page 482: Read the Petition of Thomas Brown shewing that the Petitioner hath an Increase of five persons in his Family for whom he hath had no land Granted as Yet, but being desirous to Cultivate vacant lands on a neck opposite to the upper part of SaxGotha Town'p between the Congree River and an other branch thereof, commonly called broad River, Prays his Excell'cy and their Honors two hundred and fifty acres of land be granted him under Such Quit Rents & Conditions as by his Majesty's Royal Instructions to His Excell'cy are directed & appointed &C. The Petitioner appearing and proving upon oath y'e allegations of his said Petition, the prayer thereof was Granted and y'e Deputy Secret'ry ordered to prepare a Warrant accordingly.

Pp. 482-483: Read the Petition of Richard Richeson shewing That he having Six Persons in Family for whom he has not as Yet obtained any land humbly prays his Excell'cy and their Honors that three hundred acres of land in Craven County in Prince Fredericks Parish on the north side of a Swamp Called Gumswamp be granted him. The same being Considered, the Prayer thereof was Granted on the Petitioner's appearing and Swearing to y'e Truth of his allegations, the deputy Secret'ry ordered to prepare a Warrant accordingly.

Pp. 484-485: Read the Petition of Samuel Lines shewing That the Petitioner a native of Carolina being now out of his apprenticeship & married has five in Family and being willing to Settle and Cultivate Land in his native Country, prays That his Excell'cy and their Honors, by virtue of his said Family Right may order him a Warrant for Two hundred and fifty acres on y'e north side of Santee River adjoining to y'e Land of Rich'd Jackson, for which the Petitioner as in duty &c. The s'd Petition being Considered, and y'e Petitioner appearing, and Swearing to the Truth of his allegations, the prayer thereof was granted and the Dep'ty Secretary ordered to prepare a Warrant accordingly.

Page 485: Read the Petition exhibited by Charles Radcliffe humbly shewing that the Petitioners in most humble manner pray That a Warrant be Issued to y'e s'd Charles Radcliffe for running fifty acres of vacant land on both sides of Simse's Creek Joining his own land, in the Wateree Town, Fredericksburgh Township, for building and setting up a Water mill whch will be of great benefit and service to the Whole Inhabitants and others. signed Alex'r Rattery, Samuel Hudson, Wm. Bellen[?] and 9 more subscribers. The said Petition being Considered and the Petit'rs appearing and swearing to the Truth of y'e allegations of his said Petition, the prayer thereof was granted and the deputy secret'ry orderd to prepare a warrant accordingly.

Pp. 485-486: Read the Petition of Mary Hyde of Berkley County widow humbly shewing That her late Husband having begun a Settlement and being prevented by his death, to take up land in his Family right, humbly prays that for the mantenance of her self and three children his Excell'cy and their Honours would be pleased to grant her two hundred acres of land fronting the north-east bank of Santee River opposite to SaxGotha Township, and Joining Lands laid out to Nicholas Haynes &c. The Petit'r appearing before his Excell'cy in Council and proving upon oath the allegations of her said Petition,the prayer thereof was Granted....

Page 486: Read the Petition of John Wolf humbly shewing that the Petitioner with is Family came from Bern in Swisserland with intention to reside in this Province but now having them money to pay his freight, was together with his wife obliged to enter into y'e Service of Anthony Stack of SaxGotha for three years but as it appears on the back of the Indenture he & his Wife are Legally discharged from the said service, Therefore Humbly prays his Excell'cy & their Honors that he may have one hundred acres of land laid out for him in Orangeburgh Township and also his Majesty's most gracious Bounty. The Petition being considered and the Petitioner producing his own and his Wife's discharge from their service, under the hand of the s'd Anthony Stack at the same time proving upon oath the Truth of the allegations the prayer thereof with regard to both land and Bounty was Granted...

Pp. 487-488: Read the Petition of Philip Pool, a German, humbly setting forth That the Petitioner abt Two Years ago, Embarked in Holland with his wife & four children on board the ship Elizabeth for this Province, with an Intention to Settle with his Family among his Countrymen in SaxGotha Township, but the ship putting in to Frederica in Georgia was without any pretended Crime detained by General Oglethorpe there for the space of 18 months, when upon his Petitioner the General for a pass to be allowed to Come to South Carolina, He was put in to y'e Guard house without the allowance of bread and water, neither while in Prison nor at any time during his detention for the Eighteen months, so that the money the Petitioner had brought with him, to buy negroes here, to the amount of ninety six pistoles, he was forced to expend in Georgia for maintaining himself and the other five in his Family, so that now, having nothing wherewith to Subsist, Humbly prays his Excell'cy and their Honours will be pleased to grant him three hundred acres of Land in SaxGotha Township and his Majesty's Bounty, he intending to erect a poutting [sic] mill there, for making fine flour, for y'e market, also prays that his Excell'cy and their hon'rs will be pleased to take his Confinement and hardships in Georgia under consideration, and procure him what relief therein as may seem meet in their wisdom, more especially as several of his Countrymen are at present detained in Georgia, notwithstanding they intended & do intend to Come and Settle in this province &c. March 29th 1744. Which Petition being duly Considered, and the Peti'r appear before his Excell'cy in Council, and Swearing to the Truth of y'e allegations in the s'd Petition, the prayer thereof was Granted both as to y'e land and the bounty....

Page 488: Read the Petition of Hans Conrade Verley humbly Shewing That y'r Pet'r came some Years ago with his Father and his Family to Settle at Purysbourgh, but as yet has not any land Granted him on account of his Family right but being desirous to Settle in Purysbourg Town'h humbly prays that his Excell'cy & their Honors would order him a Warrant for fifty acres to be admeasured there, and his Majesty's Bounty &c. The Petitioner appearing y'e Board and Swearing to the Truth of the allegations of his Petition, the Secretary was ordered to prepare a Warrant for the Land prayed for and that the Commis'ry Genl defray the charges of Petition, Warrant &c but no other Bounty to be allowed him.

Pp. 488-489: Read the Petition of John Jacob Gieger Shewing That the Peti'r came into this Province seven years ago and is now married, therefore prays That one hundred acres of Land be by virtue of his family right laid out to him over against Santee River opposite to SaxGotha Township where he has already begun to clear Ground, and almost finished a house. The Pet'r appearing y'e his Excell'cy in Council and Swearing to the Truth of the allegations of his Petition, the prayer thereof was Granted and the Deputy Secret'ry ordered to prepare a Warrant accordingly.

Pp. 502-503: Meeting of 29th November 1744

Read the Petition of Samuel Hudson, planter, humbly Shewing that your Peti'r about a year since arrived in this Province with desire of settling himself and family therein, having a wife, six children and six negroes for whom no family rights have been granted. He therefore humbly prays y'e Excell'cy and Honours that a Warrant may issue for surveying & admeasuring to y'e Petitioner vacant land in St. Johns Parish, bounding on Horse fords land, near Webbs Creek, agreeable to the family right which on Examination shall appeared he is entitled to &c. and the Peti'r begs leave to shew... that Thomas Powell had three hundred acres of land Surveyed for him at or near the place in the within Petitioner mentioned on the 3d day of June 1741, the Plat whereof as yet remains in the Survey'r Gen'ls Office and the same was advertise among the Plats by order of the Hon'ble Wm Bull Esq'r Lt. Gov and his Majesty's Honble Council in the Supplement to the Gazette for 2 Augt

1743 wch required all Persons claiming such lands to apply for and take out the same, on or before y'e first day of Jan'ry last, and in case of their neglecting so to do, their failure therein should be taken as a disclaim, Wherefore your Pet'r prays that his Excell'cy & Honors will be pleased to order the Survey'r General to certify the land in said Plat in y'r Petitioners name as part of y'e Warrant of Survey within Petitioned for. Samuel Hudson. Ordered That the Survey'r General do Certify if y'e Plat mentioned be in his office.

Page 503: Read the Petition of John Wildermoot from Wirtembergh in Germany Shewing That some short time ago he arrived in this Province from Holland upon y'e Encouragement of his Majesty's bounty and with design to Settle here, in Amelia Township, Therefore Prays for fifty acres of land and his Majesty's Gracious bounty. The Pet'r appearing before his Excell'cy in Council and Swearing to his said right, the pray'r of his said Petition with regard to y'e Land was Granted but not the Bounty....

Pp. 503-504: Read the Petition of Mary Bear widdow shewing That she came over here about Eight years ago, with her husband a Swiss, in Capt. Montague's Ship, that for want of money to pay her passage, she with her said Husband were obliged to service Col. Pury for four years, but her husband being since dead, she is now at Orangeburgh Township & having one Child prays for one hundred acres of Land in y'e s'd Town'p and his Majesty's Gracious Bounty. The Pet'r appearing before the Board and Swearing to her said right, the pray'r of his said Petition with regard to y'e Land was Granted but not the Bounty....

Page 504: Read the Petition of Jacob Spuhler of SaxGotha shewing That Lt. Gov'r Bull granted him a Warrant for one hundred acres of Land, the 2d March 1742, wch warrant not being as Yet executed, and the Pet'r finding that the Surveyors are not authorized to execute the same, being out of date, prays that a fresh Warrant may be granted for y'e s'd 100 acres and fifty more or acct of Encrease in his Family, in the s'd Town'p of SaxGotha. The Warrant mentioned in y'e petition, being produced and read, the prayer thereof was granted the Pet'r appearing and swearing to his family right....

Read the Petition of John Mathys of SaxGotha shewing That he has 3 Persons by virtue of Family right for whom he has not obtained any Land, therefore humbly prays his Excell'cy and their Hon'rs to Grant him one hundred and fifty acres of Land in the Fork between Santee & Wateree Rivers over against the Township of Saxgotha. The Pet'r appearing and Swearing to y'e truth of his allegations, the prayer of his s'd Petition was Granted on Condition that the land prayed for be not in any of the reserved lands nor in any already Granted away to another.

Pp. 504-505: Read the Petition of Jacob Young shewing that he with his family being five in number intend to settle in SaxGotha Township over Santee river therefor prays that five hundred and fifty acres of land there may be granted. The Pet'r appearing before his Excell'cy in Council and Swearing to his said Family right, the prayer of his said Petition with regard to the land was Granted upon Condition that it be not in any of y'e reserved lands nor in any already Granted away to another.

Pp. 505-506: Read the humble Petition of Paul Harlson & others shewing that the Peti'rs family consists of nine White Persons who being lately arrived in this Province with design to Cultivate & Settle 400 and 50 acres of land, therefore prays that his Excell'cy and their Honours to grant him a Warrant for y'e same by virtue of his family Right in Fredericksbourgh Township and the said Paul Harelson with 'ye under written Inhabitants humbly pray that the Board would grant ye s'd Harleson fifty acres more of land on a Creek called Sanders's Creek for y'e building & setting up a Water-mill in y'e frontiers of Fredericksburgh Town ship and whch mill is of extraordinary benefit to y'e distressed subscribers and further pray that an order be Granted for a road to be Cut to y'e said Town'p of Fredericksburgh whch will enable them to Convey their Small produce to y'e market.... Signd Paul Harleson, Mark Catterton about 24 more Subscribers. The Petitioner appearing before his Excell'cy the Gov'r in Council and Swearing to y'e Truth of the allegations of his Petition, the Pray'r thereof with regard to the land was Granted....

Page 506: Read the Petition of Jeffrey Summerford humbly Shewing That his family Consists of four persons for whom he has had no Land assigned him, Prays that his Excell'cy and Their Hon's would Grant him 200 acres of Land on y'e Wateree River in the upper part of Fredericksburgh Township. The Pet'r appearing before y'e Board and swearing to y'e Truth of his allegations the pray'r of his said Petition was Granted....

Read the Petition of Oliver Mahaffey Shewing That the Pet'rs Family Consists of three white persons for whom he has not had any Land assigned him, but being desirous to Cultivate land in this Province humbly Prays that one hundred and fifty acres of Land be granted him on a Creek called Granney's Quarters being of all sides vacant &c. The Pet'r appearing before his Excell'cy i Council and proving upon oath y'e allegations of his said petition, the Prayer thereof was Granted....

Pp. 506-507: Read the Petition of Gideon Ellis shewing That the Petition'r upon y'e Encouragem't given by the Board for building of mills has settled and made Several Improvem'ts and hath goth a frame for a saw-mill and grist mill, and dug y'e well and it being upon vacant land, on the south west side of Pedee River on a Creek called Bare-Creek intending to raise a Saw mill and Grist mill as soon as possible prays that a Warrant be Granted him for Six hundred acres of land upon y'e said Bare Creek in the Welch Tract. Ordered That the s'd Petition be Considered when the Pet'r himself comes to attend the Board.

Page 507: Read the humble Petition of John Fairchild shewing That Whereas his hon'r the Lt. Gov'r Bull did on the 10th of August 1742 grant to y'e Pet'r a Warrant of Survey for four hundred acres of Land in Craven County on the north side of Santee River below Jack's Creek to be returned in 12 months but no survey having been made thereof, according to y'e tenor of y'e s'd Warrant the time being now Expired, Prays for a Grant of the Lands prayed for and obtained & that it be admeasured anew wch lyes on the north side of the Congree River opposite to SaxGotha Township a few miles distant from Lands laid out to James Crokatt Esq'r and Wm. Howell's Lands &c. The Petit'r produced the Warrant from y'e Hon'ble Lt. Gov'r Bull mentioned whereupon It was ordered that this Petition be reconsidered when the Peti'r shall attend himself.

Pp. 507-508: Read the Petition of several Inhabitants on Santee River in favour of John Lessly, humbly Praying for a Certain quantity of Land lying on the half way Swamp on the north side of Santee River for building a Water mill, and saw mill by y'e s'd John Lessly which they apprehend will be of very public benefit to those remote parts and that Encouragement be given to the s'd Lessly to compleat his mills, and that the Lands he now in possession be exchanged for those he now prays for. The Pet'r appearing and proving upon Oath the allegations of his said Petition at the same time producing the Warrant he had obtained for y'e Land he now Possesses, It was ordered that y'e said Land be Exchanged...

Page 508: Read the humble Petition of Richard Haynsworth shewing That the said Pet'r has seven Persons in Family for whom as yet no land has been assigned him, but being desirous to cultivate and settle three hundred and fifty acres of vacant land there, by virtue of his said Family Right &c. The Petit'r appearing before his Excell'cy in Council and proving upon oath the Truth of his allegations of his s'd Petition, the prayer thereof with regard to the land was Granted...

Pp. 508-509: Read the Petition of William Baker of SaxGotha shewing That the Pet'r has an Increase of four persons in his Family for whom he hath not as yet had nay Land assigned him, but being desirous to settle on, and cultivate vacant land on the north side of Santee river opposite to SaxGotha Township, humbly prays his Excell'cy and their Honours That a Warrant be Issued for admeasuring two hundred acres of land there by virtue of his s'd Family right &c. The Petit'r appearing before the Board and swearing to his said Right, the pray'r of his said Petition was Granted...

Page 509: Read the Petition of Anthony Wright shewing that the Peti'r has a Family of nine Persons for whom he hath hitherto had no Land but being desirous to Cultivate some of his Majesty's Lands that are Vacant where he is now settled, with his said family on Wateree river opposite to Fredericks bourgh Township and as at pres't the Peti'r is sick and distressed with old age has sent his Wife humbly to present his s'd Petition to his Excell'cy and their

Honours Therefore humbly prays the Board would be pleased to accept of the proof of his allegations from his Wife as he is not able to undergo the fatigue of a Journey to Charles Town and to Grant thereon a Warrant for y'e Survey of the land in proportion to his Family right &C. The Pet'rs Wife appearing and making oath as to y'e allegations of her husbands Petition, It was ordered that y'e pray'r of ye said Petition be Granted....

Pp. 509-510: Read the petition of David Amstutz and his Wife humbly Shewing that the Peti'r from Bern in Swisserland arrived lately in this Province in Captain Ham's Ship on the Encouragem't given to Forreign Protestants to settle here, and as their Intention in leaving their native Country was to Settle here, humbly Pray That one hundred acres of Land be granted them in Orangeburgh Township and his Majesty's Gracious Bounty &c. ordered That y'e s'd Petition be reconsidered to morrow morning, and that Captain Ham be also ordered to attend this Board.

Page 510: Read the Petition of Jeremiah Racine humbly shewing That the Peti'r about four weeks since arrived in this Province with his wife and one male child of the age of three years with design to settle therein and having been very long on his passage hither from Germany is in Great necessity. Wherefore he most humbly prays his Excell'cy and their Honors that a Warrant be Issued for surveying & Admeasuring to him vacant land in Orangeburgh Township and his Majesty's most Gracious Bounty. The Peti'r appearing at y'e Board and proving upon oath of y'e allegations of his s'd Petition, the Prayer of his Petition with regard to both Land and y'e Bounty was Granted...

Pp. 510-511: Read the Petition of George Michel Renfer a Protestant of Swisserland praying for fifty acres of Land in Orangeburgh Township, and his Majesty's Gracious bounty. The Peti'r appearing before his Excell'cy in Council & Swearing to the truth of his allegations in his said Petition, the Pray'r thereof was Granted with regard to y'e Land not the Bounty but the Charges of his Petition, Warrant, &c be defrayed by the Publick....

Page 511: Read the Petition of Ila Orley shewing That some few weeks ago, the Peti'r arrived together with some others of her Country People from Bern in Swisserland, in Capt'n Ham's Ship, on the Encouragem't given by the King to Forreign Protestants who shall reside here, and as she designs forthwith to settle in Orangeburgh Township, Prays that 50 acres of land may be Granted her there and his Majesty's Gracious Bounty &c. The Petit'r appearing before y'e Board and swearing to the allegations of her said Petition, y'e prayer thereof both as to y'e Land and Bounty was Granted...

Read the Petition of Ulrick Stoker shewing That on acc't of y'e Encouragem't the King gives to Forreign Protestants who shall come and reside here, he is a few days ago arrived in Capt'n Ham's ship from Chafhausen[?] in Swisserland, with intention to settle in one of the Townships and therefore prays his

Excellency and their Honours to Grant him fifty acres of Land in Orangeburgh Township and his Majesty's Gracious Bounty &c. The Petit'r appearing before the Board and swearing to the allegations of his s'd Petition, the prayer thereof both with regard to y'e Land and Bounty was Granted...

Page 512: Read the humble Petition of George Pitcairn shewing that being possessed of an estate in the Island Ounst in Scotland, but by misfortunes being reduced to poverty prays for relief. That this Petition ly on the Table.

Page 513: Read the humble Petition of Anna Barbara Gallochor praying for leave to apply to the charity of Christian people. Ordered That the said Petition ly on the Table.

Pp. 516-517: <u>Meeting of 30th November 1744</u>

David Amstuts a German lately arrived her Capt. Ham's ship attended the Board, according to Summons together with his wife Margaret as mentioned in the minutes of yesterday, as did also Capt' Ham who produced the Indenture made for binding the sd Margar't for four Years, servant to Mr. Evance of Charles Town, and the Law being read, it was recommended to him, to accept of the money which he had payed to Mr. Ham for the Service of y'e said Woman and give up the Indenture to wch Mr. Evans who was present agreed, Whereupon the Petition of the sd Amstutz was reconsidered who appearing and proving upon Oath the allegations of his Petition, the prayer thereof with regard to both land & bounty was granted....

Page 517: Read the Petition of Hans Boden of Swisserland and his wife, who arrived here lately in Captain Ham's Ship, praying for one hundred acres of land in Orangeburgh Township & The Bounty. The Petitioners appearing and swearing to their Family right and the allegations of their s'd Petition, the prayer thereof with regard to the land and also the bounty are Granted them...

Read the Petition of Rudolph Buchter and four children all forreign Protestants praying for two hundred acres of Land in SaxGotha Township and his Majesty's Bounty for himself and four children. The allegations of the said Petition being proved upon oath before the Board, the prayer thereof was Granted...

Page 519: Reconsidered that Petition of Samuel Hudson as mentioned in the minutes of Yesterday, who appearing before his Excellency and the council and proving upon oath the allegations of his said Petition and at the same time producing the Survey'r Generals Certificate of the Plat mentioned in his said Petition, being in his office, the pray'r thereof was Granted.

Pp. 519-520: Read the Petition of Nathaniel Snow Sen'r Planter Shewing that the Peti'r hath in his Family two White Persons and ten negroes for whom hitherto he hath not had any warrant for land, and being desirous to Cultivate and settle Six hundred acres prays that a Warrant may be granted, for running out Six hundred acres of Land in a Tract or Tracts which is now Vacant on or near Cooper River adjoining to Mr. George Chickens's land. The Petitioner appearing before the board and Swearing to the Truth of y'e allegations of y'e said Petition, the prayer thereof was Granted on Condition That it is not on any of the reserved lands nor any lands already granted, nor fronting any other Persons land on that river...

Page 522: Meeting of 1st December 1744

Read the Petition of Abram Colson shewing That the Pet'r has an increase or 12 persons in family for whom he has not had any Lands assigned him, but being desirous to Settle in the Welch Tract, and to Cultivate lands there, humbly Prays that a Warrant be ordered him for admeasuring six hundred acres of land in that tract bounding on the north side of Pedee River near the land of John Hicks & the Pet'r produced a Certificate from several Inhabitants of y'e Welch Tract & signed by them in favor of y'e Pet'r. The Pet'r appearing before his Excellency in Council and swearing to the truth of y'e allegations of his Petition, the prayer thereof was Granted....

Pp. 519-520: Read the Petition of William Pressley shewing That he came into this Province along with his Father from Ireland above Six years ago on y'e Encouragem't of the King's bounty. That his Father obtained a Warrant for Two hundred acres of land in Williamsburgh Township, wch since his Father's death he has endeavoured to Improve but as y'e same was entirely pine barren the Pet'r has ever since spent his Labour and Substance upon it without ever being able to make any advantage thereof, or Support his family thereby. That he has a Family of Seven persons for whom he never as Yet hath taken up any land, or hath he any other land in y'e province but as before mentioned. And the Pet'r being willing to surrender up y'e former Grant, humbly prays that his Family right be granted him on the first vacant land within the said Township... The Pet'r appearing before his Excell'cy in Council and proving upon oath y'e Truth of y'e allegations of his said Petition the pray'r thereof viz three hundred & fifty acres of Land be granted him in y'e Town'p prayed for....

Pp. 531-532: Meeting of 4th December 1744

Read the Petition of Jacob Axon[?] shewing that he hath nine Persons in family for whom as Yet he has not obtained any Grant of land and being desirous to Cultivate land and settle with his Family in the Welch Tract humbly prays that an order be issued for admeasuring to him four hundred and fifty acres of land in the said Tract by virtue of his Family right &c. Ordered That this Petition be reconsidered at another meeting.

Pp. 549-550: Meeting of 8th December 1744

Read the Petition of Michael Zoug a native of Bern in Swisserland humbly Shewing that the Pet'r has been some time in this Province and served his Brother as an apprentice at Purysburgh in order thereby to pay the freight for his coming over but being now free, humbly prays his Excellency & their Honors that by virtue of his family right he may have one hundred and fifty acres of land opposite to the Township of SaxGotha and his Majestys most Gracious bounty. The Petit'r appearing before his Excellency in Council and proving upon oath the allegations of his Petition, the prayer thereof with regard to ye land was Granted but not the Bounty....

Page 550: Read the Petition of Conrade Buntzler a German humbly Shewing That he has an Encrease of Family of five children and therefore prays that he may have a Warrant for Laying out to him two hundred and fifty acres of land by virtue of his s'd Family right, over against SaxGotha Township, over Santee River. The Peti'r appearing before his Excell'cy y'e Gov'r in Council and swearing to his said Family right, the Prayer of his Petition with regard to y'e Land was Granted....

Pp. 549-550: Read the Petition of Hans Dietrick a German most humbly shewing That the Peti'r had the misfortune of having his House and Barn burned down to ashes with Every thing what was in it as may be seen by the Inclosed Certificate, therefore great necessary obliges him to pray his Excell'cy & their Honors that his lamentable Condition be taken under their Consideration &c. His Excellency by and with y'e advice of his Majestys Hon'ble Council signed an order on the Treasurer for fifty pounds Currency to be payd to the said Hans Diterick it was also signed by the Eldest Councillor present.

Page 11: Meeting of 2d January 1744/5

His Excellency also acquainted the Board that the Palatine Protestants to the number of one hundred, who had lately arrived in Capt. Brown's Ship came on the 31st of December last, in a Body to the Council Chamber and took the State Oaths to His Majestys, all of them having determined to remain and settle in this Province.

Page 13: Meeting of 17th January 1744/5

Read the Petition of Gideon Ellis praying for 600 acres of land upon Bare Creek in the Welch Tract in order for the building a Saw and Grist mill thereon. The Peti'r appearing and swearing to his family right, only to the amount of 200 acres, that number only was granted....

Read the Petition of Richard Palmer shewing that the Petitioner's Father Colonel Palmer by his last will bequeathed to him a Plantation of land on Combahee River consisting of 4 Plats, for which warrant was obtained to the petitioner's Father, and the Platts returned into the Surveyor's Office as will upon Enquiry appear, but as the petitioner's Father died before the Grants were signed for the said lands, he humbly prays that 2 Portions of the said land vizt 525 acres already surveyed in Granville county Octo'r 1st 1737 & 300 d'o signed Jan'y 10th 1738 be granted him, as also the marsha land fronting the same &c. The above Petition being read the Petitioner was ordered to give in a more perfect State of the Case to the Board.

Page 17: Meeting of 18th January 1744/5

Read the Petition of Roger Gibson of Williamsbourgh, Planter, humbly shewing That 250 Acres of land was surveyed in the foresaid Township on the 6th day of January 1740 in pursuance of a Warrant from the late lieutenant Gov'r Broughton, for Jannet McBride, who dying, the Petitioner trustee for her son John McBride, prays for a Grant in trust for the said Orphan, the Platt of which lands lyes now in the Surveyor General's Office, that he may be ordered to certify that Platt. To this was annexed a Certificate under the hand of the said John McBride, empowering the said Roger Gibson to act for him, whereupon It was ordered that the Surveyor General do certify the said Platt in his office....

Read the Petition of Andrew Buck a foreign Protestant, who arriv'd in the Ship St. Andrew, Captain Brown, Master, praying that on acc't of Family Right 400 Acres of land be laid out to him in the Township of Sax Gotha, and for the usual Bounty... the prayer thereof was Granted and the Deputy Secretary ordered to prepare a Warrant, and the commissary to pay the bounty.

Read the Petition of Michael Augston, a foreign Protest't who arriv'd here on Captain Brown's Ship, abo't a month ago, & who having a Wife & 1 Child humbly prays y't 150 acres of land be laid out for him in Sax Gotha Towns'p as family Right & Y't he may have y'e usual Bounty.... the prayer thereof was granted and the Dep'y Secre'y ordered to prepare a Warrant, and y'e Commissary to pay him the bounty.

Page 18: Read the Petition of Melchior Sower a foreign Protestant of Germany who having three Persons in Family prays that 150 acres of land be granted him in the Township of Sax Gotha, and the usual Bounty... the prayer thereof was Granted and the Deputy Secretary ordered to prepare a Warrant, and the commissary to pay him the Bounty accordingly.

Read the Petition of Jacob Giegher a foreign Protestant who lately arrived here in the Saint Andrew, Captain Brown, Commander, who having 3 persons in family prays that 150 Acres of land be laid out to him in the Township of Sax Gotha and the usual Bounty... the prayer thereof was Granted and the Deputy Secretary ordered to prepare a Warrant, and the commissary to pay the Bounty accordingly.

Page 24: Meeting of 19th January 1744/5

Read the Petition of Richard Palmer, being a more full State of his Affair relating to land prayed for as in the minutes of Jan 17th last vizt [blank] Ordered that the Prayer of the said Petition be granted and that the Surveyor General be directed to make out a special Certificate on the platts survey'd, and that the Attorney general prepare a special fait, pursuant to the devise in the will of Collonel Palmer. N.B. This Original Petition endorsed on the Back was delivered to the Petit'r to be carry'd to the Surveyor's Office, but he never did return it nor can it be found in any of the Offices.

Page 26: Meeting of 21st January 1744/5

In pursuance of an Order of this Board of the 25th day of Nov'r 1752, George Hunter Esq'r Surveyor General, made a Return of the resurvey of the Outline of 6 Tracts of land said to contain in the whole 3300 Acres of land, in Craven County belonging to the Hon'ble John Cleland Esq'r & Mary his wife, by which it appears that there is contained within the bounds of the same an Overplus of 696 Acres in which is contained the Town & Common of George Town, which is now set apart for the public use of a Town, it is therefore further ordered that the said Surveyor Gen'l do prepare and certify a platt of the whole Quantity of land contained within the outlines of the said platt and distinguishing the particular situation of the said 696 acres of land on the said platt, that a Special Fiat may be prepared for a Grant to pass for the whole 3996 acres of land at the Quit Rent the s'd 3300 Acres of land were granted, in the Original Grants thereof, viz't at 12 pence proclamation money P 100 acres, proof being made that the said Original Grants were destroyed by Fire.

Page 28: Read the Petition of Gaspar Kantz a Protestant Palatine most humbly shewing that a few weeks ago he arrived in this Province in the Ship

St. Andrew, Captain Brown, Commander, & having a wife & 4 Children humbly prays that as he is determined to settle in this Province, 300 acres of land may be laid out to him in the Township of Sax Gotha, and that he may have the usual Bounty... the prayer thereof was Granted and the Deputy Secretary ordered to prepare a Warrant, and the commissary to pay the bounty accordingly.

Read the Petition of Jacob Sneider a German Protestant, humbly shewing that as he is come over to settle in this Province, as he has a Wife and two Children in family he prays that 200 acres of land be laid out to him, and that he may obtain the usual Bounty... the prayer thereof was Granted and the Deputy Secretary ordered to prepare a Warrant, and the commissary to pay the bounty accordingly.

Pages 28-29: Read the Petition of Michael Sneider a Protestant of Germany, shew'g y'at as he intends to settle in this Province, he having 3 Persons in Family, prays y't 150 acres of land be laid out to him in y'e township of Sax Gotha & y't he may be allowed the usual Bounty... the prayer thereof was Granted and the Deputy Secretary ordered to prepare a Warrant, and the commissary to pay the bounty accordingly, viz't 100 acres of land for himself and 50 acres for Barbara Sleigher his Sister in law.

Page 29: Read the Petition of Jacob Deerer a Foreign Protestant praying that in Consideration of his having come over to settle in this Province with his Family which are three in number, 150 acres of land in Sax Gotha Township or Amelia Township be granted him, and the usual Bounty... the prayer thereof was Granted and the Dep'ty Sec'ry ordered to prepare a Warr't, and the Commiss'y to pay y'e Bounty.

Pages 30-31: Read the Petition of John Frasher shewing that the Petit'r has an Encrease of one child in Family for which no land has been assigned him, that there are 49 acres a Remainder of 100 as P'r Warrant unexecuted, the whole Quantity not to be had where the rest was laid out. Prays that a warrant may issue for surveying 99 acres of land where the Petit'r is now settling on the Low Ground of Santee or Congree River, opposite to Sax Gotha Township, and that the Hon'ble Board would accept of the proof of this Petition of Hans Jacob Reminspergher whose daughter he has married; The warrant mentioned and annexed being produced and Jacob Reminspergher called upon & made oath as to the truth of the Allegations in the said Petition the prayer thereof was granted, and the Surveyor ordered to run the land out accordingly.

Page 31: Read the Petition of Thomas and Nathaniel Green, humbly shewing, That the Petitioners Father Daniel Green did obtain from Gov'r Johnson the 10th day of January 1731 a Warrant of Survey for one thousand five hundred acres of vacant land in this Province, but had not any more survey'd thereof but 110 acres bounding eastward on the lands of Wm. Cochran, N. W. by the land of Edmond Bellinger, S. W. by the land of William Townsend and

Southward by the lands of Noah Hurst as appears by the annex'd platt returned, and as Gov'r Johnson died before the Grant for the said 110 Acres was Signed, The Petitioners humbly pray His Excellency & their honours to order a Warrant to be issued... ordered That the Petitioner be referred to Jacob Mote, Esq'r, that he give an Acco't of the right that those Petit'rs have under the will of Daniel Green's widdow and report the same to this Board.

Pages 31-32: Read the Petition of William Hutson and Mary his wife shewing, that the late Lords Proprietors of this Province on the 25th day of September 1705 did grant unto John Palmer since deceased two tracts of land contain'g 500 & 382 acres in Colleton County, joyning upon y'e north side of Combahee River under the yearly rent of 1 shill'g for every 100 acres, which s'd 2 Tracts by sundry Mesne Conveyances & other Assignm'ts in y'e law, together w'th y'e last will & testm't of Mr. Rich'd Woodward deceas'd y'e Petit'r Mary's Father duely made & executed, now in y'e hands of y'e Peti'rs ready to produced to his Excell'cy & hon'rs the Estate, Right & Titles and Interest of, in and to is become vested in Mary the Petit'r and her Heirs. That the Petit'r Mary apprehending there is an Overplus of land within the bounds of the said two tracts is desirous to procure his Majesty's Grant for the same on the Condition prescrib'd by the Quit-Rent Law. Wherefore the Petitioners humbly pray his Excellency & their Honours would be pleased to grant an order to the Surveyor General to cause the said two tracts of land to be resurvey'd and to make a Return of the same, in order that the Petit'r Mary may obtain a Grant for such Overplus as shall be found within the bounds of the said two Tracts, to Her, her Heirs, and Assigns. Signed William Hutson, Mary Hutson. The above Petition being considered the prayer thereof was granted.

Page 35: Meeting of 23d January 1744/5

Read the Petition of James Bourdeaux of St. Tho's Parish shewing, That the Petitioner is possessed of 787 Acres of land, formerly granted by the Lords Proprietors situation in the Parish & County aforesaid, and on the north side of Wandow River, that he is apprehensive there may be an overplus within the Bounds of the same, and therefore, he prays that an order may be given directing the Surveyor Gen'l to cause the said Tract to be resurveyed, that in case there should be an Overplus he may obtain his Majesty's Grant for the same, agreeable to the Quire rent Law &c. James Bourdeau. The said petition being considered, the prayer thereof was Granted.

Page 42: Meeting of 25th January 1744/5

The Petition of Tho's & Nathaniel Green which was laid before this Board and read as in the Minutes of the 22'd instant was reconsidered, having been referred by Jacob Motte Esq'r who sent back the following Certificate, viz't. "The Petition of Tho's & Nathaniel Green being referred to Jacob Motte he hereby certifies that by the will of Elizabeth Green the real Estate of the said Testatrix is devised to him in trust, and for the use of her children, Elizabeth, Thomas and Nathaniel. the 24th of January 1744. Jacob Motte." Whereupon it appearing that Elizabeth the Daughter of the Testatrix mentioned in the report, being equally interested in the lands prayed for by the petitioners, the prayer of their Petition cannot be regularly granted.

Page 55: Meeting of 26th January 1744/5

Read the Petition of Michael Keener, a Protestant Palatine, shewing that He and his Family about seven in number, are come over to settle in this Province & humbly prays that 350 Acres of land be laid out to him in Orangebourgh Township and the usual Bounty... the prayer thereof was Granted and the Deputy Secretary ordered to prepare a Warrant, and the commissary to pay the Bounty accordingly.

Page 64: Meeting of 29th January 1744/5

Read the Petition of Cornelius Miller a German, humbly shewing, That he came over here from Germany about 4 Years ago with several of his Relations now settled in Orangebourgh Township upon the Encouragement of His Majesty's Bounty, that he was obliged to enter into Service to pay his passage, and was one Year with Mrs. Dryton in Service and 3 Years an Apprentice with Mr. Williams a Carpenter at Ashley Ferry, and having now served his time, prays that 50 Acres of land be granted him in Orangebourgh Township and the usual Bounty... the prayer thereof was granted & y'e Dep'y Secret'ry ordered to prepare a Warrant, & the Commiss'y Gen'l to pay the Bounty accordingly.

Read the Petition of Solomon McGrave an Inhabitant on Santee River, opposite to Sax Gotha Township, shew'g That the Petit'r has 4 persons in Family for whom no land has hitherto been assigned him, therefore prays that 200 acres be admeasured to him on the north side of Santee River agreeable to His Majesty's Royal Instructions. The Petit'r appearing and swearing to his s'd Family Right the prayer thereof was granted and the Dep'ty Secret'ry ordered to prepare a Warrant accordingly.

Pages 64-65: Read the Petition of James Anderson humbly shewing That he has two in Family viz't himself and Wife, for whom no land has been assigned him, and therefore he humbly prays that His Excellency and their Honours would be pleased to order that 100 acres be admeasured to him on the north side of Santee River, over against the Township of Sax Gotha... the prayer of his Petition was Granted and the Deputy Secretary ordered to prepare a Warrant for the land accordingly.

Page 65: Read the Petition of Edward McGrave humbly shewing, That the Petit'r has 4 persons in Family for whom as yet no land been assigned him, and humbly prays his Excell'cy and their Honours that 200 acres may be laid out to him on the north side of Santee River opposite to the Township of Sax Gotha, where the Petitioner now resides. The Petit'r appearing and swearing to the Truth of His said Family Right the prayer of his Petition was granted and the Dep'ty Secret'ry order' to prepare a Warr't for y'e land accordingly.

Pages 65-66: Read the Petition of Archibald Campbell shewing That the petit'r had obtained a Warrant for 100 acres of land in Williamsbourgh Township with a lot there, date Aug'st 25th 1736 that the same was laid out to him by Anthony Williams, but that he cannot procure a platt thereof, from him in order to obtain a Grant for the same, tho' the petit'r has improv'd & lived on the land above Seven years. That William Campbell, his Brother, had, before his Decease, obtained a Warrant of Survey to him for 300 acres of land there, of which the said Williams made also a Survey who never returned that platt into the Surveyor's Office, but a plat of a different Tract of 300 acres at 4 Miles distance from the former, for which a Grant has passed to the said William Campbell, since his Death, w'ch distinct survey the petit'r is well assured his Brother knew nothing of, he having lived in the House with the petit'r from his Arrival to His Death: whereupon he prays that an order be sent to the said Dept'y Surv'yr to make a return of the Plat of 100 acres with the warrant into the Survey'rs Office, y't he may certify the same that a Grant may pas accordingly, also that he make a return of the 300 acres Plat in the name of Wm. Campbell, aged 20 years, son to Wm. Campbell deceased, in whose name the warrant was issued, That a Grant may pass to him for the same, The Grant affixed to the Petitioners platt having passed since the Death of the Grantee, the partys concerned being willing to make a Surrender of any claim they have thereby, or that other Measures be directed for the redress of the petit'r & his nephew who lives with him, They having for s'd land ever done public Services &ca. The above Petition being considered the prayer thereof was granted.

Pages 65-66: Read a Petition from Childermas Croft Esq'r shewing that Kennedy Obrian in his life time obtained a Warrant of Survey for 650 Acres of land from the late Lieut. Gov'r Broughton date April 8th 1737 & in pursuance thereof had a Survey of 400 Acres, part thereof performed on the 22d day of July 1737, & a plat of the same returned into the Survey'r Gen'ls hands, where it now remains, which land was afterwards sold by the said Obrian for a valueable Considerat'n, by proper Conveyances, obliging him, Heir Heirs, Executors & Administrators to obtain a Grant for the same. Therefore prays that an order be issued to the Survey'r Gen'l to certify y'e s'd platt in the name of George Gayrchin, and that His Excell'cy & their Honours would be pleased to grant it accordingly, he having purchased, settled & improv'd the same. Signed Childermas Croft executor of Kennedy Obrian. Ordered that the s'd petition be reconsidered at another meeting.

Page 68: Meeting of 31st January 1744/5

Read the Petition of Henry Snelling, humbly shewing that the Petit'r has three Persons in Family for whom he has not had any lands assigned him, and being desirous to cultivate some of His Majesty's vacant lands, was to where he now lives on the north side of Santee River, prays a Warrant may issue for laying out to him 150 acres of land there, by virtue of his said Family Right. The Petit'r appearing & being examined upon oath as to his said Family Right, and on finding he had included his Sister in law for whom he had no right to desire land, One hundred Acres only were granted him.

Read the Petition of Hugh Murphy, shewing That the Petitioner has an Encrease of five persons in Family viz't Three Children and two Negroes, for whom no land has been assigned, therefore he humbly prays that on Acco't of his said Family Right 250 Acres of land be laid out to him on the North side of Santee River, opposite to the Township of Sax Gotha. The Petitioner appearing and swearing to the truth of the Allegations of the said petition, the prayer thereof was granted and the Deputy Secretary ordered to prepare a warrant accordingly.

Read the Petition of William Janeway shewing That the Petit'r has in Family himself and wife for whom no land has been assigned, therefore he humbly prays that a warrant for admeasuring 100 acres of land on the north side of Santee River, where the Petit'r resides and opposite to the Township of Sax Gotha.... the prayer thereof was granted.

Pages 68-69: Read the Petition of Bethwell and William Dewes humbly shewing, that Mrs. Selia Haig, Guardian to the Petit'rs, did in the year 1731 obtain a Warrant dated the 20th of January from his late Excell'cy Gov'r Johnson for 350 acres of land being in proportion to the said Family right, agreeable to His Majesty's Royal instructions, pursuant to which warrant James St. John Esq'r then Surveyor General issued his precept for surveying the same, agreeable to which Precept Mr. John Stephens, Deputy Surveyor, did survey the said land & platted the same, but on the petitioners taking possession of their Estates, and looking over their papers, to their great Surprize could find no Grant for their land, tho' Tax had been paid for it for several Years before, and upon searching the office found their Guardian had neglected taking out a Grant for the Same. The Petitioners therefore most humbly pray... issue a Grant for the same. The Certificate of the Deputy Surveyor annexed to the Petitioner being read & the petition considered, the prayer thereof was granted.

Page 69: Read the Petition of John Jacob Giegher of Sax Gotha, humbly shewing, That being seperated from his Father's Family, and intending to settle his won, consisting of three persons, humbly prays that 150 Acres of land be laid out to him in the Fork between Broad River and Congree River in the neighbourhood of Sax Gotha.... the prayer of his said Petition was granted....

Read the Petition of John Ulrich Bachman humbly shewing, That having an Encrease of One in Family for whom no land has been assigned, prays that 50 acres of land be laid out to him in Sax Gotha Township... the prayer thereof was granted....

Page 75: Meeting of 14th February 1744/5

Read the Petition of Tho's Dale Esq'r shewing That the petitioner has ten persons in Family for whom he has not taken up any land in this Province and being desirous to improve some, prays that a Warrant be issued... for a survey of 500 acres of land being vacant marsh land adjoining to that in possession of the petit'r in the Parish of St. James's Goose Creek... the prayer thereof was granted....

Pages 75-76: Read the Petition of Elizabeth Seller for herself and her husband nicholas Seller of Germany humbly shew'g That the petitioners have been nine years in this Province & have not obtain'd any lands of Bounty, that they served here 4 Years, but now being both discharg'd from any Service are desirous to settle in Orangebourgh Township, among their Country people and they have a Family consisting of seven Children & Five Negroes in all 14 persons, humbly pray, that an order may issue from this Hon'ble Board that 700 acres of land be admeasured out to them in the s'd Township, and that they may have the usual Bounty.... the prayer thereof, as to the land was granted, but not the Bounty.... for the land in Amelia Township.

Page 76: Read the Petition of John Gardner of Amelia Township humbly shewing, That in the year 1742, the Petitioner on the 7th of October obtained a Warrant of Survey for 400 acres of land upon Maybrick's Creek in Amelia Township also another warrant for 150 acres in Craven county between the Wateree & Santee Rivers near the Widdow Russels, and the lands of Miles Swiney as appears by the two annexed Warrants. That the Petit'r has hitherto not made use of any of the s'd two precepts of the surveyor in pursuance thereof, and is now desirous to take up & settle one Tract of 550 acres of land in Amelia on the point of Santee River adjoyning to David Brown's land, purchased from the said David Brown by the petit'r. Therefore he humbly prays to grant him a new warrant for 550 acres of land .... Ordered that the said petition do lye on the Table until the Petit'r do attend at the Board.

Pages 80-81: Meeting of 15th February 1744/5

Read the Petition of Deitrick Miller a foreign Protestant of Germany, shewing that he came over to this Province in the Ship St. Andrew about 8 weeks ago on the Encouragement given by His Majesty to foreign Protestants that he intends to settle in Orangebourgh Township & having 4 in family prays that an order may issue for his having 200 acres of land admeasured to him in the said Township & the usual Bounty.... the prayer thereof was granted....

Page 85: Meeting of 16th February 1744/5

Read the Petition of Anna Baker, widdow & Executrix of William Baker, late of this Province, deceased, planter, That in his life time he was possess'd of a Warrant for the Survey of 1600 acres of land under the hand of the Hon'ble Tho's Broughton late Lieut. Gov'r date Decem'r the 8th 1736. That in pursuance thereof, he had laid out to him 586 acres of land, now improved by Anthony Gracia. That the said Baker having agreed to make Anthony Gracia a proper Conveyance to the said land and the remaining part of the said Warrant, died before he compleated the same. The petit'r therefore prays that his Excellency and their Honours would order the Surveyor General to certify a platt of the said 586 acres of land, now lying in his office, in the name of the said Anthony Gracia, and grant him a warrant directed to the Surveyor General for the survey of 1016 acres upon surrendering the Original Warrant. Ordered that the said petition do lye in the Table till the Affair be more fully enquired into.

Page 93: Meeting of 19th February 1744/5

Read the Petition of John Hitchcock, Planter, of Craven County, humbly shewing that he has 4 Persons in Family for whom he has not had any lands assigned him but as he intends to improve land in proportion to his Family Right he humbly prays a Warrant for 200 acres of land may be issued to him on Pedee River on the Lower end of Marsh's Bluff on which the Petit'r at present reside,s he further remonstrates that it is with the good will & desire of the Welch people that he is to love on the land petition'd for as appears by a Certificate annexed & which was produc'd & read being signed by several Inhabitants of the Welch tract... the prayer thereof was granted....

Pages 104-105: Meeting of 26th February 1744/5

Read the Petition of George Kirch a Protestant German, humbly shewing, That the Petit'r came over in the ship St. Andrew, Cap't Brown, Commander, about 9 weeks ago upon the Encouragement which is given His Majesty to foreign Protestants and intends to settle in one of His Majesty's Townships, Therefore humbly prays that 400 acres of land may be assigned him in the Township of Orangebourgh, as his Family Right, he having a Wife & 6 Children, & Also prays for his Maj'tys Bounty... the prayer thereof with regard to the land for himself, wife & 3 of His children as also His Majesty's Bounty were granted, but not for the three other Children who are at present in Service....

Page 120: Read the Petition of Hans Ulrich Sporley, a German, shewing That at his first settling in the Township of Sax Gotha 50 Acres of land were allotted him, which proving very poor, unfruitful land and subject to be for the most part overflown with water from a Creek raised for the use of a mill, the Petit'r was obliged to raise Provisions on other people's Lotts, but the proprietors thereof not being willing to permit that any longer, prays that 100 acres be granted him in Sax Gotha Township and the usual bounty. To this Petition was annexed the following Certificate from George Haig and Stephen Crell of the said Township vizt; We do hereby certify that the above Petit'r Hans Ulrich Sporley is a poor industrious man, and that 50 acres allotted him on his first coming in, has prov'd a poor barren Soil. Signed Geo Haig, Steph:

HEMPSTEAD COUNTY LIBRARY
HOPE, ARKANSAS

Crell. Sax Gotha Township y'e 16th Feb'ry 1744. ... the prayer thereof was granted as to 50 acres but not the Bounty.

Read the Petition of George Mitchell, humbly shewing, That the Petit'r hath in his Family 24 Persons whose Rights to the land he has not yet laid out, wherefore he humbly prays that a Warrant may be granted him for running out their rights or any part of them upon lands vacant on the west side of South Edistoe or Pon Pon River adjacent to the lands of Mr. Joseph Andrew Jun'r, Miss Henry & Wm. Livingston & y'e said George Mitchell... directed to state his Allegat'ns more fully in another Petition.

Pages 129-130: Meeting of 13th March 1744/5

Read the Petition of Martin Friday a German Protestant shewing, that he has 2 Persons in his family for whom he has not had any land assigned him in this Province, his Family consists of a Young Child and an Orphan whom he maintains, therefore humbly prays that he may have a Warrant for 100 acres of land opposite to the Township of Sax Gotha... the Prayer thereof was granted....

Page 130: Read the Petition of John Jacob Friday humbly shewing that he has a Family of three children for whom no land has been assigned him, therefore prays His Excellency and their Honors that 150 Acres of land be admeasured to him on the opposite side of the River to Sax Gotha Township... the prayer thereof was granted....

Read the Petition of John Keithley shewing that the Petitioner has 5 in Family for whom as yet he hath not had any land in this Province and being desirous to cultivate as much as in proportion belongs to him by virtue of Family Right, Prays 200 and fifty Acres of vacant land be alotted him in the Welch Tract, near to the Causeyneck there. John Keithley (I)... the prayer thereof was granted....

Pages 130-131: Read the Petition of John Williams of Fredericksbourgh Township, Planter, shewing, that the Petit'r has a Family of Seven Persons for whom on lands have as yet been granted, therefore humbly prays His Excell'cy and their Honours, That 350 acres be laid out to him in Fredericksbourgh Township as his Family Right... the prayer thereof was granted.

Page 131: Read the Petition of Gasper Fants a German, shewing, That he came into this Province on the Encouragement of His Majesty's Bounty to foreign Protestants Residenters here, and as he did serve three Years in the Province for his Passage and now free and since married, and has two Children, humbly prays that 200 acres of land be granted him in the Fork of Congree, and the usual Bounty... the prayer thereof was granted as to the land but not the Bounty, but that the Expence of His Petition, Warrant, Grant &C be defray'd by the public.

Read the Petition of Paul Harlestone humbly shewing, That the Petit'r at great Expence & labour to Himself hath built and compleated a strong Mill on a good stream of Water in Fredericksbourgh Township not with Expectation of great advantage or Profit but principally to encourage the Settlement of the said Township by industrious Inhabitants. Wherefore he humbly prays y'r Excell'cy & Hon'rs to grant him the Bounty & allowance for his Labour & service therein as shall be agreeable to the Laws of this Province... order'd the Treasur'r to pay the Petit'r 50£ curr'cy out of the Township fund as a Bounty to the Petit'r after Mr. Haig or any other Evidence concern'g y'e build'g these mills shall to morrow attend w'th y'r Petit'r to certify y'e Utility thereof....

Page 132: Read the Petition of John Newberry, humbly shewing, That the Petit'r for some Years past hath been an Inhabitant on the Welch Tract, and at his great Labour and Expence hath built and finished a Grist mill and saw mill on Muddy Creek in the Welch Tract, which have been of great service to the Inhabitants thereabout settled, as by the annexed Certificate.... The Petit'r therefore most humbly prays... that the usual Bounty be allowed.... Ordered that the Petit'r attend to morrow, with George Haig & Paul Harlestone.

Meeting of 15th March 1744/5

Mr. Geo: Haig according to a Resolution in the minutes of yesterday waited on His Excellency in Council & declared that he had heard of the Petition of Paul Harleston & Will'm Newberry... he had heard a very good Account of the great Usefulness of these mills.

Page 134: Meeting of 16th March 1744/5

Reconsidered the Petitions of Paul Harlestone as also that of John Newberry... give an order on the Commissary to pay £50 Curr'y to each of these Petit'rs.

Pages 134-135: Read the Petition of Alex'r McCrea, humbly shewing That the Petit'r is one of the unfortunate men who have been compelled by James Aikin Esq'r to quit possessio of the land he claims as his own, in Compliance with his Ejectment That the Petit'r has built a small Habitation on a Tract containing 8 acres on the head of black Mingo branches, in the parish of Prince Frederick Winyaw, bounding on the land of John Peter Sommerville, since which the land has unjustly and illegally been claimed by one Will'm Snow, in behalf of his Brother deceased, tho' upon due Enquiry by the Petit'r in the Office, it appears that neither Warrant nor Grant, nor any the least Evidence is upon Record, to shew the Claimer or his Brother have any manner of title thereto. The Petit'r therefore humbly prays His Excell'cy and their Honours that he may have a Grant for 150 Acres of the land whereon he has built and which he has already cultivated, on the same footing as the Township lands. Alex'r McCrea... the prayer thereof was granted as to the 150 acres of land, free of all Charges for the Petition, warrant, Grant &C but not free of not paying the Quitrents & Taxes...

Page 136: Tho's McCrea was admitted before his Excell'cy in Council who had exhibited a Petition to this Board date the 14th January 1743 and acquainted the Gov'r & Council That he had quitted possession of the lands on which he had formerly resided, belonging to Mr. Aikin, and as he is now old and has been at great Expence in prosecuting his Right to the said land, and his frequent attendance in Town about it, humbly prays his Excell'cy & their Honours that they would be pleased to grant him some Relief & in particular the 100 acres of land belonging to Mr. George Austin be purchased for him.

Pages 136-137: Mr. George Austin being sent for acquainted His Excell'cy in Council that the said land was the property of Mr. James Bunion and that he had a mortgage on the same, and would write to Mr. Bunion about it, & lay his Answer before His Excell'cy.

Page 137: Read the humble Petition of Jacob Drafts, shewing That the Petit'r came into this Country in Capt. Brown's ship, the St. Andrew, about 2 months age, and has in family six persons, viz't Himself, wife & 4 Children, and being desirous to cultivate & improve land here, on the Encouragement His Majesty gives to foreign Protestants, humbly prays Your Excellency & Honours that 300 acres of land be admeasured to him in Sax Gotha Township ,and that he may have the usual Bounty.... the prayer thereof was granted.

Pages 137-138: Meeting of 18th March 1744/5

Read the Petition of Michael Craft of Wirtemberg a Protestant, shewing, That the Petit'r a few weeks ago arrived in Capt. Brown's Ship the St. Andrew, on the Encouragem't given by Him Majesty to foreign Protest's to settle in this Province & hav'g 6 in family he prays y't 300 acres of land be admeasur'd to him in Sax Gotha Towns'p by virtue of his s'd Family Right & that he may have the usual Bounty... the prayer thereof was granted, both as to the land & bounty....

Page 139: Meeting of 19th March 1744/5

Read the Petition of Johannes Rester, a foreign Protestant of Wirtembergh, shewing That the Petit'r arrived in Capt. Brown's Ship, the St. Andrew, with an intention to settle in this Province on the Encouragement given to foreign Protestants, and having himself, wife and three children, in all, five in family humbly prays for 250 acres of land in sax Gotha Township, on 12 Mile Creek by virtue of his said Family Right, and that he may obtain the usual Bounty... the prayer thereof was granted both as to the land and the Bounty....

Pages 139-141: Read the following Petition of Edward Barnes, humbly shewing, That the Lords Proprietors Deputies on the 28th June 1714 did for the consideration mentioned, to Geo: Chicken Esq'r deceased, a tract of land containing 170 acres, butting and bounding to the north on lands of Mr. Kinloch, and to the S on Thoroughgood's land, which said Tract by a Resurvey of the same, and of the adjoyning lands appeared to be ascertained in a wrong place, because the line of the said Tract, next to Mr. Kinloch's land & Mr. Kinloch's line appeared by the said Resurvey to be the same, but that there was left out on the south side, of the said Thoroughgood's land 106 acres which in lieu of the said 170 acres were survey'd & laid out to the said Geo: Chicken by the Hon'ble Wm. Bull Esq'r then Deputy Surveyor General, and the certified platt thereof by him, annexed to the Original Grant of the said 170 acres. That the said Geo: Chicken by virtue of the before recited Title held and possessed the said lands and paid the usual Taxes and Quit rents for the same, until the time of His Death, when the said lands descended to his Son and Heir Geo: Chicken of this Province planter, who held and occupied the same, upon the said Title, until the 18th day of Dec'r in the year of our Lord 1742, when for the consideration of 405 pounds currency he conveyed the same to the Petitioner. That the Petit'r believing the same to be good has been at great pains in improving & building upon the said land, but of late has been advised that his Title hitherto, tho' bona fide & For good Consideration purchased, is precarious, for want of the s'd survey made by the Hon'ble Wm. Bull Esq'r being annex'd to a new Grant of the same, and therefore humbly prays His Excellency and their Honours that on mature Consideration of the premises and the particular hardships of his Case, a special Grant of the said 162 acres may be given him, upon the same Quit rents, as are express'd in the original Grant to the s'd George Chicken, which your Petitioner has in his hands, ready to be produced for further Satisfaction therein &C. Which Petition being considered, the Prayer thereof was granted....

Page 142: Meeting of 20th March 1744/5

Read the humble Petition of Thomas Elerbee shew'g That the Petit'r has 20 Persons in family for whom no land has been assigned him, as Family Right, and being desirous to cultivate & improve land in proportion to the s'd Right, humbly prays yo'r Excell'cy & Honours that one Thousand acres of Land be laid out to him in a Tract or Tracts within the Welch Tract &C... the Prayer of His Petition was granted.

Read the Petition of Geo: Starrat humbly shew'g That about Six years ago he came into this Province with an intent to take up land according to the laws of this Province, and to settle thereon, but finding that all the good land was taken up or surveyed has had labour'd under several Disadvantages since, for want of land, and now finding a Piece of vacant land in Kingstone Township, commonly known by the name of Long Township Bluff, prays His Excell'cy & their Honours that a Warrant be issue to the Petit'r for his Family Right being 16 in number to be laid out thereon &c. The Petitioner appearing and proving his Right for fifteen persons on oath, the Deputy Secretary was ordered to issue a Warrant to Him for Seven hundred & Fifty acres of land only.

Page 144: Meeting of 22nd March 1744/5

Read the humble Petition of Samuel de Saurence shewing That the Petit'r having an Encrease of Family of 13 Slaves is willing to cultivate and improve land in proportion to the s'd Family Right, Therefore he humbly prays His Excell'cy & their Honours that 650 acres of land be laid out to him in different tracts within the Welch Tract where the petitioner resides at present with his Family &c... the prayer of his Petition was granted....

Pages 144-145: Read the Petition of John Eberly, humbly shewing That the Petit'r has five Persons in Family, viz't Himself, wife, son in law, a white servant & two negroes, therefore by virtue of the said Family Right, he prays His Excell'cy and their Honours that 250 acres of land be laid out to him over Santee River opposite to the Township of Sax Gotha &Ca... the prayer thereof was granted....

Page 145: Read the Petition of Wm. Harris shewing That the Petit'r has 5 Persons in Family for whom he has not had any lands assigned him, and being desirous to cultivate some within this Province in proportion to his s'd Family Right, he humbly prays His Excell'cy & their Honours that 250 acres of land be ordered to be laid out to him on the north side of Wateree River near Sparrow Spring &c. The Petit'r appearing and swearing to his s'd Right, except for one, whom he owned was a hired servant, 200 acres only were allowed him....

Pages 145-146: Read the Petition of Thomas Wallexelleson humbly shewing That the Petit'r having settled himself and Family in Craven County on Santee River with a design to obtain from the Government a Title to the Rights of his family, according to law, but that contrary to law and the intent of un hospitable neighbour, Gilbert Gibson now residing on the River, above said has fraudulently obtain'd certain Quantity of Rights for land, as appears by a Warrant lately granted to him in the behalf of himself, his mother & his sisters &C who have had their Rights of land taken up & dispos'd of some years past by the s'd Gilbert's Father, John Gibson deceased, as also some part by himself and notwithstanding the illegal Acquisition of the land, the said Gilbert Gibson now possessor hath depriv'd the Petitioner of the chiefest part of its Timber by running the line of his land, contrary to the intent of a Lawful Division of the same, & deceiv'd the Surveyor by a false Information from the Petit'r of his Concession to the same, who otherwise would not have run the line in such form, the Petit'r therefore humbly prays for redress. On considering the above Petition the same was referred to the Surveyor General that he do enquire into the allegations of the same and report to his Board.

Pages 146-147: Read the humble Petition of James Gillespie, planter, shewing That the Petit'r has seven Persons in his Family for whom as yet no land has been assigned him, but being desirous to cultivate and improve land in Proportion to his said Family Right, humbly prays His Excellency and their Honours that 350 Acres of land be laid out to him in the Welch Tract. And as the Petit'r has been very assisting in contributing towards the settled of the said tract, and building a Grist mill therein, which by the annexed attestation of several Considerable Inhabitants there, the said mil has been of great service.... it was resolved by the board that a Warrant do issue for 350 acres of land to the Petit'r as his family Right and other 200 acres of land near to the Petit'rs Plantation....

Page 147: Read the Petition of George Shleppy humbly shewing, That the Petit'r about three months past did apply to his Excell'cy & their Honours for 200 acres of Land in the Township of Sax Gotha, but finding none as he has himself and wife only in Family, he humbly prays that 200 acres of land may be admeasured and laid out to him over santee River opposite to the s'd Township of Sax Gotha &c... the prayer thereof was granted.

Pages 147-148: The Surveyor General according to an Order in the minutes of this morning laid before the Board the follow'g Report, upon the Petition to him referred, viz't That upon perusal of Tho's Wallexelleson's Petition, to His Excell'cy & Honours complaining of the useage of Gilbert Gibson, &c I find that the said Gibson did obtain a Warrant of Survey from Your Excellency on the 6th day of October last, on a Copy thereof I gave a Precept of the same date, if any Survey has been made by virtue thereof, no Platt has been returned into this office. With Submission I think that if your Excellency grants the said Wallexelleson a Special warrant for the lands by him settled and improved according to His Family Right, I shall recommend it to Mr. Haig to remove his Grievance who I doubt not is both capable & willing if he has been imposed on by s'd Gibson &C. Signed George Hunter.

The Petitioner appear before His Excellency in Council, and declaring that he had not obtained any Warrant or Grant for the s'd land prayed for in his Petition, he was directed to prepr another Petition setting forth His family Right, so as that the said land may be legally assigned him.

Page 155: Meeting of 23d March 1744/5

Read a second Petition from Tho's Wallexelleson, planter, shewing that he has six persons in family for whom he has not had any land assigned him & prays that 300 acres be laid out to him in Craven County near the land of Mr. Fairfax. The Petit'r appearing & swearing to his said Right, the prayer thereof was granted, and the Deputy Secretary ordered to prepare a warrant accordingly.

Pages 157-158: Meeting of 25th March 1745

Read the Petition of the Inhabitants of the Welch Tract settled on Pedee River near the disputed Bounds of North & South Carolina, shewing That there are several persons settled on that River who have escaped from the Northerly Colonies to avoid being brought to Justice for Horse Stealing, and other felonies laid to their Charge and have killed Cattle, Stole Horses &

Robbed Houses, and go armed threatning to kill any that will molest them. That Samuel Goodman, one of His Majesty's Justices for Bladen County, in the Province of No Carolina, bro't to this River a Proclamation from under the hand of His Excell'cy the Gov'r of Virginia for the taking no less than twenty ,most of whom have been on this River and many of them are here still who have gone so far as to release Gilbert and Edward Turner with others who were kept Prisoners by the said Goodman by virtue of the said Proclamation, and put the said Goodman in Irons, and took him with them for some time and as we are informed swore the said Goodman that he shoul'd not molest them in nay shape, and then set him at Liberty. The Persons are John McCoy, William Turner, Edward Turner, Gilbert Turner, Carey Kibble, Thomas Red, &c., who have sworn damnation to themselves, if they did not ruin the whole River.

That the Petitioners humbly conceived that they bounds not being run between this Province & that of North Carolina is the chief reason that this wicked Gang settle on this River, it being far from the Inhabitants of Cape Fear, that it is difficult to suppress them & those in the Welch Tract conceive that they are not safe in going further than the disputed Bounds of this Province unless there was a power granted to protect them. How much such a set of bad People have it in their power to deprive his Majesty's peaceable subjects of their lives and Interest is obvious, not being safe to go about their lawful Business, more especially as Gilbert Turner one of the Gang ___ the Deponent Jo: Hickman to tell Captain James to raise all his Company, swearing they were men enough if the whole Inhabitants of the River came after them, to encounter them & Therefore bid them defiance. The Petitioners therefore humbly pray his Excell'cy & their Honours to take their Cause under Consideration, and grant them such relief and protection as they in their great Wisdom shall think meet &c. Signed. Samuel Goodman, Abraham Paul and about 17 others.

To this Petition was annexed a printed copy of the Virginia Gazette, wherein there is a Placard issued by William Gooch Esq'r Lieu't Gov'r of Virginia for apprehending these Robbers with a reward of ten pounds for apprehending any one of them, each of the names being named.

There was also annexed two Affidavits, one of John Hickman, giving account upon Oath of the outraged of those Robbers, in rescuing their Associates from the said Samuel Goodman, and their putting hand Cuffs on him & Carrying him off with the Prisoners &C. The other affidavit of Samuel Goodman was to the same purpose.

Pages 158-159: Read also the humble Petition of the Welch and Pensylvanians and others the Inhabitants of the Welch Tract shewing, that the Petit'rs return their humble thanks w'th their grateful Acknowledgements for the several Favours bestowed upon them by the Hon'ble William Bull Esq'r late Lieutenant Governour and his Majesty's Hon'ble Council in continuing to reserve the lands appropriated for them from time to time & Lastly to y'e 13th

August next. That the Petitioners confess there comes not the Compliment of people as was expected to settle the lands reserved for them, by reason of the War, and danger of the Seas. That the Petitioners humbly conceived that the reserving the lands for the said Welch and Pensylvanians has been rather a Benefit than a Prejudice to the Government, especially to this River and the neighboring Inhabitants since the Petitioners have rather encouraged then discouraged any of his Majesty's Subjects to Settle among them if they bore a good Character, or were like to be of service to the Country.

That there are at this time several Persons now on their river near the disputed Bounds of north Carolina who have transported themselves from the northerly Colonies to avoid their being brought to Justices, who killed several Cattle, stole horses from the inhabitants & broke open several houses and go armed, threatning to kill any that do molest them to the great annoyance of the Inhabitants...

The Petit'rs therefore humbly pray his Excell'cy & their Honors to take their Case into deliberate Considerat'n & Grant them such longer time as they in their wisdom shall think meet &c. Signed Will'm James, James Gellespie & about 40 more hands. [Governor's response by letter included]

Pages 160-161: Read the Petition Johan Christopher Hauser shew'g That the Petit'r came over to this Province in the Ship St. Andrew, Cap't Brown master, on the Encouragem't granted by his Majesty to foreign Protestants & having four Persons in family, prays that 200 acres of land be assigned him in the Township of Sax Gotha by Virtue of his s'd Family Right & the usual Bounty. The Petit'r appear'g & Swear'g to the truth of the Allegations in his said Petition, the Prayer thereof was granted, and the Deputy Secretary ordered to prepare a Warrant and the Commissary to pay the Bounty accordingly.

Pages 189-190: Meeting of 27th April 1745

Read the Petition of Fremiah Cook, widdow, shewing, That the Petitioner's late husband with his Family being Protestants came from Switzerland in order to settle in this Province, the Peti'r husband dying leaving her a daughter for whom not any family Right or Bounty have been granted. Wherefore the Petit'r humbly prays his Excell'cy and Honours that a Warrant may issue for laying out land for the Petit'r and her Daughter on the north side of Congaree River, opposite to Sax Gotha Township, and that His Majesty's most gracious Bounty may be granted to them also &c... the petition was granted.

Page 190: Read the Petition of Hans Polly, a German shewing That the Petit'r came into this Province about two Years ago on the Encouragement given by his Majesty to foreign Protestants, and having serv'd for his passage to this Country & now free is desirous to settle in the Township of Orangeburgh & having a Wife & one Child prays that 150 acres of land be assigned him in the said Township as his Family Right, and that he may have the usual Bounty. The Petit'r appearing and swearing to the truth of the Allegations of his said

Petition, at the same time producing his Discharge from his Indenture, the prayer thereof was granted....

The Petition of Gasper Nagely humbly shewing, That the Petit'r came into this Province about one Year & a half ago, on the Encouragement given by his Majesty to foreign Protestants, and as he designs to settle among his Country People, in the Township of Orangeburgh he humbly prays that 50 acres of land be assigned him in the said Township & the usual Bounty... the prayer thereof was granted....

Pages 190-191: Read the Petition of Joseph Cook shewing That he and his Wife being Protestants came from Switzerland to this Province on the Encouragem't given by his Majesty to foreign Residenters being Protestants, that he served for his passage and being now free Intends to settle in the Township of Orangeburgh and by virtue of Family Right prays that 100 acres of land be assigned him in the said Township, on the north side of Congree River, and the usual Bounty... the prayer thereof was granted...

Pages 199-200: Meeting of 30th April 1745

Read the Petition of Anna Thompson, widdow, humbly shewing, That John Thompson, late of this Province deceased, the husband of the Petit'r having in his Life purchased land of the Cheraw Indians on Pedee River within the Bounds of this Province for a valuable Consideration paid by him to these Indians and received Conveyances from them to him, by virtue whereof your Petitioner's s'd husband became possessed of the s'd land, but His Majesty's Council being informed thereof & judging the same might become prejudicial to His Majesty and the Province, summoned the Petitioner's husband to appear before them, to answer the Premises, who when he had made his appearance and been examined concerning the said purchase, freely and willingly gave up and relinquished his right and Title to the said land by virtue of the s'd Conveyance to His Majesty's use for the profit and advantage of His Majesty and the Province. In consideration whereof the Council granted to the Petit'rs husband the sum of seven hundred pounds Curr't money & One Thousand Acres of land, either in one tract or in many as he pleas'd and where he should think property to make his Choice, within the said purchased land, the Petit'rs husband having made his choice to take the same in two Parcels each containing 500 acres, obtained Warrants and had the said land surveyed and returned the Platts according to law and made several valuable Improvements thereon but was taken sick and died before he could obtain his Majestys' Letters patents for the same, but having made and ordained in his last will and Testimony in writing under his hand and seal did give and bequeath the said two Parcels of land to his youngest daughter named Jane; The Petit'r therefore has duely paid Taxes for the said land, ever since, nothing doubting but the same was free & secure from the Claims or Encroachments of any other Person, as being the Special Grant of His Majesty's said Council, but now the Petit'r is credibly informed that certain disaffected Persons have proceeded to obtain Patents for the said land on purpose to defraud that said Orphan of her just right & title to the said land, by virtue of her Father's said last will and Testament, the Petit'r thereof in behalf of the said Orphan, humbly prays that His Excellcy and their Honours may be pleased favourably to consider the premises and put a Stop to such unjust proceedings and grant to the Petit'r his Majesty's Letters Patents in the said Orphan's name for the said two parcells of land... The above Petition being read it was ordered that the same be reconsidered.

Pages 207-208: Meeting of 3d May 1745

Read the Petition of Herman Ghiegher of Sax Gotha township setting forth, y'e whereas a Tract of land contain'g 50 acres was laid out in y'e Towns'p of Sax Gotha unto Jacob Rudolph & a Grant hath been prepar'd for y'e same, condition'g y'e cultiva'n of y'e s'd land or settling, and where'as y'e s'd Jacob Rudolph before or about the time that y'e s'd Grant was issue is gone off the Province & hath been now about nine Years past, without having taken posses'n of y'e s'd Tract of land & without making or causing to be made any improvem't thereon & therefore by virtue of a Provision in y'e s'd Grant, y'e s'd tract of land is to be reputed vacant & whereas the Petit'r has encrease of Family of one Son, for whom no land hath been granted, he therefore humbly prays that his Excell'cy would assign 50 acres in the Township of sax Gotha being behind and formerly laid out & grant to Jacob Rudolph and reverted to His Majesty's as aforesaid. To this Petition was annexed two several Certificates declaring that Jacob Rudolph had deserted the Township & gone off the Province about the year 1735 or 36 & by common Report gone back to Switzerland and that the tract of land laid out to him was never settled by him nor no other Persons & lies still not improved. Whereupon it was ordered that the Grant for the said land pray'd for shall not pass to any other Person but the Petit'r who in the mean time may feed his Cattle thereon.

Page 208: Read the Petition of Michael Zang of Sax Gotha Township, a Protestant of Switzerland, humbly shewing, That the Petit'r came over upon the Encouragement of His Majesty's gracious Bounty, and on arriving was bound for 6 Year's Service for the discharge of His Passage, after the Expiration of which term, finding himself in want of all Necessaries, was obliged to serve three years more on small wages, but being since married & having three Persons in family, he had 150 acres of land already granted him by his Excell'cy in the Township of Sax Gotha, whereon he hath built a small house and clear'd some land, but now finds himself in the utmost necessity for want of means to subsist himself and family, and therefore most humbly prays his Majesty's Gracious Bounty of one Year's provision be granted him which as yet he hath not obtained &C. The above Petition being considered the Prayer thereof was not granted.

Pages 208-209: Read the humble Petition of Frederick Goat of Sweiberg in Germany, shewing, That y'e Petit'r about 9 Years ago came to this Province w'th an intent'n to settle w'th his Wife and Family on the Encouragement given by His Majesty to foreign Protestants, that he and his wife served John

Fryton two Years and three Months for his & her Freight in coming over, then served the Hon'ble Joseph Blake Esq'r as Overseer for three Years, and being now free is desirous to settle his family, which consists of 5 Persons, in the Township of Orangeburgh, therefore humbly prays his Excellency & their honours to order 250 acres of land to be laid out to him in the said Township and that he may have the usual Bounty. The Petit'r appearing and swearing to His Family Right, the prayer of his Petition with regard to the land was granted, but not the Bounty.

Page 209: Read the Petition of Samuel de Saurence humbly shewing That the Petit'r having 8 Slaves in his Family for whom he has not had any land assigned him by virtue of Family right, therefore he humbly prays that 400 acres of vacant land be laid out to him within the Welch tract, in a traced or tracts on Pedee River &c. ...The Petition be granted provided that he take out the Extant of the land prayed for in different warrants.

Page 217: Meeting of 6th May 1745

Read the Petition of Isaac Chanler, shewing, That the Petit'r has 12 Persons in Family for whom no lands have been assign'd & Being willing to cultivate land to the whole extant of his pres't additional Family Right in the Welch Tract on Pedee River, prays his Excell'cy & their hon'rs y't 600 acres of L'd be laid out to him, by virtue of y'e s'd Right in y'e tract. The said Petition being considered the prayer thereof was granted....

Page 222: Meeting of 8th May 1745

Read the Petition of John Rogers, Planter, humbly shewing, That the Petit'r has eight persons in Family for whom no land has been assigned him in this Province, and being willing to cultivate & improve to the Extent of his said family Right, He humbly prays His Excell'cy & their honours that 400 acres of land be laid out to him by two different warrants betwixt Santee River & Wateree River &c.... the prayer of his s'd Petit'n was granted....

Page 228: Meeting of 11th May 1745

The Petition of John Baxter humbly shewing That the Petit'r since the last warrant he obtain'd for land, has an encraese of one White man & 25 Slaves in his Family, in Consideration of which the Petit'r humbly prays That a warrant may be issued for laying out 1300 acres of land in one or more tracts near Black Mingo Swamp on Pedee River and that on Consideration of the very low price of Rice, and the Expectation of applying to the making of Pitch, he also prays that considering the small and uncertain value of Pine barren or Pitch land, he may have the same granted at as low and moderate Quitrents as may be judged reasonable and agreeable to his Majesty's Royal Instructions &C... the lands pray'd for were granted on Condition that the Petit'r take out the same in two different Warrants.

Page 229: Read the humble Petition of John Duvall, Inhabitant of the Town of Beaufort, Port Royal shewing, That the Petit'r has purchased of John Evans, son of Randolph Evans, 2 lots in Beaufort Town known by the number 202 & 203 for the Consideration of 600 currency of which the Petiti'r is willing to give Evidence & proof if demanded, for which two lots, as appears in the offices and upon the list in the Council Chamber a warrant was granted to Randolph Evans in Oct'r 25th 1718 & a certificate signed March 15th 1719, but no Grant was signed. The Petit'r therefor humbly prays His Excellency and their Honours that they would be pleased to order warrants to the Petit'r for the s'd two lots in right of his purchase &c. On considering the above Petit'n it was orderd that the Petit'r go to James Grame Esq'r to get a Certificate whether the Warrants of John Evans were lost or not.

Read another Petition of Wm Osborn, Pilot, shewing That the Petit'r having a Plantation near Beaufort, Port Royal, is desirous to settle there with his Family in order to be as useful as he can in the Navigation to and from that Harbour & therefore humbly prays ... a warrant for the vacant Lot No. 356 in s'd Township of Beaufort &c. This Petition being considered, it was ordered that the Petit'r do apply for another number, the number he prays for being granted to another.

Page 238: Read the Petition of Joseph Ash shewing That the Petit'r being Heir to considerable lands near to Port Royal and intending to settle in Beaufort Town, and to carry on a trade there, he humbly prays that the lot 360 be granted him there. The above Petition being considered the prayer thereof was granted, and the Deputy Secretary order'd to prepare a Warrant accordingly.

Read the Petition of Thomas Parmenter, shew'g That the petit'r has prepar'd a House of lawful dimensions in order to be built in Port Royal Town and being desirous to accomplish the same, as soon as he can, he humbly prays that the lot 331, if not laid out already, may be granted him. Which petition being considered, the same was granted, on Condition that the Petit'r make it appear that Mr. Lewis to whom it formerly had been granted is dead.

Pages 238-239: Read the Petition of Stephen Bull, Esq'r, humbly shewing, That the Petit'r has been an Inhabitant near the Town of Port Royal many years & having no lands in the Town & being desirous to build a House & improve a lot therein, Therefore humbly prays a Warr't may be issued to lay out to him y'e vacant lot No. 256, that he may be entitled to obtain his Majesty's grant for the same &c. The said Petition being considered, that prayer thereof was granted and the Deputy Secretary order'd to prepare a Warrant accordingly.

Order'd that Wm Osborn, Pilot, who petition'd for the same Lot, do look out for another vacant Lot in Beaufort, that it may be granted him.

Pages 239-240: Meeting of 13th May 1745

The petit'n of John Duvall was reconsidered as mention'd in the minutes of the 11th Instant & the Petit'r being called upon, acquainted the Board that he had been with Mr. Grame to enquire concerning the Warrants for the two Port Royal Lots as he was directed last Saturday but that Mr. Grame cannot recollect what has been done with these Warrants. Whereupon the Petit'r was directed to apply to Mr. Evans, son of Randolph Evans, & to take his Affidavit y't he never had made out these Warrants to any other person besides the Petit'r & that the Petit'r do lay the said Affidavit before this Board.

Pages 261-262: Meeting of 21st May 1745

Read the Petition of Thomas Cooper of Charles Town, merchant, shewing, That the Petit'r obtained a Warrant of Survey for 1850 Acres of land from the Hon'ble Wm Bull Esq'r President dated 28th January 1737 directed to the Surveyor General, and his Precept thereon for executing the same dated 2'd Feb'ry 1757, but has not hitherto obtained any Survey in pursuance thereof; And whereas several Platts still remain in the Surveyor General's Office, which were advertised in a supplement to the Gazette for August the 15th 1743, together with an order from the Hon'ble Wm Bull Esq'r Lieu't Gov'r in Council, requiring all Persons their Heirs & C claiming or interested in such lands so advertised to apply for the same one or before the 1st January 1743, and upon neglect or failure therein they should be deemed as vacant land & granted to any other Person y't should apply for the same. Whereupon the Petit'r prays His Excellency & Honours to order the Surveyor Genl to certify in the name of the Petit'r a Plat of thirty eight Acres now in his Office, survey'd for Laurence Mellichamp on the seventh day of May 1733 in Colleton County as appears by the said Supplement to the Gazette and that he may endorse the said Quantity on said Warrant as part thereof and that the same may be granted accordingly &C. Signed Thomas Cooper. To this Petition was annexed the following Certificate of the Surveyor General, vizt. I do hereby certify that no applicant has been made to me for the plat above mentioned & that it has been in the Office above Eleven Years. George Hunter, Survy'r Genl. The above Petition being considered the prayer thereof was granted.

Page 277: Meeting of 22d May 1745

Read the Petition of Alex'r Brown, Planter, shewing That the Petit'r, a native of Carolina, has ten persons in family for whom he has had no lands assigned him & being desirous to cultivate lands to the Extent of his s'd Family Right, He humbly prays that 500 acres of land be admeasured to him in Prince Frederick's Parish, Winyaw butting and bounding to the Eastward on land belonging to Matt'w Quash &c... the prayer was granted....

Pages 278-279: Read the Petition of Geo: Mitchel humbly shewing That the Petit'r hath in his family 24 Persons for whom he formerly obtained a Warr't from the Hon'ble Wm. Bull Esq'r Lieu't Gov'r directed to James St. John Esq'r to lay out 1200 acres of land on the east of Edistoe River date Jan'ry 29th 1741, out of which the Petit'r has surveyed him 50 acres only by Tho's Clifford Dep'ty Surveyor, March the 2d 1741. The Petit'r therefore humbly prays that his former warr't may be cancelled & a new Warr't granted for running out the remaining Rights or vacant Lands on the west side of Edistoe River adjoyning to the lands of Joseph Andrew Jun'r, Mess'r Henry and Will'm Livingston and the Petitioner. Within the said petition was the former Warrant, which together with Mr. St. John's order to the Dep'ty Surveyor were read... the prayer thereof was granted.

Pages 280-281: Read the Petition of Geo: Pawley shewing That the Petit'r on the 27th day of August 1738, then a Deputy Surveyor, did, by virtue of a precept from James St. John, Surveyor General, survey unto Daniel Dausnal a tract of land containing 200 acres on James's Neck as is expressed in the Body of the Plat, and that it lyes there is confirmed by other Platts on James's Neck bounding on Dausnal's s'd Platt, and agreeing therewith in Course and Station trees, but by mistake was certify'd by the Petit'r to be in Queensborough Township, agreeable to the return made and accordingly a Grant passed from His Excellency on the 2'd March 1743, placing it in Queenborough, tho' James's Neck lies at some distance, which difference in the description & situation may affect the Validity of the Title, Whereupon the Petit'r at y'e request of the s'd Dan'l Dausnal, who is willing that the Quit rents should commence from the date prays the mistake may be rectified ion the Grant.... ordered that the platt returned into the Surveyor's Office be certified to him, that he may have a new Grant and that the Auditor have notice thereof that he not be charged with double quitrents.

Page 282: Meeting of 23d May 1745

Read the Petition of Isaac Nicholas, planter, shewing, That the Petit'r has ten persons in family for whom no lands have been assigned him, and being desirous to cultivate land to the Extent of his s'd family right in this Province, he humbly prays His Excell'cy and their Honours that 500 acres of land be laid out to him by virtue of his said Right in the Welch Tract... the prayer thereof was granted.

Pages 350-351: Meeting of 6th December 1745

Read the Petition of James Griffeth humbly shewing, That the Petit'r came into this Province about two Years ago, with his wife and 9 Children, in order to settle and cultivate Land, & having found a tract unoccupied, consisting of about 400 acres in the Welch Tract on Pedee River bounding on the lands of John Hicks & David Roche, humbly prays that a Warrant may be issued for laying out the same to him, being the lands on which the Petit'r resides, provided no Platt thereof, has been returned into the Surveyor General's

Office, by virtue of any Survey, preformed above a Year ago, and that the Remainder may be laid out elsewhere to him, in the Welch Tract, &c. Dec'r 4th 1756. signed James Griffeth.

To this Petition was annexed the following Certificate, shewing, That John Hicks had 350 Acres survey'd in the Welch Tract by Geo: Pawley Dept'y Survey'r on the 14th day of Decem'r 1751, and David Roach had 300 acres in the Welch Tract surveyed by s'd Dep'ty Survey'r on the same day, both bounding on Pedee; & on all other sides on vacant Land as P Record Book fo. 148, whereby it appears there was then vacant land between the said Tracts & Believe if any Survey has been made thereon, since that time, no return has been made. Sign'd Geo: Hunter, Survey'r General. Dec'r 3'd 1745.... the petition was granted.

Page 351: Read the Petition of Jacob Rote, A Protestant Palatine, shewing, That the Petit'r came into this Province with his Family on the Encouragement given by his Majesty to foreign Protestants, and having a Wife and two Children prays that 200 acres of vacant land may be laid out to him in Orangeburgh Township and that he may have the usual Bounty. The Petit'r producing a Certificate from John Chivellette, one of His Majesty's Justice of the Peace in the foresaid Township, that the s'd Jacob Rote is lately become a Setler with his wife and two Children in the Township of Orangeburgh, date July 31st 1745... the land was granted but not the Bounty, only it was ordered that the Charges of his Petition, Warrant & Grant be defray'd by the Public.

Read the Petition of Andrew Moak, shewing That the Petit'r came over to this Province with Capt. Stedman & for defraying his freight became an indented Servant to Benjamnin Goddin Esq'r and being discharged from his said Service & intending to settle in this Province prays that by virtue of family Right 250 acres of land be laid out to him in Sax Gotha Township. The Petit'r appearing and no producing any discharge from Mr. Godin, the prayer of his Petition until such a discharge be produced was not granted.

Pages 1-2: Meeting of 8th January 1745/6

Read the Petition of Andrew Howel humbly shewing That the Petit'r has three Persons in family for whom not any lands have been assigned, and being desirous to cultivate vacant land in proportion to his said right, prays that one hundred & fifty acres be laid out to him between Santee & Wateree Rivers by virtue of family right.... the prayer thereof was granted.

Page 2: Read the Petition of Thomas Howell shewing that he has a family of four Persons, vizt. himself, his wife & two children, for whom he has not any lands assigned him & being desirous to cultivate some in proportion to his said Right, prays that 200 acres of vacant land be laid out to him in the Fork of Santee & Wateree Rivers, where the Petit'r now liveth... the prayer thereof was granted....

Read the Petition of Margaret Oneal, shewing that the Petit'r has a Family of two Persons, viz't negroes, for whom not any land has been assigned, and being willing to cultivate vacant land in proportion to the said Right humbly prays a warrant my issue for laying out a hundred acres adjoyning to Refae Barony... the prayer of her Petition was granted...

Read the Petition of Patrick Welch, shewing That the Petit'r has 6 persons in Family for whom not any lands have been granted & intending to cultivate land in proportion to his said right, prays that a Warrant do issue for laying out 300 acres of vacant land at a place called Ninety Six. The Petit'r appearing & making Affidavit of the truth of the Allegations in his said Petition, the prayer thereof was granted....

Page 3: Meeting of 9th January 1745/6

Read the Petition of John Turk, Thomas Turk & Michael Taylor humbly shewing, That the Petitioners begin lately arrived in this Province from the Northern parts of America, and being desirous to settle with their familys in this Province, have therefore undertaken to setle themselves at a place called Ninety Six & Coronaka, being at present vacant lands, but are informed by the Inhabitants dwelling thereabouts That the Indians claim a right to the said land, but believe upon some small Acknowledgement from His Excellency and their Honours they will readily give up and relinquish the right they claim.

The Petit'rs do therefore humbly pray that your Excell'cy and Honours may be pleasd to take the same into Consideration.... that they may be assured of a settlement for themselves & familys upon their return again into this Province. The Consideration of this Petition was postponed till to Morrow morning.

Pages 3-4: Read the Petition of Henry Long, a Protestant Swiss, shewing that the Petit'r came into this Province on the Encouragement given by His

Majestys to foreign Protestants, & not being then able to pay for his passage, about 4 years ago he served on his Arrival Mr. John Cordes all that time & Being at present free from his said service prays that 50 acres of land be laid out to him in Orangeburgh Township, and that he may be allowed the usual Bounty.... the prayer thereof was granted....

Page 4: Read the Petition of Michael Boomer, a Protestant Palatine, shewing That the Petiti'r came into this Province on the Encourgment given by His Majesty to foreign protestants, and having two in family vizt himself & his wife, for whom not any lands have been assigned as family right: Prays that one hundred ares of land be laid out to him in Sax Gotha Township, and that he may be allowed the usual Bounty. The Petit'r appearing & making Affidavit and producing a discharge indenture from the Hon'ble Benjamin Whitaker Esqr for his own & wife's services, the prayer of his Petition was granted....

Pages 5-6: Meeting of 10th January 1745/6

Reconsidered the Petition of John Turk, Thomas Turk & Michael Taylor, as mentioned in the minutes of yesterday's Journal, and they having further pray'd His Excell'cy & their Honours that such lands as they had already pitched upon & which they might be entitled to by virtue of their family right, might not be granted to any other for some time, The Gov'r & the members of His Majest'ys Hon'ble Council assured them that their request should be complied with, together with all suitable Encouragement they desired. The lands pitched upon by the Petitioners are as under, viz't, 500 acres near the North side of Coronaka Creek for Robert Turk, Father of Thomas Turk, about three quarters of a mile from the trading path near our Indian hunting Camp, where the Indians have a few houses, that they resort to in hunting time, about 200 miles from Charles Town. For Thomas Turk about three quarters of a mile below the Path, upon the same Creek, 400 acres of land. For Michael Taylor, 200 acres of land laying between the forementioned places. For John Turk, 200 acres of land, seven miles above Ninety Six upon the south side of the trading path, at a large Spring, two hundred more in the fork between Ninety Six and Wilson's Creek or thereabouts, being a place that was known by the name of Johnny Cook's place.

Page 6: Read the Petition of John Tyler shewing That the Petit'r has been a Residenter for two years in the Province & having 3 in family for whom no lands have been assigned & being willing to cultivate land in proportion thereto, prays His Excell'cy and their Honours that 150 acres of vacant land be laid out to him on the north side of Pedee River joyning to the lands of Abraham Colson & John Elerby &c. The Petitioner appearing to proving his Right to 2 persons in Family, the Deputy Secretary and order'd to prepare a warrant for 100 acres only.

Read the Petition of John Singleton, shewing, That the Petitioner has been a Residenter about 3 years in this Province, and having 3 Persons in family for whom no land has been obtained, prays that 150 acres of vacant land be laid out to him on the north side of Pedee River, joyning to the Lands of Abraham Colson & John Elerby &c, one hundred acres only were granted.

Read the Petition of Jacob Ernest, a Protestant Pallatine shewing That the Petit'r came to this Country about a twelve month ago, on the Encouragement which is given by his Majesty to foreign Protestants, but being them not able to pay for his passage was obliged to serve Mr. Fellaback & his time being now expired, having a wife & a child intends to settle in SaxGotha Township, therefore prays a Warrant may issue for 150 acres of land to be laid out to him in the above Township & that he may have the usual Bounty. The Petit'r appearing & swearing to the truth of the Allegations in his said Petition, the prayer thereof was granted & the Dep'ty Sec'ry order'd to prepare a warrant and the Commiss'ry Genl to pay the Bounty accordingly.

Page 8: Meeting of 11th January 1745/6

Read the Petition of Hardy Counsel, shewing That the Petit'r hath been here since March last past, he coming from Virginia, with an intention to settle with his wife and Children in this Province and to cultivate land here in proportion to his family right, and he having eight persons in family for whom no lands have been assigned him, prays that 400 acres of land be laid out to him in the Welch tract, in one or two tracts on Pedee River. The Petitioner appearing & Swearing to the truth of the Allegations in his said Petition the prayer thereof was granted and the Deputy Secretary order to prepare a warrant accordingly.

Read the Petition of Henry Roche, shewing That the Petit'r hath been in this Province seven years, having come from Pennsylvania in order to settle here, and to cultivate some of his Majesty' vacant land, and having three persons in family for whom no land has been assigned, prays His Excell'cy and their Honors that 150 acres of land near Buckle's Creek be laid out to him, by virtue of his said family right. The Petitioner appearing and swearing to the truth of his said Petition, the prayer thereof was granted, and the Deputy Secretary ordered to prepare a Warrant accordingly.

Meeting of 14th January 1745/6

Pages 9-10: Upon reading the Petition of Thomas Turk, John Turk & Michael Taylor, humbly praying that certain lands in this Province at a place called 96 might be reserved for the use of such new Settlers as should come to settle thereon, from the back pats of Pensylvania and Virginia, and that such steps may be taken by this government for quieting such persons as should become Settlers there in regard to the Indians and that such further Encouragement might be given to such Settlers as to his Excell'cy and the Hon'ble Council should seem meet, and thereupon it was Resolve, that this Government will forthwith use Endeavours for the satisfaction of the Indians, touching the said

Settlements, and that this Government will grant to such persons from the back parts of Pensylvania and Virginia, who shall come into this Province, and become settlers therein, fifty acres of said lands for every person, man, woman, and child, white or black in the Grantee's family. That after one hundred familys shall have become settlers on the s'd lands, this Government will exempt all the Settlers on the said lands from all provincial taxes, for slaves, for the term of ten years from the date hereof, and that this Government will from time to time give such further Encouragements and Exemptions to such Settlers, as to this Government shall seem reasonable and necessary, and it was thereupon ordered that the Clerk of this Board do certify a true copy of these Resolutions to be delivered to the said Thomas Turk under the seal of this Province...

Page 11: Read the Petition of John Kolp shewing That on the 18th of Sept'r 1740, on the Petitioner's Application to this Hon'ble Board for a gratuity for building and compleating a Corn Mill in the Welsh Tract where he now lives, and which is of great public Utility to the Inhabitants there, it was ordered that on his producing a Certificate of its being compleatly finished, he should have £200 currency allowed him out of the Township fund, and as the said Mill is now compleatly finished as by the Certificate hereunto annexed doth appear, he humbly prays that he may have the gratuity mentioned. There was also annexed a Certificate signed by Abraham Buckles That his Brother had seen the said Mill compleated and in use, as also a Certificate signed by John Hicks, Cornelius Dewees & Evan Vaughan, declaring that the said Mill is now compleated, built & of public Benefit to the Country thereabouts, Whereupon it was resolve that the Petit'r have an order for £140 the which with the sum of £60 he has had in order for from his Excell'cy the Gov'r will be in full for the sum of £200 agreed to be paid him on his finished the mill aforesaid.

Read the Petition of John Rowel shewing That the Petit'r having been a Residenter in this Province for about two years, having come from the West Jerseys being willing to settle in this Province, on order to cultivate some of his Majesty's vacant land, having 6 persons in Family for whom no lands have been assigned, he humbly prays that 300 acres of land be laid out to him in one or two tracts in the Welch Tract, joyning to the lands of Samuel Saurency at the upper end of the Long Bluff on the west side of Pedee River. The Petit'r appearing Swearing to the truth of allegations in his said petition, the prayer thereof was granted & the Deputy Secretary ordered to prepare a warrant accordingly.

Pages 11-12: Read the Petition of Saml Wilds, humbly shewing that the Peti'rs father Saml Wilds obtained a Warrant of Survey for 550 acres of land in Queensborough Township on the Bounty from the Hon'ble Thos Broughton Esq'r Lieut. Gov'r dated Jan'ry 21st 1736, That before the same could be executed he died, whose widow the said Petitioner's mother obtained an order from the Hon'ble Lieut Gov. aforesaid in Council dated April 8th 1747 requiring the survey of 550 acres of land for her & her children, which was accordingly executed by John Oldfield Dec'r 10th 1737 as appears by his Plat thereof lodged in the Surveyor General's Office, since which survey she died also, whereupon the Petit'r humbly prays that your Excell'cy and Honours would order the Surveyor General to certify the said plat in the name of the Petitioner, being eldest son to the partys aforesaid deceased, and that it may be granted him non the County accordingly &C. Signed Samuel Wilds, July 1st 1745. The Petit'r appearing after a due Examination it was ordered that the Surveyor General make out two plats of the plat aforesaid of 550 acres, vizt one plat for 350 acres for the Petit'r, the other for 100 acres of land for the Petitioner's Brother Abel Wilds.

Page 12: Read the Petition of Evan Vaughan shewing That the Petit'r is a Welchman and settled upon the Welch Tract, That he has two persons in family for whom as yet no land has been assign'd him and being desirous to cultivate vacant land in proportion to his said Family right, prays that one hundred acres of land be laid out to him in the Welch Tract &c. The Petit'r appearing and swearing to the truth... the prayer thereof was granted and the Deputy Secretary ordered to prepare a warrant accordingly.

The Petition of John Hicks, planter, humbly shewing That the Petit'r having eight persons in family from whom no land has been given, and being desirous to cultivate Land in proportion to his said family Right, humbly prays that 400 acres of vacant land be laid out to him in the Welch tract &c. The Petit'r appearing and not being able to prove the Qualifications which entitle him to have the prayer of his Petition granted, the same was rejected.

Pages 12-13: Read they Petition of Owen David humbly shewing That the Petit'r is a Welchman, lately come from Pensylvania, and being desirous to become a Residenter in this Province, and to cultivate land, prays that 50 acres of land, by virtue of his right, be laid out to him in the Welch tract on the western of part Pedee River commonly called the old Indian Field &c. The Petit'r appearing and swearing to the truth of the Allegations of his said Petition, the prayer thereof was granted and the Deputy Secretary ordered to prepare a warrant accordingly.

Page 13: Read the Petition of George Austin of Cha's Town, merchant, shewing That the Petit'r in right of his wife Ann, late the widdow and Relict of Philip Dawes, late of Berkley County, Esq'r deceased, is entitled unto a plantation or Tract of land, situate on Charles Town Neck about one mile distant from Charles Town, which heretofore, that is to say, some time in or about the year 1684, was granted to Bernard Schenking, Esq'r and was said to contain 102 acres, and was butting and bounding to the north west upon land laid out to Collonel John Godfrey and Joseph Dollin, to the southwest upon land laid out to the Hon'ble Landgrave Joseph West, and the said Collonel John Godfrey, to the south east on land laid out to Capt John Cummings, and to the north west on Cooper River, as by the records in the Surveyor General's office may appear, that the land in the above description said to be the lands of the Hon'ble Landgrave West, is now, as your Petit'r is informed vested in Collo. John Smith and others, and your Petit'r hath been informed that the said Collonel Smith hath exhibited his Petition to His Excellency and their Honours for a Grant of certain vacant land, supposed to be within his marks and boundaries, that as your Petitr's said land is said to butt and bound on the lands of the said Smith, to the southwest, he is advised and humbly conceives that he hat a forceable[?] right to any vacant lands that may happen to be found between your Petitioner's lands and the true and real lines of the said Collonel Smith's lands, on the north east of the s'd Coll'n Smiths land. Your Petit'r therefore humbly prays that an order may be issued to the surveyor general to resurvey your Petitioner's lands at the time he shall resurvey the lands of the said Smith and at the same time to report to our Excellency and Honours whether the lands prayed for by the said Collonel Smith is within his or your Petitioner's boundary &c, that the said vacant lands, if any shall be found upon said resurvey may be ordered to be granted to your Petitioner or to the said Smith, as to your Excellency and Honours shall seem meet &C. Signed Geo Austin. On reading the said Petition, it was ordered that the Consideration thereof be pospond till Collonel Smith's Petition be read and considered.

Pages 13-14: Read the Petition of John Froely, A Protestant, Swiss, shewing That the Petit'r came into this Country about 5 years ago, on the Encouragement which is given by His Majesty to foreign protestants, and being then unable to pay for his freight, was obliged to serve 4 Years to Mr. Cattell, but as his servitude has expired, having a wife & five children, in all seven persons, prays that 350 acres of land be laid out to him in Orangeburgh Township & that he may be allowed the usual Bounty. The Petit'r appeared before the Board and producing a discharge of his Indenture from Mr. Cattell, and having swore to the truth of the Allegations in the said petition, the prayer thereof was granted, and the deputy secretary ordered to prepare a warrant and the Commissary General to pay the Bounty accordingly.

Page 14: Read the Petition of Edward Trusler shewing That the Petit'r having seven persons in family for whom he has never received any land, and being desirous to settle and cultivate in proportion to his said Right, prays that 350 acres of land be laid out to him on the north side of Pedee River, butting upon the said River, joyning to the lands of Abraham Colson & John Booth &c. The Petit'r appearing and swearing to the truth of his said Petition, the prayer thereof was granted, and the deputy secretary ordered to prepare a warrant accordingly.

Pages 15-16: Meeting of Thursday AM the 16th of Jan'ry 1745/6

Read the following Petition of John Smith, shewing, That the Petitioner's Father, Wm. Smith late of Charles Town in this Province, merchant, deceased, was in his life time, & at the time of his decease, seized and possessed of a certain plantation or Tract of land & marsh, situated, lying & Being on

Charles Town Neck, in the Parish of St. Philip, Berkley County, in the said province, which plantation was originally granted to one James Martell Goulard Esq'r deceased the 14th March 1695 (as by the said Grant now in Your Petitioner's Custody, ready to be produced to your Excellency and Honours Relation being thereto had may appear) for 200 acres, that is to say, as appears by the Certificate and plat of the Surveyor General to the said Grant annexed 153 acres of land & 47 acres of marsh, That the whole plantation or Tract aforesaid by sundry mesne Conveyances and assignments in the Law duely made and executed, became vested in your said Petit'rs father, the said Wm. Smith, as aforesaid, in fee simple... said Wm Smith made his will dated 10 August 1710 and among other things did devise the said plantation, in these words following, that is to say, I give, devise and bequeath unto my loving wife Elizabeth Smith, all that plantation on which I now live, containing about 350 acres of land, with the mansion house I now live in, on the same standing... during her natural life and after her deceased, then in case my son William Smith My son John Smith or either of them, or the survivor of them, do pay or cause to be paid or secure to be paid to my two daughters Elizabeth Smith and Amarinthea Smith the sum of £100 each, at the age of 21 years or marriage, which shall first happen & in case of the death of either of them, then the 200 pounds to the survivor, then I do give the same plantation and houses to my two sons William Smith & John Smith to be equally divided between them... that your Petit'rs mother the above named Elizabeth Smith widow and relict of Wm Smith deceased, your petitionr's said father, is still living and in possession of the said plantation and is tenant for life by the said will, that your Petitir's Brother the above named William Smith is dead, that he made his will and has left issue, five children, being daughters. That your Petit'r hath reason to believe that there are more acres of land and marsh contained within the bounds of the above mentioned plat or the marked trees and stakes specified in the said plan that is expressed in the said Grant. Wherefore the Petit'r prays to pass an order to the Surveyor Genl to order the said tract of land and marsh to be resurveyd and a plat thereof to be duely made and returned, and that thereupon your Petit'r may be allowed to take a new grant for all the overplus land and marsh....

At which time was considered the Petition of Mr. Geo Austin as mentioned in the minutes of the 14th instant, upon reading the above Petition concerning the plantation on Charles Town Neck... It is ordered that the Surveyor General do cause the said lands to be resurveyed...

Pages 16-17: Reconsidered the Petition of Samuel Wildes as in the minutes of Jan'ry 14th, whereupon it was ordered that the Commissary General at the public charge do defray the Expence of the Petitioner's Warrant and Grant and that the Clerk certify the same to the Commissary

Page 17: Read the Petition of Geo: Kitts, in behalf of himself and his wife Christian Barbara Kitts, shewing that the foresaid Barbara Kitts about three years ago bound herself servant to Henry Izard, Esqr., of Goose Creek for four years, as appears by the discharge of the annexed Indenture, that the Petit'r Geo: Kitts did buy the Freedom of the said Barbara Kitts & Married her, whereby the law of the Province, she is entitled to His Majesty [Bounty] to foreign protestants. That the said Barbara had one female child whose freedom George Kitts the petitioner did also purchase. That since the Petition's said Marriage with his wife, he has one more in family, in all three persons, for whom no lands have been granted as family Right, therefore humbly prays that 150 acres of land be laid out to him in the Township of Orangeburgh, and that his wife Barbara may have the usual Bounty. The Petitioner appearing and swearing to the Allegations in his said Petition, at the same time shewing the discharge of his Wife's Indenture, the prayer thereof was granted, and the Deputy Secretary ordered to prepare a warrant and the Commissary to pay the Bounty accordingly.

Page 18: Read the Petition of Edward Trusler shewing That the Petit'r has eleven persons in family for whom as yet he has not received any Grant of lands, therefore prays by virtue of Family Right, that a warrant may issue for 550 acres of land to be laid out to him near the lands of Gibson Ellis, on the south side of Pedee River. Ordered that the said Petition do lye on the Table.

Pages 19-20: Meeting of Friday AM the 17th of Jan'ry 1745/6

Read the following Report of John Champneys Dep't Sec'ry pursuant to an order in the minutes of yesterday's Journal, vizt

John Champneys Dep'ty Secretary who was ordered to examine into the case of John Hicks by an order of Council date the 16th instant, Reports on enquiry the said John Hicks had his plat out of the Surveyor General's Office the 14th Dec'r 1742, but cannot find any record of a Fiat for the same, in the Attorney General's Office, that he has carefully looked over the Fiats in the Secretary's Office and finds some of the above date and thereabouts, but not in the name of the said Hicks, That John Wheeler several times in the Year 1743 and in the begining of 1744[?] did apply to me for the said Grant, and has for answer as he sets forth in his Affidavit, That I have since searched the office for the plat or Fiat, and cannot find the one or the other. John Champneys, Dep'ty Secretary. Jan'ry 17th 1745.

Upon reading the said report, it was ordered that the Surveyor General make out a new plat, in order for a Fiat from the Attorney General and that the Secretary prepare a Grant to be laid before the Board and as it appears upon Oath that the Fees for passing the Grant have been payed into the Secretary's Office, it is ordered that the Deputy Secretary defray the Expence of the new plat, Fiat and Grant.

Page 24: Meeting of Wednesday the 22d of Jan'ry 1745/6

Read the Petition of Andrew Johnson, planter, humbly shewing, That the Petit'r has been a Residenter in this Province about nine years and has never received any land on acco't of family right and having forty two persons in Family and being willing to cultivate and improve some of his Majesty's vacant land in proportion to his Right, prays... for 2100 acres of land in one or two tracts lying on the west side of Pedee River, one tract near to the plantation of Francis Young, the other near the lands of Hugh Swinton. The petit'r appear'g & swear'g to his s'd family Right, the prayer of his petition was granted, and the Dept'y Sec'ty ordered to prepare a Warrant accordingly.

Page 25: Read the Petition of Anthony Caufman, a protestant pallatine, humbly shewing, That the Petit'r came a few years ago into this Province on the Encouragement which is given by his Majesty to foreign protestants and being then not able to pay for his passage, he was obliged to serve Collonel Vanderdussen in order to discharge the same, being now free & having 4 persons in family, viz't himself Wife & two Children, for whom he has received no land, humbly prays that a Warrant be issued for laying out to him 200 acres of vacant land in SaxGotha Township, and that he may obtain the usual Bounty. The Petit'r appearing Swearing... the prayer thereof was granted....

Read the Petition of Phillip Pool of the Township of SaxGotha, planter, shewing That the petit'r has been an Inhabitant in the Township of SaxGotha for near two years past, & by great application and Industry hath raised wheat and at great Expence erected a Mill for grinding Wheat, that the Petit'r hath made several hundred weight of good Flower, but for want of a bolting Cloth, is unable to bring it to a due perfection, altho' the grain raised, and the mill for grinding the same wholly answers the intents to perfect the same he humbly prays his Excellency and Honours to assist him therein for the Good of the public &C. The Board on considering the said petition ordered that upon Mr. Haig at SaxGotha giving him a Certificate, confirming the truth of the allegations in the said petition ,that they the proper officer shall pay him £20 currency, to enable him to perfect his said mill as above prayed for, and that the Clerk of the Board furnish the Petiti'r with a copy of the above minute and order.

Page 34: Meeting of Saturday AM the 25th of Jan'ry 1745/6

Read the Petition of Jeremiah Theus, humbly shewing That the Petit'r ever since the 17th of Jan'ry last, has constantly been employed in Interpreting for the poor Palatines, who come to settle in this province on the Bounty, whose several petitions have been wrote by the hand of the petit'r and which when granted he constantly he conducted them to the several offices, and often supply'd them in their necessitys &c. He therefore humbly prays that the premises may be taken under Consideration and some small allowance be given him for the said services &c. The said petition being considered, it was the opinion of His Majestys Council, that an order be issued to the Commissary to pay forty pounds to the Petit'r in Consideration of his said Services, out of the Township fund, and His Excell'y the Gov'r and the Honbl'e Lieut Gov'r signed an order on the Commissary to pay the said sum accordingly, At the same time Mr. Theus has given to understand that he was not to expect any further pay for any Service of that kind from this Board, but must look for payment from those who employ him.

Page 35: Meeting of Friday AM the 31st of Jan'ry 1745/6

Read the petition of Mary Wright, on behalf of her husband Anthony Wright, shewing, that the Petit'r about a twelve month ago petitioned the Board for a Warr't to be issued for laying out 450 acres of land on Wateree River, and obtained the same, date the 3'd September 1744, here annexed, but upon executing the same, the Petit'r found that the said land could be of little or no Service to her, by reason of the River's not being navigable there, but obstructed by great floats of wood which cannot be removed without vast Expence, Therefore prays that an order be issued for laying out an equal quantity of land by a new arrant in exchange of the former, upon a neck of land in the Fork of Wateree River, where the Petitioner resides &c. The former warrant mentioned in the said Petition was produced, read and examined, whereupon the prayer of the petition was granted....

Read the Petition of Luke Gibson, shewing that the Petitioner's Family consists of three persons, viz't himself, his sister and one slave for whom as yet no lands have been obtained and being desirous to settle on the west side of Wateree River in Craven County opposite to Fredericksbourgh Township near or joyning the lands of Anthony Wright, prays that their Excell'cy and Honours would grant him 150 acres at the place mentioned. The petit'r appearing & Swearing to his right to two persons only, one hundred acres in right of himself & Sister were allowed him....

Read the Petition of Nicholas Miller, a German, shewing that the Petit'r late Servant to Edward Fenwicke, Esqr., and Leonara the Petitioner's wife, late servant to Mr. Chas Shepherd, who have both duely served their times out, hath four persons in family, for whom hitherto he hat had no lands, and being desirous to settle and cultivate 200 acres of vacant lands within the Township of the Congarees, amongst his Countrymen, prays he may obtain the same by virtue of his said Family right, he also prays that the usual Bounty to granted him. The petit'r appearing and swearing to the truth of the Allegations, the prayer thereof was granted...

Pages 35-36: Read the Petition of Samuel Loier, a German Protestant, shewing that the Petit'r having 3 persons in family viz't himself, his wife, and One child for whom as yet no lands have ben assigned, and being desirous to settle and cultivate land in proportion to his said right, humbly prays that 150 acres be laid out to him in the Congrees Township, and that he have the usual Bounty. The Petit'r appearing an swearing,... the prayer thereof was granted....

Read the Petition of Daniel Burgard, a Protestant Swiss, humbly shewing that the Petit'r came over to this Province about 9 years ago, with an intent to settle in one of his Majesty's Townships, but never did settle, but being determined to reside here with his Family, humbly prays that 150 acres of land be laid out to him in the Township of SaxGotha. The Petit'r appearing and swearing to the truth of the allegations... it was ordered that he get a Certificate from the Surveyor General, certifying that his former Warrant has not been executed, and is out of date, in which case, the prayer of his said petition to be granted.

Read the Petition of Adam Shelite, a German, humbly shewing That the Petit'r has 4 Persons in Family, viz't himself, his wife, and child, as also an Apprentice for whom as yet he hath not obtained any Grant of land, and being desirous to cultivate land that is vacant in proportion to his said family Right, prays that 200 acres of land be granted him in the Congaree Township on his Majesty's bounty. The Petit'r appearing & swearing... the prayer thereof was granted.

Read the Petition of Daniel Kilm, a Protestant pallatine, sheweth That the Petit'r came over to this Province some years ago on the Encouragement which is given by his Majesty to foreign Protestants, and being freed from service, humbly prays, as he has 4 persons in family, for whom not any land has been assigned him, that 200 acres of land be laid out to him in the Township of SaxGotha, & that he may have the usual Bounty. The petit'r appearing and swearing, the prayer thereof with regard to the land was granted him....

Pages 36-37: Meeting of Saturday AM the 8th of Feb'ry 1745/6

Read the petition of Cornelius Reine shewing that the Petit'r has eight Negroes in Family for whom he has had no land assigned & being desirous to cultivate some in property to his said family right, prays that 400 acres of land be laid out to him in one or two tracts in the Welch Tract near the land of Nathaniel Evans. The petit'r appearing & Swearing to the truth of the Allegations of the said petition, the prayer thereof was granted....

Read the Petition of William Hughs, a native of Wales, shewing That the Petit'r has one person in family for whom as yet he hat not obtained any land by virtue of family right and being willing to cultivate 50 acres of land in the Welch Tract on Pedee River, humbly prays his Excellency & their Honours that a Warrant for laying out the same to him, near the lands of Mr. Keatley, may be ordered to be issue. the prayer thereof was granted.

Read the Petition of Job Edwards, a Welchman, setting forth that he has two persons in family for whom he hath not obtained any lands Being desirous to cultivate vacant land in proportion to his s'd right, humbly prays that one hundred acres of land be ordered to be laid out to him in the Welch tract near the land of John Rowel... The petit'r appearing being sworn and it appearing that he had but one person in family, fifty acres were ordered to be granted him...

Read the Petition of Edward Boikin shewing that the petit'r has seven persons in family for whom as yet not any land hath been assigned and being willing to cultivate some of his Majesty's vacant land in proportion to his said Right, humbly prays that an order may be issued for laying out to him 350 acres of land in one or two tracts in the Welch tract bounding between the lands of Capt. Buckles & Pedee River.... the prayer thereof was granted.

Pages 37-38: Read the Petition of James Price shewing that the petit'r having left his native Country of Wales in order to settle in this Province, on the Encourgem't given by his Majesty & by that Province, has made choice of a piece of vacant land on Pedee River in the Welsh Tract, near to the land of John Elerby & John Benson, but that the Petit'r is in danger of loosing the improvements he has already made by other persons who without any Warrants threaten to take possession thereof, the petit'r therefore prays that a warrant be issued for laying out to him 150 acres of land in the Welch tract by virtue of his Family Right, that he may thereby be enabled to secure the same & as the petit'r is a poor man & not having money to bear his Expences, he humbly desires dispatch. The petit'r at the same time produced a Certificate from Wm. James, Justice of the Peace in the Welch tract, certifying that the s'd petit'r is a poor man & has been settled some time in the Welch tract, did therefore make bold to recommend him to His Excell'cy & the Hon'ble Council. The petit'r appearing & Swearing.. the prayer thereof was granted.

Page 38: Read the following petition of William Deloach, shewing That the Petit'r has seven persons in family, viz't himself, wife & five children, for whom as yet he hath not obtained any land, & being determined to settle here with his s'd family humbly prays His Excell'cy & their Honours that by virtue of his said family right 350 acres of land may be laid out to him in one or two tracts in the Welch tract on Pedee River bounding on the lands possessed by Edward Boikin and for which the petit'r has paid a Consideration of £100 currency for the good will of the then possessor altho' the said possessor had then neither Warrant nor Grant for the same, moreover as your Petit'r does intend to erect a Grist Mill for the grinding of Corn on one of the said tracts which very much favours the same, & by which not any of his Neighbours will be encroached upon. On reading the above Petition, the petit'r appearing & Swearing to the truth of the Allegations therein contained, the prayer thereof was granted.

Read the Petition of Isaac Hickman setting forth That the petit'r has 10 persons in Family for whom he has not had any land assigned him & Being desirous to cultivate vacant land in proportion to his said Right, prays that 500 acres of land be ordered to be laid out to him in the Welch tract, in one ore two tracts on Pedee River near to the lands of James Jones &c. At the same time the petit'r produced a certificate from Wm. James, Magistrate in the Welch tract, impart'g that the s'd petit'r obtained a Certificate some time ago shewing that he came from Pensylvania & that his family did really consist of 10 persons, viz't himself, wife, seven children & one slave, that he was an honest man &c. The petit'r appearing & Swearing to the Allegations, the prayer thereof was granted.

Page 39: Read the Petition of William James shewing that the Petit'r is a Residenter in the Welch tract & having 5 persons in family, viz't one Child & four slaves, for whom he has not received any land on acc't of family right but being willing to cultivate some that is vacant in proportion of the s'd Right, humbly prays... 250 acres on Pedee River &c.... the prayer of his Petition was granted....

Pages 39-40: Read the following petition of James Jones setting forth that the Petit'r on the 7th of Nov'r 1744 left a petition in the hands of the Clerk of this Hon'ble Board, praying that by virtue of family right he might obtain a Warrant for 300 acres of land in the Welch tract, bounding on the land of John Booth & the Beaver Dam, but as the s'd petit'n was delivered in about the time of the Council's rising, and as the petit'r could not possibly remain in town above one day or two but obliged to return to the Welch tract about other private business, fully intending to come to Town on the then next sitting of the Council, was hindered therefrom by several unforeseen accidents that intervened in the summer time and by the Yellow Fever in the autumn following & whose private affairs could never permit him to come to town till now to sollicit for the land prayed for, but in the mean time was greatly surprized to find that the very same land then prayed for by your Petit'r has been petitioned for, by & Granted away to another & that but very lately, to one Trusler a Butcher, who is not an Inhabitant of that place and who as we can testify by the neighbours present in Town, intends to sell that very land to one John Tyler, Wherefore as your humble Petit'r can shew to this Hon'ble Board by the annexed Certificate under the hands of the Rev'd Mr. Philip James & Several other very creditable Inhabitants of that Tract, that he, a considerable time before his application to the Hon'ble Board, in his first application had the Good will & approbation of the said Inhabitants to live among them, and your Petit'r humbly begs leave to refer himself & character to the Surveyor General of this Province, touching the premises & humbly prays that Your Excellency & honours would be pleased to order a Warrant to be issued for the land before prayed for in one or two Tracts for the Conveniency of erecting a Mill & that your Excell'cy & Hon'rs would be pleased to give what orders with regard to the premises.... The Petition referred to given in to the Clerk of this Board on the 7th of Nov'r 1744 was produced by the Clerk and the following certificate...

We whose names are hereunder mentioned, Livers & Inhabitants of the Welch Tract, on Pedee River, Craven County, South Carolina do hereby certify that we gave our Consent above a Year since that Jas Jones the Bearer hereof might obtain land & settle amongst us in the said tract & further that the said Jones sayeth that he did leave a Petition with the Clerk... Jan'ry 24th 1745. Phillip James, Abel James, Michael James & 4 others.

It was ordered that the order made to survey the same land prayed for to Mr. Trusler as in the minutes of Jan'ry the 14th last past be set aside and that notice be given by the Clerk of this Board to the Survey'r Genl accordingly. Ordered also that the Warrant dated Jan'ry 1745 to survey a hundred acres of land to John Tyler be set aside....

Pages 41-42: Meeting of Friday AM the 14th of Feb'ry 1745/6

Read the following Petit'n of Wm. James in behalf of Jos: Allison a minor, shewing that Oliver Allison deceased, Father of Joseph Allison did in the year 1741 obtain an order from this Hon'ble Board of survey for 300 acres of land to be laid out in the Welch Tract by virtue of family right & Did obtain a warrant for the same, date Jan'ry 16th 1741, signed by James St. John Esq'r the Surveyor General, the which is here annexed, and as the warrant which was returnable in a twelve month & which by reason of the intervening sickness of the said Oliver was not returned within the limited time, the said Oliver thereof did prefer a Petition before this hon'ble Board setting forth the Reasons above mentioned, and praying for a warrant or rather an Exchange of warrant for the said land, but as the said petition was delivered to the Clerk of this Board, at the time the council was not sitting, and as the said Oliver did never return to attend his said petition, nor was he able on acc't of sickness so to do, & is now deceased your Petit'r therefore humbly prays your Excell'cy & honours than an order may be issued for the exchange of the said Warrant & that the said land be surveyed & granted for the use of the aforementioned Joseph Allison the Eldest son of the deceased Oliver &C. William James. The Petition mentioned to have been by the deceased Oliver Allison delivered to the Clerk & this Board was by the Clerk produced & read as referred to, as was also produced & read the Warrant of survey from the sd St. John Esq.r then Surveyor General, dated Jan'ry 7th 1741. The Petit'r James appearing & being duely interrogated relating to the truth of the allegations in the said Petition the prayer thereof was granted.

Page 42: Read the Petition of John Pearson setting forth That the Petit'rs family consists of five persons viz't himself, his wife, one Child, & two negroes for whom no lands have been granted, and as the petitioner is resolved to cultivate vacant land in proportion to his said family right, prays for 250 acres of vacant land to be laid out to him on the north side of Santee River, opposite to Sax Gotha Township... the prayer thereof was granted.

Pages 42-43: Read the Petition of William Evans shewing That the petit'r having resided 8 years in this Province & having 5 persons in Family, vizt himself, his wife, and three children for whom as yet he has not receiv'd any Grant of land by virtue of family right & being determined to settle in this Province & to cultivate & improve some of his Majesty's vacant lands, humbly prays his Excellency & their Honors to grant him 250 acres of vacant land being in proportion to his said Right, in one or two tracts in the Welch Tract on Pedee River, one Tract near the plantation of Abel James, the other joyning the lands of Hardy Counsel, on the opposite side of the River, in the said Welch Tract... the prayer thereof was granted.

Page 43: Read the Petition of George Michael Rainford, a Protestant Pallatine humbly shewing, That the petit'r came into this Country about five years ago on the Encouragement which is given by his Majesty to foreign Protestants & being desirous to settle himself and family which is three in number in one of the King's Townships, prays the 150 acres of vacant land be laid out to him in the Township of Sax Gotha That he may be allowed the usual Bounty... the prayer thereof was granted as to the land but not the Bounty and it was order'd that the Commissary Genl do defray the charges of this Petition, the warrant & Grant.

Read the Petition of Thomas West Sen'r humbly shewing that the Petit'r having eleven persons in Family, viz't himself, wife & 9 children, for whom he hath not had any Grant of land, and being resolved to cultivate land to the Extent of his said family Right, prays that 550 acres of land may be laid out to him on the south side of the Wateree River, Joyning to Mr. Anthony Wrights lands. The Petit'r appearing and swearing to the truth of the allegations of his said petition ,as one of his sons is of age, 500 acres of land were only granted, for which the Deputy Sec'ry was order'd to prepare a Warrant.

Read the Petition of John Kirkwell, a German Protestant, shewing That about 4 years ago the petit'r came into this Province, & having 5 in Family, viz't himself, wife & three children for whom no lands have been assigned him, prays that 250 acres of land be laid out to him in the Township of Orange-burgh, & that he may have the usual Bounty... the prayer thereof was granted with regard to the land but not the Bounty....

Read the Petition of John Perkins shewing That the Petit'r has been a Residenter 7 years in this Province & having 4 persons in family, viz't himself, his wife, & two Children, for whom no lands have been assigned by virtue of family right, & Being desirous to settle din the Welch tract, to cultivate land in proportion thereto, humbly prays that 200 acres of vacant land be laid out to him in the said Tract opposite to Causeway Neck &c... the prayer thereof was granted.

Pages 43-44: Read the Petition of John Pettinger humbly shewing, That the Petit'r has been a Residenter in this Province nine Years, & having nine persons in family, viz't himself, his wife, one child, & six Negroes for whom as yet he hath not obtained any land, being determined to repare with his family into Amelia Township & to cultivate land in proportion to his said Right, humbly prays for 450 acres of vacant land, on Santee River, opposite to the land of Mr. Baker &c... the prayer thereof was granted.

Page 44: Read the Petition of Daniel Manahan shewing That the petit'r has been a Residenter eight years in this Province & having one Person in family, viz't a son for whom as yet he hath not obtained any land & being desirous to cultivate some of his Majesty's vacant lands in the Welch tract, where already he has made Improvements on the lands already assigned him, humbly prays that 50 acres of land be laid out to him in the said Welch Tract near to Chandler's line... it was granted.

Read the following petition of the above Daniel Manahan in behalf of himself & others his Neighbors & Inhabitants of the Welsh Tract, That on the 7th day of July 1739 an order was issued from the Honbl'e board to James St. John Esq'r Surveyor General, that no plats returned by Mr. Mr. ____ & James Gillespie Deputy Surveyors should be certifyed for Surveys made by them in the Welch Tract or any others in Craven County, unless it should manifestly appear to the Surveyor General, by the Buttings & boundings or upon oath, that the lands represented in such platts are not within the said tract, but that all Surveys should be made by one Deputy Surveyor only ,who should be approv'd of by this Hon'ble Board; But contrary to this order, Mr. Blythe did make a Surveyor in the Welch tract in favor or one Paul Trapier for himself & others, without mentioning the Buttings and boundings, as are required in the said order, nor indeed were than any such buttings & boundings possibly then to be found, because the land there had not been granted to any one, as will appear by the Declaration of Mr. Wm. James, Inhabitants in the said Tract, at present in Chas Town, therefore the petit'r humbly conceives that whatever Warrant or Grant may have been given to the s'd Trapier or others on the foresaid acco't is itself void & of no effect, more especially as several Residenters in the said Welch Tract besides the humble petit'r did petition for land, viz't Thos Ellerby & Wm. Jones, entirely in Compliance with the order of Council, already mentioned, who had then ____ Collo Geo: Pawley, as the only Surveyor approved of by the Board, for laying out any lands whatever in the Welch Tract, wherefore the said Pawley did lay out three tracts of land, ___ upon & partly very near to the land which had been illegally & in contempt of the foresaid order & other orders of Council. The legal and regular Surveys were to Daniel Monahan, the petitioner, Thomas Ellerby, and William Jones, as appears by the annex'd Draught of the Survey. The humble Petitioners therefore pray his Excellency & their Honours, that as the three last mentioned Inhabitants of the Welch tract have had their several tracts laid out to them in Conformity to the various orders of this Hon'ble Board, the premises may be taken into Consideration, and such relief granted the petitioners, as to his Excellency & their honours wisdom shall seem meet &c.

On considering the above Petition & the minutes of Council referred to therein produced and read, as also the plat of the Petitioners, and the illegal one of Paul Trapier inspected, and as it was difficult to deprive Trapier of what had been granted, it was ordered That the above Petit'rs may have laid in any other part free of charges.

Page 46: Meeting of Tuesday AM the 20th of February 1745/6

Read the Petition of Abraham Frisbe, humbly shewing, That the Petit'r came into this Province last August with an intention to settle here with his family, having 4 persons in it for whom as yet not any lands have bee granted & being willing to cultivate vacant land in proportion to his said family Right, humbly prays his Excell'cy & their Honours that 200 acres of vacant land be laid out to him in the Welch Tract upon Pedee River joyning to the lands of David Horry & John Evans or any vacant land thereabout &c... the prayer thereof was granted....

Read the Petition of Malachi Murphy, shewing That the petit'r is a native of this Province & having 14 persons in family viz't himself, Cousin & 12 Negroes, for whom as yet he hath not obtained any land in this province on acc't of family Right, & being desirous to cultivate & improve vacant land in proportion to his said Right by playing Indigo, humbly prays his Excell'cy and their Honours that a Warrant may be issued for laying out to him 700 acres in one or two tracts in the Welch Tract on Pedee River, below Collonel Pawley's plantation or any other vacant land thereabout &c... the prayer thereof was granted excepting land to the Cousin....

Read the Petition of Anthony Ernest humbly shewing that the Petit'r came to this Country on the Encouragement given by his Majesty to foreign Protestants, "& being willing to settle in the province, humbly prays that 50 acres of land may be laid out to him in the Township of Saxgotha & Also that he may obtain a Town Lot there & the usual Bounty &c... the prayer of his Petition was granted....

Pages 49-50: Meeting of Saturday AM the 22d of February 1745/6

Read the following Petition of Mr. Geo: Seaman, shewing, That Hugh Wire of Port Royal in the province aforesaid Storekeeper sometime about the latter end of the year of our Lord 1740, did privately & clandestinely withdraw himself & his Effects from this Province & remove to part unknown to the petitioner. That the said Hugh Wire at the time of his departure was & still is indebted to y'r petit'r in the sum of £6444.19.4 current money & upwards.

That the said Hugh Wire sometime before his departure from this Province was seized & possessed of several Lots of land, in the Town of Beaufort at Port Royal aforesaid, that is to say one lot of land N'r 133, which the said Hugh Wire purchased from John Lanbury, one other Lot of land No. 303, which he purchased from one Radolph [sic] Evans, one other lot of land No. 400, which he purchas'd from Thos Juno & one other lot of land No. ___ which he purchased from Ann Conant, as in and by certain Assignments & other writings delivered by the parts aforesaid to the said Hugh Wire, & now lodged in the hands of the Clerk of the Council for the perusal of your Excellency & Honours, reference being thereunto had may more fully appear. That the said Hugh Wire was also possessed as your Petit'r is informed & believes of three other Lots, in Beaufort aforesaid, No. 173, 302 & 333, which, as your Petit'r humbly apprehends, the said Hugh Wire held by virtue of some Authority from the Hon'ble The Gov'r & Council of this Province. That the said Hugh Wire being indebted to the petit'r as aforesaid did on the 26th day of Oct 1739 in Consideration thereof, by his certain Bill of Sale or Mortgage, bargain, sell, assign, transfer & set over to your Petition all & singular the foresaid Lots of land, with the several houses and buildings standing & being thereon, & all rents due & to grow due for the same, as a Security for the payment of his Debt aforesaid, due to the Petit'r as aforesaid, as in & by the said Bill of Sale or mortgage also lodged in the hands of the said Clerk of the Council for the perusal of your Excell'cy & Honours, reference being thereunto had may more fully appear. That the Petit'r after departure of the said Hugh Wire, immediately possessed himself to the s'd Lots, & hath continued in the same ever since, but on enquiry found, That the said Hugh Wire's title to several of the Lots herein before mentioned was not perfect & compleat, but was made to him by little imperfect Bills of Sale & some by the bare delivry of the party's precept or Warrants for taking up the same, which obliges your Petit'r to apply for the aid & assistance of your Excellency and Honours. Wherefore as no other person has any legal or equitable claim to the said Lots of land, the petit'r humbly prays his Excell'cy & Honours to direct a Grant or Grants of the same to be prepared in the name & for the benefit of your petit'r which from the Justice of the Case, and in as much as he is so great a sufferer by the said Hugh Write he humbly hopes he may be thought entitled unto &. George Seaman.

Upon reading the above petition it was orderd that the Consideration thereof be postponed.

Pages 50-51: Read the Petition of Collonel Alexander Vanderdussen shewing That the petit'r is lately arriv'd in this Province commissioned by his Majestys for the defence thereof & as several of his Majesty's soldiers raised & to be rais'd for the Defence will with their officers be quarter'd at Beaufort Town, Port Royal, your Petit'r prays Y'r Excell'cy & Honors will be pleased to grant him the Lot No. 354 whereon he intends to build & reside for the better promotion of His Majesty's Service &c. Signed Alex'r Vanderdussen. The prayer of the said petition was granted....

Page 51: Read the petition of Capt Paschal Nelson shewing That the Petitioner is lately arrived in this Province commissioned by his Majesty for the defence thereof, and as several of his Majesty's Soldiers raised & to be raised for the said defence will with their officers be quartered at Beaufort Town, Port Royal, the petit'r prays his Excell'cy & Honours will be pleased to grant him the Lot No. 155 whereon he intends to build & reside for the better promotion of His Majesty's Service &c. Signed Paschal Nelson. The prayer of the said petition was granted....

Read the petition of Capt Robert Hodgson shewing That he being lately arrived in this Province commissioned by the King for the defence thereof, and as several of the Soldiers under his Command will be stationed at Port Royal prays that the vacant Lot 156 be granted him in the said Town of Beaufort. Signed Robt Hodgson. The prayer of the said petition was granted....

Read the following Memorial of Geo: Hunter Esq'r Surveyor General, shewing that the Memorialist received an Order rom the Clerk of this Board by Command of the Board, requiring the petit'r to certify a platt of 211 ares of land in Craven county in the same & for the use of Robert Newman, pursuant to his petition read & granted the 25th day of May 1755, which lands were survey'd by Matthew Drake, Dept'y Survey'r on the 10th day of May 1733, in pursuance of a precept from James St. John Esq'r Surveyor General, dated Jan'ry 31st 1732 for Wm. Newman to whom the petit'r is son and Executor, the Memorialist upon perusing s'd plat so survey'd of reference finds the same erroneous & prays than an order from his Excell'cy & honours may be directed to him to admeasure or cause to be admeasured the said tract of land, according to the marked tress, that he may certify the same, that a Grant may pass according to the prayer of the said petition. Signed Geo: Hunter, Surveyor General. On considering the above memorial the prayer thereof was granted & an order issued accordingly.

Pages 51-52: The s'd Surveyor General also represented to the Board that an order passed from the Council in March 1744, requiring Anthony Williams formerly a Deputy Surveyor to return a plat of 500 acres surveyed for William Campbell in Williamsbourg Township, which said Williams never returned, but a plat of some useless lands at some miles distance, which has been since granted him, since his death, and left with the Memorialist by his Brother Archibald Campbell who petitioned in behalf of his nephew, that the actual survey by said Williams to whom he convey'd the chain, as proved by him, before your Excell'cy & Honours would grant the same to the said petitioner's nephew, and that your said petitioner (as appears by his Letter herewith submitted) served the said Williams with the said Order, to which, as appears thereby, he paid no deference thereunto, Whereupon your Memorialist prays in behalf of the said petitioner that his Excell'cy & Honours would do what seems in their wisdom meet & convenient. Signed, George Hunter, Surveyor General.

The above Memorial being considered it was ordered, That Anthony Williams on the 10th day of March ensuing do attend this Board with the plats & Field works mentioned, & That the Clerk of this Board do summon him accordingly.

The Surveyor General also represented to His Excell'cy & Their Honours that he received a Letter herewith annexed from John Livinston one of his Deputys, informing him that Wm Snow had surveyed some of his Majesty's lands, which he, no Deputy Surveyor, was not empowered to do, whereby the proper Officers for executing your Excellcy's & Honours Orders in the land office are obstructed, by finding Lines, which if made by lawful Surveyors they are not to cross, Whereupon the Memorialist prays his Excellency & Honors to do in those cases what shall seem meet & Convenient. George Hunter, Surveyor General.

Pages 52-53: The Letters referred to in the above Memorial being produced & read it as ordered, that the Surveyor General do publish in the Charlestown Gazette that he has receiv'd directions from the Gov'r & Council, that he give notice that the Attorney General will be directed to prosecute any person who shall presume to mark Trees or run out land, not being a regular Surveyor, or not having Legal authority....

Mr. Anthony Williams, Sir. I am order'd to acquaint you that his Excell'cy requires & Commands you to appear before him in Council on the 10th day of the ensuing month of March & Then & There to produce the plat & Field works of 300 acres of land & The Town Lot in Williamsbourgh Township formerly surveyed by You for William Campbell deceased, where of you will not fail on your peril.

Pages 55-56: Meeting of Wednesday AM the 12th of March 1745/6

Read the petition of James Babor shewing That the petit'r has been a Residenter about 9 years in the Charraws upon Pedee River, but on account of the frequent Incursions & Violences of Northerly Robbers who infest & plunder the Inhabitants there, of their Horses & Cattle &C, in so much that out of 25 Hogs of which the petit'r was possess'd those Robbers killed & destroyed the whole excepting six, for this reason & For the Charraws being as is claim'd a part of North Carolina, Your Petit'r having paid to tho's Jones, Surveyor of North Carolina, £45 currency for his land there, as will appear by his Receipt, Your Petit'r therefore being obliged to come down to Settlements that are lower, and having 8 persons in Family, viz't himself, wife, and six Children, for whom no land hath been assigned him, humbly prays that 400 acres of vacant land may be laid out to him in one or two tracts in the Welch tract on Pedee River near the Buckle's Line &c. The petit'r appearing & Swearing to his said Right the prayer of his petition was granted & y'e Deputy Sec'ry order'd to prepare a Warr't accordingly.

Read the Petition of Thomas Kesee shewing That the petit'r has resided with his Family in the Country of the Charraws upon Pedee River about a Twelvemonth, but was forced to remove from thence on account of the incursions of the Northerly Robbers, who not only plundered him & broke open his House, but forcibly took from him all His Cloaths, wearing apparel, bedding & furniture and all his working Tools which obliged him & his Family to come down to the lower Settlements on English Santee, as well for protection as subsistance, and having four persons in Family viz't himself, Wife & two Children, for whom no manner of land has been assigned, humbly prays your Excell'cy & Honours that 200 acres of vacant land be laid out to him on Santee River near to the lands of Parson Merit, free of all charges Expences and that Your Excell'cy & Honours will be pleasd to take his deplorable sufferings into Consideration and grant him such relief therein, as to your Wisdom & Justice shall seem meet & c. The prayer as to the land was granted and the Commissary General order'd to defray all charges....

Read the Petition of George Green shewing That the Petit'r is come with his Family into this Province in order to reside and cultivate vacant land in proportion to his Family right, which being two persons in Number, viz't himself & his Wife, humbly prays that 100 acres of vacant land be order'd to be laid out to him in Williamsbourgh Township about 3 miles above the lands of Matthew Bennett, but as your Petit'r in transporting himself & Family from Virginia into this Province is quite exhausted of his Money, & unable without some Encouragem't from the Governm't to make any Settlement at all, humbly prays that some allowance may be made him to enable him to cultivate the land prayed for &c. The prayer was granted as to that land, but order'd that the petit'r pay all the charges....

Pages 56-57: Read the Petition of Saml Wiggins, shewing That the petit'r has been a Residenter in the Welch Tract for above two years & having 4 Persons in Family for whom no lands have as yet been assigned him, viz't himself, his wife and Child and an infant Relation, whom your Petit'r has always mantaind & Brought up in his family & Does still at present Educate, and being willing to cultivate vacant land in proportion to his said family right he humbly prays his Excell'cy & their Honours that 200 acres of land be laid out to him in the Welch Tract upon Pedee River in one or two Tracts, near to the land of John Evans. March 11th 1745. The petit'r appearing & Swearing to the truth of his family right, with regard to three persons, the prayer of his Petit'n for 150 acres was granted.

Page 57: Read the Petition of Benjamin Rogers shewing That the petit'r has been in this province 3 Years & having seven persons in family besides himself, viz't a Wife & Six Children for whom as yet he hath not receiv'd any land on acc't of family right, but being desirous to settle and cultivate some of his Majesty's vacant lands humbly prays his Excell'cy & Honours would be pleased to give a Warr't for laying out to him 400 acres of vacant land, being in proportion to his said family right, in one or two tracts in the Welch Tract on Pedee River, near to the lands of John Lake, &c. March 11th 1745/6. The prayer of the petition was granted.

Read the Petit'n of Wm Smith shewing That the petit'r has been a Residenter in this province about 6 Years & having 3 persons in family for whom he hath never receiv'd any lands by virtue of family Right & being willing to cultivate & improve some vacant lands, humbly prays for 150 acres of vacant land in one or two tracts in the Welch Tract on Pedee River &c... the pray'r was granted....

Read the Petition of Wm. Hemsworth, shewing That the petit'r has been a Residenter in this Province in the Welch tract about 3 years & having 3 persons in family, vizt. himself, his wife & child, for whom as yet he hath not receiv'd any land, & being willing to cultivate & improve some of his Majesty's vacant lands in proportion to his said Right, prays in Excell'cy & their Honours that a Warrant may be issued for laying out to him 150 acres of vacant land in said Welch tract, on Pedee River, near to the lands of Mr. James Gallespie &c. .. the prayer was granted.

Pages 57-58: Read the Petition of Jacob Theiler of SaxGotha Township, setting forth that the Petit'r has an increase of three children in his family for whom as yet he hath not had any land assigned him by virtue of Family Right and therefore humbly prays his Excell'cy & their Honours that 150 acres of land be laid out to him in the Township of SaxGotha, joyning to the land of the Savannah Hunt Mill... the prayer of his petition was granted.

Page 60: <u>Meeting of Thursday AM 13th March 1745/6</u>

Read the petition of Daniel Hoch, a Swiss Protestant, setting forth That he had served Peter Taylor Esq'r in this Province for the payment of his passage & being now out of his time prays a Warrant for 150 acres of land and a Lot in Orangeburgh and the usual Bounty. It appearing to the Board upon Oath that the said Hoch had no more in family than himself and one negroe, it was ordered that he have a warrant for 100 acres of land & a Lot in Orangeburgh & the usual Bounty....

Page 61: Read the Petition of John Candy setting forth That he came from England with his Family consisting of 4 persons, viz't himself wife and two children & having been 4 Years in this Province & willing to cultivate in the same, humbly prays That a warrant may issue for admeasuring two hundred acres of land unto him next to the plantation of Philip Hicks in Pon Pon Parish. The said John Candy having swore to the truth of his Petition it was order'd y't y'e prayer thereof be granted.

Read the Petition of James Jenkins shewing That the Petit'r having a family of 5 Persons for whom no grant has been obtained, prays that 250 acres be laid out in Sax Gotha Township, joyning the lands of Geo Haig & a warr't was ordered to be prepared accordingly.

Pages 63-64: Meeting of Tuesday PM 18th March 1745/6

Read the following Petition of Thos & Nath'l Green & Elizabeth Jenkins, formerly called Elizabeth Green, showing That the petit'rs Thos & Nathaniel Green did on the 22d Jan'ry last past exhibit a Petit'n to this Hon'ble Board setting forth that the petitioners Father obtained from the late Gov'r Johnson a Warrant of Survey for 1500 acres of land, whereof 110 acres were surveyed, as Gov'r Johnson died before a Grant for the said 110 acres was signed, the said two pet'rs prays for a warrant for the said 110 acres & as the petit'n was referred to Jacob Motte Esq'r and his annexed report read, his Excell'cy & Honours were thereupon of Opinion that Elizabeth sister of the two Petitions, daughter of the Testratrix mentioned in the s'd Report, was equally interested in the lands prayed for, as now she humbly joyns in the present petition, humbly praying that the said 110 acres designed as mentioned be admeasured out to the three Petitioners... Thomas Green, Nathaniel Green, Elizabeth Jenkins.

Page 64: Read the Petition of Hans Jacob Annerhanely of Sax Gotha Township, showing that he had 4 Persons in Family for whom as yet no land has been assigned, viz't for his wife & 3 Children, humbly prays that 200 acres of land be laid out to him, on the north side of Santee River... the prayer of his Petition was granted....

Page 65: Meeting of Thursday AM 20th March 1745/6

Read the Petition of James McKelvy, planter, shewing That the petit'r has been an Inhabitant in this Province for 25 years & having 4 Persons in Family Viz't four male slaves for whom as yet no land has been assigned, & being desirous to take up land in proportion thereto, humbly prays his Excell'cy & their Honours that 200 ares of vacant land be laid out to him near Jackson's Creek on the north side of Santee River, and opposite to Sax Gotha Township &c... the prayer was granted & a Warr't ordered.

Page 66: Meeting of Friday PM 21st March 1745/6

Read the Petition of Thomas Eberard a protestant Pallatine, shewing That the Petit'r came into this Country about 2 Years ago, with Capt. Steadman, having now two persons in Family for whom as yet not any land has been granted viz't himself & wife, therefore humbly prays his Excell'cy & their Honours, that 100 acres of land be laid out to him in Amelia Township, & That he may be allowed the usual Bounty. the Petit'r appearing & Swearing to the truth of his Family Right, and the other allegations in his said petition, the prayer thereof was granted...

Page 68: <u>Meeting of Saturday AM 22d March 1745/6</u>

Reconsidered that Petition of Mr. Geo: Seaman, as mentioned in the minutes of the 22d day of Feb'ry last past, whereupon it was orderd that the prayer thereof be granted...

Pages 68-69: Read the Petition of James McGirt, planter, humbly shewing, That the petit'r hath for several years past been settled on a tract of land duly granted & laid out, adjoyning to which is vacant land convenient for erecting and setting up a water mill, which if compleated, will be of great Benefit to many of the Inhabitants of this Province, & be means of causing much vacant land to be settled and cultivated, That the petit'r has begun the work of the said Mill and finds he can be able to bring it to perfection if he had a Grant for some vacant land suitable for erecting it on, and having since his family right last granted, an increase of one white person & eight negroes, humbly prays a warrant may issue for surveying 450 acres of vacant land to the petitioner, butting and bounding on his own plantation & on the north side of Santee River in Craven County &c... the prayer thereof was granted...

Page 101: <u>Meeting of Friday AM 18th April 1746</u>

Read the following Petition of Kenneth Michie, merchant of Charles Town, shewing, That the Petit'r has five persons in Family for whom no land has been assigned him, and therefore on account of family Right prays that 250 acres of vacant land & marsh fronting a tract of land lately purchased by the petit'r be laid out to him there... the prayer of his s'd petit'n was granted....

Page 128: <u>Meeting of Wednesday PM 11th June 1746</u>

Read the Petition of Peter Lequeax of St. James's Santee, showing, That the petit'r hath 13 in family for whom no lands have been assigned, his Family consists of himself, three Children & 9 Slaves, prays that a Warrant may issue for surveying 650 Acres of land on the south side of Santee River, bounding on the lands of Charles Cantey & Jane Sinclair... the prayer thereof was granted....

Page 131: <u>Meeting of Saturday AM 14th June 1746</u>

Read the Petition of Maurice Keating, son and heir at Law of Edward Keating, late of the province of South Carolina, planter, deceas'd, shewing That the Petitioner's Father, did in his Life time, that is to say on the 6th of Feb'ry in the year 1735, obtain from the Hon'ble Thos Broughton, Esqr., then Lieuten't Gov'r, a Warrant under his hand & Seal, directed to James St. John Esq'r, then Surveyor General, requiring & Directing him to admeasure & lay out to the said Edward Keating, a Tract of land containing 750 acres, situated in Berkley County, that in pursuance of the said Authority, the said land was surveyed, butting & bounding on all sides on lands not laid out, & on the 5th of Jan'ry 1736 did certify a plat thereof, in the Secretary's office, as appears by a plat thereof now in the hands of the Secretary, & herewith produced: That soon afterwards, and before a Grant could pass of the said land, Edward Keating died. The petit'r therefore prays that the Secretary of the Province be directed to prepare a Grant of the said 750 acres to the petit'r, His Heirs and Assigns.... the prayer thereof was granted.

Pages 135-136: Meeting of Wednesday AM 18th June 1746

Read the Petition of Elias Horry of Craven County, Planter, shewing That y'e aforesaid Elias Horry in his life time did by his Petition represent to Lieut. Govr. Broughton & the Council, that he had for many years been possess'd of certain lands containing 1500 acres in Craven County, & granted by the Lords Proprietors, at the Quit Rent of one shilling proclamation money P 100 acres, but that grant was unfortunately destroy'd by fire, wherefore, the s'd Elias Horry Prayed His Hon'r the Lieut. Gov. afd. & The Council to give a new Grant for the same, & at the Quitrents in his former Grant which was destroyed.. Lieut. Govr. gave a Warrant under his hand & Seal to resurvey the said 1500 acres and return a plat thereof... that Grant might be prepared.... That the signed & recording of the grant prepared and affixed to the said plat was contrary to the intention of the said Elias Horry in his life time... That the division of the deceas'd Elias Horry's Estate was that Jno Horry sho'd have 500 acres, Anthony Bonneau 500 & y'e petition'r y'e remaining 500 acres.. prays to give a new grant to the foresaid John & Anthony Bonneau... Order'd that the petition together with the whole of the papers be referred to the Attorney General and that he report his Opinion on the said Petition to this Board.

Page 147: Meeting of Tuesday AM 16th September 1746

Affidavit of Thomas Parker. Thomas Parker a native of England being brought before his Excell'cy the Gov'r in the Council Chamber & Sworn on the holy Evangelist, deposeth That he hath been a Residenter in this Province 4 Years, and that about 6 Weeks ago he went to Philadelphia, when he arriv'd there Small Pox was in that Town, and he heard that several people died of it. That he left Philadelphia last Wednesday Fortnight as near as he can recollect, that the Crew during the whole voyage were all in good health except William Baker, who 3 days after coming from Philadelphia, sicknen'd and being ask'd whether he met with any Pilot on his arrival here, the Deponent answered that Mr. Harding's young man piloted in their vessel....

Page 151: Read the Petition of David Ledrier in behalf of himself & Jean Marie, Florence & Isabeau Margurite Ledrier, humbly shew'g that the Petitioner came lately with his Sisters above mention'd into this Province on the Encouragement given by his Majesty to foreign Protestants and being desirous to cultivate some of his Majesty's vacant lands in this Country, humbly prays that a Warrant be issued for two hundred acres & town lots to be laid out to them in Amelia Township, and that they may be allow'd his Majesty's gracious bounty.. the prayer thereof was granted...

Read the humble Petition of John Westfield, shewing, That the Petit'r has been a Residenter in this Province about 6 years & having 7 Persons in Family, viz't Seven slaves for whom as yet he has had no land assigned him, humbly prays his Excell'cy & Honours that 350 acres of vacant land be admeasur'd to him in the Welch tract, near to the plantation of Hardy Counsel &c.... the prayer thereof was granted.

Read the Petition of Edward Lovell, shewing that the Petit'r has been a Residenter in this Province for about a twelve month & having 4 Persons in family viz't himself, wife and two Children for whom as yet he has not had any land assigned him & Being desirous to improve & Cultivate some of his Majesty's vacant land, humbly prays his Excell'cy & their Honours to grant him 200 acres, being in proportion to his said family right, adjoyning to John Perkins's line in the Welch tract on Pedee River &c. Edward Lovell ...the prayer of his s'd petition was granted.

Pages 151-152: Read the Petition of William Osborn, shewing That the Petit'r has been a Residenter in this Province about 17 Years, but has not as yet had any land assigned him by virtue of family Right, & having at present 12 persons in family vizt, himself, wife, three Children & Seven slaves & being willing to cultivate and improve some of his Majesty's vacant land, he humbly prays your Excell'cy and Honours that a Warrant may issue for laying out to him 600 acres of vacant land, being in proportion to his said family Right, in one or two tracts, near to Filben's land on the north side of Santee River in Craven County, that so a Grant may pass for the same. Will'm Osborn. Septr 12th 1746.

Page 152: Read the Petition of John Jones, shewing That the Petit'r has been a Residenter in this Province about 10 Years, and having six persons in family vizt, himself, wife, & four Children & being desirous to cultivate some of his Majesty's vacant land humbly prays that a Warrant may issue for laying out to him 300 acres of land being in proportion to his s'd Family Right, between Buckhead & the 100 £ Savannah, near the lands of Anthony Gant, in Amelia Township, being land not granted to any person, and on which he at present doth reside, having made some improvements thereon, he also prays for his Majesty's gracious Bounty. John Jones. Septr 10th 1746... the prayer thereof with regard to the land was granted, but not the Bounty.

Read the Petition of John Bole, shewing That the Petitioner has been a Residenter in this Province about one Year & having two persons in Family viz't himself and wife for whom as yet not any lands have been assigned him, and being willing to cultivate & improve some of his Majesty's vacant land prays that a Warrant may be issued to him 100 acres of vacant land, near to the lands of Capt. Joseph Cantey on Santee River, that so a Grant may pass to him for the same... the prayer of his Petition was granted.

Page 162: Meeting of Thursday AM 18th September 1746

Read the Petition of John Friday, shewing That the Petit'r has lately married one Susanna Hembright, a Protestant Swisser, who was Servant to John Morton, Esqr., who came over to this Province about 2 Years ago in the Ship St. Andrew, Capt. Brown Commander, but has now got a proper discharge from her s'd Master, the Petit'r therefore humbly prays his Excell'cy and their Honours that a Warrant may issue for laying out to the Petit'r 100 acres of land in SaxGotha by virtue of family right and also that he may obtain for his said Wife the usual Bounty... the prayer thereof was granted... the Commissary Genl to pay the Bounty accordingly.

HEMPSTEAD COUNTY LIBRARY
HOPE, ARKANSAS

Page 1: Meeting of 20th November 1746

Read the Petition of Thomas Monck of Berkley County, planter, humbly shewing That the Petit'r has an Encrease of four persons in Family for whom no Family right has hitherto been Granted. The Pet'r therefore prays his Excell'cy and their Honours that a Warrant may Issue for Surveying and Laying out to him 200 acres of vacant land on the north Side of Santee river near to Prince Pond &c. Nov. 20th 1746.... the prayer of the Petition was Granted.

Read the Petition of Thomas Scott humbly shewing That the Petit'r Settled in Williamsburgh Town'h, has five Persons in Family viz a wife and three children for whom not any Lands have been granted and whereas a Tract of land containing 300 acres was Surveyed for John Carrol on the 27th day of March 1740, in the said Township and the plat thereof returned into the Survey'r Generals office, October 25th 1740, where it now lyes, and no application made for the same, tho advertised in the Gazette whereby it becomes vacant, the Pet'r therefore prays his Excellency the Governor and their Honors to direct the Survey'r General to Cause to be laid out to him 200 acres as his Family Right, it being in the said Township and Contiguous to lands whereon he lives, that a Grant may be passed to him for the Sale. Novem'r 14 1746.

To the Petition was annexed the following Certificate of the Survey'r General, viz I hereby certify that 300 acres within mentioned were Surveyed, returned, advertised, and no application made for the same. Nov 14th 1746. Geo Hunter, Survyr. Genl. ...the prayer of the petition was granted.

Read the Petition of John Purvis shewing that the Peti'r has been a Residenter above six years in this Province and having a Family consisting of Seven persons viz Himself, wife, and five children, for whom as yet, not any land has been assigned, and being desirous to Cultivate some of his Majestys vacant lands, humbly prays his Excellency and their Honours, that 400 acres be laid out to him in one or two tracts in the Welch Tract near the lands of Gideon Ellis upon the South branch of Jeffrey's Creek &c. October the 11th 1746. The Petitioner appearing and swearing to his said Right, 250 acres were only allotted him the 50 acres for one of the Persons mentioned in his Petition viz an orphan was not allowed him, wherefore the Deputy Secretary was ordered to prepare a Warrant accordingly.

Pages 1-2: Read the Petition of Anne Duyett, widdow, shewing, that the Petitioner has five children besides her self, for whom as yet not any Lands have been assigned and being desirous to Cultivate in proportion to her said Family Right, humbly prays his Excellency and their Honours that 300 acres of vacant land viz whereon she at present lives, be laid out to her in Fredericksburgh Towns'h on y'e North side of Wateree River... the prayer thereof was granted.

Page 2: Read the Petition of John Hope, shewing, That the Petit'r has been a Residenter in this Province for ab't 15 years and having a Family consisting of 8 persons, viz himself, wife and two children, an orphan, and three slaves, for whom as yet not any land has been assigned, and being willing to Cultivate and Improve some of his Majesty's vacant land humbly prays his Excellency and their Honours that 400 acres of land by virtue of his said Family right be laid out to him near the Swift Creek in the fork of Gum Swamp, by Wateree River, in Fredericksburg Township, whereon the Peti'r has made some Considerable Improvements.

The Petit'r appearing a swearing to his said right, 50 acres prayed for to the orphan mentioned were not allowed but 350 acres only....

Read the Petition of James Lesslie humbly shewing That the Pet'r has a Family consisting of Six persons, viz himself, wife, and four children, for whom not any lands have been granted, and being desirous to settle and Cultivate as much lands as he is entitled to by his Majesty's Instructions, humbly prays his Excellency and their honours, that a Warrant may Issue for Surveying to him 300 acres in two or three different Tracts on the north side of Santee River opposite to Sax Gotha Township... the prayer thereof was granted, but in one tract only....

Read the Petition of Evance Rice shewing That the Pet'r has moved himself and Wife into this Province with an intent to settle therein, and having a Family of five persons, viz himself, wife & three children, prays that Lands may be admeasured to him, in proportion to his said Family right on the north side of Congree River, opposite to SaxGotha Township, and Joining to the lands of Philip Rayford and William Horsel.. the prayer thereof was Granted....

Read the Petition of Nathan Evance, a native of Wales, shewing That the Pet'r has five persons in family, viz himself, wife & three children for whom as yet not any land has been assigned, and being willing to Cultivate and Improve some of his Majestys vacant land, humbly prays his Excellency and their Honours, that by virtue of his said Family right, 250 acres be laid out to him, Joining to Catfish Swamp on the Welch Tract, on Pedee River, in one or two tracts, viz that 200 acres be laid out as aforesaid, the other contiguous thereto, upon Maple Swamp run, upon which said last Tract, the Pet'r intends to build a Grist mill, both for the Public benefit, and his own use... the prayer for the 250 acres was Granted....

Pages 2-3: Read the Petition of William Carey shewing That the Pet'r has there Persons in family for whom as Yet not lands have been assigned and being willing to cultivate some that are vacant, humbly prays his Excellency and their Honours, that 150 acres be laid out to him, in the Welch Tract on Pedee River, opposite to Swan's Island, which land at pres't is possessed by John Newberry, who purchased the same, from one Lovell & w'h said Lovell made some improvements upon the same, without either warrant or Grant, and sold the same to the said John Newberry but they having as your Pet'r conceives, no legal title to the said Lands. The Pet'r therefore humbly prays that the said land b granted to him. The Pet'r appearing and searing to his foresaid right, it was ordered, That the Survey'r General, give notice to the Persons who are no win possession of y'e said land, that if they have any objection to a Grant passing in favour of the Petitioner, that they give notice thereof.

Page 3: Read the Petition of Robert Lindley, shewing That the Pet'r came into this Province in order to settle his Family, and to Cultivate and improve some of his Majesty's vacant lands, and having two persons in family for whom as yet not any lands have been assigned, viz himself and wife, humbly prays his Excell'cy and their Honors that 100 acres of vacant land, may be laid out to him near Cedar Creek on Pedee River.. the prayer thereof was granted...

Read the Petition of Benjamin McKennie humbly shewing that the Petitioner's family consists of 12 persons, viz 9 whites and 3 negroes, and he hath lately moved from the northward to this Province, and not taken up any lands, as he is now settled on a Tract of Land purchased from Charles Radcliffe and being desirous to Cultivate and settle 600 acres of his Majesty's vacant land, he therefore humbly prays hi Excellency and their Honours to issue a warrant for laying out to him 600 acres on the north side of Santee River in Fredericks-burgh Township, Craven County, lying on the south side of y'e Tract he now lives on, adjoining to the said tract. The Pet'r appearing and Swearing to his said family right, 600 acres were ordered to be laid out to him, but in regard that Ann Duyette has had a warrant ordered to her, of this day's date, for the land prayed for, by y'e Petition, it is ordered that the Petitioner do take up the land in any other vacant tract in the said Town'p of Fredericksburgh.

Read the Petition of John Swinney, shewing That the Petit'r has six persons in family for whom as yet no lands have been assigned, viz himself, wife and four children, and begin desirous to Cultivate some of his Majesty's vacant land, humbly prays his Excellency and their Honours, that 300 acres be laid out to him in Fredericksburgh Township, on the south side of John McCon-nals land... the prayer thereof was Granted.

Pages 3-4: Read the Petition of Daniel Devonauld shewing That the Petr has been abt nine years a Residenter in this Province, and having six persons in family, for whom not any land has ben obtained, viz three children and three slaves and begin desirous to Cultivate some of his Majestys vacant land here, humbly prays his Excellency and Honors that a Warrant do issue for laying out to him 300 acres in the Welch Tract in one or two Tracts bounding on the Petrs own land.. the pray'r of his Petition was granted, but the land to be laid out in one tract only....

Page 4: Read the Petition of Christian Timmerman, a Protestant Swiss, humbly shewing That the Pet'r came over to this Province some years ago, upon the Encouragement which his Majesty has been pleased to bestow on all poor foreign Protestants, willing to settle themselves and Familys in any of the townships, therefore humbly prays That as he has two in family for whom not any land has been assigned that 100 acres be laid out to him in Sax Gotha Town'p and also prays that he do obtain his Majestys Gracious bounty, the land prayed for being part of 150 acres formerly surveyed for Hans Jacob Stainer, since dead, the plat thereof lying in the Survey'r Generals office... the 100 acres prayed for was granted.

Read the Petition of Christian Bravant, a Protestant Swiss, humbly shewing That the Petit'r came over to this Province on the Encouragement given by his Majesty to all forreign Protestants, who come to reside in this Province ,and being now free from his Servitude, and desirous to live in Sax Gotha Township, humbly prays that 50 acres of vacant land be by warrant laid out to him in the foresaid Township, and that he may obtain the usual bounty, the land prayed for being part of a tract of 150 acres formerly surveyed for Hans Jacob Stainer, since dead, the plat thereof lying in the Survey'r Generals office... it was ordered that Survey'r General do lay off 50 acres for the Pet'r from the forementioned plat of 150 acres formerly surveyed to Hans Jacob Stainer....

Page 6: <u>Meeting of Friday AM 21st November 1746</u>

Read the Petition of Alex'r Weed shewing That he has 34 Persons in family viz 4 whites and 30 negroes, for whom as yet not any land has been assigned him, wherefore by virtue of said Family right, he prays his Excellency & their Honours, that 1700 acres of vacant land be laid out to him between Savannah Edisto Rivers... the prayer thereof was granted....

Read the Petition of Thos McPherson shewing that he has 4 Persons in family for whom he has not had hitherto any Land, he therefore prays his Excellency and their Honours that 200 acres of vacant land whereon he at present doth reside be granted him... the prayer thereof was granted...

Read the Petition of Rachel Gardner of Amelia Town'p shewing that the Peti'r has a family of Eleven persons viz her self, one child & nine slaves of her own sole right and property, for which she has not had any land hitherto therefore prays his Excelle'cy and their Honours to grant her a Warrant of Survey for 550 acres of land in Buckhead Neck, adjoining to the Petit'rs plantation in the said Town'p of Amelia... the prayer thereof was granted...

Pages 6-7: Read the Petition of Wm. McKelvie, an Inhabitant of English Santee shewing That the Peti'rs family consists of three persons viz himself, wife and one child for whom not any land has been assigned him, and being desirous of cultivating some of his Majestys vacant land, on the north side of

Santee river in the English Santee, being a tract of land run out 5 years ago but no Plat returned, in the office, joining on the NW Side of Mary Lawsons land, where she now lives, therefore prays that a Warrant be issued for laying out to him 150 acres in the place already named. Annexed to his Petition was the following Certificate of Survey of the Survey'r General viz Nov 21st. I hereby Certify that no Plat has been returned for John Lawson into y'e Survey'r Generals Office the last four years. Signed Geo Hunter, Surv'r Genl.... the prayer thereof was granted.

Page 7: Read the Petition of George Saunders, Shewing that the Pet'r has Eleven persons in family viz himself, wife and 5 children and 4 slaves for whom not any land has been assigned, and being willing to Cultivate some of his Majestys vacant land humbly prays that 550 acres be laid out to him in the Welch Tract, being land on which the Petr does at present reside and joins to Mr. Ravells [Ravenell's?] land. Nov 21st 1746. Signed Geo. Saunders... the prayer thereof was granted.

Read the Petition of John Brown, planter shewing that the Petitioner has four persons in family for whom he has not received any lands pursuant to his Majestys' Royal Bounty, and as there is a tract of land containing 800 acres surveyed above 10 years ago, for Gideon Gibson and at pres't a Plat thereof in the Survey'r General's Office, as appears by his Certificate, and is vacant, by not being applied for in the time prescribed in the Gazette, the Pet'r therefore humbly prays that the Survey'r General be directed to Certify the said Plat for the use of the Petitioner, and in his name that it may be granted him accordingly. To which was annexed a Certificate by Geo Hunter... that 200 acres of land was surveyed on the NE side of Pedee River for Gideon Gibson on the 13th day of April 1736 in pursuant of a Warrant from Gov'r Johnson, dated March 6th 1733, and that a Plat thereof was returned into the Survey'r General's Office on the 18th of June 1736 which has laid there ever since without any application made for y'e same tho advertized in the Gazette, August 5th 1743.. the prayer thereof was granted....

Read the Petition of William Farrel shewing That the Pet'r has been a Residenter in this Province about 9 Years & having two persons in family, viz two children, for whom as yet not any land has been assigned, and being willing to Cultivate and improve some of his Majesty's vacant lands, humbly prays his Excellency and Their Honours, that 100 acres of Land be laid out to him, in the Welch Tract, by virtue of Family right, in order that a Grant may pass for the same &c. Signed Wm Farrel. Nov'r 21st 1746... the prayer thereof was granted....

Page 8: Meeting of Saturday AM 22d November 1746

Read the humble Petition of Widdow Lowrey shewing That the Pet'r arrived with her Husband and Children from Ireland, in the Year 1736 and obtained a Warrant of Survey for 200 acres of Land in Kingston or Willimsbourgh

Township from the Hon'ble Thomas Broughton Esq'r Lieut' Governor, dated Feb'ry 10th 1736 which warrant has never been executed, whereupon the Pet'r prays his Excellency and Their Honors to grant a Warrant requiring the Survey of the said 200 acres in Williamsburgh Town'p whereon her husband, with her, and family lived, for the use of the Petitioner, and her children William, Robert & Jane Lowrey, and that it may be granted accordingly, free of all charges as at time Intended &c. Witness Robert Gibson. Signed Elizabeth Lowrey. To the above petition was annexed a letter form John Livingston dated Williamsburgh March 15th 1745, directed to Geo Hunter Esq'r Surv'r General, mentioning that in her Husband's time he obtained a Warrant to run out land on the Encouragem't given by his Majesty which Warrant was given to Williams Dep'ty Surv'r to run out the same which he did not perform in the meantime the Husband died... the prayer thereof was granted....

Pages 9-10: Meeting of Saturday AM 22d November 1746

Read the Petition of Paul Trapier, merchant, shewing, that the Pet'r has 20 persons in Family for whom he has not obtained any warrant of survey, therefore prays ... to certify a Plat for a thousand acres of land, surveyed for James Matthews deceased in Craven County, Prince Fredericks Parish, for which there has not been any application made, by the heirs and executors of Mr. Matthews and disclaimed by his Executrix, and that pursuant to an order of council published in the Gazette August 15th 1743, whereby such lands are declared vacant, The Survey'r General be ordered to certify the above mentioned Plat in the name & for the use of the Petitioner. At the same time the Petitioner produced a certificate singed by Geo Hunter shewing that the Plat of 100 acres of land mentioned in the Petition was surveyed as aforesaid & returned into the Surveyor Generals Office on 14th March 1737 and that no prior application has been made for the same.. the prayer was granted....

Page 12: Meeting of Wednesday AM 26th November 1746

Read the Petition of Adam Shoab, Jacob Plasy, Garson Lewis, Henry Audley which four above mentioned Petitioners not having their Familys in y'e Province were ordered to Carry back their Petitioners, to y'e Survey'r General till They should bring their familys into this Province.

Read the Petition of Leopold Clance shewing That y'e Pet'r came over to this Province on the Encouragement given by his Majesty to all forreign Protestants and having four Persons in Family for whom not any Lands have been assigned prays that 200 acres of vacant land be laid out to him in Amelia Township, he having a Wife and two children, prays also for the Bounty.. the prayer with regard to the Land was Granted, but not the Bounty, only that the Commiss'y General do defray the Expences of the offices....

Read the Petition of Gaspar Akerman, a Protestant Pallatine shewing That the Pet'r came over to this Province on the Encouragement given to forreign Protestants and has served to as that the time of his Servitude is now expired and having two Persons in Family viz himself & son, for whom not any Land has been assigned prays that 100 acres of land be laid out to him in New Windsor and he may obtain the kings most Gracious Bounty.. the prayer was Granted....

Read the Petition of Thos Rawlins humbly Shewing That the Petit'r has seven persons in family viz himself, wife & Five children for whom not and Land has ben assigned, that he has improved a Tract of land in Williasmburgh Town'p on which he now resides, and is vacant, therefore humbly prays that by virtue of Family right 350 acres be laid out to him out of the land mentioned, and in regard to his extream Poverty, that he may have his majestys bounty... the prayer thereof as to the land was granted but not the bounty...

Page 13: Read the Petition of Gershom Lewis, shewing that the Petit'r has been a Residenter in this Province between two and three years, and having 38 Persons in Family, viz himself, wife, five children, an indented Servant, & 20 Slaves, for whom not any land has been assigned, humbly Prays that by virtue of Family right 1400 acres of vacant land be laid out to him in one or two tracts in the Welch Tract on Pedee River near y'e lands of Giles Rogers.. the prayer thereof was granted, but the land in one Tract only....

Page 14: Meeting of Thursday AM 27th November 1746

Geo. Hunter Esq'r Survey'r Genl sent a paper by him signed to the Clerk of this Board acquainting that he had received his Excell'cys warrant for y'e survey of 100 acres in New Windsor for Gaspar Akerman but that not any Deputy Suvyr there, there being no Employ, no land having been surveyed in that Township for four years Past. That as the said Gaspar Akerman is on the bounty, it would be a Great charge to the Public to send a Survey'r on purpose and that y'r Excellency and their Honours would be pleased to order him to certifie 100 acres being part of a tract of 600 acres in that Township surveyed for Wm. Gascoign and by him disclaimed, he would do so accordingly that the other 500 acres has been already petitioned for viz 350 acres Adam Shoub and 150 for Conrad Fusher... they do accordingly order him to certify the 100 acres which is part of y'e 600 acres in the said Township...

Page 15: Meeting of Saturday AM 29th November 1746

Read the Petition of Henry Falcast, a Swiss Protestant, shewing that the Pet'r came into this county w'th his family on y'e Encouragem't given to forreign Protestants and having a family of 6 persons, vizt himself, wife & 4 children, humbly prays that 300 acres of vacant land be laid out to him in Orangeburgh Town'p & y'e he may obtain his Majestys bounty... the prayer thereof was granted.

Page 18: Meeting of Tuesday AM 9th December 1746

Read the Peti'n of Hugh Shannon, shewing, That the Petit'r has 4 persons in family for whom he has not received any Land, and being desirous to Cultivate some of his Majesty's vacant land humbly prays that 200 acres be laid out to him in Berkley County near Santee River at a place called Providence contiguous to the lands of Alex'r Tait... the prayer thereof was granted.

Read the Pet'n of John Grossman, a Protestant Pallatine, humbly shewing That the Peti'r came over into this Province on y'e Encouragem't which his been bestowed on all Forreigners who are desirous of settling themselves with their Familys in any of y'e Townships here, therefore humbly prays that in consideration of his servitude being expired, 150 acres of vacant land be assigned him in the Town'p of Saxe Gotha, he having a wife and a Child, and that he may obtain also his Majestys Gracious bounty... the prayer of his said Petition was granted....

On motion it was ordered that the Survey'r General do certify a Plat of 850 acres of surplus land returned into his Office, by Thos Witter, Deputy Survey'r, of James St. John late Survey'r Genl on the 17th day of Feb'ry 1738 for Mary Hutson, late otherwise Mary Chardon, widdow, situate on the north side of Combee River in Colleton County being in the boundary line of Two tracts of 500 acres and 382 acres of land heretofore, that is to say in the year 1705, granted by the late Lords Proprietors to John Palmer and by several Mesne conveyances now become vested in the said Mary Hutson and her heirs in order that a Grant of such surplus land may be passed to the said Mary Hutson and her heirs pursuant to the Quit Rent Act.

Page 19: Meeting of Wednesday AM 9th December 1746

Read the Petition of Major William Pinckney, shewing, That the has 10 persons in family for whom he has not obtained any warrant of Survey therefore prays a tract of land on Pedee river containing 494 acres, formerly surveyed for Aaron Huntscomb, and now in the Survey'r General's office, tho advertised in the Gazette, to be taken out on or before the 1st day of January 1743, whereby the same becomes vacant... signed William Pinckney. To this Pet'n was annexed a Certificate signed by Geo. Hunter Esq'r Surv'r General, declaring that a plat of 494 acres of land on the southwest side of Pedee River, was returned into the office March 14th 1737 surveyed by Geo Pawley, Dty Sury'r, Oct 28th 1746, for Aaron Huntscomb, and that the same had been advertised in the Gazette and no application made for the same, on the Contrary, when he Informed him thereof, he refused to take it out.... the pray'r thereof was granted.

Read the Petition of Isaac Motte shewing That the Pet'r in the Year 1737 obtained from the Hon'ble Thomas Broughton, Esq'r, Lieut. Govr., a Warrant of Survey, for 200 acres of land in y'e Townsh'p of New Windsor, and a lot in the said Town, as by the annexed certificate fully appears, that a Grant for the same was not made out, according to the precept, and by which your petitioner's title to the said land is become void, and the pet'r liable to the payment of quit rents for the same, long before they would have become due, had the said Grant been properly made out. That the Pet'r has built on and Improved said lands, therefore prays he may have a proper and authentic title, agreed to the said warrant... the prayer thereof was Granted.

Pages 21-22: Meeting of Friday AM 12th December 1746

Read the Petition of Gideon Gibson, shewing That the Pet'r has been a residenter in this Province ab't 15 Years, and never having taken up any Lands in this Province, and now willing to Cultivate some of his Majesty's vacant land thereon, humbly prays that a Warrant do Issue for laying out to him 50 acres in a place called the Duck pond on the south side of Pedee River. Decem'r 12th 1746. The prayer thereof was granted.

Page 22: Read the Petition of Gideon Gibson Jun'r shewing That the Pet'r has four Persons in Family viz Himself, his wife and two Children for whom as yet not any Land has been assigned him and being willing to Cultivate and improve some of his Majesty's vacant land humbly prays that by virtue of Family right that 200 acres of vacant land be laid out to him at a place called the Duck pond on the south side of Pedee River where the Pet'r at pres't resides.... The prayer thereof was granted.

Read the Petition of Josias Garnier DuPre, Setting forth that the Pet'r is a native of this Province, and having 12 persons in Family viz 3 children and 9 Slaves, for whom as yet not any lands have been assigned him, and being desirous to Cultivate some of Majestys vacant lands humbly prays that by virtue of his said Family right, 600 acres of vacant land may be granted him in one or two tracts, one tract joining to y'e lands of Colonel Pawley, on Pedee River, the other likewise on Pedee River... the prayer thereof was granted, but in one tract only.

Page 24: Meeting of Thursday AM 22d January 1746/7

Reconsidered the Petition of Isaac Motte as in the Journal of the 10th of December last past, whereupon it was ordered that the original rant referred to in his said Petition, be produced at this board.

Page 25: Meeting of Thursday AM 29th January 1746/7

Read the Petition of Martyn Kalemir, a Protestant Pallatine shewing that he came into this Province from Georgia with a Wife & their child, where he has live about 4 Years, after the expiration of five years servitude, but could not support his family there, having been promised only 50 acres of land for his whole people, out of which 8 acres were only fit to be Cultivated, but which never has been Granted whereupon he was obliged to move with his family from thence, and to come into this Province, and therefore humbly prays that 50 acres be laid out to him, for each person in his Family, viz 250 acres in all, in Sax Gotha Township, free of charges, and what bounty shall seem met, prays also that his baggage and tools be carried up to the fores'd Town'p free of Charges, he being poor as not to be able to pay the least expense &c... the pray'r of the pet'n granted as to the land but not the bounty, but that the Commis'ry General pay the expense of Petitioning &c.

Page 26: Read the Petition of Samuel Kern, a Protestant Pallatine shewing that the Pet'r came over to this Province four years ago with Captain Steadman, with an Intent to Settle on the Encouragement which his Majesty Gives to forreign Protestants, and having been here, in quality of a Servant, and the time of his servitude now expire, prays that 50 acres of land be laid out to him in Sax Gotha Town'p and that he may have the usual bounty... the prayer of the Petitioner was granted.

Read the Petition of Solomon Ade, a Protestant Pallatine, shewing that the Pet'r came into this Province from Georgia where he lived 5 years at Ebenezzar, but after which he never could obtain any bounty of the Trustees, nor land, nor the promise of any, wherefore he was induced to come here, and having a family of four persons viz himself, wife and two children, humbly prays that 200 acres of land be laid out to him in Sax Gotha Township and that he may have his Majesty's most gracious provision bounty.

Read the Petition of Henry Metz, a Protestant Pallatine, shewing That the Pet'r came over into this Province 4 years ago on the Encouragement which his Majestys was pleased to settle on all poor forreign Protestants who are desirous of settling themselves and Familys in any of the Townships here and as the time of his Servitude is now expired, and having a Family of 5 Persons, viz himself, wife and three children, prays that 250 acres of land be laid out to him in Sax Gotha Township, and that he may obtain his majestys most gracious provision bounty... the prayer thereof was granted.

Pages 26-27: Meeting of Friday AM 30th January 1746/7

Read the Petition of George Cooper humbly Shewing that the Pet'rs father Adam Cooper upon his arrival into this Province with his Family in the year 1737 obtained a warrant for the survey for 450 acres of land in any of the northern Townships dated Feb'ry 8th 1737, which warrant by neglect of the survey'r was never executed, as y'r pet'rs father is since dead, he therefore as Eldest son and Heir prays his Excell'cy and Honours upon his surrender of the aforesaid Township warrant herewith surrendered, to order a Common warrant for y'e survey of 450 acres on the north side of Black Mingo Creek, bounding on or near the plantation of Hugh McCutchen, and that a Grant may be passed for the same to the Petitioner. To this was annexed the warrant mentioned, whereupon y'e Pet'r appearing... it was ordered that 450 acres be granted to the Pet'r viz 100 acres for himself, and 350 acres in Trust for his mother Jane Rutledge & his brothers William Cooper, James Cooper, Thos Cooper, Samuel Cooper and his sisters Isabel Cooper and Mary Cooper each 50 acres....

Page 27: Read the Petition of Isaac Bradwell shewing That the Pet'r is a native of this Country, and having 34 persons in family viz himself, wife and four children, and twenty eight slaves for whom not any lands have as yet been assigned him, and being willing to Cultivate and Improve some of his Majestys vacant land humbly prays 1700 acres of vacant land be laid out to him in one or two Tracts, in the Welch Tract on Pedee River, not remote from the lands of William James, Esq., in order that a Grant may pass for the same. The said Petition being considered, it was ordered that y'e land be granted in one tract only.

Page 28: Meeting of Wednesday AM 4th February 1746/7

Read the Petition of Anna Baumgan, a Protestant Swiss woman, humbly shewing, that the Pet'r came over to this province with Captain Stedman on the Encouragem't w'ch his Majestys has been pleased to bestow on all poor forreign Protestants who are willing to settle in any of the Townships... prays that 50 acres of land be assigned her in the Town'p of Sax Gotha, and that she may obtain his Majestys Gracious bounty... the prayer thereof was Granted.

Read the Petition of Barbara Husar, a forreign Protestant Pallatine, shewing that the Pet'r came over to this province on the Encouragem't w'ch his Majestys has been pleased to bestow on all poor forreign Protestants who was desirous of settling themselves in any of the Townships, and as the time of the Petitioner Servitude is now Expired, that 100 acres of land be assigned unto her in the Town'p of Sax Gotha, she having a Child and herself in Family, and that she may have his Majestys bounty... the prayer thereof was Granted.

Read the Petition of Barbara Appeal humbly setting forth that she being about to Settle in the Township of SaxGotha humbly prays for a Grant of 50 acres of Land and a Town lot in the upper parts of the Town'p of Sax Gotha and that she may obtain from his Excellency and order for the payment of the remainder of the provision money allowed her, she having received that half thereof at her coming into y'e Province. It was ordered that the Commiss'ry General pay the other half of the bounty prayed for, and that the depty Secretary prepared a warrant for the land, and that the bounty be paid to Jacob Weaver who is impowered under the Pet'rs own hand which was produced and read at the Board to receive it on her behalf. Sax Gotha 25 Jan 1746/7. Stephen Crell.

Read the Petition of Magdalen Appeal, humbly setting forth that the Pet'r is one of the late Swiss prisoners, that was carried into the Havana, as she is here she designs to settle in the Town'p of Sax Gotha, therefore humbly prays that 50 acres of land be laid out to her and a Town lot in the said Townh'p and that an order issue for paying her the remainder of the Provision money, that other half having been payed her on her arrival in this Province &c. Sax Gotha 25 Jan 1746/7. Stephen Crell. It was ordered that the Commiss'ry General pay the other half of the bounty prayed for, and that the depty Secretary prepared a warrant for the land, and that the bounty be paid to Jacob Weaver who is impowered under the Pet'rs own hand which was produced and read at the Board to receive it on her behalf.

Page 29: Read the Petition of Henry Feisler, who came here from the Havana, where he has been a Prisoner, shewing that the Pet'r has three persons in family for whom he has not any lands assigned him, and being willing to Cultivate and Improve some of his Majestys vacant lands, humbly prays that by virtue of his said family right, 150 acres of land may be granted him, opposite to Sax Gotha Township, where hat at present resides and likewise that he may obtain the remainder of his Majestys most gracious bounty. The Pet'r having already appeared before the Board and swore to his family right, as in the minutes of the 31st of July 1746, it was ordered that the Commissry Genl pay the other half of the bounty according to the prayer of the petition and the Dpty Secretry prepare a Warrant accordingly.

Read the Petition of Rosina Shaffer, a Protestant Pallatine, humbly shewing That the Pet'r came over to this Province with her husband and two children, on the Encouragement to all forreign Protestants who are desirous of settling themselves here... that 150 acres of land be assigned to her having two children, in the Town'p of Sax Gotha and having had the misfortune of losing her husband in the time of her servitude, she also prays that she may be allowed his majestys provision bounty.. the prayer thereof was granted when she produces a discharge from her service.

Page 30: Meeting of Thursday AM 5th February 1746/7

Read the Pet'n of Elizabeth Gibbes shewing That a lot in the new plat of Beaufort newton, known by the number 2, was granted to one Reven Shardoveyn, the 27th July 1717 in the old tenure, by virtue of a Warrant dated 25 July 1717 and returned Certifyed by Francis Yonge, Esq., then Survey'r General, on the 27th July 117. That Paul Jenys did in his life time on, or about the month of April or May 1734, purchase the sd lot of one James Ruffiat who then married Chardovins widdow, and on the 2d of May aforesaid, payed the purchase money to the said James Ruffiat who then entered into bond to give a legal Title, in one Year thence next ensuing, that the Petr apprehends the said Titles were destroyed by the late dreadful fire in Charles Town. The petr therefore prays that an order be issued that a Grant be passed to Paul Jenys and Geo Jenys, the two surviving children of the said

Paul Jenys deceased, for the said lot old tenure, or grant such other relief as shall be thought meet &c. The sd petition being considered, it was ordered that it be sent to the Survey'r General, and returned by him, to this board, with the other Port Royal lots.

Rosina Shaffer pursuant to an order in the yesterday's Journal, produced a discharge of her self, and son Johannes, of her service from Samuel Perkins, whereby she was ordered to have the land and bounty prayed for, in her said petition of yesterday.

Page 31: Meeting of Friday AM 6th February 1746/7

Pursuant to an order from his Excell'cy Ja. Glen Esq'r Gov. in Council, dated Jan'ry 16th 1745 to me directed requiring the resurveys of the plantations of Geo. Austin and Jno Smith, and to return plats of the same together with what overplus may be found in either of y'e said tracts, or between them... I have accordingly resurveyed Mr. Austins plantation from y'e natural marks on the marshes of Cooper River, the Courses and distances of the Plat (not one marked tree being to be found) and find that y'e same extends Inland to the black lines; and to contain 104 acres tho the original plat and Grant say only 102 acres, also by my resurvey of ye contiguous tract, I find it to contain 20 acres tho the quantity granted is only 18 acres I have also measured from the only original marked Tree in Mr. Smith's plat, being a live oak 3X p'r March[?] an undoubted Course inland to Mr. Shubricks head line, Express by the Black lines, above mentioned and find the same to exceed the distance of Mr. Smith's Plat seven and a half chains at w'ch distance I have set off Mr. Smith's head line, distinguished by red lines in the above plat, to which I have also incerted the Plat of Mr. Witters surveys returned to me some time ago, which extends to the prickt lines, within Mr. Shubrick's proper bounds, by wch plat he makes Mr. Smiths land to contain 1091 acres and one half, tho the original plat and Grant are only for 150 acres, whereby it exceeds the quantity granted 41 acres and one half, the space between the red lines, and the prickt lines contains 28 3/4 acres of which Mr. Shubricks bounds expressed by black lines takes 3 acres the remained between the black lines and the red lines 25 3/4 acres, I apprehend to be the surplus between the s'd Tract within' ye red lines the marsh Mr. Gadsden, & Mr. Freeman's lines are contained 162 acres ¼ of one acre exceeded the quantity granted 12 acre sand 3/4 which I apprehend to be Mr. Smith's overplus, by Mr. Witters lat returned to me, this day with the figure of the old Plat very accurately laid down therein the Incorrectness of the original survey specially on the within Mr. Shubrick's line a terminus aquo, in my delineation, I have begun at an undoubted Corner Tree, on the marsh, judging it more certain and seems to be confirmed by many points of land in the old plat, compared with the new Plat, as laid down in one Plat, by Mr. Witter, herewith annexed & Submitted by Geo Hunter, Surv. Genl.

The Partys Concerned, viz Col Smith and Mr. Geo Austin, having been sent for, and Interrogated, concerning their mutual claims, it was ordered that they do attend this board on Thursday next, in the forenoon to be heard thereon.

Pages 31-32: Read the Petition of Alex'r Davidson, Executor of y'e Estate of Edward Handlen deceased, shewing That the s'd Edward Handlen on the 28th day of Oct 1735, did obtain a Warrant for 650 acres of land, to be laid out to him under the hand of the Hon'ble Thos Broughton Esq'r Lt. Gov'r 450 of which were Surveyed by James Gillespie, dty Surveyor Oct. 1st 1736 as appears under his own hand on the said Warrant hereunto annexed for which a Grant never has been passed. That the s'd Edward Handlen by his last will and testament likewise hereunto annexed, has left to his fourth son Champineau 300 acres of y'e Tract of Land mentioned in the said Warrant, the Pet'r therefore humbly prays y'r Excell'cy and Honors, that at Grant for the s'd 300 acres together with 450 more, being the whole of that Tract above mentioned, surveyed by James Gillespie as aforesaid, may be passed in y'e name of the s'd Champeneau and likewise that the remaining 200 acres not surveyed may be laid out, to the Eldest son Thomas in the Welch Tract on Pedee River &c... the pray'r thereof was granted...

Read the humble Petition of Alex'r Davidson shewing that the Pet'r having 12 persons in family viz himself, wife, one child and nine slaves, for whom as yet not any lands have ben assigned him, and being willing to Cultivate and Improve some of his Majestys vacant lands, prays that by virtue of Family right 600 acres of vacant land be laid out to him in one or two tracts in the Welch Tract on Pedee River in order that a Grant may pass for the same... the prayer of his petition as to the land was granted, but in one tract only....

Read the Petition of Mary Dorothy Herman, A Protestant Palatine, shewing That the Pet'r came over into this Province about 4 Years ago in Capt'n Stedmans ship, on the Encourgem't which his majestys has been pleased to give to all poor Protestant forreigners who are desirous of settling themselves in any of y'e Town'ps and as the time of her servitude is now expired, she humbly prays that 50 acres of land may be assigned her in the Townsh'p of Sax Gotha, she also most humbly prays that she may be allowed his Majestys Gracious bounty... the prayer thereof was granted on her producing a discharge of her Indenture.

Pages 31-32: Read the Petition of Michael Zilch, a Protestant Pallatine, shewing That the Pet'r came over to this Province, with his family abt 4 Years ago, on the Encouragement which his Majesty has been pleased to give to all poor Protestant forreigners who are desirous of settling themselves in any of his Majestys Townships Therefore y'r Pet'r humbly prays that 200 acres of land may be assigned him in the Townsh'p of Sax Gotha, he having a family of 4 Persons, viz himself, wife and two Children, the time of his Servitude being expired, he also prays that he may be allowed his Majestys Gracious bounty... producing his Indentures discharged, the pray'r thereof was granted.

Page 33: Meeting of Thursday AM 10th February 1746/7

Read the following Petition of James Anderson shewing That the Peti'r has 10 persons in family viz himself, wife, 4 children & 4 Slaves for whom as yet not any land has been assigned him and being willing to Cultivate Lands in proportion to his said Right humbly prays that 500 acres of land be laid out to him in the Welch Tract on Pedee river near Mr. Murphy's Plantation. Feb. 10, 1746. The prayer thereof was granted....

Read the petition of Benjamin Wall, planter, Shewing That the Petr has Seven persons in Family for whom not any land has been assigned him and being willing to Cultivate Some of his Majestys vacant Land humbly prays that 350 acres of land be laid by virtue of his s'd family right in the Welch Tract on Pedee in two separate warrants, viz 250 acres near Thos Elleby land and the other 200 on the north side of Pedee. Feb. 10th 1746. The prayer thereof was granted but in one tract only....

Read the Petition of William Deloch, planter, setting forth That the Pet'r since his last[?] application for land has an Encrease of one in Family viz a Child, for whom not any Lands have been assigned wherefore by virtue of family right he humbly prays that 50 acres of land be laid out to him in the Welch Tract on Pedee River near Flat Creek. Feb. 10th, 1746. The prayer thereof was granted.

Pages 33-34: Read the Petition of John Rowdy, planter, humbly setting forth, that the Pet'r has 3 persons in family viz himself, wife, and one child for whom as yet not any land has been assigned, and being willing to Cultivate some of his Majestys vacant land in proportion to his said right, humbly prays that 150 acres of land be assigned him in the Welch Tract near the lands of William Deloach. Feby 10th 1746. The prayer thereof was granted.

Page 34: Read the Petn of Jacob Burchard, one of the orphans, who arrived with Reimenspergher in the year 1742, setting forth That the Petr being lately married, and intending to settle in y'e Township of Sax Gotha humbly prays for the maintainence of himself and his wife that 100 acres of land be laid out to him in the upper part of y'e said Town'p and also a Town lot on his majestys bounty. 2d Feb 1746. Stephen Crell. The prayer thereof was granted as to the land and also that the Commi'sry defray the Expences of Petitioning & ca. the Pet'r having already received y'e Bounty.

Pages 35-36: Meeting of Thursday AM 12th February 1746/7

Read the Pet'n of Barbara Akerman, a Protestant Pallatine, setting forth That the Pet'r came over to this Province 6 years ago on the Encourgem't which his Majesty has been pleased to bestow on all such poor Protestant forreigners who are desirous of setting themselves in any of the Tonwh'p here, the Petr therefore humbly prays that 50 acres of land may be assigned to her in the

Town'p of Sax Gotha her time of Servitude being now expired, and also she most humbly prays for his Majestys Gracious Bounty. The prayer thereof was Granted.

Page 36: Read the Pet'n of Robert Council setting forth That the Pet'r has 5 Persons in family viz himself, wife & three children for whom not any land has been assigned, and being desirous to Cultivate land in proportion to his s'd family right prays that 250 acres be laid out to him in the Welch Tract on Pedee River near the lands of William Carey deceasd. Feby 11th 1746. Robt Councill. The prayer thereof was granted.

Page 37: Meeting of Friday PM 13th February 1746/7

Col. Smith and Mr. Geo: Austin pursuant to an order in the minutes of the 10th instant, P. M., attended on this Board, and upon a hearing it was ordered. That the surplus land laid down in the Plan of y'e survy'r Genl be divided between the partys equally & proportionally to the quantity expressed in their original Grants....

Page 39: Meeting of Tuesday PM 17th February 1746/7

Read the Petition of Conrad Shenis Shewing that the Pet'r came to this Country above Eighteen months ago on y'e Encouragem't to all poor forreign Protestants who are desirous of setting themselves in any of the Town'ps here, and being willing to Cultivate some of his Majestys vacant land, the Petr prays that 50 acres of land be assigned to him, in y'e Town'p of Sax Gotha, and that he may obtain his Majestys bounty. The prayer thereof was granted as to the land but not the bounty but that the charges of Petitioning be defrayed him....

Page 42: Meeting of Wednesday PM 18th February 1746/7

George Hunter Esq'r Survey'r General pursuant to an order in y'e minutes of Council, laid before his Excellency the State of the Port Royal Lots, whereupon the following Petition of Elizabeth Gibbes surviving executrix of Paul Jenys' will, was read viz

That a Lot in the Town Plat of Beaufort new town, known by the number 2 was granted to one Reven Chardovan the 27th day of July 1717 by virtue of a warrant dated 25 July and returned certifyed by Francis Yonge, Esq., then his Majesty's Survey'r Genl the said 27 day of July 1717, That said Paul Jenys did in his life time on or about the months of April or May 1734 purchase y'e s'd lot of one James Ruffiat who was then married to the widdow of the said Shardoveyn and did on the 2d day of May aforesaid pay the purchase money unto the said James Ruffiat who then entered into Bond to give a legal title in one year then next ensuing that your Pet'r apprehends the said titles were destroyed by the late dreadful fire in Charles Town, the Pe'rs therefore humbly pray that a grant may pass to Paul Jenys and George Jenys, the two surviving children of the above mentioned Paul Jenys deceased for the said lot old tenure or grant such other relief and in such manner as shall seem most meet. Chs Town 12th day of Jan 1746. Eliz. Gibbes.

Annexed to the Petition was a Certificate of the Survey'r General shewing that the lot no. 2 was granted as set forth in y'e petition, to the opinion of the Board that the same ought not to be granted de novo. That the Pet'r ought to apply to the Person under whom she now claims for a proper Conveyance.

Read the Petition of Col. Samuel Prioleau humbly setting forth That some time ago the Pet'r exhibited a Petition for Lot 31 in Beaufort Town Port Royal, but it was then adjudged to have been Granted away to another as appears indorsed on the back of the s'd Petition, and in the minutes of Council, but the Pet'r having carefully enquired into the affair, begs lave to Inform that the Lot 31 was run out to Thomas Coiniers by warrant but never was Granted, because the said Thomas Coiniers left y'e Province after obtaining the Warrant and has been dead ab't 20 years ago, nor did he live behind any Heir, whatsoever so that y'e said lot is still vacant and not granted to any one, therefore prays that as he intends to settle one of his sons, on the Lot prayed for that it be granted to him... the prayer thereof was Granted.

Pages 42-43: Read the Petition of Edward Wigg of Port Royal humbly shewing That on the 25th day of Jan'ry 1718, Ichabod Winburn had a Warrant from Gov'r Johnson, for a Lot in Beaufort No. 69, and whereas Col. Barnwell since deceasd by virtue of a deputation from Francis Yonge, Survr General about the 16th of March 1719 laid out the said Town lot 69 to Ichabod Winburn butting and bounding to the northward on a lot laid out to y'e s'd Ichabod Winborn to y'e Eastward on a lot claimed by John Wilkins to the Southward to a lot laid out to Jacob Wright and to the westward on a street named West Street, as appears in the Secretary's office in the Plat, and whereas the Pet'r did some time since become a purchaser of the said town lot, for a valuable consideration and thereby the sole property thereof is now become legally vested in him, prays that y'e said lot be granted him in his own name. The above petition being Considered, it was ordered to ly on y'e Table.

Page 43: Read the Petition of Thos Wigg humbly setting forth That about four years ago his brother Rich'd Wigg did purchase a lot in the Town of Beaufort, No. 70, of the Heirs and assigns of Jacob Wright deceased, and did Petition for a Grant of the same, w'ch petition was dated the 9th day of Feb'ry 1744, the particulars will more fully appear to the same, since which his said brother Richard is dead, and hath left a widow and three daughters behind & the Pet'r hath himself been at great Expence to build, finish and compleat the house, one house &c thereon, for the Immediate support and maintenance of the Petitioner's Brother's family but the Petitioner finding he can sell and disposed of the said lot and buildings to a Great advantage for the benefit of the said family, the rent of the houses in that part of the province being very low so as not to keep the same in repair. The Pet'r humbly prays to enable him by a Grant either to Settle or keep the said Lot and building for the sole use and support of his brothers children aforesaid. Chs Town Feb 2d 1746. It was ordered that y'e lot be granted to Thos Wigg in trust for his brother's children.

Read the Petition of Capt. Robert Taylor of the Parish of St. John humbly setting forth that The Pet'r on the 7th day of Febry 1717 had admeasured and laid out to him, two lofs in Beaufort Town, in Granville County known by the numbers 98 & 99, as by the Certificate thereof signed by Francis Yonge, Esqr. and hereunto annexed will more fully appear, That the Certificates above mentioned hath lyen unknown to the Pet'r in the hands of Captain John Trott for upwards of 12 years past, and not any Grant hath as yet been made out to the Pet'r of the sa'd lots... it was ordered that the said lots be granted to the Heir, or devisee of Robt Taylor the Petitioner.

Pages 43-44: Read the following Petition of Mary Tailfer humbly setting forth, That the Pet'rs late Husband Doctor Patrick Tailfer did some time since delivered in a Petition for a lot in the Town of Beaufort but unfortunately the Lot mentioned in the said Petition had been before Granted at which time y'r Excell'cy & Honors were pleasd to mention that he might have any other not granted and as the Pet'r is since become a residenter in the said Town, she therefore humbly prays that they would be pleasd to Issue a Warrant to survey out a lot known by number 111 to the Pet'r.... the prayer thereof was granted.

Page 44: Read the following Petition of Andrew Delagal humbly setting forth That the Petitioner being at present in his Majestys service and that most of his Father's family residing in Beaufort Port Royal at wch place he is desirous to obtain a Grant of the Lot 199 in which he forthwith intends to build and also to cultivate the said lot, prays that Lot 119 be granted to him. The prayer thereof was granted.

Read the following Petition of Richard Brickles and James Smallwood setting forth, That in Octo'r 1732 he purposed to settle in Beaufort Town, and in Compliance with Mr. Richard Brickles found vacant Lots No. 188, 199, 129, 149, & 142 and on their coming back to Charlestown were informed that the late Gov'r did not sign any Grants for Lots in That Town, but were advised to enter the numbers in y'e Secretarys office, and give bond to the Attorney General to comply with y'e Law in building &c, which they did, to Charles Pinckney Esq., who was then the King's attorney, this being all they had in their power to do, they humbly hope that have a Good claim to the said Lots and pray that they may have grants in the name of Richard Brickles. signed James Smallwood. Charles Town March 2d 1735. The above Petition being read, was dismissed.

Read the Petition of Alex'r Taylor humbly setting forth That he has been a Settler in this Province for a Considerable time and has done the duty of the same, but has not any lands therein, that he is desirous of settling, Improving and building on a lot at Beaufort Port Royal, therefore prays that either the Lot 122 or 117 be granted him. The prayer as to Lot 117 was granted.

Read the Petition of William Ferguson humbly Shewing That the Petition'r having been an Inhabitant of Granville County for many years past, is desirous to take up and building on a Lot in Beaufort Town viz No. 122 or 123, therefore prays a Warrant to cause the lot to be ascertained or laid out to him in order to obtain a grant for the same. The pray'r thereof as to the lot 122 was granted.

Page 45: Read the following Petition of James Williams setting forth that y'e Pet'r being master and part owner of the Defiance Schooner arrived with her in Prot Royal the beginning of this month, that he intending to Carry on trade there shall have occasion to build int he Town of Beaufort a dwelling house, and stores, thereof prays to lay out to him Lot No. 164 in order to obtain a Grant for the same. Beaufort, Oct. 10th, 1743. It was ordered that the Lot 164 be granted to the Pet'r if prior to any other for the same.

Read the Petition of Philip Delagal, setting forth that the Pet'r has been a residenter in this Province about 20 years and had the Honour to Command an Independent Company at Beaufort Port Royal, where at present the rest of his family does reside, and being at present in his Majestys Service, and willing to settle some of his Family in the said Town, humbly prays that the Lots known by the numbers 175 & 177 be granted him. The prayer thereof was Granted.

Read the Petition of Andrew Walker humbly shewing That the Petitioner has resided in the Town of Beaufort for some years, being in that time obliged to pay Great Rents for a house to live in, and in hopes of removing that Expence humbly prays that a Warrant may issue for surveying to him Lot 184 that he may be enable to Improve and build on said lot, and also obtain a grant for the same. July 4th 1746. The prayer of the above Petition was Granted.

Read the Petition of George Bunckle humbly setting forth That the Pet'r being by trade a Carpenter and having four apprentices is desirous to settle in Beaufort Town, provided he had a proper place allotted him for so doing, therefore humbly prays that a Warrant do Issue for his obtain Lot 237 and that a Grant do pass for the same. Beaufort. June 21st 1746. The Prayer thereof was granted.

Pages 45-46: Read the following Petition of Richard Hazelton and William Gilbert, humbly shewing That some time in or about the year 1721 one Barnabas Gilbert, then an Inhabitant of Beaufort aforesaid, did obtain the survey of a Lot in expectation that he should at proper and convenient time obtain a Grant of the said lot, to him and his Heirs, but Barnabas Gibson in or about the year 1734 died intestate, possessed of the lot, but had not any Grant for the same. and left his son the Pet'r William Gilbert his Heir at law,

That some time in or about the year 1739, the Richard Hazelton intermarried with the widdow formerly of the aforesaid Barnabas Gilbert, but then of Rich'd Franklin, and hath ever since been possessed of and lived upon y'e said lot, and made repairs and improvements thereon, that the Pet'r Richard Hazelton did about two years and a half ago prefer a Petition praying that for the reasons therein set forth, the said lot might be granted to the Petitioner, in such manner as was thereby humbly desired, but the Pet'r hath not been so fortunate yet to obtain the prayer of his said Petition... The pray'r thereof was granted.

Page 46: Read the humble Petition of John Chilcot humbly shewing that the Pet'r has lately come into this Province with a Resolution to settle and live in it, and has made a purchase of some lands in y'e Parish of St. Helena near the Town of Beaufort, therefore humbly prays that Lot 313 in the said Town be granted to him. The Petition being Considered, was dismissed.

Read the Humble Petition of Henry Lewin shewing That the Pet'r having some time resided in the Town of Beaufort and being desirous to settle with his family there, and having a lot in possession on which he has the frame of a house and is making improvements dayly thereon, prays that he may have a grant for said lot 331. The above petition being considered, the same was dismissed.

Read the Petition of Isaac Wood most humbly shewing That the Pet'r has been an Inhabitant in Beaufort Town or Port Royal Island, above 18 Years, in which time lay many vacant lots unimproved but no opportunity of getting his Majestys Grant for any. That the Pet'r begin desirous of settling there, did then fence and build on a Vacant Lot No. 332 on the presumption of obtaining y'e preference of a Grant for it, when it should be his Majestys pleasure to give directions for Granting them away, and have been adding to the buildings on said lot and dwelt on the same ever since the settling of it. On reading the above Petition and it appearing by the Indorsement that the said lot had been assigned to Doctor Ambrose Reeves, it was ordered that the said lot No 332 be granted to Ambrose Reeves.

Pages 46-47: Read the following Petition of Robert Thorpe humbly praying that lot in Beaufort No. 332 be granted him. Which being considered, the said Petition was dismissed.

Page 47: Read the Petition of John Chapman humbly Shewing that the Pet'r having been bound an Apprentice to Mr. Robert Williams late of the Island of St. Christophers, merchant, but now of Port Royal and the Petitioners time being now Expired, and he intending to follow Business and settle in Beaufort humbly prays that the survey'r General be ordered to lay out to him the lot no. 349 in order to obtain a Grant for y'e same. The Pray'r thereof was granted.

Read the Pet'n of James Duvall humbly shewing That as he is desirous to live and reside in the town of Beaufort, the lot 332 be granted to him. The s'd Pet'n being considered was dismissed.

Read the petition of John Yarworth setting forth that the Pet'r apprehending that on the arrival of one of his Majesty's 40 Gun Ships, at Port Royal, he may be called there, to Encrease in his Employment as a Ship Carpenter, and as at any rate he purposes to build on and improve a lot there, when granted, humbly prays that Lot No. 349 granted him. Decem'r 4th 1746. J. Yarwoth. The said petition being considered lot 145 was granted him.

Read the Petition of Sarah Mellichamp humbly setting forth That the Pet'r on relyance of their Honors' favor for a Grant did some time ago purchase a house on a lot in the new town of Beaufort, Port Royal known by number 352, and having since the purchase improved it, humbly prays that a warrant be issue for surveying the said lot that a Grant may be passed for the same. Feb 17 1740/1. S. Mellechamp. The prayer thereof was Granted viz that Colonel Flower shall have it in Trust for the Heirs or devizees of Mrs. Mellechamp.

Pages 47-48: Meeting of Thursday P. M. 19th February 1746/7

Read the Petition of Patrick Hindes, setting forth That the Pet'r has been a Settler in the Town of Beaufort for y'e space of four years, during which time he has been obliged to pay an Extravagant price for house-rent, but as he intends to build in y'e s'd town, prays that a warrant be issue for surveying to him, any of ye following lots viz 355, 359, of 354, or 353. Beaufort 20 May 1744. The above petition being considered, lot 353 was Granted.

Read the following petition of Hugh Anderson master of y'e Free School in Charleston, setting forth that the Pet'r has a family of children and sons here, whom he intends to settle in mercantile business, That on the 30th of May 1744 he petitioned for a lot wch said lot was said to have been granted away to y'e Honble Joseph Blake Esqr., therefore humbly prays that lot number 360 may be granted him. The prayer thereof was granted.

Page 48: Meeting of Friday A. M. 20th February 1746/7

Read the Petition of James McGoven humbly setting forth That the Pet'r has been a Residenter in this Province for y'e space of 9 years and having nine persons in family viz Three children, and 6 negroes for whom as yet not any land has been assigned him, and being willing to Cultivate land in proportion to his said family right, prays for a warrant for laying out to him 450 acres of vacant land, night to the lands of Robert Paisley. Feb 19th 1746/7. The prayer thereof was granted.

Pages 48-49: Read the petition of John Livingston, humbly setting forth that the Pet'r having been a residenter in this Province about 10 years and having four Persons in Family viz himself his wife and one child and a slave, for whom as y et not any land has been assigned him, and being willing to Cultivate and Improve some of his Majesty's vacant land, humbly prays for 200 acres of land in the Township of Williamsburgh. Feb. 20, 1746/7. The prayer of his Petition was granted.

Pages 53-53A: <u>Meeting of Friday A. M. the 13th March 1746/7</u>

Read the Petition of William Jones humbly setting forth That the Pet'r was favoured with a Warrant dated Janry 26, 1741, for the survey for 400 acres of land in the Welch Tract free of charges, which he had accordingly executed, returned and granted 18 January 1743 but to his great loss, finds that 252 acres thereof is possessed by Paul Trapier, Esq., by virtue of a prior Grant, as appears by a survey of James Gillespie, Deputy Surveyor, hereunto annexed, and that he can not have his deficiency mae up by any vacant land contiguous to the part possessed, there being only 161 acres vacant, and 148 acres of the old grant making 309 in all, whereupon the Pet'r prays that the survey'r Genl be ordered to certify a plat of the same for the Petr free of charge he having surrendered his former Grant, and therefore prays the same to be corrected in the offices of record, and as the Petr has one in family for whom he never obtained any land, prays that 50 acres allowed on that amount & the 91 acres the remainder of the former warrant making in all 141 acres may be surveyed for him at a place known by the Pine Tree in the Welch Tract... the prayers thereof were Granted.

Page 53A: Read the Petition of Daniel Day a Protestant Pallatine humbly shewing that the Pet'r came over to this Province some years ago on the Encourgem't which he majesty has been pleased to bestow on all poor Protestant forreigners, who shall come to settle in any of the Town'ps of this Province, and having two in family viz himself and wife for whom not any lands have been assigned, prays that 100 acres be laid out to him in Saxe Gotha Township and that he may have the usual bounty. The prayer thereof as to the land was granted but not the bounty.

Read the Petition of Evan Vaughan humbly setting forth That the Pet'r has one person in family for whom as yet not any land has been assigned, and being desirous to Cultivate vacant land in proportion to the said right humbly prays 50 acres be laid out to him in the Welch Tract on Pedee River. March 7th 1746. The prayer thereof was Granted.

Pages 53A-54: Read the Petition of that the Pet'r with his family are settled on the Welch Tract on the south side of Peedee river and having 7 persons in family for whom as yet not any lands have been assigned viz himself, wife, four children, and one slave, he humbly prays that a Warrant may issue for surveying and laying out to the Petr 350 acres on both sides Thomsons Creek in the Welch Tract aforesaid. March 11th 1746. The prayer thereof was granted.

Page 54: Read the Petition of Edward Sharpton humbly setting forth that the Pet'r has 9 persons in Family for whom not any lands have as yet been assigned him, viz himself, wife and seven children, and being at present settled his s'd Family on Pedee river in the Welch Tract on the south side of the s'd river, humbly prays that 450 acres of land be laid out to him on both sides of Thomsons Creek in the Welch Tract aforesaid. March 11th 1746. The pray'r thereof was granted.

Read the Petition of William Johnson humbly setting forth That the Pet'r is settled in the Welch Tract on the south side of Pedee river, and having four Persons in family viz Himself, wife and two children for whom as yet not any lands have been assigned him, he humbly prays that 200 acres of land be laid out to him in the Welch Tract. The pray'r thereof was Granted.

Read the Petition of John McIver humbly setting forth that the Petr has been a residenter in the Province about 13 Years and having 10 persons in family viz 10 negroes for whom as yet not any lands have been assigned him and being willing to Cultivate & improve some of his Majesty's vacant lands, humbly prays that 500 acres be laid out to him between Linches Lake and Black Mingo Creek in Prince Frederick's Parish, that a Grant may pass accordingly. March 13, 1746. The pray'r thereof was granted.

Pages 55-55: Read the Petition of John Seabrook setting forth that he has three persons in family whom not any lands have been assigned him and being willing to cultivate some of his majestys vacant land in proportion to his said right prays that 150 acres be laid out to him near Lynches Creek in Craven County. The pray'r thereof was granted.

Page 61: Meeting of Tuesday A. M. the 17th March 1746/7

Read the Petition of Robert Williams humbly setting forth that on the 12th day of Feb'ry 1745 one Cornelius Reine obtained y'e annexed warrant for laying out to him 400 acres of Land, 200 acres of which were bought from the said Reine, by one William Deloach lying between the lands of John and Nathaniel Evans, and wch said 200 acres y'r Pet'r did on, or about the last day of July last past, purchased from the said William Deloach for a valuable consideration and for which land, no Grant has yet been passed, since ye running out of the same, y'r Pet'r therefore prays that a Grant may pass for the s'd 200 acres in his name. Robert Williams March 17th 1746. On reading the said Petition it was rejected.

Read the Petition of William Lacey humbly setting forth that the Pet'r came from Virginia ab't 4 Years ago & having 8 persons in family viz himself, wife and 6 children, having obtained no lands in this Province is willing to Cultivate and improve 400 acres in the Welch Tract, if it shall seem meet... he is informed that a plat for 40 acres surveyed on the 14th of Oct'r 1736 by virtue of a warrant from his Excellency Rob't Johnson, dated August ye 6th 1734, from William Thompson since dead, lies in the survey'r General's Office, having been returned there Jan'ry 15th 1736 and no application made for the same tho advertised in the Gazette. Whereupon your Pet'r prays that the Survey'r General certify the said plat in the name and for y'e use of y'r Petitioner &c. To this Petition was annexed a Certificate from Geo Hunter Esqr, that what relates to the plat of Wm. Thompson mentioned is true. Date March 1746. The pray'r thereof was Granted.

Pages 61-62: Read the Peti'n of Francis Whittington humbly setting forth That y'e Pet'r has been a residenter in this Province between 18 & 19 Years, and having 4 Persons in family viz himself, wife and 2 children for whom as yet not any lands have been granted him, and being willing to Cultivate and Improve some of his Majestys vacant lands, prays that 200 acres of vacant land on the north side of Pedee River joining the lands of William Fielding so that a Grant may pass for the same. March 17, 1746. The prayer thereof was Granted.

Page 62: Read the Petition of Robert Williams humbly setting forth That the Pet'r is come into this Province with an Intention to settle his family and reside here and having 6 persons in family viz himself, wife, and four children, for whom not any land has been assigned, prays that 300 acres of his Majestys vacant land be laid out to him on the south side of Pedee River bounding on the lands of John Evance. March 1, 1746. The prayer thereof was Granted.

Page 72: Meeting of Wednesday A. M. the 8th April 1747

Read the Petition of Nicholas Millar a Protestant German in behalf of himself, and wife Leonora Millar, humbly sheweth that on the 28th of March 1746 the Pet'r and Wife laid a Petition before the Hon'ble Board praying that 200 acres of vacant land to be laid out to him, by virtue of Family right, in the Fork of Santee and Wateree Rivers, and that himself and spouse should obtain the King's most Gracious Bounty, given them, whch petition was Granted and the bounty accordingly payed, at the same time the Warrant here annexed, issued from the Survey'r General's Office for the land but by reason of a Long Sickness, the Pet'r was unable to Carry the s'd Warrant to the Dep'ty Survey'r to have it run out, in the time limited, by law for the purpose; He therefore humbly prays that a fresh order be Issued that a Warrant may be prepared for the laying out the same 200 acres as in the former Warrant. Nicholas Miller. The pray'r thereof was granted.

Pages 72-73: Read the Petition of Mathew Keymath a Protestant Pallatine shewing That the Pet'r came over into this Province about 2 years and 3 months ago, in the Ship St. Andrew, on the Encouragem't wch his majesty has been pleased to bestow on all such poor Forreigners, who shall seem willing to settle themselves in any of the Towns'ps and as the Pet'r is now free of the time of his Servitude he is desirous of settling himself in the Towh'p of SaxGotha therefore humbly prays that 50 acres of land may be ordered to be laid out to him in the said Township and that he may be allowed the usual bounty. The pray'r thereof was Granted.

Page 73: Read the Petition of William Cattel Jun'r shewing that a Warrant of Survey dated the 1st day of August 1735 was issued by the Hon'ble Thos Broughton Esq'r then Lieu't Goven'r containing 1900 acres of land in the Province in a Tract or Tracts to William Catell Jun'r by William McPherson Deputy Survey'r as appears by the plat annexed by virtue of a warrant under the hand of Geo Hunter Esq'r Surv'r General, the Pet'r prays that the Survey'r General be directed to Certify the said plat of 160 acres of land being part of the Warrant in the name and for the behalf of the Pet'r so that a Grant may pass for the same. Whereupon it was ordered that the Plat returned by William McPherson Dep't Surv'r to the Survey'r General's office bearing date 24th March 1746 for 160 acres of land, being part of the warrant for 1900 acres issued in the name of William Cattell Junr and Geo Austin jointly be issued in the name of Wm. Cattell Junr alone in order that a Grant pass for the said William Cattell Junr for the same.

Page 94: Meeting of Thursday P. M. the 14th May 1747

Read the Petition of Peter McKew humbly shewing That the Pet'r has been a Residenter in Province about 12 months having come from Pensilvania in order to settle here, with his Family consisting of six persons, viz his wife, himself, and four children, for whom as yet not any land has been assigned him, and being willing to Cultivate vacant land in proportion to his s'd family right, humbly prays y'r Excellcy and Honours that 300 acres of Vacant land be admeasured out to him in the fork on the south side of Wateree River near the lands of Anthony Wright and whereas the Pet'r is at present in low Circumstances, he humbly prays y'r Excellency and Honors that the Expences of his Petition, Warrant, and Grant may be defrayed by the Public. May 11th 1747. The Prayer thereof was granted and the deputy Secretary ordered to prepare a warrant and the Commiss'y Genl to defray the Charges of the Petition, Warrant &c.

Read the Petition of John McConnell humbly shewing that the Pet'r has been a residenter in this Province between 5 & 6 years, and having now a family consisting of five persons, viz himself, wife and three children, for whom as yet not any land has been assigned him, and being willing to Cultivate some of his Majesty's vacant land, humbly prays 250 acres of vacant land in Fredericksburg Town'p on the south side of the s'd Town'p line, near to the land of Andrew Collins and whereas the Pet'r is low in Circumstances, he humbly prays that he likewise obtain his majesty's most gracious bounty or that the expences of his petition may be defrayed by y'e public. May 11th 1747. The Prayer thereof was granted and ye Commiss'ry general to pay the charges of the Petition, Warrant & ca.

Pages 94-95: Read the following Petition of Robert McMurdy shewing that y'e Pet'r has 20 person in family, viz 4 White Persons and 16 blacks, for whom as yet he has no land assigned him and being willing to cultivate in proportion to the s'd right, prays y'r Excellency and Honrs that a Warrant may be directed to y'e Suv'r Genl for the Surveying or causing to be surveyed one thousand acres in Granville County, viz 300 acres in beech Island joining to the lands of Mr. John Tobler and 300 acres at a place called Rich-land Savannah on Savannah Road, ab't 40 miles on this side of New Windsor, and whereas a Tract containing 400 acres was surveyed for Kennedy Obrian deceased and was advertised in the Gazette, and no application made for the same, as appears by the Survey'r General's Certificate hereunto annexed, Whereby the same becomes vacant y'r Petitioner prays that the Survey'r General may be directed to Certify the said plat in the name of and for the use of y'r Petitioner and that a Grant may pass accordingly. May 11th 1747. Robert McMurdy.

The Certificate mentioned in the above Petition being produced and read is as follows viz, May 14th 1747. I hereby Certify that 400 acres of land was surveyed for Kennedy Obrian on the 22d day of June 1737 by James Gillespie, Depty Survey'r situate in Granville County bounded northwest on Town Creek, South west on Savannah River and on other sides on vacant land, which said plat was returned into the Survy'r General's office the 28th day of July 1737 where it has layen ever since, tho advertised in the Gazette, August 14th 1743 and no application made for the same. signed Geo Hunter.

The Tract prayed for containing 300 acres of land be returned in the name of the Petitioner, that he have the remaining 500 acres on Beach Island, if it be so much, and if not the remaining quantity of land be laid out to him on Rich-land Savannah as prayed for.

Page 95: Read the humble Pet'n of Rob't Rogers shewing that the Pet'r being lately arrived in this Province and having Family right of 150 acres of land prays his Excell'cy and his Honor that they would be pleased to Issue a Warrant to lay out to him 150 acres of land in the Township of Amelia. The pray'r thereof was granted.

Read the Petition of Peter Villpontoux humbly shewing That the Pet'r has two persons in family for whom as yet not any land has been assigned him, and being desirous to Cultivate vacant land in proportion to this s'd Family right prays that 100 acres of marsh land near to Commings[?] Point be laid out to him. April 10th 1747. The Pet'r appearing before his Excellency in Council and being asked to what use he Intended the said vacant land prayed for, he informs the board that he purposed to prevent any other Person but himself to gather shells thereon. The Petition being Considered it was ordered that y'e same do ly on the Table because the shells were a Common Good & was highly unreasonable and that therefore they should remain for the benefit of every person

Page 96: Meeting of Friday A. M. the 15th May 1747

Read the Petition of Doctor David Caw humbly shewing That the Pet'r has six persons in family for whom as yet not any lands have ben assigned, and being desirous to Improve land in proportion to his said Family right, Prays that 300 acres be laid out to him on WabbaCaw Island near Santee River contiguous to the lands of Noah Serree deceased and that of Mons'r Lavalette[?]. The pray'r thereof was granted.

Pages 98-99: Read the Petition of Margaret Akerman, a Protestant Pallatine humbly shewing That the Pet'r came over into this Province on the Encouragement of his Majesty to all poor forreign Protestants who shall be desirous to settle in any of the Townships the Pet'r prays that 50 acres of land be laid out to her in the Town'p of SaxGotha by virtue of her family right and also that she may obtain his Majesty's most Gracious provision bounty, the time of her servitude being expired. The prayer thereof was granted.

Page 99: Read the Petition of Jacob Pfisler a Protestant Swiss most humbly shewing That the Peti'r came over with his Family a few years ago, on the Encouragement of his Majesty to all poor forreign Protestants who are desirous of settling themselves in any of the Townships here, and as the time of is Servitude is expired, he humbly prays that 250 acres of land be assigned to him in the Town'p of SaxGotha, he having 5 persons in family viz himself, wife and three children for whom not nay land has been given, the Pet'r likewise prays for his Majesty's most Gracious provision bounty. The prayer thereof was granted.

Pages 100-101: Meeting of Wednesday A. M. the 20th May 1747

Read the Petition of Will'm Graham, Planter, humbly shewing that the Pet'r and his family arrived here from Ireland ab't Eleven years ago, in the Ship called the new built of Liverpool, that on application to the then lieu't govr for land, 450 acres were ordered to be laid out to him in Williamsburgh Town'p by virtue of family right, whereby a precept from the Survey'r General's office issued to Anthony Williams for running out the said Tract, the charges to be made by the Public, as it was on y'e King's bounty, but Mr. Anthony Williams never made any return, of y'e survey in favour of the Petitioner, notwithstanding he was very often solicited so to do, but never complied with the Survey'r Genl's order there, notwithstanding y'e Pet'r from the Encouragement he had of obtaining a Grant from the Hon'ble Board, did settled and improve the said land, and at present lives on it. The Pet'r therefor humbly prays that he has five or six times travelled down ab't 60 miles on foot to Chs Town in order to have this affair executed, occasioned always by the false misrepresentations of the s'd Williams, that at last y'r Excell'cy & Honors may compell y'e s'd Williams to do y'e Pet'r Justice and that he make a return of y'e Surveyor so that a grant may pass, whereupon y'e following certificate of the Suv'r Genl was produced and read.

So Carolina. I hereby certify that William Graham with 60 other persons obtained a warrant of survey directed to James St. John Surveyor Genl dated 25 August 1736, the quantity assigned to the said Graham was 450 acres in Williamsburg Town'p and y't no return of a Plat thereof has been ever made to the Survey'r Generals Office; to my knowledged by Anthony Williams who surveyed y'e same many Complaints of s'd Williams neglect of duty in such cases are dayly made, by people who apply to me for their Plats, upon his information them that he returned them to me, when last in Charles Town, that I have not sen him these 5 Years past, a Summons was ordered by his Excell'cy and Hon'ble Council for his attendance to answer y'e Complaint of Archibald Campbell for whose Brother William y'e said Williams surveyed some lands but after the death of s'd William Campbell Williams returns a plat of different lands by Archibald Campbell guardian to his Brother Williams children. May y'e 29th 1747. G. Hunter, Surv. Genl.

It was therefore ordered that the Survey'r General do Issue a precept to one of his Dep'ty Survey'r to survey the land mentioned and make a return of the same to y'e Survr Generals office.

Pages 102-103: Meeting of Thursday A. M. the 21st May 1747

Read the following Petition of Ebenezzar Simmons, merch't in Charlestown, humbly shewing that the Pet'r has one negro in Family for whom as yet not any land has been assigned him, Wherefore he prays that the Survey'r General admeasure to him some part of vacant marsh bounding upon the Lot No. 310 belonging to the Petitioner thereof, by the Quit Rent Laws, wch march is bounded to y'e northward by Lot No. 310 aforesaid, to the eastward by vacant marsh, to y'e northward by the north side of a Canal 30 feet wide as agreed upon by the Petitioner and Isaiah Brunel the owner of the southern part of said march, and to the westward on meeting house street, being one quarter of an acre or thereabouts, and that a Warrant be Issued in order to have a grant for the same. Ordered that the prayer of the Petitioner be Granted.

Page 103: Read the Petition of Christian Minnick humbly shewing that the Pet'r has been a residenter in this Province about 10 Years and having 8 persons in Family viz 8 slaves for whom not any land has hitherto been assigned him, and being now willing to Cultivate some of his Majestys vacant land in proportion to his said Family right, he humbly prays for 400 acres of vacant land on the south side of Wateree River joining to the Plantation of Anthony Wright. May 21st 1747. The prayer of the s'd petition was Granted.

Pages 103-104: Read the Petition of Thomas Jones humbly shewing That the Pet'r a native of this Province has 10 persons in Family viz 20 negroes for whom as yet not any lands have been assigned him by virtue of Family right and being desirous to Cultivate vacant land in proportion thereto, he humbly prays for 500 acres in Craven County near the land of John Evance. May 21st 1747. The Pet'r producing a Warrant dated the 15th day of Jany 1731 from the late Govr Johnson for a survey of 1300 acres of land in Colleton County to his mother Dorothy Jones wch warrant exception 51 acres of marsh and some small Island was never executed, the Pet'r accordingly delivered up y'e s'd warrant and renounced the title to the land, whereupon it was ordered that in consideration of the Petitioners having upon oath declared that he intended to sell the land prayed for that his prayer be rejected.

Page 104: Read the Petition of James Searls shewing that the Pet'r has lived on the Island of Port Royal above 10 years and at present keeps a school there, and having made Improvements on the Lot 210 there, humbly prays that s'd lot be granted him. The prayer thereof was granted.

Read the Petition of Samuel Newman humbly shewing that the Pet'rs father William Newman had a Tract of land containing one hundred and eleven acres in Craven County surveyed for him, returned into the Survey'r General's office and advertized in the Gazette was applied for after his decease by the Pet'rs brother Robt Newman, who obtained an order to certify the said plat in his name who finding the same erroneous did not sign it, but petitioned for an order for a survey w'ch was granted, but has not been executed by reason of the death of the s'd Robert Newman who in his life time had agreed to sell the same for a Consideration payed him by your Petitioner as appears from under the hand of Thomas Newman who was to be partly concerned in the said land, which Robert and also under the hand of Julien widdow of sd Robert Newman. Whereupon y'r Petit'r prays that as he has 5 children for whom he has obtained no Lands a Warrant will direct to the Survey'r General for resurveying the tract of 211 acres according to the marked trees in the field for your Petitioner and that a grant may pass accordingly. The pet'r producing a Certificate singed by Julian Newman, shewing that the Pet'r payed 50 pounds to her Husband for which They were to make a title to the 211 acres but as the grant neger passed it could not beg produced. Read also a Writing of Thomas Newman acknowledging that he had sold the said land to his brother. thereupon the prayer of the petition was granted.

Pages 104-105: Meeting of Thursday P. M. the 21st May 1747

Read the Petition of Robert Williams shewing that the Pet'r has resided in this Country above 3 months with his family which consists of two persons for whom no land has been granted him , viz 2 negroes and being willing to Cultivate some of his Majestys vacant lands, he humbly prays that a Warrant may be issued for admeasuring to him 100 acres of vacant land, near to the lands already granted to yr Petitioner on Pedee River. May 11th 1747. The prayer thereof was granted.

Page 105: Read the Petition of David Roche humbly shewing that Y'r Peti'r has been a residenter in this Province about 8 Years and has in his family three Persons for whom as yet he has not had any lands assigned him, and being desirous to Cultivate & improve some of his Majesty's vacant lands, he humbly prays that an order for admeasuring to him 150 acres of vacant land on the south side of Pedee River, near to the lands of Evan Vaughan, so that a Grant may pass for the same. May 21st 1747. The prayer thereof was Granted.

Pages 111-112: Meeting of Thursday P. M. the 28th May 1747

Read the Petition of Thomas Powel humbly shewing That the Pet'r, a native of England, Came into this Province with Intention to settle and cultivate some of his Majesty's vacant land had having 3 persons in family, for whom as yet not any lands have been assigned, viz himself and wife and one child, humbly prays that 150 acres be laid out to him near Pedee River, near on the little Charaws in the Welch Tract. It appearing that the wife and Child mentioned were as yet not arrived in the Province 50 acres only was Granted, the Petitioner as his own Family Right.

Pages 4-5: Meeting of Friday A. M. 5 June 1747

Read the Petition of Alex'r Sprowle setting forth that your Pet'r has been a Setler in the Town of Beaufort for upwards of a year during which time he has been obliged to pay an extortionate price for house rent which would not have been had he a proper place allotted him to build on And therefore Humbly prays a warrant directing his Maj's Surv'r Gen'l to Survey out a Lot No. 130 unto your Petitioner that he may be thereby enabled to settle and build a House in the said Town of Beaufort and likewise to obtain his Maj. Grant for the same. Alexr Sprowl. 4 June 1747. to which was annext y'e Surv'r Gen'l Cert'f. I hereby Certifie that the lott Number one hundred and thirty in Beaufort Town is vacant and petitioned for by no other person than Alexand'r Sprowl. June 4, 1747. Certified P G. Hunter, Sur. Genl. Order'd That the Dep'y Sec'y prepare a Warrant for the Same.

Page 5: Read y'e Petition of Will'm Cattle Jun'r Esq'r That your Pet'r hath one Negro in family for whom he has obtained none of his Maj. Bounty and being possessed of part of a Lott in Charles Town bounded to the South West by marsh now vacant is willing to cultivate the same. Therefore prays to direct the Surveyor Generall to admeasure and lay out to him such part thereof bounded south east on Marsh granted to Rich'd Hill Esq'r to the Southward on a Canal intended and westward on marsh petitioned for by Cap't Ebenezar Simmons and North Eastward on y'r Pet'rs Garden and that a grant may pass accordingly. Wm. Cattell Jun'r. 4 June 1747. Y'e Prayer of said Pet'n granted.

Pages 20-21: Meeting of Friday A. M. 14 August 1747

Read the Petition of Ant'o Gracia setting forth that he had bought of his Brother in law William Baker a Warrant for One thousand six hundred acres Land dated the second day of December 1736 on which Warrant five hundred eighty and six acres was run the seventh day of September 1744. The said Warrant is indorsed by the said Baker to your Petitioner and His Executrix is ready to disclame any right to the said Warrant. Therefore your Petitioner prays that your Ex'cy and Honours will order the Surveyor Generall to Certifie a Plot of the said five hundred and Eighty six Acres of land now in this office and that he may have leave to perfect his said Warrant. July 30, 1747. Sign'd Ant'o Gracia (A). Order'd that the Grant be made to the Executrix Ann Cater the late widow of Wm Baker dec'd and that the Surveyor Generall Certifie accordingly.

Page 21: Read y'e Petition of David Caw setting forth That your Petitioner obtained a warrant of Survey dated May the Sixteenth 1747 from your Excellency and Honours directed to the Surveyor Generall for the survey of three hundred acres of vacant land on Wabacan Island joyning the lands of Noah Serre deceased and Andrew Lavillette that by the Survey of the said vacant land it appears that there are four hundred and fifty acres which exceeds the quantity which the said Vacancey was thought to containe and for which the Warrant aforesaid was Issued. One hundred and fifty acres as your Petitioner has three Negros for whome he has not obtaind any lands. Therefore prays to direct the Surveyor Generall to Certifie the said Plot of four hundred and fifty acres for your Petitioner and that it may be granted accordingly to your Petitioner. Signed David Caw. July 23, 1747. My. David Caw attending the Board took the usual oath to the alegation of his Petition. Order;d that the Surveyor Gen'l Certifie the said Plat and that a Grant be made out according to the Prayer of the said Petition.

Page 22: Read the Petition of Joseph Shute setting forth That your Petitioner having purchasd a lott of land of Mr. John Harlstone on the Bay in Charles Town with all appurtenances thereunto belonging on which your Petitioner is about to build a House for his better carrying on his trade in this Town to which he intends to build a Bridge for the more convenienecy of landing his goods and Merchandize. Therefore your Petitioner prays to grant him the low water lott and that you will be pleasd to order the Surveyor General to run it accordingly. June 19, 1747. Sign'd Jos. Shute. The Prayer of the said Petition being granted.

Read a Petition of Jacob Mott Esq'r Attorney to Amey Utting seting forth That a lott in Beaufort Number 240 was order'd to be granted to Ashbey Utting Esq'r 12 November 1743 and he dying the Grant was never made out. Your Petitioner desires your Excel'y and Honours order to make out the said grant in the name of the said Amey Utting his widow and Executrix pursuant to the directions of his will. July 30, 1747. Sign'd Jacob Mott. The Prayer of the Petitioner being granted.

Page 23: Read the Petition of Thos Crotty seting forth That your Petitioner is a Shipwright and hath been this Sixteen year in the Country and hath lived most of that time at Beaufort without any Lott being granted to him. He Humbly prays your Excellency and Honours Grant of a Vacant Lott and such of the low Water lotts as may be improved by him for the heaving down of Vessells... Aug. 11, 1747. Signed Thos Crotty. Mr. Crotty not attending said Petition was order'd to be referr'd to further consideration.

Read y'e Petition of Ambr. Reeve setting forth That your Petitioner hath been an Inhabitant on Port Royall for upwards of Sixteen year and that your Petitioner has not yet had one lott granted to him on his own right and as the lot 331 in the New Town of Beaufort is now vacant your Petitioner prays that the said Lott may be granted to him. Sign'd Ambrose Reeve. Port Royall, July 18, 1747. Order;d that the said Petition be referr'd to further consideration.

Pages 23-24: Read the Petition of Solo. Ade of Saxa Gotha setting forth That some years ago he hath left Germany where he was born with an intent to setle in any of His Majesty's Provinces in America in expectation to enjoy the Bounty granted to Foreigners setling there and comeing to London he and several other of his Countrymen were order'd for Georgia with Promise made them from His Maj. part that after haveing served for their passage they should receive the Bounty Order'd by his Majesty for to be enabled to form their Setlement That your humble petitioner after haveing served five year being set free hath severall times apply'd for the said Bounty but was told and many with him that there was no money to pay them the Bounty nor part thereof. That your humble Petitioner being thus disappointed had found it impractable for him to maintain himself and his Family in Georgia and therefore was come over to this Province with his Family with an Intent to setle in one of the Township haveing that confidence in the known Generosity of this Government that he would be enabled to setle there like other of his Country men whome he Heart were in a flourishing condition. That your Humble Petitioner being detain'd by a lingering sickness almost two year in Charles Town were thereby prevented from goeing up to the Township till Last Spring when applying with an humble petition to your Excellency hath received a warrant for land in Saxa Gotha Township where he since lived on the Bounty but had no provision yet granted to him And your Humble Petitioner haveing to maintain his sickley wife and two children under age finds it impossible to make due improvements and to get into a way of living without assistance. He therefore most Humbly prays to take the premises into consideration and to grant to him His Majestys Bounty of one Years provision for Himself and his said Famely for the mentioned purpose. Signed Solomon Ade.

Page 32: Meeting of Friday A. M. 6 November 1747

Read the Petition of John Prockter Seting forth That the Petitioner being lately arived in this Province and having five Persons in family being Poor and having no way of Liveing but by Cultivating land humbly Prays a Warrant to have two hundred and fifty acres land run out in the Welch Tract on the North side of Pedee River. Dated November the 4, 1747. Signed John Prockter. The Petitioner appearing and Swearing to the Number of his Family and the alegations of his Petition Ordered that the Deputy Secretary prepare a Warrant to the Surveyor General for two hundred and fifty acres of land according to the Prayer of the said Petition.

Pages 32-33: Read the Petition of John Seller setting forth that the Petitioner came from Switzerland and hath lived with Mrs. Mary Sureau Seven years and is now desireous to setle for himself having indeavoured by his fidelity and care to purchase and honest and industerous character humbly prays for his Majestys Bounty of land and provisions as usual to Forr'n Protestants. dated July 23, 1747. Signed John Sellers. The Petitioner appearing and not being willing to setle at any of the Townships or had resolved where he would setle his Petition was referr'd to a further consideration.

Page 33: Read the Petitioner of Christian Kotiler seting forth That having agreed with Captain Wilkinson in Rotterdam to transport him to South Carolina the said Captain contrary to his Promise had landed him in

Philadelphia in the midle of January 1746 whereby his wifes sickness which last'd several months he had spent his little Substance and after his recovering was obliged to make the remaining part of his way by land to this Province where he arrived last winter in March and intending to setle in Saxagotha Township humbly prays to grant him his Majesty Bounty of One hundred acres of Land in the said Township of Saxa Gotha and one Years Provision for himself and his wife. Signed Christian Kotiler. The petitioner appearing and swearing to the allegations of his Petitioner, Orderd that the Deputy Secretary prepare a Warrant for one hundred acres of land and that the Commissary pay the Bounty.

Pages 33-34: Read the Petition of Lawrence Wetzel setting forth That the Petitioner came over into this Province on the incouragement which His Majesty has been pleased to grant unto all poor foreign Protestants who shall seem desireous of Setling in any of his Townships here Therefore your Petitioner most humbly Prays (as the time of his servitude is now expired) that two hundred acres of land may be assigned unto him opposite the Township of Saxagotha having a Wife and two Children. He likewise most humbly prays for his Majestys most Gracious Bounty. Signed Lawrence Wetzell. The Petitioner appearing and Swearing... the prayer thereof was granted.

Page 34: Read the Petition of Jacob Stackley a Protestant Palatine seting forth That the Petitioner came over into this Country on the incouragement which is given to all poor forreign protestants who shall be desireous of setling in any of his Majesties Townships in this Province that they may be inabled with their industery to get an honest livelyhood. Therefore your Petitioner most humbly prays that fifty acres of land may be assigned unto him opposite the Township of Saxa Gotha as likewise his Majestys most gracious Provision Bounty. Sign'd Jacob Stackley. The Petitioner appearing and Swearing... the prayer thereof was granted.

Page 35: Read the Petition of Anthony Cottlar setting forth That the Petitioner came into this country in 1744 with his wife and three children and hath served and his wife Mr. Joseph Shute Two years (as appears by his Indenture) for which he paid their Passage desires to setle at the Congerees with his Family to wit himself, wife and three children. Therefore prays for his Majestys bounty and that he may have his lands run out in or near Saxagotha Township. Sign'd Anthony Cottilar. The prayer thereof was granted. Ordered that the Deputy Secretary Prepare a Warrant to the Surveyor General for Two hundred and fifty acres of Land and that the Commissary pay the bounty.

Pages 35-36: Read the Petition of John Blewer setting forth That the Petitioner is arrived in this Province about Eight days ago who left his native Country to come hither on his Majestys incouragement which he was assured was given to all such persons poor forreign Protestants who shall seem desireous of settling themselves in any of his Majesty's Township here But unfortunately happened to be taken by his Majestys Ennemys the Spaniards and was carried to the Havannah in which place he was kept ever since. Therefore as your humble Petitioner has been desireous for several years past to be a Settler in one of the Townships of this Province and is still he humbly prays that one hundred and fifty acres of land may be assigned unto him in the Township of Saxagotha having a wife and child and he also most humbly prays for his Majestys most gracious Provision Bounty. Signed John Blewer. Ordered that the Deputy Secretary prepare a Warrant for one hundred and fifty acres of land and that the Commissary pay the Bounty.

Page 36: Read the Petition of John Blacey setting forth That the Petitioner has been some time ago at New Windsor where he has seen a great quantity of Good lands that is not as yet admeasured and as your humble Petitioner is very desireous of setling in the said Township, prays that such a quantity of land may be admeasured to him free of Charges as it is accustom'd in any of his Majesty's Townships having a Wife and three Children. Sign'd John Blacey. The Prayer of the Same was Granted. but as the said Blacey's Family is in Georgia it is also Order'd that the Grant for the said land be not Issued untill he shall have brought his said Family into this Province.

Page 37: Read the Petition of Noah Beller setting forth That the Petitioner has been some time ago at New Windsor where he has seen a great quantity of Good lands that is not as yet admeasured and as your humble Petitioner is very desireous of setling in the said Township, prays that such a quantity of land may be admeasured to him free of Charges as it is accustomed in any of his Majesty's Townships having a Wife and four Children. Sign'd Noah Beller (X) his mark. The Prayer of the Same was Granted. But as the said Beller's family is in Georgia it is also Order'd that the Grant for the said land be not Issued untill he shall have brought his said Family into this Province.

Pages 37-38: Read the Petition of Adam Stroub setting forth That the Petitioner has been some time ago at the Township of New Windsor where he has seen a great quantity of Good lands that is not as yet admeasured and as your humble Petitioner is very desireous of setling in the said Township, prays that such a quantity of land may be admeasured to him free of Charges as it is accustomed in any of his Majesty's Townships having a Wife and six Children. Sign'd Adam Stroub (X) his mark. The Prayer of the Same was Granted. But as the said Stroub's family is in Georgia it is also Order'd that the Grant for the said land be not Issued untill he shall have brought his said Family into this Province.

Page 38: Read the Petition of Henry Anderley setting forth That the Petitioner has been some time ago at the Township of New Windsor where he has seen a great quantity of Good lands that is not as yet admeasured and as your humble Petitioner is very desireous of setling in the said Township, prays that such a quantity of land may be admeasured to him free of Charges as it is accustomed in any of his Majesty's Townships having a Wife and one Child. The truth of the allegations of the above Petition being asserted by the three foregoing Petitioners as also that the said Anderley was then sick at Georgia and desired them to Petition for lands. Order'd that the Deputy Secretary prepare a Warrant for 150 acres of land and that Mr. Commissary Dart pay the Charges. But that the said Warrant be not delivered until the said Anderly shall have made oath to the truth of his Petition as usual and the Grant remain unissued til his Family is in the Province.

Page 39: Read the Petition of Solomon Adie, Martin Kessemajor, Henry Metz and Daniel Ladrier Setting Forth that the Petitioners having warrants for lands in Saxagotha Township and that by the Certificat of George Haige Esq'r Deputy Surveyor the lands they have made choise of is about two miles out of the said Township and that no lands is in the said Township proper for the said Persons setlements. Therefore humbly prays to add to the Warrants in such manner as you think proper that the Petitioners may have the grants of the lands you have granted warrants for and that the said Warrants may be inlarged for a longer time. dated Nov'r 4, 1747.

The Certificate. South Carolina. These are to Certifie to whom it may Concern that the bearer hereof John Anthony Cotler is lately come into this neighbourhood and partaken himself to a spot of ground opposite to the lower part of this Township as no more good Vacant land is (as I know of) to be had in this Township. Saxagotha. September the 4, 1747. George Haig.

Upon Reading the said Petition and also the Certificat of George Haig Esq'r Deputy Surveyor on the back of the said Warrants it was order'd that the Words Or in the lands thereabouts be inserted in each of the said warrants and that the time for the execution of the said Warrants be inlarged for six months from this date by indorsement on the back of the said Warrants.

Page 40: Meeting of Tuesday A. M. 10 November 1747

The said Adie comeing from Georgia was not entitled to the Provision Bounty. Order'd that the Petition be rejected.

Page 42: Read the Petition of John Abraham Schwerd Afeger from Prusia setting forth That he hath been onwards of three years in this Province in which time he hath work'd about the Country and is now desireous of setling with his Wife and one Child at the Congrees that he has improved himself in the Flax trade and intends to Cultivate the same. Humbly prays for his Majestys bounty of land and Provision as usually given to Forreigners. Signed John Abraham Schwerd Afeger. The Prayer thereof was granted and the Deputy Secretary to prepare a warrant for one hundred and fifty acres land.

Read the Petition of John Scott setting forth That the petitioner is desireous of setling in this Province having a Wife and one Child and five Negros for which he hath not had any Grant of lands and proposes to setle about Ninety Six or Saludy where your Petitioner shall be able to find such good Land as he may live on.... prays for in one tract four hundred acres land at either of the above places. Signed John Scott. Order'd that the Deputy Secretary prepare a Warrant for four hundred acres of land But that the Grant lye till further order.

Page 43: Read the Petition of William Stevens seting forth That the Petitioner had setled on some land called the Beauty Spot and had purchased of James Coward the improvement of the same but that David Goodwin has run by Warrant the said Lands your petitioner has a Wife and four Children and is desireous of settling on Pedee River. Your Petitioner humbly begs that you will order the Deputy Secretary to direct a Warrant to the Surveyor General to run out in such tracts as may be convenient for him three hundred and fifty acres on Pedee River. Signed William Stevens. The Petition was granted.

Page 45: Meeting of Wednesday A. M. 11 November 1747

Read the Petition of Alexander McGreger setting forth That the Petitioner is desireous of Settling a Plantation on Savannah River. Your Petitioner hath a Wife, two Children, and Eight Negros and hath neither for himself or family had any Land. Therefore your Petitioner humbly prays for a Warrant to run out Six hundred acres of land... Signed Alexander McGregor. Order'd that the Deputy Secretary prepare a Warrant for six hundred acres of land.

Pages 45-46: Read the Petition of Peter Varon setting forth That the Petitioner has been many years in this Country and has now setled himself on the south side of Pedee River and never had any Land granted to him humbly prays to direct a Warrant to run out fifty acres of land... Signed Peter Varon. Order'd that the Deputy Secretary prepare a Warrant.

Page 46: Read the Petition of William Fielding setting forth That he had been many years a settler himself on the Welch tract at Pedee about three year on land of his own Purchase and is desireous of Cultivating more land having a wife for whom and himself he never had any grant of land... humbly prays to direct a Warrant to run out on the North side of Pedee one hundred acres of land for his Family right ... Signed William Fielding. Order'd that the Deputy Secretary prepare a Warrant for One hundred acres of land.

Pages 46-47: Read the Petition of Nelson Grimes setting forth That the Petitioner is an old settler in the Township of Williamsburg of about ten year and hath a wife and never had any land granted to him either for himself or his wife and is desireous of Cultivating some land out of the Township... humbly prays to prepare a Warrant for one hundred acres of land for his Family right ... Signed Nelson Grimes. Order'd that the Deputy Secretary prepare a Warrant.

Page 47: Read the Petition of Thomas Jackson of Saxagotha Township setting forth That your Petitioner hath ten persons in family (to wit) his wife and Eight children for which he had no land hitherto and is desireous to take up some land of his Majesty's vacant land in the said Township where at present he lives... humbly prays to grant a Warrant for the survey of five hundred acres of land in the said Township. Order'd that the Deputy Secretary prepare a Warrant to run out said land.

Pages 47-48: Read the Petition of George Austin seting forth That the Petitioner is Possessed of two Negro men for whom he never obtained any land and being desireous to have a grant of some marsh or some vacant land in St. Philips Parish adjoyning to his own Plantation, your Petitioner prays to direct a Warrant for one hundred acres of marsh or land lying within or fronting his said Plantation toward Cooper River and the high land of the Honourable Joseph Blake Esquire whose permission he has obtained. Signed George Austin.

The annext consent of Hon. Joseph Black Esquire is as followeth vizt. Charles Town, February the 27th 1747. Whereas there is some vacant land and marsh between my Plantation and George Austin's on Charles Town neck, I agree that the said George Austin be at liberty to take it up. Signed Joseph Blake.

The prayer thereof was granted.

Pages 48-49: Read the Petition of Rodolph Buckler, David Amstutz, Michael Zoug, Ulrick Stocker, Melcher Souwr, Gasper Nantz, Jacob Shneider, Michael Shneider, Jacob Derer, Barbarah Shleighler, John George Kirsh, and Hans Michael Croft Setting Forth that the Petitioners having warrants for lands in Saxagotha Township and that it appears by Certificat and information of George Haig Esquire, Deputy Surveyor, the lands they have made choise of is without the Township and that there is not any within the Township so proper for the said Persons setlement. Therefore humbly prays to add to the Warrants in such manner as you think proper that the Petitioners may have the grants of the lands you have granted warrants for and that the said Warrants may be inlarged for a longer time. Order'd that the Words Or on land thereabouts be inserted in each of the said warrants next after the Word Township therein mentioned and that the time for executing the said Warrants be inlarged for six months from this date by indorsement on the back of the said Warrants.

Pages 49-51: Read the Petition of Childermas Crofts, Executor of the last Will and Testament of Kennady O'Brion, setting forth That in a Former Petition to your Excellency and Honours by the Petition it was set forth that the said Kennady Obrion in his life time had obtained a Warrant of Survey for Six hundred and fifty acres of land from the Honourable Thomas Broughton Esquire late Lieutenant Governor dated the eighth day of April 1737 and in pursuance thereof had a Survey of four hundred acres (part thereof) perform'd on the Twenty second of July 1737 and a Plott of the same returned into the Surveyor Generals office where it then remained which tract of land was afterwards sold by the said Obrion for a Valuable Consideration by proper conveyance obliging himself, his heirs and executors to obtain a grant for the same and therefore humbly praying to order the Surveyor General to Certifie the said Plot in the name of George Galphin and that your Excellency and Honours would be pleased to grant it accordingly he having purchased, settled and improved the same. That Archibald M'Gilvery, William Studders and others were the purchasers of the said land from the said Kenady Obrion and conveyed the same to the said George Galphin and the said Archibald M'Gilvery (the Assembly at that time setting in which the Petitioner being their Servant was obliged to attend) undertook to deliver the above recited petition to be present to your Excellency and honours and to Solicit the Same himself but he not long after departed the province & as your Petitioner heard no more of the matter he concluded that the Prayer of the Petitioner had been granted till very lately he received a letter from the said William Studders acquainting him that one Robert McMurdy had obtained a Grant of the said four hundred acres of land and then the Petitioner (upon Searching the office) found that a Grant passed the ___ day of ____ last to the said McMurdy of the said land and that his former Petition was read on the twenty ninth day of January 1744 at which time an order was made by your Excellency and honours That the same should be Reconsidered at an other meeting of which order your Petitioner never had the least notice nor can he be informed that any further Order was ever made by your Excellency and Honours on the matter of the said Petition. That no application was made by any Persons whatsoever for a Grant of the said land till the twenty ninth day of January 1744 but the Petitioner. And as the said George Galphin had paid a Valuable Consideration for the land and paid tax for and lived upon the same seven years past the Petitioner humbly apprehends that the said McMurdy must have obtaind the said Grant by surprise. your Petitioner therefore most humbly prays (the premises being Considered) to give such reliefe as therein as to your Excellency and Honours in your great Wisdom shall seem meet. Dated the 9th day of November 1747. Signed Childermas Crofts.

Ordered that the Clerk of the Council lay before the next Board the Petition of Robert McMurdy for their Consideration on the above Petition.

Page 51: Read the Memorial of Alexander Gordon, Esquire, addressed to his Excellency, setting forth that some years ago the Memorialist purchased the place of Clerk of the Council of this Province from Mr. Hammerton his Majestys Patentee, That he left two beneficial Employments in England and transported himself and family to this Country at no small charge in hopes of a comfortable subsistance and settlement. That immediately on his arrival he was comitted to the Exercise of the said office and hath ever since exercised the same to best of his skill and capacity and so constant hath his attendance been that in the course of five years he hath not been three days absent. That by his close application and some other accidents his health hath of late been greatly impaired and as his Private affairs require his presence elsewhere for some little time, He prays your Excellencys leave to be absent from his Duty for one year and that the public service may not suffer by his absence in case your Excellency shall think property to indulge him so far he hath agreed with Mr. John Brailsford a Person well Quallified to transact whatever the duty of Clerk of the council required... 19th November 1747. Signed Alexander Gordon. On which his Excellency ask'd the oppinion of the council and the Consideration of it was Postpon'd.

Page 52: Read the Petition of Arthur Baxter setting forth that he was desireous of improveing some Vacant land joyning William Anderson has two Negros and one Child for which he has not had any land. Therefore prays a warrant for one hundred and fifty acres. dated November the Sixth 1747. signed Arthur Baxter. Order's that the Deputy Secretary prepare a warrant....

Page 53: Meeting of Thursday A. M. 12 November 1747

Read the Petition of Thomas Freeman setting forth That the Petitioner hath been this two year a Settler on Pedee in the Welch Tract and hath a wife and four children but never had any land granted to him for himself and family, Therefore humbly prays a Warrant to run out three hundred acres of land in or about the Welch tract and that he may have a grant for the same. Dated the 11 day of November 1747. Signed Thomas Freeman (X). The prayer was granted....

Pages 53-54: Read the Petition of John Mixon setting forth that the Petitioner is a Setler on the Welch Tract and is desireous to have land of his own to improve and cultivate and has a wife and four children humbly prays a Warrant to run out three hundred acres of land in or about the Welch tract and that he may have a grant for the same. Signed John Mixon. The prayer was granted....

Page 54: Read the Petition of Gideon Gibson setting forth that the Petitioner had a Warrant for about Six hundred and fifty acres in the Welch tract and setled it about fifteen year ago and keept it as a Cowpen with a Servant on it for about two year and paid tax for the same, being the Plantation now Colonel Pawleys and delivered it up being in the Welch tract. And has since setled at a Place called Persimon Grove and has nine persons in Family to wit and wife, seven children and one negro for which your Petitioner never had any land but as above Expressed, your Petitioner humbly prays to order a warrant to run out the land for himself and family and that he may have Grants for the same. Signed Gideon Gibson (mark). The prayer thereof was Granted. Ordered that the Deputy Secretary prepare a Warrant for four hundred and fifty acres of land.

Pages 54-55: Read the Petition of Hans Eric Sheffer setting forth that the Petition being a German Protestant came into this Province with may other Passengers in Captain Brown in the year 1744 since which time he has lived as a servant with Docter Bull. That the Petitioner's master having given him the remaining part of the time he has to serve according to his Indenture is now at Libertie and desireous to become a Setler in this Province with his Family which consists of a wife and three Children. Therefore your Petitioner humbly prayes your Excellency and Honours will be pleased to grant him a warrant for two hundred fifty acres of land in or near Saxa Gotha with the usual Bounty provided and allowed for the Incouragement of Poor Protestants to become settlers in this Province. Signed Hans Eric Sheffer. The Prayer thereof was Granted.

Page 55: Meeting of Friday A. M. 13 November 1747

Reconsidered the Petition of Childermas Croft Esq'r and on reading Robert McMurdy's Petition of the fourteenth of May last and on Debateing on the Same, it was order'd that Mr. Crofts may have Coppys of all the Minutes relateing to said land Petition.

Page 56: Read the Petition of James McGaw setting forth That the Petitioner hath some years lived on his own lands in Christ Church Parish and having A wife, four children, and seven Negroes for whom he never had any land humbly prays an order of Council to Certifie in his name a Plot of three hundred twenty six acres formerly surveyed for Andrew Lorimer advertized in the Gazette and no application made for the same as appears by the Surveyor Generals Certificat annext and a Warrant to the Surveyor General to admeasure the remainder (videlicet) three hundred twenty and four acres of land near or adjoyning the same. Signed James McGaw.

The Certificat of the Surveyor General. I hereby Certified that three hundred twenty six acres of land in Berkly County was Surveyed for Andrew Lorimer May the tenth one thousand Seven hundred thirty Seven and was returned into the Surveyor Generals office was advertized in the Gazette November one thousand Seven hundred forty and three and no application has been made for the Same. George Hunter, S. G. November y'e 13 day 1747.

The Prayer of the Petition was granted.

Pages 69-70: Meeting of Wednesday A. M. 18 November 1747

The Humble Petition of Geo: Hicks was presented and Read setting forth That he lately arrivd from Virginia with a Family consisting of Nine White and Eleven Blacks, is willing to Settle and Cultivate part of his Majesty's Lands Praying that he may obtain Grants in Proportion to the said Number and being Informed hat a Tract of land containing 4000 acres was surveyed in the Welch Tract for James Griffith by virtue of a Warrant dated Decem'r 6th 1745 requiring the same to be returned into the Secretarys office for a grant in 12 Months, a Platt of which has passed the Surveyor Gen'l Office above a Year ago, but no Return thereof made into the Secretary's Office, and the said Griffith having some time ago left this Province as reported & generally believed has since come to an untimely End. Whereupon the Petitioner Prays to direct the survey'r General to Certifie the said Platts in his Name and that he may obtain a Grant thereof, tho' formerly certified by him for the said Griffith and also that the said Survey'r Gen'l may be directed to Certifie for y'r Petitioner two Tracts of Land in the Welch Tract one containing 200 acres, the other 100 acres surveyed for James Jones by virtue of a War't dated Feb'ry 12th 1745 requiring a Return into the Sec'rys Office in 12 months w'ch said Platts were returned into the Survey'r Genl Office March 9th 1746 where they now lie & no application made for the same Y'r Petitioner further prays that in your order to the Survey'r Gen'l you may Direct him to admeasure and lay out 300 acres of Land in the Welch Tract being in the whole 100 acres &c. Upon Examining the said Petitioner & Enquiring into his Family Right it appearing that 3 in whose Right he had Petitioned were not of his own Family 3 being his Sisters Children & the third his overseer, it was Ordered that the Survey'r Gen'l do Certifie the Platts Pray'd for in the Name of the Petitioner & That 150 acres may be survey'd for him in the Welch Tract.

Pages 70-71: The Humble Petition of John Seller... setting forth that he came from Switzerland & hath served 7 Years to Mrs. Mary Sereau & being desirous to settle in Saxa Gotha Township having endeavoured by his Fidelity and Care to purchase an Honest and Industrious Character Praying his Excellency & Hon'rs order to the Survey'r Gen'l to lay out 50 acres of Land in Saxa gotha Township & his Majestys Bounty to poor foreign Protest'ts & c'a. Ordered that the Dep't Sec'try prepare a Warr't for 50 acres of Land & that the Commissary Gen'l Pay the Bounty.

Page 72: Meeting of Thursday A. M. 19 November 1747

The Humble Petition of Jared Nelson was presented & Read... setting forth That he is a Setler on Black River, Craven County & hath a Wife and four Children, one white servant & 8 Negroes for whom he never had any Lands And being desirous of Cultivating 750 acres of land on the North side of Santee River (that is to say) 300 acres that was formerly survey'd for Sampson Ball (as by the Annex'd Certificate of the Survey'r Gen'l) and 450 acres in Lands thereabouts. Ordered that the Prayer of the Petition be Granted....

Pages 72-73: The Humble Petition of Jno Keithley was Present & Read... setting forth That having obtained a Warr't dated the 15th day of March 17444 requiring the Survey of 250 acres of Land in the Welch Tract for the Petitioner who my Sickness was detained from applying to the Deputy Survey'r for a considerable time, the Survey'r by the like cause was prevented from executing the said Warr't in the time therein Prescribed as appears by his L't to the Suv'r Gen'l therewith annex'd but did execute the same on the 25th of

March 1745 as appears by his Platt herewith also annex'd which the Sur'r Gen'l refuses to pass alledging that it not having been executed in the time prescribed to him He might thereby be liable to your Exellency & Hon's censure in so doing and objects to the Northwest Bounder not being mentioned in the Dep'rs Certificate tho on the Plat it is Praying his Ex'cy & Hon'r order to the Surv'r Gen'l to Certifie the said Platt on the day of the Date of the Deputies and his Certificate to add or rectifie the Omission of the North West Bounder's Name &C. Ordered that the Prayer of the Petition be Granted.

Pages 73-74: Meeting of Friday A. M. 20 November 1747

The Petition of Henry Son was present and read setting forth That he came into this Country from Holland about 10 years ago & serv'd Will'm Allen Esq'r 3 Years & live 2 more with him as his Hired Servant & being now desirous of setling near the Congrees having a Wife & 4 Children for whom he never had any Land or Bounty Prays the Survey'r General to lay out 300 acres of Land at the Congrees & that he may receive his Majestys Bounty to poor For'n Protestants. Ordered that the Prayer of the Petition be Granted.

Page 76: Meeting of Saturday A. M. 21 November 1747

The Humble Petition of Dan'l McDaniel was read setting forth That he is an Inhabitant of Williamsburgh Township & hath 6 Persons in family (that is to say) 3 Children and three slaves for whom he never yet has obtained any Land Praying to Grant him a warr't to the Survey'r Gen'l to lay out 300 acres of Land on the north side of Watree River, Craven County. Ordered that the Prayer of the Petition be Granted.

Pages 76-77: The Humble Petition of Eliz: Griffith was presented and read setting forth that the Pet'r being a widow with 10 Children having nothing else for herself & them to depend on save a Tract of 300 acres of Land in the Welch Tract survey'd by virtue of Y'r Ex'cy Warr't and return'd into the Sur'r Gen'ls Office and by him certified and delivered out of the said office, but not Grant having passed for the same, Y'r Petitioner understands that your Excellency & Hon'rs have ordered the Survey'r Gen'l to Certifie the said Platt in the Name of Geo Hicks that a Grant may Pass to him for the same Praying that in Consideration of her & her Family's Low Circumstances they will direct the Attorney Gen'l to prepare a Fiat & Grant for the Platt Certified for Jas Griffith since Deceased in the name of the Petitioner & her children in such Proportion as in your wisdom shall seem meet allowing to the said Hicks the like Quantity of 400 acres elsewhere in the Welch Tract. The said Petition being taken under Consideration it was the opinion of his Excellency & the Council that the order to Geo. Hicks for 400 acres of Land in the Welch tract formerly surveyed by Jas Griffith was obtained by a Surprise and therefore Ordered that the same be reversed and that the Dep't Sec'try prepare a Warrant for Eliz. Griffith for the said Tract in the following manner.

viz to Samuel her eldest son 100 acres and the remaining 300 acres to herself & 3 younger sons James, Michael & Willm. and that the fees be paid out of the Township Fund.

Page 77: The Humble Petition of Jno Hutchinson was Presented & Read setting forth that he has been an Inhabitant of Port Royal for sev'l years & being desirous of Building upon & improving a Lot in the Town of Beaufort Prot Royal where he intends to settle prays to Grant him a Warr't for Lot No. 159 in said town. Ordered that the Prayer of the Petition be Granted.

Page 78: Meeting of Monday A. M. 14 December 1747

The Humble Petition of James Omar setting forth That he is a Setler on the South side of Pedee River in the Welch Tract & hath in Family 5 Persons that is to say Himself, a Wife, and three Children for whom he never yet has had nay Land assignd him Praying a Warr't for 250 acres of Land in y'e Welch Tract. Ordered that the Prayer of the Petition be Granted.

Pages 78-79: The Humble Petition of Hugh Shannon setting forth That he is a Setler on Mill Creek on the So side of Santee River, Berkley County & hath in Family two Children for whom no Land has ever yet been assign'd, Praying to Grant him a Warr't for 100 acres of Land on the s'd So Side of Santee River. Ordered that the Prayer of the Petition be Granted.

Page 79: The Humble Petition of Tho's Ford setting forth That he is a Setler on one of the Branches of Edisto River & has in Family 13 Persons (that is to say) Himself & 12 Slaves for whom no Land has ever yet been assign'd Praying a Warr't for 650 acres of Land in or near the Welch Tract. Ordered that the Prayer of the Petition be Granted.

Page 83: The Humble Petition of Tho's Ford Sen'r setting forth That he is a Setler on one of the Branches of Edisto River & has in Family ten Persons that is to say 4 Whites and & 6 Blacks for whom as yet no Land has been assign'd Praying a Warr't for 500 acres of Land in or near the Welch Tract. Ordered that the Prayer of the Petition be Granted.

Page 93: Meeting of Wednesday A. M. 13 January 1747/8

The Humble Petition of Isaac Nicholes setting forth That he had about two Years ago obtained a Warr't for 500 acres of Land to be laid out in the Welch Tract & that only two of the s'd 500 acres had been survey'd by Virtue of the s'd Warr't Praying an Order that the remaining 300 acres may be Survey'd for him in the Welch Tract. The Prayer of the Petition Granted.

Pages 93-94: The Humble Petition of Sam'l Hollingsworth setting forth That he is a Setler on the Welch Tract & hath a wife, one Child & 3 Slaves for whom no land has been yet assign'd and that there is a Tract of about 100 acres of Land vacant joining to the Place where he now lives Praying for a Warr't to run out the above said Land & to make out the rest to the Amount of 300 acres as near the same as it can be had. Ordered that a Warr't be Prepared for running out the whole adjoining to the Tract whereon he now lives if so much can be found, if not the Deficiency to be run out where the Petitioner Prays.

Page 94: The Humble Petition of Tho's Jones setting forth That he is a Setler on Watree River, Craven County, & hath in family 4 Persons, that is to say, 3 Whites & one Negro for whom no Land has ever yet been assign'd, Praying a Warr't for 200 acres of Land on the said Watree River. Ordered that the same be Granted.

The Humble Petition of Henry Folker setting forth That he came into this Country with his Family that is to say his wife & 4 Children upon the Encouragement his Majesty has been pleased to give to poor For'n Protestants Praying for a Warr't for 300 acres of Land in one of the Townships. The Prayer of the Petition Granted.

Pages 94-95: The Humble Petition of Henry Sustrunk setting forth That he came into this Province with his Family that is to say his wife, One child & an Apprentice upon the Encouragement given by his Majesty to all poor for'n Protestants who shall settle in any of the Townships Praying his order for 200 acres of land in one of the Townships also the half part of his Provision Bounty for his Persons only. Ordered that the Dept'y Surv'r prepare a Warr't for 150 acres only & no Bounty allowed.

Page 95: The Humble Pet'n of Conrad Scheis setting forth That in behalf of his Wife which he lately marry'd he Prays to grant him a Warr't for 50 acres of Land in the Township of Saxa Gotha and also his Majestys most Gracious Provision Bounty may be given to him & his wife. Ordered that the Dept'y Surv'r prepare a Warr't for 50 acres but no Bounty allowed.

The Humble Petition of Jno Geo Lites setting forth That he hath in Family three Whites that is to say himself, a Wife & Child & that he came over into this Province from the Encouragement w'ch his Majesty has been Pleased to give to all poor for'n Protestants who shall settle in this Province Praying a Warr't in any of the Townships where he can meet with Land to support his Family and also his Majesty's Bounty of Provision. Ordered that the Dept'y Surv'r prepare a Warr't for 150 acres only & that the Commissary Gen'l Pay the Bounty for himself & Wife only.

Pages 95-96: The Humble Petition of David Amstutz setting forth That he came into this Province upon the Encouragement given by his Majesty to all poor For'n Protestants who shall settle in this Province and that he hath a Family consisting of 3 Persons that is to say himself a wife & one child

Praying a Warrant for 150 acres of land in Saxa Gotha Township. Ordered that the Dept'y Surv'r prepare a Warrant for the same.

Page 100: Meeting of Friday A. M. 22 January 1747/8

The Humble Petition of Felix Smith setting forth That he came over into this Province upon the Encouragement which his Majesty has been Pleased to give to all poor for'n Protestants who shall settle in this Province That he hath a wife & two children for whom no Land has been yet assign'd Praying a Warr't for 200 acres of land in the Congrees. Ordered that a Warr't be prepared for 200 acres of land himself Paying the Charges.

The Humble Petition of Jos Bacon setting forth That he is a Setler on Beach hill & hath in Family 26 Persons that is to say Himself, his wife, 7 Children, and 17 Negroes for whom no Land has been yet assign'd and being desirous of Cultivating & improving some [land] prays a Warr't for 1300 acres of Land to be laid out at or upon Cattell's Creek, Edisto river. The Prayer of the Petition Granted.
Pages 100-101: The Humble Pet'n of Casper Fry setting forth That he hath been setled 11 Years at Saxa Gotha & hath a wife & two child'n for whom no Land has ever yet been assign'd and being desirous of Cultivating and improving some vacant land between the Broad River & Santee River Prays a Warr't for 100 acres of land for his s'd two Children. Ordered that the Dept'y Surv'r prepare a Warrant for the same.

Page 101: The Humble Pet'n of Fr's Burloin setting forth That he is a Setler at English Santee & hath one slave for whom no Land has ever yet been assign'd Praying a Warr't for 100 acres of land on the south side of Santee River. Ordered that the Dept'y Surv'r prepare a Warrant for the same.

The Humble Pet'n of Jno Gowman setting forth That he has been a setler at Saxa Gotha 13 Years & hath six Persons in Family (that is to say) Himself, his wife & 4 children for whom no Land has ever yet been assign'd Praying a Warr't for 300 acres of land near Saxa Gotha Township. The Prayer of the Petition Granted.

Pages 101-102: Meeting of Friday A. M. 22 January 1747/8

The Humble Petition of Wm Payne setting forth That he is a Setler on Pedee River but the land on which he now lives being run out by others is desirous of Settling about Pine Tree Creek That he hath six Persons in Family (that is to say) himself, a wife, and 4 Children Praying a Warr't for 300 acres of land to be run out on the said Pine Tree Creek. The Prayer of the Petition Granted.

Page 102: The Humble Petition of Wm Nelme setting forth That he hath 11 Persons in Family (that is to say) Himself, a wife & 3 children & 4 Children that are his relations & Two Negroes for whom no Land has ever yet been assign'd Praying a Warr't for 550 acres of land near Saxa Gotha Township. The Prayer of the Petition being considered Ordered that the Dep'ty Sec'ry do prepare a Warr't for 350 acres only that is to say for himself, his three Children & 2 Negroes.

The Humble Petition of Jno Neigler setting forth That he is a son to Peter Neigler who is an Inhabitant of Orangeburgh & hath been in this Province above 5 Years & after having been an Indented Serv't to Wm. Bull Jun'r in St. Andrew's Parish, his time of service being now Expired is desirous of Settling in the s'd Township of Orangeburgh with his Father Praying the Bounty allotted to Encourage Poor Protestants to become Setlers in this Province. The Prayer of the Petition Granted.

Pages 103-104: Meeting of Saturday A. M. 23 January 1747/8

The Humble Petition of Conrad Kuntzler setting forth That he having obtained a Warr't for Land on the 10th day of Dec'r 1744 which had been before Survey'd & having now one Child more in Family Prays that 50 acres may be added to his former Warr't for 250 acres & that the same may be laid out in the Forks of Santee River. The Prayer of the Petition Granted.

Page 104: The Humble Petition of Felix Long setting forth That he came into this Province on the Encouragement which his Majesty has been pleased to grant to all poor For'n Protestants who shall settle here Praying for a Warr't for 50 acres of Land in Fredericksburgh Township & that he may receive his Majestys Bounty. The Prayer of the Petition Granted.

The Humble Petition of Ann Leutsen setting forth That She came into this Province on the Encouragement which his Majesty has been pleased to grant to all poor For'n Protestants who shall settle here Praying for a Warr't for 50 acres of Land in Fredericksburgh Township & that she may receive his Majestys Bounty. The Prayer of the Petition Granted.

Pages 104-105: The Humble Petition of Christiana Kern setting forth That She came into this Province on the Encouragement w'ch his Majesty has been pleased to grant to all poor For'n Protestants who shall settle here Praying for a Warr't for 50 acres of Land in Fredericksburgh Township & that she may receive his Majestys Bounty. The Prayer of the Petition Granted.

Page 105: The Humble Petition of Christ'n Aisler setting forth That he came into this Province on the Encouragement which his Majesty has been pleased to grant to all poor For'n Protestants who shall settle here That he hath a Family of 4 Persons that is to say himself, his wife & 2 Children, Praying for a Warr't for 200 acres of Land in Fredericksburgh Township & that he may receive his Majestys Bounty. The Prayer of the Petition Granted.

The Humble Petition of Michael Boomer setting forth That he came into this Province on the Encouragement w'ch his Majesty has been pleased to grant to all poor For'n Protestants who shall settle here Praying for a Warr't for 50 acres of Land in Fredericksburgh Township & that he may receive his Majestys Bounty. The Prayer of the Petition Granted.

The Humble Petition of Geo Felker setting forth That he came into this Province on the Encouragement w'ch his Majesty has been pleased to grant to all poor For'n Protestants who shall settle here Praying for a Warr't for 50 acres of Land in Fredericksburgh Township & that he may receive his Majestys Bounty. The Prayer of the Petition Granted.

Page 106: The Humble Petition of Jacob Warle setting forth That he came into this Province on the Encouragement which his Majesty has been pleased to grant to all poor For'n Protestants who shall settle here Praying for a Warr't for 50 acres of Land in Fredericksburgh Township & that he may receive his Majestys Bounty. The Prayer of the Petition Granted.

The Humble Petition of Jacob Mackley setting forth That he did sometime ago Obtain a Warr't for Land & Bounty for himself but having since Married a Wife w'th 4 Children that were before Servants to Mr. Thos Middleton Prays to grant him an Order for a Warr't for run out 250 acres of Land in Saxa Gotha township that he may receive his Majesty's Bounty. The Prayer of the Petition Granted.

The Humble Petition of Geo Mesner setting forth That he came into this Province on the Encouragement which his Majesty has been pleased to grant to all poor For'n Protestants who shall settle here Praying for a Warr't for 50 acres of Land in Fredericksburgh Township & that he may receive his Majestys Bounty. The Prayer of the Petition Granted.

Pages 106-107: The Humble Petition of Barn'd Sibler setting forth That he came into this Province on the Encouragement which his Majesty has been pleased to grant to all poor For'n Protestants who shall settle here Praying for a Warr't for 50 acres of Land in Fredericksburgh Township & that he may receive his Majestys Bounty. The Prayer of the Petition Granted.

Page 107: The Humble Pet'n of Roger Gibson setting forth That he hath in Family 10 Persons that is to say two Children & 8 Negroes for whom no Land has ever yet been Assign'd and being desirous of Cultivating & improving some of his Majesty's Vacant land on the Wateree River Prays for a Warr't for 500 Acres of Land on the s'd Watree River. The Prayer of the Petition Granted.

Page 121: Meeting of Thursday A. M. 28 January 1747/8

The Humble Petition of George Coohn setting forth That he came with several of his Country Men into this Province on the Encouragement his Majesty has been pleased to give to poor for'n Protestants Praying for a Warr't for 50 acres of Land & his Majestys Bounty. Ordered that the Dep'ty Sec'ty prepare a Warr't for 50 acres of Land that the Commissary Gen'l only Pay half the Bounty till he Produce a Certificate from a Magistrate of his being settled on the s'd Township.

The Humble Petition of Catherine Croft setting forth That she and her Brother came into this Province in Capt Brown on the Encouragement his Majesty has been pleased to give to poor for'n Protestants who shall settle here & being desirous of settling w'th her Relations at Saxa Gotha Township & her Bro. Geo Croft being now abt 12 years of Age is also desirous of being put Apprentice there Prays for a Warr't for 100 acres of Land & his Majestys Bounty. Ordered that the Dep'ty Sec'ty prepare a Warr't for 50 acres of Land to the said Cath'e Croft & another Warrant for 50 acres of Land in Saxa Gotha Township that the Comm'y Gen'l Pay the Bounty to them both.

Page 122: The Humble Petition of Rachel Smicher setting forth That she came into this Province on the Encouragement his Majesty has been pleased to give to poor for'n Protestants who shall settle here & she being desirous of settling among some of her Country People in Fredericksburgh Township Prays for a Warr't for 50 acres of Land & his Majestys Bounty. Ordered that the Dep'ty Sec'ty prepare a Warr't for 50 acres and that the Comm'y Gen'l Pay the Bounty.

The Humble Petition of Abraham Eichler setting forth That he came into this Country in Capt Brown on the Encouragement his Majesty has been pleased to give to poor for'n Protestants who shall settle here & being now out of his time & desirous to settle in Saxa Gotha Township Prays for a Warr't for 50 acres of Land & his Majestys Bounty. The Prayer of the Petition Granted.

Pages 122-123: The Humble Petition of George Rainsworth setting forth That he came into this Province on the Encouragement his Maj'y has been pleased to give to poor for'n Protestants who shall settle here & about 2 years ago he obtained a Warr't for 50 acres in Saxa Gotha Township which he could not settle for want of the Bounty and that he hath since married a wife & hath 2 Children Praying a Warrant for 150 acres in Saxa Gotha Township & his Majestys Bounty. The Prayer of the Petition Granted.

Page 123: The Humble Petition of John Wheeler setting forth That he is desirous of settling o some vacant land hear Pedee River that he hath a Wife & that neither for himself or Wife any land has ever yet been Granted Praying a Warr't for 100 acres of Land to be laid out on Pedee River as aforesaid. The Prayer of the Petition Granted.

Page 125: Meeting of Friday A. M. 29 January 1747/8

The Humble Petition of Mich'l Boomer setting forth That he came into this Province on the Encouragement his Majesty has been pleased to give to poor for'n Protes'ts who shall settle here and that about 2 years ago he obtained a Warr't for 100 acres in Saxa Gotha Township in right of himself & his wife, now prays a Warrant for 100 acres of Land in right of his two sons John & Jacob now servants in Charles Town and that the whole may be run out in one Tract in Saxa Gotha Township free of all charge. The Prayer of the Petition Granted.

The Humble Petition of Eve Boomer setting forth That she came over into this Province on the Encouragement which his Majesty has been pleased to give to poor for'n Protes'ts who shall settle here and having serv'd her time to Capt. Harramond is now desirous to settle in Saxa Gotha Township and that she may receive his Majesty's Bounty. The Prayer of the Petition Granted.

Page 129: Meeting of Saturday A. M. 30 January 1747/8

The Humble Petition of John Lining setting forth that he hath 4 Slaves for whom no land has ever yet been assign'd & being desirous of Cultivating & improving some of his Majesty's Vacant Land near James Island Prays an order to run out 100 acres of Land. The Prayer of the Petition Granted.

Page 136: Meeting of Friday P. M. 26 February 1747/8

The Humble Petition of Stephen White setting forth That your Petitioner hath one White Servant & the neither for himself or his said White Servant any Land has ever yet been Granted and that being desirous of Setling near Hearnes Bluff on Santee River Prays for a Warran't for 100 acres of Land on Hearnes Bluff. The Prayer of the Petition Granted.

The Humble Petition of Jno Hudson setting forth That he hath 10 Persons in Family that is to say, himself, a Wife & 8 Children & that being desirous of setling in Fredericksburgh Township Prays for a Warran't for 500 acres of Land as aforesaid free of Charge. The Prayer of the Petition Granted, the Petitioner Paying his own Charges.

Pages 136-137: The Humble Petition of Jno George Wagerman setting forth That he came into this Province w'th his Wife ab't 3 years ago on the Encouragem't which his Majesty has been Pleased to give to all poor for'n Protest'ts who shall settle here, That he hath served out his Time with Thomas Drayton, Esqr., and being desirous of setling upon some of his Majesty's Vacant Land having never had any assignd either for himself or his wife Prays for a Warran't for 150 acres of Land in Amelia or Orangeburgh Township & that he may receive his Majesty's Bounty. The Prayer of the Petition Granted.

Page 137: The Humble Petition of Everhart Kirchner setting forth That he came with his Family on the Encouragem't which his Majesty has been Pleased to give to all poor For'n Protest'ts who shall settle here, That his Wife and Children being now Dead & his time of Servitude w'th Col. Blake[?] expired as by the annex'd Certificate is desirous of setling on some of his Majesty's Vacant Land in Fredericksburgh Township on the Watrees Praying 50 acres of Land in Fred'k Township and that he may receive his Majesty's Bounty. The Prayer of the Petition Granted.

Pages 137-138: The Humble Petition of Mich'l Messinger setting forth That he came into this Province on the Encouragem't which his Majesty has been Pleased to give to all poor For'n Protest'ts who shall settle here, That he hath served his time out w'th Stephen Bull, Esq'r, & that he hath 6 Persons in Family that is to say himself, his wife & 4 Children for whom no Land has ever yet been Assign'd and being desirous of setling in Fredericksburgh Township Prays for 300 acres of Land in Fred'kburgh Township & his Majesty's Bounty. Order'd that the Dep'ty Sec'rty prepare a Warr't for 300 acres of Land as prayed for & that the Com'sr Gen'l Pay the Bounty for 4 only.

Page 138: The Humble Petition of Matthias Smith setting forth That he came into this Province with his Family consisting of 3 Persons (that is to say himself, his wife & one Child) in Cap't Brown on the Encouragem't which his Majesty has been Pleased to grant to all poor For'n Protest'ts who shall settle here and desirous of setling in Frederic'k Township Prays for 150 acres of Land in Fredericksb'h Township & that he may receive his Majesty's Bounty. Order'd that the Dep'ty Sec'rty prepare a Warr't for 150 acres of Land as prayed for & that the Com'sr Gen'l Pay the Bounty for 2 only.

Pages 138-139: The Humble Petition of Robert Austin Esq'r in behalf of & at the request of John Skene Esq'r setting forth That the said Jno Skene Esq'r obtain'd a W't & Certificate for the Lot No. 36 in Beaufort as may appear by the Accot of the disposal of the s'd Lot Lodg'd with the Clerk of the Hon'ble Council & a Grant for the s'd Lot as may appear by the Certificate of the Bounding Lots & their Grants viz the Lots No. 7, 8, 9, & 10 to the South & No. 32, 33, 34, & 35 to the North'd, the Grant with the Certificate of the s'd Lot 36 being since Lost of mislaid Praying an order to the Surv'r Gen'l to Certifie the s'd Lot in the Name & for the use of the s'd John Skeen & that a Grant may Pass accordingly.

These are to Certifie that from the Hon'ble the Lieu't Govr's List of Beaufort Lots Survey'd & Granted Lodg'd in the Council Chamber (which I apprehend to be the most accurate acco't of the same) it appears that the Lot No. 36 in the s'd Town was survey'd on the 27th day of July 1717 by virtue of a Warr't dated June 25, 1717 direct to Fr's Yonge Esq'r Sur'v Gen'l for Jno Skeen. Given under my Hand Feb'ry the 27th 1757. Signed Geo. Hunter, Sur'v Genl. The Prayer of the Petition Granted.

Pages 139-140: Read the following Petition of Henry Gray... That a Ferry hath been made use of for sev'r years past over Cooper River from Charles Town to a Place late belonging to M'r Peter Villepontoux, and now to your Petitioner. That the said Ferry is chiefly made use of by all Travellers from the Northern parts of this Province, but has not yet been established by Law. Your Petitioner therefore prays for leave to bring in a bill for establishing the said Ferry & allowing the same rates as at Hobcaw Ferry and that the same may be vested in him for such Term of Years as to your Excellency & Honours shall seem meet. Signed Henry Gray. Ordered that the said Petition be referred to the Coms House of Assembly & that it be send down by the Master in Chancery & the same was referred & sent down accordingly.

Page 143: The Humble Petition of John Garvey setting forth That he has been a Setler in and about Beaufort 10 years & has practiced the Trader of a Builder but being a present unprovided with a House Prays the Lot No. 195 at Beaufort &c. The Prayer of the Petition Granted.

Page 149: Meeting of Thursday A. M. 3 March 1747/8

The humble Petition of Geo Whitfield setting forth That he hath a Wife & 8 Negroes for whom no Land has ever yet been Assign'd & being desirous of Cultivating & improving some of his Majestys Vacant Land prays for a Warrant to run out 500 acres on the Indian Land & that a Grant may Pass for the same. The Prayer of the Petition Granted.

The Humble Petition of Wm McClure Praying for an Order for a Warr't to run out 650 acres of land amongst some Broken Islands joining to the Pet'rs Land. The Prayer of the Petition was Rejected, those Islands being of Public Benefit.

Page 153: Meeting of Friday A. M. 4 March 1747/8

The Humble Pet'n of Abraham Heizenwood setting forth That he has been a Setler in this Province 12 or 13 years ago & hath in Family 4 Persons (that is to say) himself, his Wife & 2 Children & being desirous of Cultivating and Improving some of his Majesty's Vacant Land prays for 200 acres in Orangeburgh Township & that he may have a Grant for the same. The Prayer of the Petition Granted.

The Humble Pet'n of John Farrer setting forth That he hath been an Inhabitant of this Province 13 years ago & hath in Family 6 Persons that is to say himself, his Wife & four Children for whom no Land has ever yet been Assignd and being desirous of Cultivating & Improving some of his Majesty's Vacant Land prays for 300 acres near Orangeburgh Township & that he may have a Grant for the same. The Prayer of the Petition Granted.

Pages 153-154: The Humble Pet'n of Geo Ackerman setting forth That he came into this Province with sev'l others on the Encouragem't which his Majesty has been Pleas'd to Grant to all poor For'n Protest'ts who shall settle here, That he hath Lived a Serv't with the Hon'ble Wm. Bull Esq'r and the time of his Service being now Expired he is now desirous of Cultivat'g & improving some of his Majestys Vacant Land Praying for a Warr't for 50 acres in Saxa Gotha Township & that he may receive his Majestys' most Gracious Bounty of Provision. The Prayer of the Pet'n Granted.

Page 162: Meeting of Tuesday A. M. 8 March 1747/8

The Humble Petition of Jno Townsend Darte setting forth That he is a Setler in the Welch Tract in Pee Dee & hath in Family 4 Persons (that is to say) himself, his Wife & 2 Children for whom no Land has ever yet been Assign'd Praying for 200 acres of Land on Pedee &c. The Prayer of the Petition Granted.

The Humble Pet'n of Dan'l McDaniel setting forth That he is a Setler on the Welch Tract Pedee River & hath had for himself & for his Wife 100 acres of Land but having Children for whom no Land has ever yet been Assign'd Prays for 100 acres & that a Grant may pass for the same. The Prayer of the Petition Granted.

The Humble Pet'n of Abraham Paul setting forth That he has been a Setler in this Province 5 Years & hath in Family 4 Persons (that is to say) himself, his Wife & 2 Children for whom no Land has ever yet been Assign'd Praying for 200 acres of Land on or near Thompson's Creek Pedee &c. The Prayer of the Petition Granted.

Pages 164-165: Meeting of Wednesday A. M. 9 March 1747/8

The Humble Pet'n of Jno Gordon setting forth That he hath been sometime in this Province and hath in Family 23 Persons (that is to say) himself, his Wife & 21 Negroes for whom no Land has been ever yet Assign'd Praying for a Warrant for 1150 acres in two tracts (that is to say) one at 4 holes & the other at Congrees & that a Grant may Pass for the same. The Prayer of the Pet'n Granted.

Page 165: The Humble Petition of Martin Reighler setting forth That he came into this Province on the Encouragem't w'ch his Majesty has been Pleas'd to give to all poor For'n Protest'ts who shall settle here, That he hath served part of his Time with Philip Poole & being now free (as appears by the annex'd Certificate) is desirous of setling in Amelia Township Prays for 50 acres & that he may receive his Majesty's Provision Bounty.

Certificate. The within mentioned Martin Reighler in consideration of his Age & other things to me moving I hereby give him the remainder of the time of the within Indenture & declare him as absolutely free as if he had never been Bound. Philip Poole (FP), March 9th 1747. The Prayer of the Petition Granted.

Page 166: The Humble Pet'n of Hugh McDowal setting forth That he hath lived in this Country for some years past & that he is now a Setler on Wadmelaw Island. That he hath a Family consisting of 5 Persons (that is to say) himself, his wife & 3 Negroes for whom no land has ever yet been assigned & there being some vacant land adjoining to where he now lives, he prays for a Warrant for 250 acres of land & that he may have a Grant for the same. The Prayer of the Petition Granted.

The Humble Pet'n of Jacob Weaver setting forth That he hath lived in this Country for some years past & that hath a Family consisting of two Persons for whom no land has ever yet been assigned & prays for a Warrant for 100 acres of land & near the Township of Saxa Gotha & that he may have a grant for the same free of Charge. The Prayer of the Petition Granted.

Pages 166-167: The Humble Pet'n of Jno Geger setting forth That he came into this Province some Years ago & hath a Family consisting of 3 Persons (that is to say) himself, his wife & one Child, and being desirous of cultivating & improving some of his Majesty's vacant land near Saxa Gotha prays for a Warrant for 150 acres of land & near the said Township of Saxa Gotha free of all Charge. The Prayer of the Petition Granted.

Page 167: The Humble Pet'n of Philip Poole setting forth That he is an inhabitant in Saxa Gotha Township & hath a good Mill for Grinding Corn & could if assisted on the same stream of Water make a Saw mill most humbly Praying to Grant him the Assistance of Saws & Iron for such a Building for which he is willing to pay yearly till he has repaid the sum so advanced. Ordered that the Petitioner do lay before the Board an Estimate of the Charge.

Page 170: Conrad Scheis presented the following Certificate: These are to Certifie that Catherine Scheis (late Cath: Croften from Charles Town) liveth now in this Township with her Husband Conrad Scheis a Smith. Signed Geo. Haig. Ordered that John Dart Esq'r the commissary Gen'l do pay to Conrad Scheis the Bounty for his Wife.

Pages 172-173: The Humble Petition of James Kinloch Esq'r Sheweth That in and by an Act of the General Assembly of this Province intitled An Act for Vesting the Ferry already established on the South side of Santee River on the Land of the Hon'ble James Kinloch Esq'r for the term of Seven years Passed the 3d day of April 1739 the Ferry on the South side of Santee River from your Petitioners Plantation was Vested in y'r Petitioner for the term of 7 Years and from thence to the end of the next Session of the Gen'l Assembly. That the said Act is expiring and that in and by a Clause in the s'd Act a

Ferry was established from the north side of the s'd River in Capt Abraham Micheau for the term of 7 Years, but as the Road to the s'd Ferry went thro' your Petitioners Land the said Micheau was by the s'd Act to Pay to your Petitioner a Yearly Acknowledgement for the same and that the said Clause is also expired or near expiring. Your Petitioner therefore humbly Prays leave to bring in a Bill for continuing the Ferry. Signed James Kinloch. Ordered that the s'd Petition be recommended to the Commons House of Assembly.

Pages 173-177: The Humble Petition of Ant'o Wright in behalf of himself and his Nephew Luke Gibson & Niece Susannah Gibson & also of Thomas West setting forth That your Pet'r Ant'o Wright and the said Susannah Gibson, Luke Gibson and Thomas West in the month of February in the Year 1745 did obtain from your Ex'cy Warr't of Survey for several Tracts of Land to be laid out to them respectively on Wateree River and also had from the Survey'r Gen'l precepts for the admeasurement thereof accordingly. That soon after application was made & the s'd Precepts delivered to Mr. Geo Haig, but about the time the s'd George Haig intended to have executed he s'd Warr'ts he being obliged to go into the Cherokee Nation when your Ex'cy made your Tour thither was thereby prevented from performed the said Surveys, therefor Prays to renew the Warrants and order the new warrants to be made out generally to survey any Vacant Lands that your Petitioner may be able to find and your Petitioner further Prays that 150 acres part of his tract may be added to the Warrant for his nephew Luke Gibson who at present has only 100 acres which your Petitioner conceives is too small for a Settlement. Signed Anthony Wright.

At the same time said Anthony Wright laid before his Excellency two letters from Mr. Geo Haig. [first letter dated Congrees Feby 27th 1747/8; the second dated Saxa Gotha Feby 29 1747/8]. Ordered that the s'd Petition be referred to Geo Hunter Survey'r Genl, and returned to the Clerk with the following Indorsment. With Submission I am of opinion that six months time may be allowed for executing the four Warrants... Geo Hunter, S. G.

Pages 177-178: The Humble Petition of Conrad Joseph setting forth That he came into this Country about 10 years ago on the Encouragement which his Majesty has been Pleased to Grant to all poor for'n Protest'ts who shall settle here, That he has practiced the Trade of a Weaver and that he hath a Family consisting of 10 Persons (that is to say) himself, his wife, six children & 2 Negroes for whom no Land has ever yet been Assign'd and being now desirous of Cultivating and improving some of his Majesty's Vacant Land he prays for a warr't for 500 acres of land and that he may receive his Majesty's most Gracious Bounty of Provision for himself his wife & 2 Children. Ordered that the Dep'ty Sec'ty do prepare a Warr't for 500 acres of Land as Pray'd for & that Jno Dart Esq'r the Com'sry Gen'l do Pay the Fees only.

Pages 216-217: Meeting of Saturday A. M. 16 April 1748

The Humble Pet'n of Dan'l Laroche setting forth That he hath 73 Slaves for whom no Land has ever yet been assign'd & being now desirous of Cultivating & improving some of his Majesty's Vacant Land on Pedee River he prays for a warr't for 3650 acres of land on Pedee River, Craven County as aforesaid. Ordered that the Dep'ty Sec'ty do prepare a Warr't for the same.

Page 217: The Humble Petition of Othniel Beale Esq'r (in behalf of Jane Sinclair) setting forth That his Ex'cy did the 8th day of April 1742 Grant to the Petitioner Jane Sinclair a Warr't for 1150 acres of Land on w'ch Warr't 500 acres only hath been laid out. The Petitioner therefore most humbly Prays an order to lengthen out the time & that she may have Leave to perfect the said Warr't on the North side of Santee River. Ordered that the Survey'r General direct a Precept for the Survey of 650 acres of Land, being the remaining part of her Warr't for the 1150 acres & that the same be Survey'd on the north side of Santee River & returned into the Secretary's Office on 12 Months after this Date.

Pages 225-226: Meeting of Thursday A. M. 21 April 1748

The following Petition of J. J. Remensper[ger] setting forth That as your Petitioner is now going for England under your Exell'cys direction to procure People to come & settle in the Townships & that the Improvem't of Land for Provision & raising of Cattle is absolutely necessary that there may be no want when they Arrive & your Petitioner leaves his Son in Law John Frasier in the Care of his Plantation & Stock which he'll endeavour to improve for the said Purposes and in order thereto he humbly Prays to grant him a Warr't to lay out 500 acres of Land on the North side of the Broad River about 40 miles above the Congrees where the said John Fraiser has already a stock of Cattle & built a house for himself & Family & also prays that the Grants may be half to your Petitioner & half to the said John Francis [sic] free of Charge. Apl 20th 1748. The foregoing Petitions having been read, I Jacob Remensperger who attended in the Lobby was Ordered into the Council Chamber & Was there Reprimanded by his Excell'cy for being troublesome to the board by so often repeating his Petitioners and no Order was made thereon.

Page 235: Meeting of Wednesday A. M. 27 April 1748

The Humble Petition of Owen David setting forth That the Petitioner lately arrived in the Ship Phenix, Capt. Mason from Philadelphia with an intent to settle here with his Family consisting of 5 Persons that is to say himself, his wife & 3 Children, but being in very low Circumstances he humbly Prays that his Ex'cy & Hon's w'd be Pleased to ascertain a certain Proportion of Land in the Welch Tract on Pedee River for himself & Family free of Charge. Ordered that the Dep'ty Sec'ty do prepare a Warr't for 250 acres of Land on Pedee River in the Welch Tract, & that the Pet'r pay the Fees.

The Humble Petition of James Brothro setting forth That the Pet'r lately arrived in the Ship Phenix, Capt. Mason from Philadelphia w'th an intent to settle here w'th his Family consisting of three Persons that is to say himself, his wife & one Child, but being in very low Circumstances he humbly Prays that his Ex'cy & Hon's w'd be Pleased to grant him a Warr't for 150 acres to be laid out in the Welch Tract free of Charge. Ordered that the Dep'ty Sec'ty do prepare a Warr't for 150 acres of Land on Pedee River in the Welch Tract, & that the Pet'r pay the Fees.

Page 243: Meeting of Saturday A. M. 30 April 1748

The Humble Petition of Capt. Joseph Hamar, Com'r of his Majestys Ship the Adventure at Port Royal, setting forth That he is desirous of Improving & building upon two Lots in the Town of Beaufort Port Royal Praying to grant him an Order to the Survey'r Gen'l to Certify two Lots that is to say No. 365 & No. 366 in the name of the Petitioner. Ordered that the Surv'r Gen'l do certifie the s'd Lots in the name of the s'd Jos. Hamar as Pray'd for.

Pages 243-244: The Humble Pet'n of Thomas Fleming setting forth That he hath 10 Negroes for whom no Land has every yet been Assign'd & being now desirous of Cultivating & improving some of his Majesty's Vacant Land in Craven County on the North Branch of Black River prays to grant him a Warr't to lay out 500 acres of Land on the North Branch of Black River as Afores'd Bounding on Lands Grant to Col'l Tho's Lynch Dec'd & on lands now in the possession of Rob't Futhy & that a Grant may pass for the same. Ordered that the Dep'ty Sec'ty do prepare a W't for the same.

Page 244: The Humble Petition of David Amstutz setting forth That your Petitioner did on the 20th day of Jany 1747 obtain a Warr't for 150 acres of Land to be laid out in Saxa Gotha Township & delivered the same to Mr. Haig on the 15th day of Feb'ry last, but no Land could be run out on the s'd Township as y'r Petitioner could get his Living upon. But Mr. Haig examining found & informed your Petitioner that 50 acres of Land had been run for Henry Sconce with a Town Lot in the said Township survey'd the 10th day of Septm'r 1747 by virtue of a Warr't dated the 29th of Sept'r 1746 and the said Sconce has been some years gone off the Province & is said to be Dead in his own Country. The Land & Lot was advertized in the Gazette Aug't 25 1743 & still remains unapplied for, The Pet'r therefor prays that the s'd platt of 50 acres & town lot be certified to him & that he may surrender his Warr't hereunto annex'd & obtain a new warr't for 100 acres of Land near the s'd Township & bounding on lands of Patrick Brown &c. Ordered that the Prayer of the Petition be Granted.

Page 246: Meeting of Tuesday A. M. 3 May 1748

The Humble Petition of Edward Wigg setting forth That the Petitioner sometime ago purchased of Benjamin Mortimore his right to the Lot no. 69

in Beaufort Port Royal which Lot has never yet been Granted tho several Improvements have been made thereon by your Petitioner humbly Praying to Grant him an order to the Surv'r Gen'l to Certifie the s'd Lot No. 69 in the Name of the Petitioner. Ordered that the Surv'r Gen'l do certifie the s'd Lot No. 69 in the name of Edw'd Wigg as Pray'd for.

Page 253: Meeting of Thursday A. M. 5 May 1748

The Humble Petition of Thomas Reeve setting forth That he has been an Inhabitant in P. Royal for upward of 16 Years & has not yet had one Lot Granted him Praying to Grant him the Lot No. 331. Ordered that s'd Petition do lie on the Table.

Page 254: Meeting of Friday A. M. 7 May 1748

The Humble Petition of James Allen setting forth That your Petitioner hath 13 Persons in Family that is to say himself, his Wife, one child & 10 Negroes for whom no Land has ever yet been assign'd & being desirous of Cultivating & Improving some of his Majesty's Vacant Land prays for 650 acres & that he may have a Grant for the same. Ordered that s'd Petition do lie on the Table to be considered on another time.

Page 261: Meeting of Wednesday A. M. 11 May 1748

The Humble Petition of Lockland McInItosh setting forth That your he hath a Family consisting of six persons that is to say himself, his Wife, 3 children & one slave for whom he never yet obtained a Warr't for any Land & being now desirous of Cultivating and Improving some of his Majesty's Vacant Land on the west side of Stono River in St. Pauls Parish prays for 600 acres on the west side of Stono River in St. Pauls Parish as aforesaid. Ordered that the Dep'y Sec'ty do prepare a Warr't for the same.

Page 280: Meeting of Thursday P. M. 19 May 1748

The Humble Petition of Michael Reais setting forth That he hath been for some Years a Setler in Georgia &c being now desirous of setling on some of his Majestys Vacant Land in or about Saxa Gotha &c therefore prays to grant him an order for a Warr't for 100 acres on the s'd Township for himself & his wife for whom no Land has ever yet been assign'd & that he may have a Grant for the same free of Charge. Ordered that the Dep'ty Sec'y do prepare a Warr't for 100 acres of Land & that the Petitioner Pay the Charges.

Page 291: Meeting of Friday P. M. 3 June 1748

The Humble Petition of Andrew Muck settling forth That he had a Grant for 250 acres of Land which by thro Ignorance is run in Saxa Gotha Township all Pine Barren on which he is not able to maintain his Family & that he hath one Child for whom no Land has ever yet been Granted Praying to run near Saxa Gotha 50 acres free of Charge and that he may have a Grant for the same. The Prayer of the Pet'n Granted.

Pages 296-297: Meeting of Thursday A. M. 9 June 1748

The Humble Pet'n of Dan'l Burnet setting forth That he hath a Family of 10 Persons that is to say himself his wife, 4 Children, an Indented Servant & 3 Negroes for whom no land has been yet assignd and being desirous of settling upon a Tract of Land lately in the Possession of Mr. Ja's Francis at Saludy having Purchased from him the improvements made thereon, but as there has been no Survey made of the said Land prays an order to run out 500 acres of Land on Saludy as aforesaid. The Prayer of the Petition Granted.

Page 297: The Humble Petition of Dan'l McDaniel setting forth That he hath 10 Negroes for whom no Land has ever yet been assignd praying an order to run out 500 acres of Land about the Watree River. The Prayer of the Petition Granted.

The Humble Petition of Patrick Hinds setting forth That he hath 8 Persons in Family that is to say, himself, his wife, 2 children, 3 Indented Servants and one Negro for whom no Land has ever yet been assignd praying an order to run out 400 acres of Land on the west side of Stono River. The Prayer of the Petition Granted.

Pages 297-298: The Humble Petition of Dorothy Nathamer setting forth That she came into this Country on the Encouragement given to for'n Protestants and having served near 4 Years is nor free Pray'g a Warr't to run out 50 acres of Land in Fredericksburg Township and his Majestys Bounty. The Prayer of the Petition Granted.

Page 298: The Humble Petition of Allard Belin setting forth That his Father James Belin of Craven County decd by virtue of a Warr't dated August 2d 1734 for the survey of 1700 acres of Land had a Tract of 1000 acres survey'd on the 12th July 1735 on the north side of Black River by Hugh Row Dep'ty Survey'r w'ch was survey'd, recorded and delivered by Jas. St. John, Surv'r Genl but being since lost or mislaid no Grant hath Passed for the same. Your Petitioner hath a wife, 2 Children and 17 Slaves in this Province for whom he never had any Land therefore Prays to Certifie a Duplicate thereof in his name and that is may be Granted accordingly in pursuance of your Petitioners Family Right. Ordered that the Prayer of the Petitioner be Granted.

Pages 303-304: Meeting of Friday A. M. 10 June 1748

The Humble Petition of Tacitus Gaillard setting forth That he hath a wife, 3 Children & 5 Negroes for whom no Land has ever yet been Assignd and being desirous of Cultivating and Improving some of his Maj'ts Vacant Land joining to the Place whereon he now Lives prays to Grant him an order to prepare a Warr't to run out 500 acres of Land joining to the place whereon he now lives. The Prayer of the Petition Granted.

Page 304: The Humble Petition of Rob't Rogers setting forth That he has settled and improved some of his Majesty's Vacant Land on the Watree River which he is desirous of running out having a wife, 4 Children and one slave prays to Grant him an order to prepare a Warr't to run out the said Land being about 200 acres of Land & the remaining part to make up 350 acres as near about it as he can & that he may have a Grant for the same. The Prayer of the Petition Granted.

Pages 304-305: The Humble Petition of Wm Kelly setting forth That he came into this Country from the Northward on the Prospect of being encouraged and getting good Land That he has 11 Persons in Family that is to say, himself, his wife, and nine Children for whom no Land has ever yet been Granted therefore prays to Grant him an order to prepare a Warr't to run out 550 acres of Land about Swift Creek and that he may have a Grant for the same. The Prayer of the Petition Granted.

Page 313: Meeting of Tuesday A. M. 14 June 1748

The Humble Petition of Jno Ouldfield setting forth That he hat 5 Negroes for whom no land has ever yet been assignd Praying to grant him an order to run out 250 acres of Land on the west side Pedee River. The Prayer of the Pet'n Granted.

Pages 313-314: The Humble Pet'n of Martin Herhigler setting forth That he came into this Province on the Encouragem't w'ch his Majesty has been Pleased to give to poor For'n Protestants. That he hath served his time with Mr. Mulayne at Beaufort and being now desirous of settling on some of his Majestys Vacant Land humbly prays an order to prepare a warr't for 50 acres of land to be laid out in Fredericksburg Township and is majt's Bounty. The Prayer of the Petition Granted.

Page 314: The Humble Petition of James Roisseau setting forth That he hath been for some time a Setler in the Parish of St. James Santee in Craven county & is desirous of taking up a Piece of Land in the said Country. That he hath six Negroes for whom he never yet has had any land Granted him Praying to run out 300 acres of Land in the County and Parish and that he may have a Grant for the same. The Prayer of the Pet'n Granted.

Page 316: Meeting of Wednesday A. M. 15 June 1748

The Humble Petition of George Gesendaner Jun'r in behalf of his Father Geo: Gisendaner setting forth That your Petitioners Father is the next surviving Bro. to Hans Ulric Gisendanner who had a Warr't for 550 acres of

Land Granted to him the 15th Aug't 1737 w'th Lot No. 148 in Orangeburg Township and the Platt returned by Geo Haig Esq'r on October 1737 as appears by the Surv'r Gen'ls Certificate That your Petitioners uncle being Dead without any Heirs to said Land devolves on your Petitioner's father who having 6 Children is desirous of setling the said Land Praying an Order to Certifie the said Platt of 550 acres now in his Office and that a Grant as before Granted free of Charge may pass to y'r Petitioner's Father. Ordered that the Prayer of the Petition be Granted Provided George Gesendaner the Elder be now Living in this Province.

The Humble Petition of James Sprowle setting forth That he has been a Liver ion his Trade at Beaufort about 3 years and not having any House or Ground in the Town & the Rents too dear for him by his Work to Pay he has Improved the Lot No. 131 in the said Town praying an order to run Lot no. 131 and that a Grant may pass for the same. Ordered that the Prayer of the Petition be Granted.

Page 329: Meeting of Thursday A. M. 23 June 1748

The Humble Petition of Benjamin Heap setting forth That he is Possessed of a Warr't as Heir to his Father for 550 Acres of Land Dated the 2d day of March 1731 and your Petitioner hath in his own Family a wife, one child & 4 Negroes for whom he never had any Land. That he has found some Vacant Land near where he now lives at Wappoo where he is desirous of Improving Praying to run out 900 acres of his s'd Warr't & himself and Family Right & that a Grant may Pass for the same. Ordered that the Dep'ty Sec'y do prepare a Warr't for 350 acres only for his Family right.

Pages 329-330: The Humble Petition of Joachim Zubley in behalf of John Tobler setting forth That by Virtue of a Warr't dated 30th July 1747 he had admeasured a Tract of 750 acres of Land that is to say

100 acres to & in the name of John Tobler
400 acres to and in the name of Rich'd Martin & assigned Jno Tobler
50 acres to and in the name of Lockstenslager & assigned Jno Tobler
100 acres to and in the name of John Scheffer & Lot 44 in New Windsor Bought by Jno Tobler but s'd Scheffer Died before assignd
50 acres to and in the name of Con'd Engester bought by Jno Tobler but also Died before assignd
50 acres to and in the name of Hans Ulrick who is Dead intestate & without heirs as by the annexed Platt Certified 4th May 1748 and now the 8th April last by the present Surv'r Gen'l

Praying that a Grant may pass to him for the above 750 acres of Land and as before on the Bounty it may be free of Charge. On considering the forgoing Petition some Papers were though necessary to be Produced and therefore an

Order on the s'd Petition was Postponed till such Papers should be laid before the Council.

Page 371: Meeting of Tuesday A. M. 19 July 1748

The Petition of Ann Thomson in behalf of her Husband William Thompson and the rest of her family setting forth That your Petitioner has been settled about 2 Years and a half on English Santee when your Petitioner by the help of the neighbourhood hath built a house & got the means of Living and Supporting their Family of 6 children, her husband being now infirm and worn out with Labour in this Country so not Capable of settling another Place. That Stephen White has by virtue of a Warr't run out this spot of Ground and threatens to turn of your Petitioner and their Great Family which must bring them to extream want and application to the Parish for subsistance, Praying that the Plat for 100 acres being the Ground your Petitioner has been so long settled on & now in the Surv'r Gen'ls Office may be certified to your Pet'rs Husband praying the Charge of Surveying it to the said Stephen White. Ordered that the Dep'ty Sec'ty prepare a Warr't for 100 acres and that the Survey'r Gen'l do not Certifie the Platt in the name of Stephen White.

Pages 371-372: The Petition of John Bealer setting forth That he came into this Country on the Encouragem't given to for'n Protestants hath serv'd out his time with Mr. Joseph Shute who hath Certified his freedom and being desirous of settling in Fredericksburg Township Prays an order to run out 50 acres of Land & that he may have the Provision Bounty. Ordered that the Prayer of the Pet'n be Granted.

Page 372: The Petition of Martin Talmer setting forth That he came into this Country with his Family on the Encouragem't given to For'n Protestants That he with his Wife hath serv'd their time out with Mr. Doct'r Caw as P his annexed discharge is desirous of settling in Fredericksburg Township hath a wife & one child that he brought with him & one Child since Born here Praying an order to run out 200 acres of Land and that he may have the Provision Bounty for himself, his wife & one child. That the Prayer of the Petition Granted.

INDEX

Index prepared by James D. McKain